FRENCH REVOLUTION.

944. 04

D1374559

5F.

Hertfordshire

7/12

Please renew/return this item by the last date shown.

So that your telephone call is charged at local rate, please call the numbers as set out below:

The French Revolution

J. F. BOSHER

The French Revolution

Weidenfeld and Nicolson
London

First published in Great Britain by
George Weidenfeld & Nicolson Limited,
91 Clapham High Street, London SW4 7TA

The text of this book is composed in Baskerville, with display type
set in Garamond. Printed in Great Britain by Butler & Tanner Ltd,
Frome and London.

The table on pp. 88–90 is reprinted from Jean Egret, *The French
Prerevolution, 1787–1788*, Chicago, 1977, p. XII. By permission of the
University of Chicago Press, © 1977 by the University of Chicago,
all rights reserved.
Material in the map on p. 224 is adapted from Timothy Tackett,
Religion, Revolution, and Regional Culture, Princeton University Press,
1986, p. 54, by permission of Princeton University Press © 1986.

To
Sylvie and Lise,
Kate and Hal

Contents

MAPS

Preface

The French Revolution has become a modern fable written and rewritten for people who imagine they already know the story even before they have read it. In particular, a fabulous inevitability pervades the tale, and it comes not from historical evidence but from an inclination to assume that what happened was meant to happen. Anyone who approaches the subject with scientific doubt and detachment, however, may find a generation of revolutionaries whose deeds were not premeditated and a series of events that do not seem inevitable. All the people, great and small, who took part in revolutionary events were free to act otherwise than as they did. Few of those active in the 1780s foresaw what was to come. So regarded, the events of those early years and their circumstances take on a great significance, and five of the twelve chapters in this book are therefore devoted to them. The storming of the Bastille on 14 July 1789 is not reached until Chapter 6. I could not summarize in one chapter the fall of a monarchy that had lasted for a thousand years.

In writing this book, I have tried to maintain a measure of independence. To read or write about the French Revolution is to enter a world of rival factions past and present, each with a different view of events and people. Ideology colors most of the writing on the subject, whether it be of the eighteenth century or of the twentieth. The individual is hard pressed to take sides. Nobody, or almost nobody, wants to let us think for ourselves. Independent opinions are hard to form and then still harder to defend. The unwary are quickly recruited by the French nationalists, by the Marxists, by the royalists, or even by the feminists. Most university people in our time are easy prey for socialists or republican democrats. I followed in their train for many years.

Even the most independent thinker will be tempted nowadays to side with the popular movement of the time, simply in the name of social justice, and to see the Revolution as an epic struggle between the common people and their oppressors.

A historian with a humble family background like mine may be tempted to sympathize with the popular cause. One of the pitfalls in that approach, however, is that the poverty, ignorance, and violence of the populace may come to be seen as virtues rather than as misfortunes. These may appear to qualify the masses for citizenship and government rather than merely for sympathy, patience, and help. It is easy to forget that such peace, plenty, and good government as the world enjoys have been due to the leadership of small elites, not to the masses. It is easy to forget that the ferocious killing, the terror, and the waves of fanatical hatred that racked France in the years 1792 to 1794 were mainly the work of the populace and of leaders who took up the popular cause.

The liberal ideals of the years 1789 to 1792 are more appealing and enduring than the republican democratic ideals that followed. Liberty, civil rights, the rule of law, and constitutional government echo wonderfully in people's hearts around the world. True, a broad measure of liberal government had already been established, and with less fanfare and fewer lapses, in the Dutch Republic, Great Britain, and the United States of America. True, the French National Assembly did not solve the social problems of the masses, or even formulate them, any better than other liberal regimes did. But now in the 1980s, when most people in the world are ruled by tyrannies and dictatorships claiming republican democratic support, it may be time to look afresh at the principles laid down in the Declaration of the Rights of Man and the Citizen and at the history of the National Assembly that drew up a constitution for the French monarchy in 1791.

These reflections have led me to write as though the educated middle and upper classes were no less worthy than the poor and ignorant masses. I cannot follow those who take for granted that France was "ripe for revolution." There are no grounds for assuming that insurrection was beneficial because some were rich and many were poor, or that the ruling classes were evil by definition, or that social differences were based only on wealth, or that killing was normal and necessary because the killers were poor and unfortunate. To refuse those assumptions is to be left with the difficulty of explaining popular insurrection. I have tried to do this in Chapters 2 and 9 with reference to popular culture or civilization as well as to politics.

Every student of an independent mind must seek to discover whether the revolutionary struggles were between different social groups or between different political groups of similar people. The complexity of this problem, on which a great deal has been written, drove me to take refuge in eighteenth-century categories at once political, social, and cultural: the "public" *(le public)*, and the "populace" *(le peuple)*. Though lacking in precision, these terms have proved to be more flexible and robust than terms like "bourgeoisie," "noblesse," and "working class." Objections to these categories will no doubt be raised now in the twentieth century, especially by those academic elites that pretend to oppose elitism, but I find hearty support among eighteenth-century thinkers and independent scholars of every age.

The French Revolution was made by men and women, as well as by committees, crowds, clubs, and factions, but the individuals flicker past in the course of narrative and analysis. I have therefore compiled biographical notes on many leading figures and on people chosen as examples from among the terrorists, nobles, journalists, clergy, and other groups.

Various chapters have had the benefit of criticism by friends and colleagues, to whom I am sincerely grateful, especially Roger Boulton, Joseph Ernst, David Higgs, T. J. A. Le Goff, and George V. Taylor. It is a pleasure to acknowledge help and hospitality given in Toronto by Jack and Mary Harris and in Paris by Michel Bruguière, to whom I also owe stimulating conversation on many issues. Jack P. Greene and Donald S. Lamm, president of W. W. Norton & Company, have been marvelously patient and have commented usefully on several chapters. As one who works best at home, I thank my family for putting up with the fuss and mess of French history as a cottage industry, and I dedicate this book to my children.

J. F. B.
TORONTO

A Chronology of Events

Dates

1774

10 May   Death of Louis XV.
20 May   Louis XVI recalled Maurepas to court.
9 June   Vergennes made secretary of state for foreign affairs.
12 June   Choiseul returned to court.
24 August   Maupeou and Terray disgraced; Turgot named controller general of finances.
27 September   The parlements recalled.

1775

27 April–   The "Flour War."
10 May
21 July   Malesherbes named secretary of state for the royal households.
27 October   Saint-Germain named secretary of state for war.

1776

12 March   Turgot's six reforming edicts registered.
12 May   Turgot dismissed.
14 May   Maurepas named president of the Royal Council of Finances.
29 June   Necker named director general of the royal treasury.
22 October   Necker named director general of finances; many financial reforms followed.

1777

August   Edict abolishing 481 offices of domains and forests.

1778

6 February	Franco-American Treaty of Alliance.
18 October	Decree *(arrêt)* rationalizing accounts.
November	Edict abolishing twenty-seven venal offices in War and Marine ministries.

1779

7 January	Declaration rationalizing pension payments.
July	Edict abolishing eighteen venal accountants in the royal households.

1780

9 January	Reform of the tax farms and *régies*.
April	Edict abolishing the forty-eight venal receivers general.
28 May	Direct taxes to be managed by a twelve-man commission *(régie)*.
24 August	The *Question préparatoire* torture abolished
24 December	Decree *(arrêt)* requiring Crown guarantee of accountants' credit notes.

1781

19 February	Publication of Necker's *Compte rendu au roi*.
19 May	Necker resigned.
21 May	Joly de Fleury named minister of finance.
October	The forty-eight offices of receiver general revived.
16 October	Every receiver general allowed to issue his own credit notes *(rescriptions)*.
9 November	Maurepas died.

1782

January	The 418 offices of receiver revived.
July	Offices created for second treasurers general of war and marine; sale price, 1.6 million livres.

1783

20 February	Vergennes named chief of the Royal Council of Finances.
29 March	Lefèvre d'Ormesson, controller general of finances.

3 September	Peace treaty signed to end the American War of Independence.
13 November	Calonne, controller general of finances.

1784

March	Calonne created two offices of receiver general for Paris to sell for 1.6 million livres each.
September	Calonne created twenty more offices of *payeur des rentes* to sell for 300,000 livres each.
December	Publication of Necker's *De l'administration des finances de la France.*

1785

January – mid-1786	The Diamond Necklace Affair.

1786

26 September	The Anglo-French Trade Treaty
31 December	*Le journal de Paris* announced an Assembly of Notables.

1787

January– June	Five major accountants went bankrupt.
13 February	Vergennes died.
22 February	The 144 Notables assembled at Versailles.
8 April	Louis XVI dismissed Calonne and Miromesnil.
3 May	Laurent de Villedeuil, controller general of finances.
25 May	Closing of the Assembly of Notables.
10 August	Calonne fled to England.
12 August	The Parlement of Bordeaux exiled to Libourne.
15 August	The Paris Parlement exiled to Troyes.
30 August	Claude Lambert, controller general of finances.
28 September	The Parlement returned to Paris: demonstrations and riots.
19 November	The Parlement received the law granting civil status to Protestants.

1788

29 January	The Parlement registered the law on Protestant civil status.

12 February	Lamoignon's decree abolishing the *Question préalable* torture.
March	Reform of the royal treasury began.
27 April	The first French budget, with Loménie de Brienne's *Compte rendu au roi.*
8 May	Lamoignon's coup against the parlements.
10 May	Riots at Rennes (Brittany).
7 June	Riots at Besançon (Franche-Comté) and at Grenoble (Dauphiné), the *journée des tuiles.*
19 June	Riots at Pau (Béarn).
9 July	The intendant at Rennes fled to Paris.
8 August	The Estates General convoked for 1 May 1789.
25 August	Loménie de Brienne resigned.
28–30 August	Demonstrations in Paris at Loménie de Brienne's resignation.
23 September	Celebrations and riots at the return of the Paris Parlement from exile.
6 November– 12 December	The second Assembly of Notables.
27 December	The Royal Council decided to double the numbers of the Third Estate but did not change the old system of voting Estate by Estate.

1789

24 January	Official regulations for the elections to the Estates General; elections followed in February, March, and April.
26–27 January	Riots at Nantes.
23 March	Riots at Marseilles.
30 March– 3 April	Riots at Besançon.
15 April	Riots at Montlhéry (Seine-et-Oise).
27–28 April	Reveillon riots in Paris.
4–6 May	Riots at Limoux (Aude).
5 May	The Estates General opened at Versailles.
9 June	The Third Estate in conflict with the others.
13 June	Three priests joined the Third Estate.
17 June	The Third Estate proclaimed itself a National Assembly (henceforth NA).
20 June	The Tennis Court Oath.
23 June	The royal session in the Estates General.

26 June	First orders given to troops to gather around Paris and Versailles.
27 June	The king ordered the upper Estates to join the Third.
28 June	The Gardes françaises mutinied in Paris.
8 July	The NA protested against the troop concentrations near Versailles and Paris.
5–9 July	Demonstrations in the courtyard of the Palais Royal in Paris.
11 July	Louis XVI dismissed Jacques Necker.
12 July	Public anxiety and popular demonstrations at the news of Necker's dismissal; Camille Desmoulins harangued a crowd at the Palais Royal; the Royal Allemand Regiment charged into the crowd at the Tuileries Palace.
13 July	Forty of the fifty-four Paris gates (barrières) burned or wrecked; the Saint-Lazare Convent pillaged; the crowd began to search for weapons; the Paris electors formed a standing committee and a bourgeois militia, the National Guard.
14 July	A crowd invaded the Invalides Military Hospital, took the Bastille, and murdered the governor of it; Louis XVI ordered the troops out of Paris.
16 July	The Royal Council invited Necker to return and ordered the troops around Versailles to leave.
17 July	Louis XVI visited the Paris town hall, fixed a cocarde tricolore to his hat, and so gave informal recognition to the Revolution.
22 July	A crowd murdered Berthier and Foulon.
Late July	The Great Fear swept across rural France.
4–5 August	The NA effusively gave up seigneurial rights.
11 August	Decrees abolishing seigneurial rights (but not the dues).
26 August	The NA adopted the Declaration of the Rights of Man and the Citizen.
5–6 October	A crowd with many women went from Paris to Versailles; the king signed the Declaration of the Rights of Man and the Citizen; the king, court, and National Assembly were persuaded to move to Paris.
2 November	The NA decreed that ecclesiastical property was at the disposal of the nation.
7 November	The NA decreed that its members could not be appointed ministers of the Crown.

21 December	Decree founding the Caisse de l'extraordinaire.
24 December	Decree allowing Protestants to hold public office.

1790

8 February	The Jacobin Club adopted its constitution.
15 February	Decree dividing France into eighty-three departments.
19 February	The Marquis de Favras hanged.
14 March	The *gabelles* suppressed.
15 March	All remaining serfs ordered freed.
17 April	*Assignats* became legal tender.
21 May	The NA reorganized Paris in forty-eight sections and adopted the distinction between active and passive citizens.
22 May	The NA renounced all military conquests.
19 June	Decree abolishing nobility.
12 July	The Civil Constitution of the Clergy; Avignon and Venaissin occupied.
18 August	Royalist gathering at the Château de Jalès.
9 September	Necker resigned and emigrated.
11 September	The intendance of the treasury united with the treasury.
September	The NA took control of government finances.
5 November	The internal customs duties abolished.
14 November	Receivers and receivers general abolished.
27 November	Decree enforcing the clerical oath.

1791

19 February	Duties on wine at Paris city gates abolished.
2 March	The *aides* excise duties abolished.
11 March	The pope denounced the Civil Constitution of the Clergy.
27 March	Abolition of the General Farm of Taxes and the Régie générale.
2 April	Mirabeau died.
27 April	Founding of the ministries of the Interior and Public Contributions.
16 May	The NA decreed its own members ineligible for election to the Legislative Assembly (LA).
26 May	The king confined to a civil list of 25 million.
20–21 June	The royal family's flight to Varennes.
11 July	Voltaire's remains carried to the Panthéon.

16 July	About 300 monarchists quit the Paris Jacobin Club.
17 July	"Massacre" on the Champ-de-Mars.
27 August	Declaration of Pillnitz.
3 September	The NA adopted the constitution.
13 September	The NA declared a general political amnesty.
14 September	Louis XVI signed the constitution.
24 September	*Payeurs généraux* established in departments.
27 September	Jews admitted to citizenship.
30 September	The NA disbanded, its work done.
1 October	First session of the LA.
17 October	60 counterrevolutionaries killed at Avignon.
29 December	The LA renounced all military conquests.

1792

January	Royalist uprisings in many provinces.
20 April	The LA declared war on Austria and Prussia.
28 March	General Dillon defeated, murdered by his troops.
30 May	The regiment of the king's guards disbanded.
20 June	The Paris populace invaded the Tuileries Palace.
5 July	The enemy approaching, national emergency declared.
30 July	The *fédérés* arrived in Paris from Marseilles.
3 August	The Duke of Brunswick's manifesto made public.
10 August	A revolutionary municipal assembly *(commune)* formed in Paris; the Tuileries was invaded, the royal family arrested, and the Terror began with the murder of monarchists and moderates.
11 August	The LA decreed the election of a National Convention by universal manhood suffrage.
17 August	Revolutionary Tribunal appointed to judge royalists and moderates.
18 August	Decree abolishing orders of monks and nuns.
20 August	Lafayette emigrated; Longwy fell to the enemy.
2 September	Verdun fell to the enemy.
2–7 September	The September massacres.
8 September	Massacre at Orléans.
20 September	A French victory at Valmy; the Convention's first meeting.
21 September	The Convention abolished the monarchy.
22 September	First day of the republic.
10–14 October	The Montagnards expelled Brissot and all other dissenters from the Jacobin Club.

6 November	A French victory at Jemappes.
27 November	Savoy annexed.
3 December	The Convention decided to try the king.

1793

21 January	Louis XVI executed.
31 January	County of Nice annexed.
1 February	France declared war on England and Holland.
March	Belgium annexed.
2 March	Principality of Salm annexed.
7 March	France declared war on Spain.
16 March	A royalist revolt broke out in the Vendée.
18 March	The Battle of Neerwinden.
25 March	A Committee of General Defense formed.
30 March	Territory between the Rhine and the Moselle annexed.
4 April	Dumouriez emigrated.
6 April	A Committee of Public Safety (Comité de salut public) formed.
8 April	All government payments to be in *assignats*.
10 May	The Convention moved to the Tuileries Palace.
31 May– 2 June	Thousands of *sans-culottes* surrounded the Convention and forced the expulsion of the Girondins.
7 June	Open rebellion at Lyons against Paris.
22 June	Open rebellion at Marseilles against Paris.
13 July	Charlotte Corday murdered Marat in his bathtub.
17 July	Seigneurial dues suppressed without compensation.
18 July	Open rebellion at Toulon against Paris.
23 August	General mobilization ordered (*levée en masse*).
24 August	Cambon announced a *Grand livre de la dette publique*.
25 August	Marseilles fell to the army.
27 August	General Custine executed.
17 September	The Law of Suspects voted to speed up trials.
22 September	The first day of Year II; the revolutionary calendar adopted.
29 September	Maximum wages and prices established.
9 October	Revolutionary forces recaptured Lyons.
16 October	Queen Marie-Antoinette guillotined.
22 October	Emergency Food and Supplies Commission founded.
31 October	Thirty-one Girondin leaders guillotined.
8 November	Madame Roland guillotined.
22 November	Paris churches officially closed.

4–7 December	Three hundred and sixty civilians murdered in repression at Lyons.
5 December	Two hundred and eight civilians murdered by Javogues.
18 December	Toulon fell to the army.
19 December	Decree ordering universal primary schooling.

1794

24 March	The Hébertists guillotined.
5 April	The Dantonists guillotined.
8 May	Farmers general and other financiers guillotined.
26 June	Belgium regained by a French victory at Fleurus.
27–8 July	Robespierre and eighty-two other Jacobin leaders arrested and guillotined.
6 October	Köln (Cologne) occupied.
14 November	The Paris Jacobin Club closed.
16 December	J. B. Carrier executed.
23 December	The Vendean army defeated at Savenay.

1795

20 January	French forces took Amsterdam.
21 February	Decree separating Church and State.
2 March	Barrère, Billaud-Varenne, and Collot d'Herbois arrested.
20–24 May	A Paris crowd subdued by the army.
31 May	The Revolutionary Tribunal abolished.
5 June	About 100 Jacobins massacred at Marseilles.
8 June	Louis XVII died at age ten.
21 July	A royalist force defeated at Quiberon.
22 August	The constitution of 5 Fructidor adopted.
1 September	The École polytechnique founded.
1 October	Belgium annexed again.
5–6 October	A Paris crowd subdued by the army (General Bonaparte's "whiff of grapeshot").
26 October	The Convention disbanded; a general amnesty for political crimes.
8 December	Surviving Girondins returned to the Convention.

1796

19 February	No more *assignats* to be printed.
25 February	Stofflet executed.

20–21 May	A *sans-culotte* uprising.
5 October	A royalist uprising.

1797

27 May	Babeuf executed.
4 September	An antiroyalist purge.
17 October	Treaty of Campoformio.

1798

28 January	Mulhouse annexed.
14 February	Berne occupied.
21 February	Pierre Sotin, minister of police, dismissed.
11 May	An anti-Jacobin purge.
19 May	General Bonaparte set out for Egypt.

1799

16 May	Sieyès became a director.
5 August	Royalist uprising in the southwest.
16 October	General Bonaparte arrived in Paris.
9 November	The coup d'etat of 18 Brumaire brings General Napoleon Bonaparte to power.
15 December	Napoleon Bonaparte's constitution proclaimed.

1801

16 July	Concordat signed by Napoleon and Pope Pius VII (published 18 April 1802).

Who's Who in the
French Revolution

AIGUILLON, Emmanuel-Armand de Vignerot du Plessis de Richelieu, Duc d' (1720–88). He fought in the War of Austrian Succession, became a peer on his father's death (1750) and then commander in chief in Brittany. La Chalotais in the Parlement of Rennes was a bitter enemy, and Aiguillon was removed in 1770 to take Choiseul's place in Paris. But he was disgraced with Maupeou and Terray on Louis XVI's accession.

AMAR, Jean-Pierre-André (1755–1816). Born at Grenoble to a mint official, he became a lawyer (*avocat au parlement*), a magistrate *trésorier de France*, and (in 1790) a member of the new district administration of Grenoble. He was elected to the Convention and became a Jacobin enemy of the Girondins and an active terrorist on missions into the provinces. From 16 June 1793 to 6 October 1794 he was a leading member of the Committee of General Security and planned many arrests and executions. An opponent of Robespierre in July 1794, he had much to do with the fall of the Committee of Public Safety but remained a Jacobin terrorist throughout the life of the republic. He survived an association with Babeuf in the "conspiracy of equals," retired from politics, dabbled in Swedenborgian mysticism, and died in a fit of apoplexy.

ANDRÉ, Antoine-Balthazar-Joseph d' (1759–1825). A lawyer serving the Parlement of Aix, he represented the nobility of Provence in the Estates General. A liberal nobleman, he was a friend of Mirabeau and Lafayette and president of the Feuillants in 1792, shortly before emigrating to London after 10 August. As an émigré he worked as a constitutional royalist in various parts of Europe, returned home in 1814, and held offices under Louis XVIII. (W. R. Fryer, *Republic or Restoration in France*, 1794–97?, Manchester, 1965.)

ANTRAIGUES, Emmanuel-Louis-Henry de Launay, Comte d' (1753–1812). Born at Montpellier, his mother the daughter of the intendant of Languedoc, Saint-Priest, he was sent at fourteen years of age to serve in the royal guards at Versailles. He left the army, traveled widely, lived on his feudal estate, and was elected to the Estates General by the nobility of the Vivarais, who hated Protestants as he did. In the National Assembly he was an outspoken royalist opponent of the Revolution, was embroiled in the counterrevolutionary plot of the Marquis de Favras and fled abroad in February 1790. From Switzerland he built up a remarkable network of spies and informers in France through whom he plotted and tried to influence affairs. His counterrevolutionary work was not only against revolutionaries and Protestants but also against Louis XVI and the Bourbon monarchy that had, he and his kind believed, usurped the governing authority of feudal noble families.

ARTOIS, Charles-Philippe, Comte d' (1757–1836). Louis XVI's youngest brother, he emigrated in the Revolution and took an active part in counterrevolution. From 1824 to July 1830 he reigned in France as Charles X and was the last Bourbon to rule.

BABEUF, François-Noël, called Gracchus (1760–1797). The son of a poor clerk and laborer of Saint-Quentin (Aisne), he became a domestic servant and seigneurial clerk near Roye (Somme). Taking an interest in the intellectual life of the time, he wrote, corresponded with the secretary of the Academy of Arras, made reforming plans, helped write the *cahier des doléances* of Roye in 1789, and went as a Patriot to Paris. There he kept a wineshop, protested against the Paris duties on wine, tried to found a journal, and spent time in prison. He, Sylvain Maréchal, and others worked out a communist doctrine, formed an insurrectional committee, and made so many enemies that he lost his various jobs in Paris and the Somme Department. He was arrested under the Directory on 10 May 1796 and executed on 27 May. He is remembered, and revered in left-wing circles, as an early communist (see R. B. Rose, *Gracchus Babeuf*, Stanford, 1978).

BAILLY, Jean-Sylvain (1736–93). Born in Paris, he was taught at home by his mother and became a scientist and intellectual. Named assistant astronomer to the Academy of Science (1763), he did original work on the satellites of Jupiter, joined the French Academy (1784), and wrote several books, including a criticism of Paris slaughterhouses (1788). When he was elected to the Estates General for Paris, Louis XVI said, "I'm pleased. He is an honest man." Chairman of the Third Estate, he presided over the meeting in the Tennis Court (20 June 1789), and was acclaimed mayor of Paris on 12 July, a post he passed on to Pétion de Villeneuve on 18 November 1791. As mayor he was hated by both left and right, held responsible for the "massacre" on the Champs-de-Mars on 17 July 1791, and executed on 11 November 1793.

BARBAROUX, Charles-Jean-Marie (1767–94). The son of a Marseilles merchant, he studied law and science and even took a course in optics from Marat in Paris. In the Revolution he became an executive secretary to the Marseilles town government, which sent him in February 1792 to report to the Legislative Assembly on the city's state. Elected to the Convention, he soon began to speak with the Girondins against the Paris Commune, against Robespierre and the Jacobins. He was purged with other Girondins and fled to Caen, where he met Charlotte Corday, and on to Brittany and then by sea to Bordeaux. In 1794 he was with Buzot and Pétion at Saint-Émilion, was arrested and guillotined on 25 June.

BARÈRE de Vieuzac Bertrand (1755–1841). Born at Tarbes, son of an attorney, he became a lawyer, followed the intellectual life of his time, and joined the academies of Montauban and Toulouse. Elected to the Estates General in 1789 for the Third Estate of Bigorre, he founded a journal, *Le point du jour*, on 27 April 1789 and continued to published it until 1 October 1791. Meanwhile, on the committee of *lettres de cachet* with Mirabeau and others he reviewed lists of prisoners in thirty-two state prisons and freed many. He was elected to the Convention for the Hautes-Pyrénées, was friendly with the Girondins, and sat in the center. He slowly moved leftward, voted for the king's execution (having interrogated Louis XVI for three hours on 11 December 1792), and became a member of the Committee of Public Safety on 6 April 1793. (Leo Gershey, *Bertrand Barère, Reluctant Terrorist*, Princeton, 1962.)

BARNAVE, Antoine-Pierre-Joseph-Marie (1761–93). Born at Grenoble, he studied under Abbé Laurent (a future constitutional priest), but grew up a sociable, worldly lawyer. Active in Dauphiné politics with Mounier, he was elected to the Estates General, sat on the left in the National Assembly, and spoke brilliantly and without notes. With Duport and the Lameth brothers he tried to save the constitutional monarchy, was arrested on 19 August 1792, and was executed on 29 November 1793. While in prison, he wrote an *Introduction to the French Revolution*.

BARRAS, Paul-François-Jean-Nicolas, Vicomte de (1755–1829). Born into an old noble family of Languedoc, he joined the army at sixteen and fought in India in the American War of Independence. Early in the Revolution he became an administrator in the Var Department. Elected to the Convention, he voted for Louis XVI's death and in 1793 went on several missions with Fréron. They were generally regarded as corrupt. Suspect to the Committee of Public Safety, he turned against them on 9 Thermidor (27 July 1794) with Taillien, Fouché, and the Paris army, which he commanded at that time. He then became a leading figure in the Thermidorian regime. Elected to the Directory, he remained on it until the regime fell with Napoleon's coup d'etat on 18 Brumaire. His career declined thereafter, and he lived three years as an exile in Rome.

BILLAUD-VARENNE, Jacques-Nicolas (1756–1819). Son of a lawyer to the presidial court of La Rochelle (Charente-Maritime), he studied in Paris and Poitiers and in 1784 settled in Paris as a lawyer with literary interests. An early Patriot and Jacobin, he wrote on public questions and was elected to the Convention in September 1792. He voted for the king's death, went out to the Île-et-Vilaine and Côte-du-Nord departments on recruiting and political missions, and then joined the Committee of Public Safety. On 17 February 1794 he was put in charge of an expedition to seize the island of Jersey, but it failed. After Thermidor he was deported to the colony of Cayenne, where he was enraged to learn that his wife in France had married an Englishman named Johnson. Freed after Brumaire, he bought a small property and stayed several years, then died on Saint-Domingue (Haiti) after visiting New York.

BOISGELIN DE CUCÉ, Jean-de-Dieu Raymond de (1732–1804). Born at Rennes, he attended the Saint-Sulpice Seminary and the Sorbonne and so became a priest (1755), bishop of Lavaur (1764), and archbishop of Aix (1770). An orator and capable administrator, he presided over the Estates of Brittany, entered the French Academy (1776), and wrote. He was elected to the Estates General, wherein he opposed the confiscation of Church property and the Civil Constitution of the Clergy. He fled to England in 1792 but returned as bishop of Tours in 1802, became a cardinal (17 January 1803) and a Napoleonic senator.

BOISSY D'ANGLAS, François-Antoine (1756–1826). Born to a Huguenot family at Saint-Jean-Chambre (Ardèche), he became a lawyer in the Paris Parlement and bought an office in one of the royal households. Turning to literature, he was elected to the academies of Nîmes, Lyons, and La Rochelle. He was a Patriot when elected to the Estates General in 1789 and a moderate republican when elected to the Convention. He spoke up against the royalist movement at the Château de Jalès and went on missions against the Chouans. But he sat with the moderate majority opposing the Jacobins, voted against the king's execution, and spoke against Marat. After Thermidor, he was elected to the Five Hundred and was active in liberal causes until banished, unfairly, as a royalist on 4 September 1797. A distinguished statesman in the empire and the restoration, he suffered from a severe stammer but remained a firm liberal, moderate, discreet, and courageous in the defense of liberty.

BOURBON, LOUIS-HENRI-JOSEPH DE CONDÉ, Duc de (1756–1830). He came of a mother from the Rohan-Soubise family, was hostile to the Revolution, and emigrated in July 1789. He joined the princes' army in the Austrian Netherlands (Belgium) and fought at the Battle of Jemappes (6 November 1792). When the Duc de Condé's army disbanded in 1801, he settled in England but returned to France in 1814 as an army commander.

BOURDON, Louis-Jean-Joseph-Léonard (1754–1807). Born in Alençon, son of a clerk in the royal government's service in Paris, he joined the Jacobin Club, was elected to the Convention, became a follower of Hébert, and helped bring down Robespierre in July 1794. He ended his career as a civil servant under Napoleon I.

BRETEUIL, Louis-Auguste le Tonnelier, Baron de (1730–1807). Born at Azay-le-Ferron, son of a noble officer, he went into the army. Louis XV then sent him to Copenhagen, Cologne, St. Petersburg, and Vienna in his secret service. From 1783 he was secretary of state for the royal household, though hostile to Calonne, and took up philanthropic and humane causes. In 1788 and 1789 he wanted to take firm antirevolutionary steps and therefore emigrated when Necker was recalled on 12 July 1789. At Hamburg and other places he was a counterrevolutionary diplomat, but he later returned to Paris and died there, poor and forgotten.

BRISSOT de Warville, Jacques-Pierre (1754–93). Born at Chartres, the thirteenth son of a restaurant keeper *(traiteur-rotisseur),* he became one of those literary men active in the shadow of the philosophes. Full of vague ideas and plans, he traveled to London and the United States, wrote books and pamphlets, spent two months in the Bastille (1784) for libel, worked as a police spy in literary cases, joined the mesmerist sect, founded a journal, *Le patriote français* (on 6 May 1789), and joined the Jacobin Club, where he made brilliant speeches. Elected to the Legislative Assembly and the Convention, he expressed the republican ideas he had first learned abroad. He was one of the leaders of the so-called Girondins. "Brissot," Danton used to say in fun, "you are a Brissotin." He was arrested with the others and guillotined on 31 October 1793. (On his early life see Robert Darnton, *The Literary Underground of the Old Regime,* Cambridge, Mass., 1982, ch. 2, and *Mesmerism and the End of the Enlightenment in France,* Cambridge, Mass., 1968, passim.)

BURKE, Edmund (1729–97). A British statesman and Member of Parliament who wrote a celebrated critical review of the French Revolution,

Reflections on the Revolution in France (London, 1790), and shorter essays on the same subject.

BUZOT, François-Nicolas-Léonard (1760–94). Born at Évreux, he became a lawyer, a magistrate, and a deputy to the Estates General and sat in it on the extreme left with Robespierre, Prieur de la Marne, and Dubois-Crancé. In 1792 he was elected deputy to the Convention for the Eure Department and acted with the Girondins, with whom he was later driven out and declared a traitor. He killed himself on 18 June 1794.

CABANIS, Pierre-Jean-Georges (1757–1808). Born at the Château de Salaignac near Brive (Corrèze), the son of an *avocat au Parlement,* he became an intellectual and a scientist of the revolutionary generation. Anticlerical, he was in the revolutionary years a leader of the Auteuil circle of Ideologues who tried to work out a general science of man and human behavior. He was elected a deputy to the Council of Five Hundred, wherein he was committed to stabilizing the republic in that moderate phase, and he worked for universal primary education, national public assistance, and hospital reform. (M. S. Staum, *Cabanis,* Princeton, 1980.)

CADOUDAL, Georges (1771–1804). Born into a peasant family on the manor of Kerléano near Auray (Brittany), he attended college at Vannes and became a notarial clerk. In 1793 he and other members of his family joined the Vendean army at Fougères. He was seized organizing an uprising at Brest on 30 June 1794, escaped after Thermidor, and had a long career as a Vendean and Chouan chief. He was strong and capable and had a prodigious memory. In 1800 Louis XVIII made him commander of the counterrevolutionary armies in the west. Napoleon thought him a serious enemy, caught him on 9 March 1804, and executed him on 25 June.

CALONNE, Charles-Alexandre de (1734–1802). Born at Douai, he became a master of requests (1765), intendant of Metz (1766) and Flanders (1778), controller general of finances (3 November 1783, and resigned on 8 April 1787. He married twice into financial families and cultivated financial and noble connections. In 1787 he emigrated to England to escape arrest by the Parlement of Paris, and became an active émigré enemy of the revolutionary governments.

CAMBON, Pierre-Joseph (1756–1820). Son of a cloth merchant of Montpellier, he took over his father's business in 1785. He was elected in error to the Estates General but stayed at Versailles, signed the Tennis Court Oath on 20 June 1789, and went home in January 1790 to be a municipal official and Jacobin. After the king's flight to Varennes he became a republican and was elected to the Legislative

Assembly and the Convention, where he became a leading expert in financial reform. The Thermidorians eventually accused him as a terrorist, and to avoid being arrested, he hid until the general amnesty of 26 October 1795. A frank, capable, rough person, he survived much criticism and even personal assaults and retired to Brussels when the Bourbon restoration brought royalist confiscations of his property.

CARNOT, Lazare-Nicolas-Marguerite (1753–1823). Born at Nolay (Côted'Or), he was schooled in military engineering and artillery and became an officer of exceptional ability. An intellectual, he wrote an *éloge de Vauban* and was elected to the Academy of Arras (1787). In 1791 he was elected to the Legislative Assembly, in 1792 to the Convention, but spent much time at the battlefronts and was soon the government's leading military expert. On 14 August 1793, on Barère's recommendation, he was brought into the Committee of Public Safety, where he directed the armies of the republic with brilliant success and survived the intrigues to which others fell victim.

CARRA, Jean-Louis (1742–93). Born at Pont-de-Veyle (Ain), son of a commissioner of seigneurial rights, he worked as a secretary in Moldavia, then for the cardinal de Rohan, then at the royal library. He and Mercier founded an influential journal, *Les annales patriotiques*, on 3 October 1789. He was active in the Paris Jacobin club but lost friends on 4 January 1792, when he tried to persuade the club that Louis XVI should be replaced by an English royal prince. After 10 August 1792 he became a republican, and in September he chose the Saône-et-Loire out of eight departments which wanted to elect him to the Convention. There he was sent off on many missions, but he worked with the Girondins and was one of the thirty-one executed on 31 October 1793.

CARRIER, Jean-Baptiste (1756–94). Born at Yolet (Cantal), the son of a prosperous tenant farmer, he became a lawyer, a member of the local National Guard (1789), and a deputy to the Convention. On 14 August 1793 he was ordered to combat the counterrevolutionary movements in Brittany, and there, at Rennes and Nantes, he ravaged and massacred with a ferocity that earned him a reputation. Arrested after Thermidor, he was guillotined as a terrorist on 16 December 1794.

CASTRIES, Charles-Eugène-Gabriel de la Croix, Marquis de (1727–1801). Brought up as a soldier by an archbishop uncle, he fought at Dettingen (1743), Rossbach (1757), and Minden (1759). A worldly nobleman, he became lieutenant general of the Lyonnais (1766) and secretary of state for the navy (1780), and he was at Brest on 13 March 1781 to inspect the expeditionary force for America. A reformer and friend of Necker, he soon fled from the Revolution, first to Coppet (Necker's house near Geneva), then to Coblenz and a place in the counter-revolutionary armies. He directed Louis XVIII's cabinet in 1797.

CHABOT, François (1756–1794). Born at Saint-Geniez (Aveyron), son of a cook at the Collège de Rodez, he became a Capuchin monk at Rodez, but after reading the philosophes, he was glad to take the oath in the Civil Constitution of the Clergy, to marry, to sit in the Jacobin Club, the Legislative Assembly, and then the Convention. There he opposed the king very early and voted for his death, and he was an enemy of the Girondins. A member of the Committee of General Security, he was sent on many missions. An unprincipled and corrupt intriguer, he was arrested with Fabre d'Eglantine and guillotined on 5 April 1794.

CHAMPION DE CICÉ, Jérôme-Marie (1735–1810). Born at Rennes, he became abbé of Chantemerle (1760), bishop of Rodez (1770), archbishop of Bordeaux (1781), keeper of the seals (3 August 1789), and rich in the process. A good administrator, an innovator, a friend of Turgot, he was in the liberal or Patriot groups at the Assembly of Notables (1787) and the Estates General and was one of the first bishops to join the Third Estate in June 1789. He fled to Holland and England in 1792 but returned to France in 1802 as archbishop of Aix.

CHARTRES, DUC DE. An early title of Philippe-Égalité and then of his son, who in 1830 became King Louis-Philippe.

CHAUMETTE, Pierre-Gaspard-Anaxagorus (1763–94). Born at Nevers, he became a writer and journalist, a member of the Cordeliers Club, and a *sans-culotte* leader in the Théâtre-français Section of Paris. Though not a strong Patriot, he was named to the Commune of 10 August 1792 and became *procureur* to the Paris municipality. He was guillotined in 1794.

CHOISEUL, Étienne-François, Comte de Stainville (1719–85). Born at Nancy, son of a courtier in the service of the Duc de Lorraine, he served as an infantry officer, governor in the *pays des Vosges*, ambassador to the papacy (1753) and to the Habsburg emperor (1757). Louis XV appointed him secretary of state for foreign affairs (3 December 1758 to 12 October 1761 and 10 April 1766 to 24 December 1770), *ministre d'état* (10 December 1758), secretary of state for war (27 January 1761 to 24 December 1770), and secretary of state for marine and colonies (13 October 1761 to 10 April 1766). From 1758 to about 1770 he and his friends, including many financiers and one of their daughters, the king's mistress Madame de Pompadour (1721–64), had decisive influence on many matters at court, but he lost influence in time and was disgraced on 24 December 1770.

CLAVIÈRE, Étienne (1735–93). Born at Geneva, he became a banker but joined the democratic cause and was driven into exile in 1782. In Paris he made a fortune in various businesses and speculation but turned to politics and joined Brissot and Mirabeau in the early Revolution. Like his compatriot Necker, he was an expert in banking, public and private. A Girondin, he was minister of public contributions under Roland (March 1792), was dismissed on 20 June and reinstated on 10 August. On 2 June 1793 the Piques Section of Paris arrested him, and on 8 December, after six months in prison, he stabbed himself to death.

CLOOTS, Jean-Baptiste, called Anacharsis (1755–94). He was a cosmopolitan banker born about 1755 in Cleves, under Prussian rule, to a family of Dutch origin enriched in West Indian trade. He was educated in Brussels, Mons, and Paris. In 1775 he returned to Paris and became a Patriot and an anticlerical tract writer. A friend of Jean-Louis Carra, he became a Jacobin, and the Legislative Assembly made him a French citizen on 25 August 1792. He was elected to the Convention and there championed French imperial expansion in the name of a "universal republic." He was arrested with a group of the Cordeliers Club on 14 March 1794 and guillotined ten days later.

COLLOT D'HERBOIS, Jean-Marie (1750–96). Born in Paris, son of a goldsmith, he became an actor and playwright, director of the theater in Lyons (1787), where he took the name d'Herbois. In 1789 he settled in Paris, and his play *La famille patriote ou la fédération* was played there in 1790. He joined the Jacobin Club and took up the defense of soldiers being punished for indiscipline. His *Almanach du Père Gérard* won a prize offered by the Paris Jacobin Club in September 1791. A member of the revolutionary Paris Commune of 10 August 1792, he was elected to the Convention, which, on his motion, formally abolished royalty on 21 September 1792. He was sent out on various missions, notably to Lyons, where he and Fouché savagely suppressed counterrevolution, and on 6 September 1793 was named to the Committee of Public Safety with his friend Billaud-Varenne. His role on that committee is obscure. After Thermidor, he was arrested and deported to French Guiana, where he fell ill of a fever and died right after drinking a whole bottle of rum.

CONDÉ, Louis-Joseph de Bourbon, eighth Prince de (1736–1818). As governor of Burgundy (1754), he gave a prize to Lazare Carnot for a memoir on Marshal Vauban. A lieutenant general in the Seven Years' War, he married Godefride de Rohan-Soubise and was an archroyalist. He emigrated in July 1789 and long commanded counterrevolutionary armies: in the Rhineland (1792–96), in the Russian czar's army (1798), and in England (1801). His son Louis-Henri-Joseph (1756–1830), the last Prince de Condé, was with him much of the time. He was capable enough but hampered by the many quarrels among the princes and their allies. He returned to Paris in 1814 and held high office under Louis XVIII.

CONDORCET, Marie-Jean-Antoine-Nicolas Caritat, Marquis de (1743–94). He was born in Dauphiné to an army officer, schooled in Rheims by Jesuits and at the College of Navarre (Paris), where he took up science and mathematics. He published on these subjects, was named to the Academy of Science (8 March 1769) and the French Academy (1782), and moved in the circles of the *Encyclopédie* and the salons. He developed the current passion for the public good and worked much of his life as a social scientist in public life. Elected on 18 September 1789 to the municipal assembly of Paris and appointed an inspector of the public treasury, he passed into the republican camp at the king's flight to Varennes (21 June 1791), joined the Cercle social, and was elected to the Legislative Assembly and the Convention, wherein he was active in educational and constitutional reform and was counted a Girondin. The Girondin constitution of 15 February 1793 was largely his work. He was arrested as a Girondin and an academician and died in a prison at Bourg-la-Reine (Seine).

CONTADES, Louis-Georges-Erasme, Marquis de (1704–95). Born at Angers, he married into a rich merchant family of Saint-Malo (Magon de la Lande, 1724). A *maréchal de camp* (1740), he fought in the War of Austrian Succession and commanded the armies in Germany during the Seven Years' War. Made *maréchal de France* (1758), he had a public dispute with the Duc de Broglie over the defeat at Minden (1759) and retired. He was named governor of Lorraine (May 1788), arrested in Paris in the Terror, freed after Thermidor, and died on 19 January 1795 in the house of Madame Hérault de Séchelles. He is not to be confused with his relative Erasme-Gaspard de Contades (1758–1834), a career officer who fought in the counterrevolutionary armies and left memoirs of the Quiberon expedition in which he took part.

CONTI, Louis-François-Joseph de Bourbon, Prince de (1734–1814). He fought in the Seven Years' War. Sly and profligate, he made his way at court by flattering Mesdames de Pompadour and du Barry and then the ministers Maupeou, Terray, and Maurepas. In the second Assembly of Notables (1788) he opposed doubling the numbers of the Third Estate. He emigrated in 1789 disguised as a peasant, but he returned in 1790, was imprisoned in Marseilles in April 1793, and was freed in August 1795. He went to Spain in 1797 with a duchess and died there.

CONZIÉ, Louis-François-Marc-Hilaire de (1732–1804). Born at Château de Pommier (Ain), he became a priest (1759), bishop of Saint-Omer (1766) and of Arras (1769). He refused to attend the Estates General in 1789, emigrated to Turin (1790), and became almoner to the counterrevolutionary Prince de Condé.

CORDAY, Marie-Anne-Charlotte (1768–93). Born into a poor noble family of Saint-Saturnin-des Ligneries near Vimoutiers (Orne), she was boarded at the abbey of La Trinité in Caen, where her aunt was a nun. When the abbey was closed in March 1791, she lived with her father and near an aunt who owned books by Voltaire, Rousseau, Raynal, and the Encyclopedists. An independent, proud, and intelligent person, she learned to hate Marat and the Paris Commune. On 9 July 1789 she left Caen by coach for Paris, leaving word that she was going to England. In Paris she rented a room in the rue des Vieux-Augustins and drew up an *Adresse aux français* . . . in which she announced Marat's death. Gaining access to Marat's house on 13 July, she found him in the special bathtub in which he sat to ease a skin disease. She listened to him say that he would soon guillotine the Girondins and then stabbed him to death with a butcher's knife. In her prison, whence she was soon taken and guillotined, she wrote a letter to her father: "Pardon me, my dear Papa, for disposing of my existence without your permission. . . ." On 19 October 1793, her father was imprisoned in Caen with her grandfather (aged ninety) and grandmother (eighty-three), but they were released.

COUTHON, Georges-Auguste (1755–94). Born at Orcet (Puy-de-Dôme), he became a lawyer and was elected to the Legislative Assembly and the Convention. He went out on various missions and was named to the Committee of Public Safety on 30 May 1793. By then he was a cripple in a wheelchair, probably as a result of meningitis, though he had first lost the use of a leg after hiding in the wet and cold under a girl's window after her father had unexpectedly come home. In spite of his infirmities, he was one of the dominant members of the committee along with Robespierre and Saint-Just, siding with them in internal quarrels. He was guillotined with them on 28 July 1794.

CUSTINE, Adam-Philippe, Comte de (1740–93). Born at Metz into a noble military family, he fought in the Seven Years' War and in the American War of Independence as a colonel in America, and in the Estates General he sat on the left. A lieutenant general in October 1791, he was an officer in the army of the Rhine in spring 1792, commander in chief of it by November, and commander of the *armée du Nord* on 13 May 1793. A strict general, he was not good at politics and was arrested on 22 July 1793 on suspicion of foreign links and guillotined on 28 August.

DANTON, Georges-Jacques (1759–94). Son of a lawyer in the *bailliage* of Arcis-sur-Aube, he was schooled by the Oratorians at Troyes, became a Paris lawyer, and bought a royal office of *avocat au conseil du roy* for 78,000 livres. In July 1789 he joined the National Guard and also presided over the Paris district of Cordeliers until it was suppressed, whereupon he and his friends (including Desmoulins and Billaud-Varenne) founded the Cordeliers Club. He became a municipal official. Energetic, resourceful, and devious, a big, ugly man with a loud voice and an arresting manner, he became a famous orator and one of the leaders of the Paris populace. A prominent Jacobin, he helped plan the insurrection of 10 August 1792 and was named minister of justice right after it. He was elected to the Convention on 6 September and was already one of the organizers of the war effort. He played a leading part in the Convention until, in a political conflict among the revolutionary chiefs, Robespierre and his friends succeeded in discrediting him. He was accused of corruption and conspiracy and guillotined on 5 April 1794 with Desmoulins and others. (Norman Hampson, *Danton*, London, 1978.)

DARTIGOEYTE, Pierre-Arnaud (1763–1812). Son of a notary at Mugron (Landes), he became a lawyer and was elected to the Convention, where he sat on the Mountain with the Jacobins. On 9 March 1793 he was sent on missions in the south and southwest to recruit troops, fight against counterrevolution, and generally represent the dictatorial regime, and he did these ruthlessly, especially by violent measures against priests.

DAVID, Jacques-Louis (1748–1825). Son of a Paris iron merchant, he became an artist, famous for large canvases with classical themes, and was named to the Royal Academy in 1781. He attended the Jacobin Club, was elected to the Convention, sat with the Mountain, and voted for the execution of Louis XVI. He sat on various committees and performed various tasks but is noteworthy for his pictures of revolutionary occasions and people, such as a sketch of the Tennis Court Oath, Marat dying in the bathtub, Barère interrogating Louis XVI before the Convention, and a portrait of Jeanbon Saint-André. Arrested after 9 Thermidor as a friend of Robespierre, he was eventually released. Napoleon visited his studio, and made him a chevalier of the empire on 10 September 1808. In 1816 he went into exile in Brussels, but after his death his remains were transferred to the Père Lachaise Cemetery in Paris.

DEFFAND, Marie de Vichy-Chamrond, Marquise du (1697–1780). A worldly, cynical, egotistical woman who lived the dissolute life of the aristocratic circles she moved in and entertained intellectuals at her famous salon in Paris.

DESMOULINS, Camille (1760–94). Born at Guise (Picardy), he knew Robespierre, and they attended the Collège Louis-le-Grand at the same time. In Paris in 1789 he soon became a popular radical leader. He was prominent among those who harangued the crowd in the Palais Royal on 12 July 1789, one of the first and strongest leaders of the movement to bring the king to Paris on 5 and 6 October, and a founding member of the radical Cordeliers Club. He submitted a petition on the Champ-de-Mars on 17 July 1791, went into hiding during the subsequent repression, and was elected to the National Convention in fall 1792. Meanwhile, he won a large following by his elegant but inflammatory writing in his journal *Révolutions de France et de Brabant*. During the Terror he became a moderate Jacobin, notably in the six numbers of his journal *Le vieux Cordelier*, which first appeared on 5 December 1793. After criticizing the *enragés* and the Robespierrists, he was denounced and guillotined on 5 April 1794. Robespierre, who had often defended him, described him as "a bizarre mixture of truths and lies, of policies and absurdities, of sane views and vague personal projects."

DILLON, Arthur Richard (1721–1806). Born at Saint-Germain-en-Laye to an Irish family, he attended the Saint-Sulpice Seminary, wrote a thesis on the validity of Anglican ordination, and made a career as priest (1748), bishop of Évreux (1753), archbishop of Toulouse (1758) and of Narbonne (1763). Politically active, in the first Assembly of Notables (1787) he favored giving up clerical financial privileges and in the second (1788) voted for doubling the Third Estate. He lived like a rich nobleman and gave generously to the poor. In 1791 he refused the oath, emigrated in June, and lived and died in London with a noble nephew, Lord Dillon, who also kept other French clerics.

DOBSEN, Claude-Emmanuel (1743–1812). Born near Soissons, the son of an iron merchant of Noyon (Oise), he became a lawyer (*avocat*), was defeated in the elections of 1789, but elected an officer of the National Guard in 1790. He became a judge at Épernay, then in the sixth arrondissement of Paris, and active in the politics of his section. Head of the Central Revolutionary Committee which directed the insurrection of 31 May–2 June 1793, he became a leader of the *enragé* group of extremists and was in prison from 2 April 1795 to the amnesty of October. He conspired with Babeuf but escaped arrest and served in the new French court set up in the conquered territory of Trèves. He and Jeanbon Saint-André founded a Masonic lodge, Les amis de l'humanité. (Morris Slavin, *The Making of an Insurrection*, Cambridge, Mass., 1986, p. 76.)

DUFRESNE, Bertrand (1736–1801). A shoemaker's son born at Navarrenx (Basses-Pyrénées), he worked as a clerk in shipping firms at Bayonne and Bordeaux until the banker Jean-Joseph de Laborde (1724–94) found him a job in Paris. He worked his way up through various financial services in Paris until he impressed Jacques Necker, who made him *premier commis* in charge of the royal treasury (1777) and director general of the public treasury (9 September 1790). He lost his post and was arrested during the Terror. He was elected to the Five Hundred (April 1797) and named director of the public treasury by Napoleon (17 August 1800).

DUMOURIEZ, Charles-François du Périer, called Dumouriez (1739–1823). Born at Cambrai, the son of a war commissioner, he joined the army in the Seven Years' War and had a long military career under Louis XVI. In 1790 he joined the Jacobin Club. He served as minister of foreign affairs from 15 March to 12 June 1792, then as minister for war for a few days. Owing to his roots in Cambrai, he was devoted to the liberation of Belgium, not to French hegemony. After a period at the head of the French armies in 1792 and 1793, he went over to the invading armies in April 1793 as a counterrevolutionary and was declared an outlaw on 3 April. He retired to England in 1803, died at Turville Park (Bucks) in England, and his name is inscribed on the north side of the Arc de triomphe in Paris.

DU PONT DE NEMOURS, Pierre-Samuel (1739–1817). Born in Paris to a Huguenot clockmaker to the king, he rebelled against his father and studied political economy. He fell in with Dr. Quesnay, the Physiocrat, who encouraged him to publish; with Turgot, who named him inspector general of trade in 1774; and then with Vergennes, who put him to work on the trade treaty with England (1786). He was secretary to the Assembly of Notables (1787) and elected to the Estates General for Nemours (hence his titled name). A Huguenot, a Freemason, and a Patriot, he was in favor of confiscating Church property, but he believed in law, order, and the constitutional monarchy. On 10 August 1792 he fought to defend the king in the Tuileries and then hid in the dome of the observatory at the Collège des Quatre Nations (now the Institut). Elected to the Council of Ancients (October 1795), he decided to create a utopian colony in Virginia, published a prospectus, and sailed away on 2 October 1799. A letter from Thomas Jefferson awaited him at Newport, Rhode Island, where he landed on 1 January 1800, and he played a part in the Louisiana Purchase and other diplomacy. In 1803 he returned to Paris and was elected secretary to the Chamber of Commerce. At the restoration of the Bourbons he returned to the United States and died at Eleutherian Mills, where his son was working a gunpowder plant.

DUPORT, Adrien-Jean-François (1759–98). Son of a magistrate in the Paris Parlement, he became a lawyer (1778) and an intellectual of his time: a disciple of Montesquieu, Rousseau, Beccaria, and the Physiocrats; a Freemason and a mesmerist; a Patriot and a deputy for the Paris nobility in the Estates General. With Barnave and Alexandre Lameth he sat on the left in the National Assembly and spoke eloquently for the liberal cause of the constitutional monarchy. In one speech he stressed the importance of protecting mail from being opened by government or anyone else. He spoke up for giving citizenship to Jews. In 1790 he was a leader in the Jacobin Club and opposed Lafayette's group, but he and his friends founded the Feuillants Club and became conservatives and monarchists.

ESPAGNAC, Marc-René-Marie d'Armazit de Sahuguet, abbé d' (1752–94). Born at Brive-la-Gaillarde (Corrèze), became a Bachelor of Theology and a tonsured cleric and then turned to financial speculation, writing, and the fashionable circles of Paris. As a friend of Calonne, he and his brother, Jean-Frédéric-Guillaume, Comte d'Espagnac (1750–1817), made profits in Indies company shares and went on speculating into the Revolution, as did many others. Accused of complicity with General Dumouriez in 1792, he was several times imprisoned and eventually guillotined in 1794 with Danton, Desmoulins, and Chabot.

ESTERHAZY, Valentin-Ladislas (1740–1805). Grandson of a Hungarian officer who settled in Lorraine, son of an officer at the court of Stanislas Leszczynski, Duc de Lorraine, he became a page to Stanislas and then fought in the Seven Years' War. An envoy in the negotiations for the marriage of Louis XVI and Marie-Antoinette, he won their favor and was loaded with decorations and honors. In 1790 he emigrated to England but settled in Russia in 1791.

FABRE D'ÉGLANTINE, Philippe-François-Nazaire (1750–94). The son of a merchant draper of Carcassonne, educated by priests at Toulouse, he became an actor and playwright. In his career he traveled a good deal and directed theaters at Arras, Douai, Geneva, Lyons (where he met Collot d'Herbois), and Nîmes (1786). In 1787 he went to Paris, where several of his plays were put on in the next few years. He joined the Cordeliers Club, befriended Danton and Camille Desmoulins, and after 10 August 1792 followed Danton into the Ministry of Justice as a clerk. Elected to the Convention, he sat and voted with the Jacobins, served on the Committee of General Defense, and helped draw up the revolutionary calendar, adopted on 24 October 1793, in which the new seasonal names for the months were his idea. He helped bring down the Girondins, the Hébertists, and many financial speculators, but he made many enemies and was denounced and guillotined on 5 April 1794.

FAUCHET, Abbé Claude (1744–93). Born at Dornes (Nièvre), he entered an order of monks attached to the parish of Saint-Roch, Paris, and then became vicar general to the archbishop of Bourges. Becoming an enthusiastic revolutionary, he identified Christianity with democracy, joined the provisional Commune of Paris (1790), led the democratic party in 1789 and 1790 with two journalists, Camille Desmoulins and Elysée Loustalot, founded the Amis de la vérité, the Minimes popular society, and a journal, *Les bouches de fer*. In April 1791 he was elected constitutional bishop of Calvados but returned to Paris as a deputy to the Legislative Assembly and stayed as a deputy to the Convention. His views in 1792 and 1793 were moderate. He spoke up for the king, founded a moderate journal, *Le journal des amis*, and was guillotined with the Girondins on 31 October 1793.

FOUCHÉ, Joseph (1759–1820). Born at Le Pellerin (Loire-Maritime), the son of a ship's captain, sent to be a monk in the Oratory, he taught logic at Vendôme and physics at Arras (where he knew Robespierre), was elected to the Convention, and then married. He voted for Louis XVI's death, worked on the Committee on Public Instruction, and went to Nantes and elsewhere on Jacobin missions. In fall 1793 he and Chaumette led the dechristianizing movement in the Allier and Nièvre departments, confiscating property, sending seventeen trunks full of valuables to Paris, and forcing priests to marry. At Nevers he removed crosses from the cemetery and put up a large sign: DEATH IS AN ETERNAL SLEEP. To the left even of Robespierre, he never ceased to intrigue but survived the 9 Thermidor and an involvement with the communist Babeuf, and he became Napoleon's chief of police with the title of Duc d'Otranto (15 August 1809). Maneuvering like Talleyrand, he survived the restoration and even held high office but was banished in 1816 and died in Trieste.

FOUQUIER-TINVILLE, Antoine-Quentin (1746–95). He was born at Hérouel (Aisne) to a magistrate related to the family of Camille Desmoulins. They helped him to get a post in the Châtelet criminal court in Paris, which he needed to support the six children he had by two wives. His cousin Camille Desmoulins, whom Danton brought into the Ministry of Justice, got him a post on the tribunal created on 17 August 1792 for judging royalists arrested after the insurrection of 10 August, and on 13 March 1793 he was elected to the post of public prosecutor in the new Revolutionary Tribunal. There he had the authority to send prisoners to the guillotine, and he used it relentlessly. Beginning at 8:00 A.M., he read files and directed court proceedings. Tall, strong, stooped, with black hair, a bluff, vulgar manner, a harsh voice, and a terrifying stare, he sent hundreds of people to their deaths. When eventually arrested after Thermidor, he defended himself vigorously, arguing that he had only been carrying out orders. He was guillotined on 7 May 1795.

FOURCROY, Antoine-François (1755–1809). Born in Paris, son of the Duc d'Orléans's pharmacist, he became a doctor (1780) and a distinguished chemist, entering the Academy of Science in 1785. He became a left-wing Jacobin, replaced Marat in the Convention on 25 July 1793, worked with Guyton de Morveau and other scientists at gunpowder production, public instruction, and other tasks for the Committee of Public Safety, and served briefly on that committee after Thermidor. He was anticlerical until the empire, when he became a Roman Catholic.

FRÉRON, Louis-Marie-Stanislas (1754–1802). He was born in Paris, son of Élie Fréron, an enemy of Voltaire and founder of *L'année littéraire*. Author of the violent left-wing journal *Orateur du peuple,* he was elected to the Convention and joined Barras in suppressing counterrevolution at Marseilles and Toulouse with great violence. In July 1794 he helped bring down Robespierre and became a leader in the Thermidorian reaction, in the *jeunesse dorée* movement, and in the White Terror in southeastern France.

FROMENT, François-Marie (1756–1825). Born at Nîmes, he became a lawyer, a financial receiver to the clergy, and active in politics. A fanatical Roman Catholic, he sided with clerical and landed interests, hated Protestants, and resented their revolutionary gains at Nîmes. In December 1789 he emigrated to Turin and became an agent of the princes' counterrevolutionary forces. After the Revolution he was a leader in the White Terror against revolutionaries in the Gard Department.

GENSONNÉ, Armand (1758–93). Born at Bordeaux to an army chief surgeon, he attended the Collège de Guienne and was named secretary general of Bordeaux by Louis XVI on 20 September 1787. He refused this post but agreed to sit in the first elected municipal council of Bordeaux (1790) and was elected judge in the Gironde Department (1791). He was elected to the Legislative Assembly and the Convention, where he became a leading Girondin moderate and opposed Robespierre and his friends. Upright and firm, he did not even try to hide and was guillotined with others on 31 October 1793. His portrait by Greuze hangs in the Louvre.

GRÉGOIRE, Abbé Henri-Baptiste (1750–1831). Born near Lunéville (Meurthe-et-Moselle), son of a poor tailor, he showed ability enough to attend the Jesuit college at Nancy and to become a priest (1775). He studied, wrote, became a Jansenist, a Richerist, and a Patriot. He was one of the radical clergy ready to join the Third Estate at the

Assembly of Notables. In the National Assembly he was a republican as early as June 1791, an early champion of black slaves and Jews, was elected bishop of Blois in 1791, to the Convention in 1792, and to the Five Hundred in 1795. He was learned and idealistic, an enemy of superstition, and an enlightened Roman Catholic. David painted his portrait. (R. F. Necheles, *The Abbé Grégoire*, Westport, Conn., 1971.)

GUADET, Marguerite-Élie (1755–94). Born at Saint-Émilion (Gironde), he was sent by a rich patron to the Collège of Guienne, and after studying law in Bordeaux, he worked in Paris as secretary to a lawyer, Élie de Beaumont, friend of Voltaire. He was elected administrator of the Gironde Department (1790), president of the criminal court (1791), and deputy to the Legislative Assembly and the Convention. With a Voltairean sense of justice, he was a strong opponent of Marat, of Robespierre, and of the entire Jacobin left wing. He became a leader of the Girondin faction with Buzot and Gensonné. On 2 June 1793 he escaped the arrest of the Girondins and went to the Gironde in disguise. Discovered a year later, he was arrested and was executed at Bordeaux on 20 June 1794.

GUENOT, Nicolas (1754–1832). Born at Voutenay (Yonne), the son of a river worker, he went to Paris (1771) as a timber and dock worker, enlisted (1775) in the Gardes françaises, where he was trained in violence, and after many adventures became a police spy. In 1793 he spied for the police in the Piques Section of Paris, near the Palais Royal, and began to serve the surveillance committee of the Paris Department. In 1794 he also worked for the Committee of General Security, denouncing and arresting, among others, the writer André Chénier. A terrorist who enjoyed the Terror, he was cruel, vindictive, and self-serving, but he managed to carry on under the Directory. Dismissed and imprisoned twice for embezzlement, he eventually took to the woods and lived a wild life for many years. (Richard Cobb, *Reactions to the French Revolution*, Oxford, 1972, p. 75.)

GUIBERT, Jacques-Antoine-Hippolyte, Comte de (1744–90). Born at Romans (Drôme) to an officer who became governor of Les Invalides in Paris, he entered the army, fought in the Seven Years' War and against Paoli in Corsica (1768–1769). He published an influential *Essai général de tactique* (1772), Saint-Germain called him to the War Ministry (1775) to reform the army, and the Comte de Brienne again (April 1787) to reform military administration. The French Academy elected him on 13 February 1786. Brilliant and original, he wrote several more books.

GUILLOTIN, Joseph-Ignace (1738–1814). Born at Saintes (Charente), he became a Jesuit teacher at the Collège des Irlandais in Bordeaux and then a medical doctor in Paris (1770). Elected deputy for Paris at the

Estates General, he worked at reforming medicine and pharmacy, and on 10 October 1789 urged that public executions be made more efficient. His name came to be used for the guillotine, but in fact, that apparatus was designed and built under the direction of Dr. Louis, secretary of the Academy of Surgery. Arrested in the Terror, he was released and went on with his medical work.

GUYTON DE MORVEAU, Louis-Bernard (1737–1816). The son of a law professor of Dijon, he became chief lawyer to the Parlement of Burgundy, wrote books (such as *Memoir on Public Education* [1764]) and then devoted himself to science. In 1776 he published *Elements of Theoretical and Practical Chemistry* in three volumes and sat in the Academy of Dijon. Elected to the Legislative Assembly and the Convention, he sat on their finance committees, went out on missions, voted for the king's death, and served briefly on the Committee of Public Safety in its early stages. He busied himself with armaments, aerial balloons, and education. He sat in the Five Hundred, was a founding member of the Institute, taught chemistry at the École polytechnique, and received the Legion of Honor and a baronetcy from Napoleon.

HANRIOT, François (1759–94). Born at Nanterre, the son of a domestic servant, he served on the staff at the gates of Paris, and the Paris Commune put him in charge of the National Guard on 31 May 1793. In this post he played a major part in the events of 2 June by surrounding the Convention and enforcing the policy of the Revolutionary Central Committee. He was hostile to Ronsin and his Revolutionary Army, formed in September 1793. On 27 July 1794 he took Robespierre's side, and the Revolutionary Tribunal had him executed the next day.

Hassenfratz, Jean-Henri (1757–1827). He served on a warship, then studied mathematics and mining and worked in Lavoisier's chemistry laboratory. He became a Patriot and a Jacobin, was active in the insurrection of 10 August 1792, and sat in the Paris Commune then formed. He soon turned to war production and also served on the commission confiscating machines, tools, and weapons for the republic. In 1797 he began to teach at the École polytechnique.

HÉBERT, Jacques-René (1757–94). Born to a poor family of Alençon (Orne), he went to Paris in about 1785, earned a precarious living, became a Patriot, and began to write pamphlets. By September 1790, glib and fluent, he was writing a popular journal, the scurrilous, violent *Le Père Duchesne*. Through it he became an influential leader of the popular cause, a member of the Paris Commune formed on 10 August 1792, and one of the Cordeliers Club of revolutionary socialists, including Ronsin, Vincent, Momoro, and Frédéric-Pierre Ducroquet. Late in 1793 these Hébertists began to antagonize the Committee of Public Safety, which soon arrested them and a dozen followers, charged them with inciting the populace to revolt, and guillotined them on 24 March 1794.

HÉRAULT DE SÉCHELLES, Marie-Jean (1759–94). Born in Paris, the son of a noble officer killed at the Battle of Minden (1759), he was intelligent and well educated. Because of the patronage of the Polignac family, the queen made him *avocat du roi* in the Châtelet criminal court (1777) and then *avocat général* in the Parlement of Paris (1785). He broke with the royal court as soon as it got into difficulties, was in the attack on the Bastille (14 July 1789), was elected judge (1790) and then deputy to the Legislative Assembly and finally to the Convention (for Seine-et-Oise). Eloquent, elegant, something of a dandy, with an easy grasp of public affairs, he was a fervent Jacobin in the Terror but not committed to any party. He was elected to the Committee of Public Safety on 10 July 1793 and with Barère directed diplomatic affairs. Foreign and aristocratic connections exposed him to the suspicion of treason, which Fabre d'Églantine falsely accused him of, and the Committee of Public Safety had him tried and guillotined on 5 April 1794.

HUGUENIN, Sulpice (1764–?). Formerly a clerk in the customs service at the gates of Paris, he was one of the influential members of the Paris Commune after 10 August 1792. He was an unprincipled adventurer, whose main purpose was to make his own fortune; cruel and troublesome, he had much to do with the massacre of Swiss Guards in the courtyard of the Hôtel de Ville on 10 August 1792. Pache put him in charge of military clothing and equipment, and when he was publicly criticized in July 1793 for making a fortune, Pache and Marat defended him.

ISNARD, Henri-Maximin (1758–1825). Born at Grasse (Alpes-Maritimes), he went into business with his father, a wholesale merchant of oil, wheat, silk, and soap until he was elected to the Legislative Assembly for the Var Department. He threw his eloquent and stormy character into the anticlerical cause ("The law, there is my God, I know no other") and associated with the Girondins. Elected to the Convention, he went on missions and sat on the Committee of General Defense, opposed the Jacobins, but survived, though his property was confiscated and his business ruined. After Thermidor he was a leader of reaction against terrorists and famous for a speech at Aix: "If you have no weapons, take sticks; if you have no sticks, dig up the bones of your relatives to strike the terrorists." He was elected to the Five Hundred, and in 1804 Gaudin found him a place in the financial administration. At the restoration he retired to Grasse.

JAVOGUES, Claude (1759–96). Son of a notary and *avocat au* Parlement of Bellegarde (Loire), he became a soldier, a legal clerk, and then a deputy to the Convention. Sent on a mission to the Saône-et-Loire Department, he was notorious for rigorous repression, though not as cruel as Carrier. He came into conflict with Couthon, but they were soon reconciled. Sometime after Thermidor he was denounced for his work as a representative on mission, sentenced, and executed on 10 October 1796. (Colin Lucas, *The Structure of the Terror,* Oxford, 1973.)

JEANBON SAINT-ANDRÉ, André (1749–1813). The son of a Protestant fuller of Montauban, he attended a Jesuit college and then became a ship's captain. Discouraged by a shipwreck on a voyage to the West Indies, he went to Lausanne and became a Calvinist minister (20 April 1773). He served at Castres and Montauban, met some Girondin leaders, was elected to the Convention for the Lot Department, and sat with the Girondins until their attacks on Paris grew too much for him. With an eye to national causes, he became a leading Jacobin, active in the war effort, especially in naval affairs. He joined the Committee of Public Safety on 12 June 1793 and directed naval warfare. Practical and talented, he survived the events of Thermidor, became French consul at Algiers (1795) and Smyrna (1797), and survived three years of imprisonment at Constantinople after war broke out. Returning to Paris in 1801, he became one of Napoleon's prefects, a member of the Legion of Honor, and Baron of Saint-André (1810). David painted his portrait.

LACOMBE, Claire (1765–?). A merchant's daughter born at Pamiers (Ariège), she became a beautiful actress and played at Lyons, Marseilles, Toulon, and Paris, where she arrived in March 1792. Already a republican, she founded (with Pauline Léon) a women's club, the Société des citoyennes républicaines révolutionnaires (10 May 1793), which played a brief but colorful part in the political life of Paris, notably in the insurrection of 31 May–2 June 1793. She survived long enough to act in the Grand Théâtre de la République in April 1797.

Lafayette, Marie-Joseph, Marquis de (1757–1834) Born at the Château de Chavaniac (Haute-Loire), he became an army officer and a general in the French forces sent to America during the War of Independence. Impressed by American ideas, he led a liberal faction in the Assembly of Notables and headed the Paris National Guard in 1789 and 1790. He was soon leading a party of constitutional monarchists and was hated therefore by the extreme right and left. In 1792 he took up an army command but soon emigrated and was interned by the Austrians. When released, he served the counterrevolutionary cause of constitutional monarchy. True to his principles, he refused to serve Napoleon, and under the restoration sat on the left in the Chamber of Deputies. Opposed to Charles X and the ultraroyalists, he left in 1824 to tour America. In 1830 he helped put Louis-Philippe on the throne and sat in the Chamber of Deputies almost until his death on 20 May 1834. He was not brilliant but was a man of strong character and firm principles, one of the great liberals of the age.

LAMBALLE, Marie-Thérèse-Louise de Savoie-Carignan, Princesse de (1749–92). Born at Turin, charming and educated, she married the Prince de Lamballe, *grand veneur de France* (1767) and became a friend of Marie-Antoinette. She was killed in a massacre on 3 September 1792.

LAMETH, a family of three brothers, all born in Paris, all called "Comte de Lameth." All served in America as commissioned officers during the War of Independence, all imbibed certain liberal ideas but remained constitutional monarchists, and all played similar parts in the Revolution. (1) Théodore (1756–1854) was elected to the administration of the Jura Department (1790) and then to the Legislative Assembly, where he sat on the right and was one of the few to remain after 10 August 1792. Later he fled to Switzerland and did not return to France until 1814, when he again entered public life. (2) Charles-Malo-François (1757–1832) sat in the Estates General for the nobility of Artois, was one of the first to join the Third Estate, and sat on the left in the National Assembly. In 1792 he fled to Hamburg and spent years in a counterrevolutionary movement. He served Napoleon as governor of Würzburg and in other posts. (3) Alexandre-Théodore-Victor (1760–1829) had a career much like his brother Charles, but served in the army of the Nord from April 1792 until emigrating with General Luckner. He was a prefect under Napoleon and a deputy in the Chamber of Deputies during the restoration.

LAMOIGNON DE BASVILLE, Chrétien-François II de (1735–89). The son of Chrétien-Guillaume de Lamoignon (1712–59), a magistrate in the Paris Parlement, and of a granddaughter of the Huguenot banker Samuel Bernard, he was a seventh-degree nobleman and soon became a magistrate himself. In 1758 he married the daughter of Nicolas-René Berryer (1703–62), the rigorous lieutenant general of police. He was a cousin of the great Malesherbes, and the family was a rival of the Maupeous. In the coup of 1771 Chancellor Maupeou banished him to Thizy, a tiny Rhône village where there was only one decent house and (as he wrote) "nothing grows but potatoes." He was intelligent and enlightened enough to propose judicial reforms of his own to the king as early as 1784, especially reforms of criminal justice, and on 8 April 1787 Louis XVI appointed him keeper of the seals (after Miromesnil) at a critical moment in the struggle between the

Crown and the parlements. Rising to the occasion, he planned sweeping changes, which the king announced on 8 May 1788. Removed from office with Loménie de Brienne in September 1788, he was found dead in his park on 16 May 1789; there was a gun nearby, and his family decided there had been a hunting accident. (Marcel Marion, *Le garde des sceaux Lamoignon et la réforme judicaire de 1788*, Paris, 1905.)

LANTHENAS, François-Xavier (1754–99). Son of a Paris wax merchant, he was apprenticed to a Lyons firm (1770) and then traveled on business in Holland, Germany, and Italy. He met Roland and his wife, who arranged for him to study medicine, and he became a doctor at Rheims (1784) with a thesis on education as a cause of illness. Through the Rolands he later wrote for *Le patriote française*, joined the Jacobin Club, and was elected to the Convention. Like other Girondins, he voted for Louis XVI's death but opposed Marat, Robespierre, and the Paris Commune. When the Girondin leaders were arrested on 2 June, Marat saved him by taking his name off the list on the ground that he was not worth thinking about. He escaped the Terror and was elected to the Five Hundred in 1795. He wrote several books, admired and translated Thomas Paine, and was an active member of the Amis des noirs.

LEBRUN, Charles-François (1739–1824). Born at Saint-Sauveur-Lendelin (Manche), of which his father was *syndic-perpétuel*, he went to England, learned English, and studied English institutions. He became a lawyer (1762), a *payeur des rentes* (1768), and secretary to Chancellor Maupeou (1770) and was asked to draw up "a uniform code of jurisprudence," for which he received 6,000 livres a year (B.N., Joly de Fleury papers, 1437 fol. 104). He was a noble deputy to the Estates General, sat on the right in the National Assembly, and worked mainly at financial reform. In the Terror he was arrested on 10 September 1793 but survived. Under the Directory he was elected to the Council of Ancients (1795). Under the consulate he was briefly one of the consuls. Napoleon made him a peer, Duc de Plaisance (1808), and entrusted him with treasury matters. His memoirs are interesting.

LE CHAPELIER, Isaac-René-Guy (1754–94). Born at Rennes to a lawyer, he became a lawyer himself and was elected to the Estates General. An orator active on the Constitution Committee and a firm liberal, he tried to have the postal service guaranteed against police searches and drew up the decree abolishing nobility and the law against guilds, strikes, and workers' meetings (14 June 1791) that bears his name. A firm champion of constitutional monarchy, he joined the Feuillants and was arrested on 22 April 1794 with two like-minded colleagues, Jacques-Guillaume Thouret (1746–94) and Jean-Jacques IV Duval d'Espremenil. They were guillotined together.

LECLERC, Jean-Théophile-Victor (1771–?). Born at Montbrison (Loire), the son of a civil engineer, he joined the National Guard at Clermont-Ferrand (1789) and then (March 1790) went as a merchant's agent to Martinique, where he joined the Patriots. The governor arrested them and sent them back to France, where he soon joined the army of the Rhine, then the army of the Alps at Lyon, and the Jacobin Club, which sent him to Paris (9 May 1793). Active in the life of the sections, he played a part in the insurrection of 31 May–2 June 1793 and became one of the extremist group the *enragés*. He married the *sans-culotte* feminist Anne-Pauline Léon on 18 November 1793. When his friend Jacques Roux was arrested, he escaped arrest by going to the battlefront as a soldier.

LEGENDRE, Louis (1752–97). Son of a Versailles butcher, he worked for ten years as a sailor, then as a butcher at Pointoise and Paris, and was a popular leader in Paris from 1789. With Danton and others he founded the Cordeliers Club and spoke to it loudly and often. In December 1791 he led a delegation to the Legislative Assembly to ask for the distribution of pikes. Becoming an assiduous Jacobin, he spoke with Marat-like tones, proposing, e.g., in 1792 that priests who would not take the oath should be drowned in the sea. He later claimed to have hidden Marat for two years in his cellar. On the night of 9–10 August 1792 he presided over the Luxembourg Section, sitting between two open barrels of gunpowder as a precaution against arrest. Elected deputy to the Convention, he voted for the king's death and wanted his head carried on a pike to the battlefronts as a warning to the counterrevolutionary leaders. After several missions he served from 16 June 1793 for two months in the Committee of General Security. He had the courage to speak in defense of Danton, but being contradicted by Robespierre, he collapsed in fear and discouragement. After 9 Thermidor he became a vigorous Thermidorian serving on the Committee of General Security in its reactionary phase. But the complexities of the warring factions confused and demoralized him again before his death.

LÉON, Anne-Pauline (1768–?). Born in Paris, the daughter of a chocolate manufacturer, she became a revolutionary activist in summer 1789 and in February 1791 led a party of women to sack the Fréron household, "where they smashed a bust of Lafayette and threw the pieces out of the window." (R. B. Rose, *The Making of the Sans-culottes,* Manchester, England, 1983, p. 113.) On 17 July 1791 she went with her mother and another woman activist, the cook Constance Évrard, to sign the republican petition on the Champ-de-Mars. She attended the Cordeliers Club, the Société fraternelle, later the Luxembourg Society; in 1793 she was one of the founders of the Société des citoyennes républicaines révolutionnaires, a feminist society devoted, among other things, to recruiting a legion of armed women to be part of the revolutionary forces.

LINDET, Jean-Baptiste-Robert (1746–1825). Born at Bernay (Eure), the son of a merchant, he became a legal official *(procureur du roi)* there, was prominent in official revolutionary circles, and was elected to the Legislative Assembly in 1791. He voted on the left, but on 10 August 1792 hid and saved a colonel of the Swiss Guards. Elected to the Convention, he quit the Girondins and joined the Jacobins, was elected (7 April 1793) to the Committee of Public Safety, where he worked at matters of provisioning, supply, and finance. He survived Thermidor and was elected to the Five Hundred, to the Ministry of Finance (1799), retired to private life under the empire and later regimes, and was buried in the Père Lachaise Cemetery.

LOMÉNIE DE BRIENNE, Étienne-Charles de (1727–94). He was born in Paris, schooled at the Sorbonne, and became bishop of Condom (1760), bishop of Toulouse (1763), archbishop of Sens (1788), and a cardinal (15 December 1788). Active in literary circles, he was received in the French Academy (1770); benevolent and generous, he endowed a hospital at Toulouse, dug a canal, assisted poor students, and did other good works; a vigorous administrator, he had much influence in the quinquennial Assembly of the Clergy. When Calonne fell out of favor, Louis XVI appointed Loménie chief of the Royal Council of Finance on 1 May 1787 and principal minister on 26 August. He resigned on 25 August 1788. In 1790 he took the oath and was elected bishop of Yonne. During the Terror he lived quietly at Sens until arrested on 9 November 1793. Bullied and punched by some drunken soldiers guarding him in prison, he died on 16 February 1794. During his term of office as king's minister, his brother Louis-Marie-Athanase de Loménie, Comte de Brienne, was minister for war.

MAGNIEN, Vivent (1744–1811). Born a baker's son at Chalon-sur-Saône, he worked his way up through the General Farm of Taxes and into the group working on customs reform. He published *Recueil alphabétique des droits de traites uniformes, de ceux d'entrée et de sortie des Cinq Grosses Fermes . . .* (Avignon, 1786, 4 vols) and became an adviser to the National Assembly on customs reform and then one of the customs directors *(régisseurs)*, 1791–1794 and 1796–1811. He was a Freemason.

MAHY DE CORMERÉ, Guillaume-François (1739–94?). Born to a receiver general of domains and forests at Blois, he became head *(chef)* of the customs reform bureau in the controller general's department during Jacques Necker's first ministry (1776–81). Devoted to customs reform, he worked at it on the committees and commissions of the years 1780–1790, left many manuscript memoranda, and published many books. The National Assembly based its customs reforms on his work and that of Magnien. When his brother, Thomas de Mahy, Marquis de Favras (1744–90) was executed for conspiracy on 19 February 1790, he emigrated to Saint-Domingue (Haiti) in 1791 and later spent some time in Baltimore Maryland, where he published a memoir on the crisis in Saint-Domingue. (J. F. Bosher, *The Single Duty Project*, London, 1964.)

MALESHERBES, Chrétien-Guillaume de Lamoignon de (1721–94). Born in Paris to an old family of magistrates, son of the chancellor, he was schooled by Jesuits, and served as a liberal and enlightened director of the censorship service (*librairie*) (1750–63) and president of the Cour des aides (1750–76). He traveled on foot through France, Holland, and Switzerland disguised as a "Monsieur Guillaume." He became a popular reformer, rescued many people jailed for debt by financiers, and on 18 February 1771 drew up a famous remonstrance against Maupeou's abolition of the parlements. Louis XVI called him to the ministry (with Turgot) in 1774 and again briefly in 1787. Famous in his own time, he was elected to the academies of Science (1750) and Inscriptions (1759) and to the French Academy (1775). He had studied botany under Jussieu, and his hobby was gardening at Malesherbes, where he had a famous collection of exotic shrubs and trees. In 1792 and 1793 he tried to defend Louis XVI before the Convention and stayed faithfully with him until the execution. He was himself arrested with his family in December 1793, and they all were guillotined on 22 April 1794.

MANUEL, Pierre-Louis (1753–93). The son of an itinerant potter who settled at Montargis in the mercery trade, he attended a seminary and became a teacher and tutor. He became a police clerk in Paris and a Jacobin and saved several people during the September 1792 massacres in the Paris prisons, just before his election to the Convention. There he courageously blamed the Paris populace in general for the massacres, and took sides with Louis XVI. With his moderate views, he was soon shut out of the Cordeliers and Jacobin clubs, arrested, and guillotined on 14 November 1793. Joseph Ducreux painted his portrait.

MARAT, Jean-Paul (1743–93). Born in Sardinia, he worked as tutor to the children of a Bordeaux merchant, Paul Nairac, as a student of medicine and a writer in London, and as a dilettante scientist and journalist in Paris. He was elected in 1789 to the electoral committee of one of the sixty Paris districts and soon became a popular leader and agitator. He founded a left-wing journal, *L'ami du peuple*, in autumn 1789, was soon promoting violence and revolt, and had to hide from the police until 10 August 1792. Then he was elected to the Convention, where he was one of the strongest popular leaders, an opponent of the Girondins, and a tireless denouncer of counterrevolutionaries. Among his friends were three other left-wing journalists, Fréron, Desmoulins, and Prudhomme. One of the most prominent of revolutionary leaders, he was stabbed to death at the height of his career, on 13 July 1793, in his bathtub, by Charlotte Corday, a scene painted by David.

MARÉCHAL, Pierre-Sylvain (1750–1803). Son of a Paris wine merchant, he became a lawyer in the Parlement and then a writer and revolutionary intellectual. Prolific and versatile, he published poetry, history, and many political tracts. He befriended such radicals as Chaumette and Babeuf but managed to avoid their fate.

MAUPEOU, René-Nicolas-Charles-Augustin de (1714–92). Born at Montpellier to a magistrate in the Paris Parlement, he followed his father's career, and was named chancellor of France on 18 September 1768. Intelligent and determined, he and the controller general of finance, Abbé Terray, struck at the troublesome parlements in 1770 and 1771 and abolished them. When Louis XVI was crowned, he sacrificed Maupeou to a reconciliation with the parlements and banished him on 24 August 1774 to his Château de Thuyt (Eure) in Normandy. As chancellor he was appointed for life and so had to be removed. The keeper of the seals *(garde des sceaux)* then became acting chancellor.

MAUREPAS, Jean-Frédéric Phélypeaux, Comte de (1701–81). Descendant of a family of magistrates and royal ministers, son of Louis XIV's chancellor, a member of several academies, he was secretary of state for the navy and colonies (1723–49). Disgraced and exiled on 24 April 1749, he was recalled by Louis XVI on 20 May 1774 and became the king's chief adviser and chief of the Royal Council of Finance until his death on 9 November 1781.

MERCY D'ARGENTEAU, Florimond-Claude, Comte de (1727–94). Born in Liège, he served as Austrian ambassador to France from 1766 and played a part in arranging Marie-Antoinette's marriage to Louis XVI. He thereby became an intimate with the royal couple, especially the queen, and advised her in accordance with Austrian policy. Leopold II recalled him in 1790 to serve as governor of the Austrian Netherlands (Belgium). Thereafter he did counterrevolutionary work.

MIRABEAU, Honoré-Gabriel, Comte de (1749–91). Born at Bignon (Loiret) to Victor-Riqueti, Marquis de Mirabeau (1715–89), he led the life of a wayward noble son, criticized the regime in his *Essay on Despotism* (1776), and was imprisoned in the Bastille for debt and disobedience. In 1788 he visited Prussia, where he met King Frederick

II. Rejected by the nobility in 1789, he was elected for the Third Estate of Aix and spoke for the constitutional monarchy with intelligence and brilliant eloquence. He was severely scarred by smallpox in his youth, lived a dissolute, self-indulgent life, and died on 2 April 1791. The left wing in and out of the Assembly had already marked him as an enemy.

MIROMESNIL, Armand-Thomas Hue de (1723–96). Born at Mardié (Loiret) to a marquis and cavalry captain, he became a master of requests (1751), a magistrate in the Parlement of Rouen (1757), and keeper of the seals (24 August 1774) on Maupeou's disgrace. He was neither very interested nor very capable and retired on 20 February 1781.

MOMORO, Antoine-François (1756–94). A cultivated master printer and bookseller, interested in social problems, he became an administrator of the Paris Department and the most influential member of the Marat Section of Paris. Informed and determined, he was often president of the Cordeliers Club and had a following among the *sans-culottes* until he was guillotined with Hébert and his followers on 24 March 1794.

MONGE, Gaspard (1746–1818). Born at Beaune (Côte-d'Or) to a humble family, he studied so well that at sixteen he was teaching physics at Lyons. He became a famous mathematician, the founder of descriptive geometry, a professor at Mézières and then Paris. In the Revolution he was politically active and directed the manufacturing of cannon until he was denounced in the Terror and fled briefly abroad. He and Berthollet went on Napoleon's Egyptian campaign, and then he taught at the École polytechnique. He lost his post at the restoration.

MONTMORIN DE SAINT-HEREM, Armand-Marc, Comte de (1745–92). Born in Paris, he was attached to Louis XVI's retinue before the reign and held high office under the king: ambassador to Madrid (1777), commander in chief in Brittany (1783–86), and secretary of state for foreign affairs (14 February 1787). One of Necker's friends, he was dismissed briefly with him on 11 July 1789. He was close to the king, gave him much advice, and issued a passport under a false name for the royal family's planned escape in disguise on 21 June 1791. Suspected of counterrevolutionary plots, he was replaced by Antoine-Nicolas Valdec de Lessart (1741–92) in November 1791 and had to hide after 10 August 1792. He was found eleven days later in the house of a laundress, sent to the Abbaye prison, and murdered there by a mob on 31 August.

MORRIS, Gouverneur (1752–1816). Born near New York, his mother descended from a Huguenot family named Gouverneur, he lived in fashionable circles in Paris from February 1789 until autumn 1794. This was longer than the visits of most of the Americans, more than a hundred of them, who lived in Paris during those years. At first he represented American business interests and kept Thomas Jefferson informed of French affairs, but late in 1791 he was appointed American ambassador. A colorful person in some ways, he had a wooden leg and many lady friends, particularly the beautiful Comtesse de Flahaut (who already had an illegitimate son by Talleyrand-Périgord, bishop of Autun), and he led as busy a social life as possible in those times. A collection of his letters, with his news of revolutionary events, has been published.

MOUNIER, Jean-Joseph (1758–1806). Born at Grenoble, the son of a merchant, he became a learned and liberal lawyer (1779). An active Patriot in the 1780s, a prominent member of the Company of Thirty, he was elected to the Third Estate in 1789 and proposed the Tennis Court Oath on 20 June. A constitutional monarchist, he emigrated to Switzerland in 1792. He refused a post as a judge in Canada that the British government offered him in 1793, but in 1795 he accepted employment at the court of Weimar, Germany, where he organized a school. He returned to France in 1801 and Napoleon made him prefect of Île-et-Villaine in 1802 and a councillor of state in 1804. His principles of liberty and justice were sorely tested during the Revolution.

NECKER, Jacques (1732–1804). Son of a German teacher trained in law who settled at Geneva, he became a banker and made a fortune as partner in the banking firm of Thellusson et Necker (1756) and then in Germany, Girardot et Compagnie (1772). He came to public notice partly through his wife's salon and partly through a book on the grain trade. Though he was a Protestant, a commoner, and a foreigner, Louis XVI made him director general of finances (1776–81), and he made many enemies by his sweeping reforms in the financial administration and then by his popular books on French public finance. The public in general, impressed by his books and his reforms, liked him, and Louis XVI recalled him in August 1788. He remained in command of the finances until 1790, when the National Assembly took control, and he then retired to his house at Coppet on Lake Geneva to write more books. His daughter became famous as Madame de Staël. (J. F. Bosher, *French Finances 1770–95*, Cambridge, England, 1970; R. D. Harris, *Necker*, Berkeley 1979.)

PACHE, Jean-Nicolas (1745–1823). An expatriate Swiss, born at Oron (Vaud), and a soldier's son, he was patronized by Necker, who found him an office as controller of the royal households and secretary of the navy, working under Castries. In the Revolution he became a secretary and friend to the Rolands, then an employee in the ministries of the Interior and War. On 10 August 1792 he became a member of the Paris Commune and served as Girondin minister of war from 3 October 1792 to 4 March 1793. On 4 November he, Roland, and Monge set up a purchasing agency for the three ministries of Interior, War, and Navy. He quarreled with the Girondins, secretly supported Marat and the Paris Commune, and went over to the Jacobins. He was elected mayor of Paris. Arrested soon after 24 May 1794, he was saved by the amnesty of 24 October.

PAINE, Thomas (1737–1809). Born at Thetford (Norfolk), the son of a Quaker farmer and staymaker, he proved unstable and incompetent at various occupations but impressed Benjamin Franklin, who gave him a letter of introduction to people in Philadelphia. During the colonies' quarrel with the government he wrote *Common Sense* (1776), became an aide to General Nathanael Greene and a secretary to the Continental Congress in 1777. In 1781 he went to France with Henry Laurens of the Congress. During the French Revolution he wrote *The Rights of Man* (1791) and *The Age of Reason* (1794), was welcomed in Paris, but returned to America and died in New York a celebrated patriot and radical.

PANIS, Étienne-Jean (1757–1832). Born in Paris, he worked with an uncle who was a cashier in the royal treasury, studied law, and was accredited as a barrister *(avocat)* to the Parlement of Paris on 7 March 1782. But he was not typical of this conservative profession. As an elector in the Arsenal Section of Paris, he became a radical Patriot and a friend of Danton and Marat. Elected a judge and then a police official in the Paris municipality, he was on the Comité de surveillance and able to play a part in the uprisings of 20 June and 10 August 1792. Elected to the Convention and to its Committee of General Security (10 September 1793), he stood up for Marat and for Santerre, whose daughter he had married, and himself escaped from the retribution following Thermidor. He became an obscure pensioner and survived quietly into the July Monarchy.

PAOLI, Pasquale (1725–1807). Born at Strettade-Morosaglia (Corsica), he was proclaimed commander in chief by the Corsican clans in 1755 to lead in wars of independence against the Genoese and then the French. When 22,000 French defeated him at Ponte-Nuova on 9 May 1769, and France annexed Corsica, he fled to England, where he drew a pension of £1,200 on the civil list for twenty years and was befriended by Joshua Reynolds, Dr. Johnson, Edmund Burke, and Oliver Goldsmith. In 1790 he went to Paris, addressed the National Assembly, and was made military commander of Corsica by Louis XVI. He fell out with the republican government, turned Corsica over to British forces, and in 1795 retired to London, where he lived and died at 200 Edgware Road. There is a marble bust of him in the south aisle of Westminster Abbey.

PÉTION DE VILLENEUVE, Jérôme (1756–94). Born at Chartres, he became a lawyer, like his father, and then the Chartres subdelegate to the intendant of Orléans. Elected to the Estates General, he joined Buzot, Dubois-Crancé, Prieur de la Marne, and Robespierre on the extreme left. He was no orator but made a good public impression, and on 16 November 1791, when he was even more popular than Robespierre, he was elected mayor of Paris. A moderate monarchist, he was suspended as mayor by the Paris Department on 6 July 1792 and by the king on 12 July, but by turning against the monarchy in August, he persuaded the revolutionary Commune to restore him as mayor. He did nothing to stop the September 1792 massacres. He was reelected mayor (4 October 1792) but resigned to take up a seat in the Convention. There he sided with the Girondins against Robespierre, was eventually denounced with the rest, escaped with his friend Buzot, but took his own life at Saint-Magne (Gironde) on 18 June 1794.

PHILIPPE-ÉGALITÉ (Louis-Philippe-Joseph, Duc d'Orléans) (1747–93). A descendant of the princely family of Orléans, he was a deputy to the National Assembly and elected to the National Convention. A radical revolutionary Jacobin, in spite of his social position, he voted for the execution of his cousin Louis XVI in January 1793, but he himself was arrested and executed later that year. His son, Louis-Philippe (1773–1850), Duc de Chartres, served in the army as an officer at the battles of Valmy (1792), Jemappes (1792), and Neerwinden (1793) and ruled as the last King of France from 1830 to 1848.

PRIEUR DE LA CÔTE-D'OR, Claude-Antoine (Prieur-Duvernois) (1763–1832). Born at Auxonne (Côte-d'Or), son of a receiver of finance, he became an officer in the army engineers and reached the rank of captain (1 April 1791). By then he was a member of the Academy of Dijon busy with applied science, and the Côte-d'Or Department elected him to the Legislative Assembly and then to the Convention. He was prominent in organizing the armies in many parts of France and was named to the Committee of Public Safety (14 August 1793). Industrious, intelligent, and no intriguer, he survived Thermidor, was elected to the Five Hundred, and worked on weights and measures, education, internal waterways, and fortifications. During the empire he retired to his writing and a quiet life on a tiny pension.

PRIEUR DE LA MARNE, Pierre-Louis (1756–1827). Born at Sommesous (Marne), he became a lawyer at Châlons-sur-Marne, where he was elected to the Estates General. He sat on the left and worked at judicial and administrative reforms. A vigorous Patriot with a loud voice, he presided over the elections to the Convention at Châlons with a double-barreled gun on the desk, to be ready, he said, for enemy forces if they came. He himself was elected, served on the Committee of General Defense, went out on several missions, and was named (10 July 1793) to the Committee of Public Safety. There he served the cause in many ways, organized military bands and youth groups, and denounced the English in wild Napoleonic terms. He survived Thermidor, hid when his arrest was later decreed, became a hospital administrator and, under Napoleon, a lawyer. In 1816 he fled to Brussels, where he died.

PROVENCE, Louis-Stanislas-Xavier, Comte de (1755–1824). Louis XVI's next brother, he emigrated in 1791, returned to rule France in 1814, and was succeeded at his death by the youngest brother, Charles-Philippe, Comte d'Artois.

PUISAYE, Joseph, Comte de (1755–1827). Born at Mortagne (Orne) the son of an army officer from an old family of Perche, he followed his three brothers into the army and in 1789 became head of a National Guards battalion at Évreux (Eure). A Patriot ready to plant trees of liberty, he remained a constitutional monarchist and commanded an army of Federalists *(fédérés)* who were ready to resist the Paris dictatorship formed by Jacobins on 2 June 1793. His 2,500 men were defeated at the Battle of Brécourt (13 July 1793). He hated the Paris Commune, Marat, and the whole republican-democratic movement and soon came to hate the Jacobins, who sent *commissaires* on violent missions out into the provinces and put a price of 3,000 livres on his head, dead or alive. He became a counterrevolutionary leader in touch with émigrés and with the British government often through the Channel Islands. He commanded the disastrous Quiberon expedition which landed at Carnac, Brittany, on 27 June 1795. (Maurice Hutt, *Chouannerie and Counter-Revolution*, Cambridge, England, 1983, 2 vols.)

Robert, François (1763–1823). Born at Gimnée (Namur), Belgium, he became a barrister in France and moved to Paris in August 1789. He settled on the Left Bank in the Cordeliers district and married Louise-Félicité Guinement de Keralio (1758–1821), a writer from a noble Breton family who had known Robespierre in the Academy of Arras. She was working for the *Journal d'état et du citoyen*, and when Robert joined its staff with Jean-Louis Carra and others, the journal soon became the well-known *Mercure national*. Its staff were educated middle-class people working for social equality by spreading revolutionary ideas. They were among the founders of the Cordeliers Club, and Robert was secretary of the central committee they set up in May 1791 to coordinate insurrection in the forty-eight sections. One of the first republicans, he drafted the petition the Cordeliers used on the Champ-de-Mars on 17 July 1791. He was elected to the Paris Commune in August 1792 and to the Convention in September, and he was active in denouncing and trying Louis XVI. His career was damaged by illegal sales of rum, which he kept in his cellar, but he went on various missions to Liège and Belgium, where he eventually returned and died a merchant. (J. R. Censer, *Prelude to Power: The Parisian Radical Press, 1789–1791*, Baltimore, 1976.)

ROBESPIERRE, Maximilien Marie-Isidore (1758–94). Born in Arras (Pas-de-Calais), the son of a barrister, who soon abandoned the family, and of a brewer's daughter, he went to school at Louis-le-Grand in Paris, became a lawyer (1781), and was elected to the Estates General (1789) for the Third Estate of Arras. He became the leader of the left wing in the National Assembly and in the Jacobin Club, was elected (5 September 1792) to the Convention and (27 July 1793) to the Committee of Public Safety. There he presided over the war effort and the organization of the revolutionary republic until 28 July 1794, when he was guillotined with his colleagues Couthon and Saint-Just. His biographers, like his contemporaries, disagree about his character and his work, but all see him as the leading figure in the Revolution. As a man, he was thin, frugal, hardworking, uncompromising, intense, fanatical, and psychologically complex. Of the many biographies, those by J. M. Thompson, David P. Jordan, and Gérard Walter are intelligent, readable, and nonpartisan. The shorter ones by Norman Hampson and R. R. Palmer *(Twelve Who Ruled)* are also entertaining.

ROEDERER, Pierre-Louis (1754–1835). He followed his father in an office in the Parlement of Metz and was elected to the Estates General in 1789. A member of the Jacobin Club, in 1791 he became an administrator and then a councillor in the Paris Department and took a special interest in tax reform. A liberal monarchist and a moderate, he went into hiding after 10 August 1792 and played no further part in public affairs until after the Terror, when he emerged as a liberal journalist, editor and half owner of *Le journal de Paris*. He consorted with Benjamin Constant, Madame de Staël, and Thibaudeau and threw his energies into the struggle to stabilize the regime, to establish an ordered liberty, and to thwart the efforts of extremists. He supported the coup d'etat of Brumaire and served as one of Napoleon's *notables* and trusted aides until 1815, when he retired and then went into the Chamber of Peers. (K. Margerison, *P.-L. Roederer: Political Thought and Practice During the French Revolution*, Philadelphia, 1983.)

ROHAN-SOUBISE-GUÉMÉNÉE. This great clan included (1) Louis-René-Édouard de Rohan, Prince de Soubise, cardinal and archbishop of

Strasbourg (1734–1803), a nobleman of dubious reputation eventually tried by the Parlement of Paris for his involvement in 1787 in the scandalous Affair of the Diamond Necklace, for which see Alfred Cobban, *Aspects of the French Revolution*, London, 1968, ch. 4; (2) Ferdinand-Maximilien Mériadec de Rohan-Guéménée (1738–1813), archbishop of Bordeaux; (3) Maréchal Charles de Rohan, Duc de Rohan-Rohan, Prince de Soubise (1715–87); (4) Jules-Hercule Meriadec, Prince de Rohan-Guéménée, whose wife was governess to the royal children and who in 1782 suffered a notorious bankruptcy of some 33,000 livres which ruined even many humble families; (5) the attractive Louise-Julie-Constance de Rohan-Rochefort, Comtesse de Brionne by marriage, who was Choiseul's mistress. Among these are examples of the nobles whose scandalous lives began to bring the royal court, especially the queen, into disrepute in the 1780s.

ROLAND, Jean-Marie (1734–93). Born at Thizy (Rhône), he became an inspector of manufactures under Louis XVI, played a part in promoting French industry, and became minister of the interior after Louis XVI fell on 10 August 1792. A prominent Girondin, wealthy and educated, he was arrested with the others, escaped, but killed himself on 10 November 1793 on hearing of his wife's death and the trend of national affairs.

ROLAND, Jeanne Manon, née Phlipon (1754–93). Wife of the above, she was intelligent, ambitious, and a distinguished hostess with a salon where the Girondin leaders met until they were arrested and executed, she with them.

RONSIN, Charles-Philippe (1751–94). Born in Soissons (Aisne), son of a master cooper, he joined the Aunis regiment (1768) and left with the rank of corporal (1772). He then wrote plays, studied the theater, was patronized by the painter David, by Protestant notables of Nîmes, and by the Duc de Chartres. His play *La fête de la liberté*, in praise of Lafayette, was put on in 1790 in a theater on the rue de Richelieu. In July 1789 he became captain of the National Guard in the Saint-Roch district of Paris, then joined the Cordeliers Club, where he met Momoro, Pache, and others. He went out on missions for Roland (1792), denounced corruption in Dumouriez's army, commanded troops at La Rochelle and in the Vendée (1793), where he was savage in repression of counterrevolution, and finally commanded the civilian *armée révolutionnaire* of Paris. He was executed on 24 March 1794 in a huge roundup of suspects.

ROUX, Jacques (1752–94). Born at Pranzac (Angoumois), he was ordained a priest in 1776 and settled in Paris as parish priest of Saint-Nicolas-des-Champs. He lived in the Gravilliers Section in June 1791, preached revolution from the pulpit and in print, and played a leading part in the Cordeliers Club and as one of the *enragés* group. He was irritable and fierce in argument, and tended to exaggeration. Arrested with the other *enragés*, he killed himself on 10 February 1794.

SAINT-GERMAIN, Claude-Louis, Comte de (1707–78). Born at Vertambon (Jura), he became a Jesuit and then an army officer and had wide experience of war under various flags during the War of the Austrian Succession (1743–48) in Hungary, Bavaria, and Flanders. He made a reputation especially at the Battle of Rossbach (1757). Then he was employed in Denmark, to reform the Danish army. Louis XVI named him secretary of state for war in 1775, and he made many enlightened reforms. His hobby was gardening on his little estate near Lauterbach in Alsace, until his banker went bankrupt and left him with financial cares.

SAINT-JUST, Louis Antoine (1767–94). Born at Decize (Nièvre) to a cavalry officer, he became a local ne'er-do-well and writer, and, after a journey to Paris in 1789, a lieutenant colonel in the National Guard. In 1791 he made an impression with his book *Spirit of the Revolution and of the Constitution of France* and was elected to the Convention for the Aisne Department on 2 September 1792. A friend of Robespierre, he became the youngest member of the Committee of Public Safety, went out on various missions, was especially active in promoting and assisting the armies of the republic, and was guillotined with Robespierre on 28 July 1794. He was proud, hard, clever, and fanatical.

SANTERRE, Antoine-Joseph (1752–1809). Born in Paris, he became a brewer in the Faubourg Saint-Antoine, and was one of the Paris electors in 1789. Commander of the Paris National Guard for the Enfants Trouvés district in August 1789, later a prominent member of the Cordeliers Club and a leader in the attack on the Tuileries Palace on 10 August 1792, he became commander of the Paris National Guard after 10 August 1792 and a leader in the Quinze-vingts and Montreuil sections. He was sent out on missions, imprisoned in September 1793 but freed and then retired to a quiet life.

SARTINE, Antoine-Raymond-Jean-Galbert-Gabriel de (1729–1801). Born at Barcelona to a financial councillor of Philip V of Spain, he became a *conseiller* in the Châtelet criminal court (1752). He served as lieutenant general of the Paris Police (1759–67) and secretary of state for the navy (1774–80). Thereafter he was a councillor of state. For much of that time he was of Choiseul's party and a favorite of the queen.

SÉGUR, Philippe-Henri, Marquis de (1724–1801). He saw a great deal of fighting in the mid-century wars, was wounded many times, and lost an arm. Louis XVI made him *maréchal de France* (1781) and secretary of state for war. He was imprisoned in the Revolution.

SIEYÈS, Abbé Emmanuel-Joseph (1748–1836). Born at Fréjus (Var), he attended the Seminary of Saint-Sulpice and was a curé at Chartres. A Patriot in 1787 and 1788, he wrote some famous pamphlets, notably *What Is the Third Estate?* (January 1789), and became a radical leader in the Estates General. He soon took up the defense of the clergy and was a conservative in the Convention. Under the Directory he was elected to the Five Hundred, but served as ambassador to Berlin (1798) and then as one of the directors of the republic. A central figure in the coup of Brumaire, he brought Napoleon into it and became a senator and a nobleman in the empire. He was deported from France in 1815 but returned after 1830 and died in Paris.

STOFFLET, Jean-Nicolas (1751–96). Born at Lunéville (Meurthe-et-Moselle), a soldier's son, he joined the royalist army in the Vendée. There he later organized guerrilla bands of the Chouans until he was taken and shot at Angers on 15 February 1796.

TALLEYRAND-PÉRIGORD, Charles-Maurice de (1754–1838). Born in Paris, he attended the Seminary of Saint-Sulpice and the Sorbonne and became general agent for the French clergy (1780–85), bishop of Autun (1788), and a noble deputy to the Estates General (1789). Intelligent, liberal, worldly and cynical, he accepted the Civil Constitution of the Clergy, gave up his clerical career (1791), and turned to politics and diplomacy. He was ambassador to London (1792), toured the United States (1794), played a major part in the coup d'etat of Brumaire, and advised Napoleon on foreign affairs. He broke with Napoleon and in 1814 became president of the provisional government and sat in the Congress of Vienna (1815). Under Louis XVIII he sat in the Chamber of Deputies with the opposition. Louis-Philippe made him ambassador to Great Britain. He died in Paris on 17 May 1838, one of the remarkable figures of his time.

TALLIEN, Jean-Lambert (1767–1820). Born in Paris to the *maître d'hôtel* of the Comte de Bercy, he became a lawyer's clerk. He turned revolutionary journalist, joined the Jacobin Club and then the Paris Commune on 10 August 1792, and was elected to the National Convention for the Seine-et-Oise Department. He suppressed counterrevolutionary forces in the Gironde Department in 1793. One of the conspirators who brought down Robespierre in July 1794, he became a leader of the Thermidorian reaction and then a deputy to the Council of Five Hundred. He had married the fashionable daughter of a rich banker, Étienne Cabarrus. He was captured by British forces at one time. He died poor in Paris.

TERRAY, Abbé Joseph-Marie (1715–78). Born at Boën (Loire) into a family of magistrates and financiers, he took office in the Paris Parlement (1736) and served as minister of state (1770), secretary of state for the navy (1770), director general of royal buildings (1773), and, most important of all, controller general of finance (22 December 1769 to 24 August 1774). Worldly and determined, he and Chancellor Maupeou abolished the parlements in 1770 and 1771 in a firm stroke of royal authority, but Louis XVI undid this work. Terray's brother was in the Paris Cour des Aides, and his nephew was an intendant.

THÉROIGNE DE MÉRICOURT. The pseudonym of Anne-Joseph Terwagne (1762–1817), a feminist leader who in 1793 organized women in the faubourg Saint-Antoine, Paris.

TOUSSAINT L'OUVERTURE, François-Dominique (1743–1803). Born a black slave near Cap Français, Saint-Domingue (Haiti), he became a Roman Catholic convert and a steward on his plantation. In time he took seriously the Declaration of the Rights of Man and, in 1793, joined Spanish rebels against the French authorities. In May 1794, by which time he was the leader of a large army of rebellious slaves, he changed sides and helped drive out the Spanish. After some years Napoleon sent a force that captured him and brought him to France, where he died in the Fort-de-Joux prison in the French Alps.

TURGOT, Anne-Robert-Jacques (1727–81). Born in Paris into a family of royal officials and parlement magistrates, he went into the Paris Parlement and then became a royal master of requests and intendant at Limoges. A friend of the Physiocratic writers and a capable and enlightened reformer, he held various ministerial posts at Versailles and was Louis XVI's first controller general of finances (1774–76). He planned various reforms but fell before they could be implemented. His written works and correspondence, edited by G. Schelle, fill 5 volumes (Paris, 1913–23).

VADIER, Marc-Guillaume-Alexis (1736–1828). Son of a tithe collector of Pamiers, he fought in the Piedmont Regiment in the Seven Years' War and in 1770 became a magistrate in the presidial of Pamiers. There he acquired a hatred of the ruling classes, who treated him as a contemptible upstart, and this passion ruled his career as a deputy to the Estates General and later to the Convention. On 14 September 1793 he joined the Committee of General Security, wherein, until he left it on 1 September 1794, he was able to bring terror and death to untold numbers of enemies and others.

VARLET, Jean-François (1764–1832). Born to a prosperous Paris family, studied at the Collège d'Harcourt and then worked in the post office. An active Patriot in the early years of the Revolution, he joined Marat and the Jacobin and Cordeliers clubs and became a republican (in June 1791), and then one of the *enragé* extremists, favoring direct democracy and a kind of socialism. A popular activist on most of the great *journées*, he was a leader in the *sans-culotte* insurrection of 31 May–2 June 1793. He was in prison from 5 September 1794 to 4 November 1795.

VAUDREUIL, Louis-Philippe de Rigaud, Marquis de (1724–1802). Born at Rochefort (Charente-Maritime), he became a lieutenant general (1782), a conservative in court circles, a noble deputy to the Estates General, and an émigré officer.

VERGENNES, Charles Gravier, Comte de (1719–87). Born into a noble family of Dijon magistrates, he became a leading French diplomat, especially in Turkey, eastern Europe, and Sweden. Louis XVI made him secretary of state for foreign affairs (1774) and chief of the Royal Council of Finance (1783) and took his advice on many matters until his death on 13 February 1787.

VERGNIAUD, Pierre-Victurnien (1753–93). Son of a bourgeois of Limoges who was a friend of Turgot, he became a lawyer at Bordeaux and secretary to Charles Dupaty, president of the Bordeaux Parlement (1781). Recognized as a brilliant orator, he became a Patriot early in the Revolution, joined the Bordeaux Jacobin Club, and there made an eloquent speech on the death of Mirabeau. He was elected an administrator in the Gironde Department and then elected to the Legislative Assembly and the Convention, where he soon became one of the leaders of the Girondin faction and shared an apartment with another, Jean-François Ducos (1765–93). He supported Brissot's campaign for the declaration of war (20 April 1792) and spoke up against the Paris Commune soon after the September massacres. Hated by Robespierre and Marat, he was arrested on 2 June 1793 with the other Girondin leaders and executed on 31 October.

VINCENT, François-Nicolas (1766–94). Son of a concierge at a Paris prison, he became secretary-general of the War Office during the Revolution. A passionate Patriot, close to the *sans-culottes*, violent like Marat and Ronsin, he joined the Cordeliers Club. On 17 December 1793 he was arrested with his friend Ronsin and held until 2 February 1794. With Hébert and Momoro he tried to lead the Cordeliers Club against the Committee of Public Safety in spring 1794, and these leaders were arrested on 14 March 1794. He was guillotined with them ten days later.

VOLTAIRE, François-Marie Arouet (1694–1778). Author, playwright, poet, historian, humanitarian, one of the leading intellectuals of the French eighteenth-century Enlightenment.

WESTERMANN, François-Joseph (1751–94). He joined the Esterhazy Regiment in his native Alsace in 1767 and later became a municipal official at Strasbourg and Hagenau. He went to Paris in May 1792, joined Danton, and put himself at the head of the *fédéré* forces from

Brest to march on the Tuileries Palace on 10 August 1792. Named adjutant general to the army in the Ardennes on 14 September 1792, he helped Dumouriez in negotiations with the Duke of Brunswick and then became adjutant general to the army in Holland in February 1793. He was arrested with Dumouriez but was sent to fight in the Vendée. Arrested with Danton, Desmoulins, and others on 3 April 1794, he was executed with them.

WICKHAM, William (1761–1840). He studied at Christ Church, Oxford, and the University of Geneva, where he married the daughter of a mathematics professor. Lord Grenville sent him again to Berne in November 1794 as British consul general and, secretly, as an intelligence officer. There he played a major role in informing the British government and in counterrevolutionary circles of émigrés. In 1802, his projects largely unsuccessful, he returned home and became chief secretary for Ireland. The French regarded him as their most dangerous foreign adversary on the Continent. (H. Mitchell, *The Underground War Against Revolutionary France*, Oxford, 1965.)

The French Revolution

ONE *The French on the Eve of the Revolution*

A T THE time of the French Revolution there were 27 or 28 million French people. This was the largest population of any country in Europe, and since the beginning of the eighteenth century it had risen from 22 million by nearly 25 percent.[1] The total figure was imposing, but in the later eighteenth century the French population was growing less quickly than the smaller populations of countries such as Sweden, Russia, England, and Ireland. The French share of the European population had fallen from nearly one-quarter to about one-fifth of it. Being unified and wealthy in a fertile, temperate part of the world, however, the French were potentially the most powerful nation in Europe, *la grande nation,* as they proved in their imperial expansion between 1792 and 1815. The ultimate effect, then, of the eighteenth-century increases in population was to supply soldiers in unprecedented numbers. The excess population did not emigrate from France as it did from some countries; in the main, it only went abroad in the huge armies of the Revolution and the empire.

Not until 1792 and later years did the drafting of soldiers into the army ease the pressures of a rising population. Until then France suffered the social effects of more and more people crowding into towns, wandering about the countryside, pressing upon limited food supplies and upon a settled economy not flexible enough to make room for them. Here is one of the circumstances contributing to the French Revolution, though certainly not a cause of revolution. The rising population caused some groups among the middle and upper classes to be younger and younger. The magistrates in some of the parlements were younger than usual, and the king's finance minister, Jacques Necker, believed that the outbreak of revolution owed something to young men with general ideas, little experience, and less judgment who had "become dominant." And once the Revolution had taken hold, in the National Convention (1792–95), "political leadership was in the hands of younger rather than older men, commonly in their thirties."[2] Although it is doubtful whether there was anything clear enough to be called a "demographic revolution" in eighteenth-century France, there were many more Frenchmen than ever before, and the average age of certain ruling groups was falling.

France was just over 200,000 square miles (528,000 square kilometers), a hexagon slightly bigger than the state of California or the province of Newfoundland, slightly smaller than Texas or Manitoba. On the map there are roughly 600 miles between Bayonne and Strasbourg, Bayonne and Dunkirk, Marseilles and Dunkirk, Brest and Strasbourg. People lived everywhere in this fertile, temperate country, but especially in the northern provinces of Artois, Hainaut, Cambrésis, Flanders, Picardy, Normandy, Maine, Perche, Île-de-France (including Paris) and Brittany, in the northeastern provinces of Alsace and Lorraine, in the central provinces of the Lyonnais, Forez, and Auvergne, and in the western provinces of Saintonge and Aunis (including La Rochelle).

The pattern of these more densely populated regions did not markedly coincide, as one might have expected, with the paths of the four great river systems, the Seine, the Loire, the Garonne, and the Rhône, though the Seine ran through Île-de-France and Normandy, the Loire ran through southern Brittany, and the Rhône bordered the Lyonnais, all thickly peopled. Nor was the population altogether sparse in the mountainous regions, for although the Alps and the Pyrenees were thinly peopled, the Massif Central contained the rising population of the Auvergne, Forez, and parts of the Lyonnais. The Massif armoricain of the Breton peninsula was scarcely mountainous, but it was rocky enough not to support the moderately dense population it had in the eighteenth century.

English Channel

Dunkerque
Calais
Dieppe
Somme
Le Havre
Rouen
Beauvais
Marne
Meuse
Rhine
Strasbourg
PARIS
Seine
Vosges
La Beauce
Saint-Malo
Massif
Armoricain
Orléans
Angers
Loire
Nantes
Saône
Jura
La Rochelle
Geneva
Cognac
Lyon
Charente
Massif
ATLANTIC OCEAN
Central
Bordeaux
Dordogne
Rhône
Garonne
Adour
Bayonne
Toulouse
Marseille
Pyrénées
Mediterranean Sea

The Geography
of France

0   40   80   120   160   200 Miles

Corsica

Many different factors determined where people lived and multiplied. They may be summed up by observing that this was an agricultural, preindustrial economy somewhat like that which prevails today in parts of Africa, Asia, South and Central America. Some three-quarters or five-sixths of the people lived in the country districts, or *pays*, as peasants, or *paysans*, and most of the rest lived in small market towns of no more than 10,000 or 15,000 people. The countryside, like the towns, was inhabited by rural artisans, clergy, notaries, and people with small independent incomes, but most of the countryfolk were peasants wresting a living from small plots of land. Some peasants lived in isolated farms and hamlets, with a small town (bourg) in the middle of each parish, as in the bocage region of western France with its myriad fields enclosed in hedgerows. Some lived in substantial farming villages, as on the northern plains, where they worked open fields, or in the many wine-producing districts in the southern half of the country, where they tended the vineyards. Those in the grain-growing Beauce region lived in huge, isolated farmhouses. In country districts nearly everywhere there were peasants in huddled villages or hamlets wresting livings from small plots of land nearby. The truly urban people of Paris, Lyons, Marseilles, Bordeaux, Nantes, and a few other cities were a tiny fraction of the population. The vast majority of Frenchmen were born and bred in rural families; the main wealth of the nation, and hence the substance of the middle and upper classes, came from agricultural rents and revenues.

I. The Country People

Does not a preindustrial agricultural economy, whether in eighteenth-century France or in twentieth-century Africa, tend toward inevitable poverty? There is no doubt that a large proportion of the countryfolk were miserably poor in Bourbon France: over half in the north in 1789, writes Lefebvre; between three-quarters and four-fifths in Auxois, writes Robin; never less than one-third in the Vannetais district of Brittany, writes Le Goff; between a third and a half of the entire population in 1789, writes Hufton; a half, of whom one-fifth were beggars, thought Louis XIV's observant military engineer Marshal Vauban.[3]

More than three out of four peasant plots were too small to support a family. A peasant family in Flanders, for instance, needed about 12 acres (5 hectares) of land, but only one out of every seven families had that much. A family of five in the Auxois district of Burgundy might harvest less than twelve U.S. bushels of wheat per acre. They needed nearly sixty bushels for a year's supply, or with the triennial rotation of crops, about 15 acres of land for food, even if they hired themselves out to work. A family in the Beauvaisis could not be economically independent on less than 30 acres (12 hectares) and really needed more. Only a small fraction of the rural population had as much. An average peasant holding in Brittany was between 6 and 15 acres (2.5 and 6 hectares) of land. Small holdings were a feature of life at Azereix near the Pyrenean town of Tarbes.[4]

Such facts are only straws in the wind as a guide to conditions among the peasantry, because yields varied from region to region with the quality of soil and climate. Some regions supported greater populations than others. The northwestern side of the hexagon of France, the most densely populated by far, was the best for producing grain, then as now, in particular the region bounded on the north by Dunkirk and Maullogne in Hainaut, on the west by Caen in southern Normandy, on the south by Châteaudun, and on the east by Provins in Brie. Wheat and rye grew in open fields on the plains of Flanders and Picardy, in the Pays de Caux and the Pays d'Auge in Normandy, all sloping down to the English Channel, and, farther inland, in the Paris basin watered by the Seine and its tributaries, the Oise and the Marne, and southwest of Paris the dry, windswept, but fertile plain of the Beauce descending almost to the Loire at Orléans. In this northwestern region wheat was usually planted in October and harvested in the spring; rye, barley, and other lesser grains then planted on the wheat stubble plowed under; after the harvest the fields lay fallow, according to the medieval system of triennial crop rotation.

Although the north and northwest were the most productive of food, grain grew in most parts of France, on the drained marshes near La Rochelle, on the little fields of the western bocage country of Normandy, Maine, Anjou, and Poitou, laced with hedgerows and often with lakes, ponds, and pastureland, and even in the more arid parts of Languedoc and Provence. Different rhythms of rotation were practiced in different parts of the country, fields lying fallow every fourth, fifth, or sixth year, according to local custom. This was not a large-scale commercial production of grain, but a small-scale peasant production on plots of widely varying size. Nor were agricultural habits all the same or devoted entirely to grain. Cattle, pigs, goats, geese, ducks, bees, and orchards of apples and pears all flourished, and there were forests everywhere.

A kitchen garden of vegetables and fruit was usually the mainstay of the peasant family.[5] Nevertheless, dried peas, beans, lentils, barley, rye, and especially wheat were the most nourishing and portable foods with the longest storage life and the most domestic uses in that age, providing even a fair measure of protein, and lasting through the winter and early-spring months when little or nothing grew in gardens. For townspeople, dried grains were essential staples and so became a form of wealth, a commodity to be stored, hoarded, and monopolized. Even today, after all the changes of the last two centuries, bread is still a staple in the French diet, lentils are a widely respected dish, and crepes, often made of buckwheat, commonly grown in western France in the eighteenth century, are everywhere recognized as a traditional Breton food.

The more densely populated parts of southern France also depended on grain for food and tended toward a biennial rotation of wheat one year and fallow crops the next. Maize or corn had been added to the food grains of the southwest in earlier times and was widely grown in the eighteenth century. In some parts of the country people were beginning to grow potatoes. But the greatest exception to a grain diet was in the mountainous Massif Central, where the peasants of Auvergne, Vivarais, the Cévennes, Limousin, La Marche, and parts of Languedoc lived for long periods on chestnuts. The chestnut in those regions, the English traveler Arthur Young observed in 1788, "Is the exact transcript of the potatoe in Ireland."[6]

The long coasts of the Mediterranean, the Atlantic, and the English Channel offered a useful variety of seafoods, though it remains to discover how far inland they were eaten in quantity.

Certainly large numbers of fishermen worked out of all, or nearly all, French ports, and even the Newfoundland fisheries attracted ships from many ports large and small. In the autumn dried cod from the fisheries of North America was delivered by the fishing fleets of Saint-Malo and Granville to the bigger southern ports, especially Marseilles, and partly distributed inland, and salt or green cod, mackerel, sardines, and perhaps other fish were sent up the Seine to Paris and used in the northern towns generally. But fish, like livestock and poultry sold in local markets or at regional cattle fairs, was a food supplement for most people and eaten in plenty only by the prosperous few. The populace in general fed mainly on grain and on garden produce in season. Even of these there was seldom enough.

This rural poverty was owing partly to the absence of markets and capital, partly to constraints and inequalities of the age-old seigneurial system of land tenure, partly to the subdivision of land among children from generation to generation, and partly to inefficient farming methods and the scarcity of manure and other fertilizer. In the reign of Louis XVI government officials and groups of enlightened observers were well aware of these shortcomings. Societies of agriculture were formed, journals and reports published, and efforts made here and there to bring about improvements like those already well advanced in the Netherlands and in England. A few noble landlords tried to improve crops and yields. But peasants are slow to change and fond of their ancient methods.

The feudal kingdom and principalities of the Middle Ages had bequeathed systems of land tenure in which a noble landlord usually turned the management of his estates over to big farmers (*fermiers* or *fermiers généraux*). These systems of tenure were complicated by local and regional variations, but in general the seigneurial farmer and his descendants, known as *censitaires* because they paid the feudal *cens* to the landlord, had a firm claim on the land so long as they fulfilled their seigneurial duties to their feudal landlords. Some were poor, some rich, and some even became noblemen; but the *censitaires* as a whole were the stable element among the French peasantry. The great majority of peasants, however, held plots of land from the *censitaires* or from their noble landlords under the terms of short leases, seldom longer than nine years and by no means always renewable. Here and there, as in French Canada, the peasant tenant held his land directly from the landowner or seigneur and so became himself a *censitaire,* or an *habitant,* as they were called in French Canada.[7] But few French peasants enjoyed such security, and most depended upon the terms of leases which varied a good deal from time to time and from place to place. A detailed account of feudal land tenure in practice may be read in Robert Forster's study of the Tavanes estates in Burgundy on which the seigneurial farmers collected the rents of the peasant tenants in kind at a fixed rate per acre.[8] Whether payment was in kind or in cash, this system of rental leasehold *(fermage)* seems to have been common in many parts of France, but prevalent in the west and common enough elsewhere was the sharecropper leasehold *(métayage)* with the tenant paying a proportion of his crops.

Sharecroppers like those in the Gatiné district of Poitou lived in poverty on tiny farms *(métairies),* almost the slaves of the seigneurial bailiffs. In the region of Toulouse most peasants were sharecroppers, many of them paying 60 percent of their crops to their landlords and some with leases as short as one or two years. To take a different example, nearly one-fifth of holdings in lower Brittany, west of a line from the Bay of Saint-Brieuc in the north to Penerf on the Vilaine River in the south, were by *fermage,* but the other four-fifths were by a regional variation, the *domaine congéable,* by which the landlords owned the land and leased it for cash to the tenants, who owned the buildings, crops, fruit trees, and other stock. These had to be paid for by a landlord wanting to get rid of a tenant, and the effect of this system was to make most of Lower Brittany a country more of peasant proprietors than of tenants.[9]

Whatever the system of land tenure, the peasant tenant had to give a certain amount of his labor to the landlord or to the seigneurial farmer and to pay various seigneurial dues—the *cens et rentes, lods et ventes,* the *dîme seigneurial,* and others. All these varied widely from district to district and appear to have been light in some parts of the kingdom and burdensome in others. The same may be said of the *taille,* the tithe collected by the Church, and other taxes collected by the Crown and by the provincial estates in the *pays d'états.* Salt, so necessary in farming, had to be bought at fixed prices, often very high, from profit-making financial companies of tax farmers.

Since 1789 it has been easy for people with humane sympathies and modern ideas of social justice to assume that the 20 to 23 million French peasants were poor, often starving, and hence rebellious, because they were oppressed by noble landlords and governments composed of noble landlords. There is, of course, much truth in this assumption. The seigneur, or his farmers, worked part of his land himself, the *domaine,* and was thus a competitor of his peasant tenants, and he owned and managed the extensive forests which peasants would have liked to use more freely for fuel, timber, and pastureland. He tended to press farmers and tenants for rents and to replace them if they could not pay, and he seldom made any improvements to the estates or took an interest in farming.

Relations between lords and tenants were often bad by English standards, as that traveling farmer Arthur Young pointed out. The enlightened self-interest of English landlords and the trust of English tenants were rare in France. "I don't believe your tale of misery," the Marquis of Mailly wrote to the bailiff on his Picardy estates in 1772, a time of crisis. "All the seigneurs who have land in your neighborhood talk of abundant wheat. In spite of this, you imagine you can make me believe that people there are dying of hunger."[10] No doubt the opulence of certain noble and middle-class elites was a gross affront in the midst of such poverty.

Yet much of the poverty was due not to those elites but to high birthrates in families trying to support themselves independently on small plots of land. The family was, it is true, an economic unit able to survive collectively when a single adult could not. But in the long term there was scarcely room on the land, statistically speaking, for more than two children in a family to replace the parents, and although about half of the children died before reaching adulthood, there remained too many children to feed, children with poor prospects of earning their livings when they grew up.

One result was that the children could not and did not marry until relatively late, men until they were twenty-seven or twenty-eight years old, women until twenty-four or twenty-five. The child marriages of popular legend were those of aristocratic or wealthy families. Peasants could not marry until they could support themselves or hope to do so. The Church held, of course, that young people might marry at puberty, twelve for girls and fourteen for boys, but most had to put off marriage until deaths had made room for them on the land, or somewhere in the agricultural economy. When plague or famine brought a periodic demographic fall to a certain part of the country, there was suddenly more room in the economy, the marriage rate rose briefly, the marriage age fell, and the population rose accordingly. Thus, unmarried people were a sort of "marriageable stock whose function was to allow society to maintain the more or less constant number of families based on the more or less constant economic units of land."[11] If called upon, the population could have increased its birthrate by perhaps 50 percent merely by marrying younger.

The agricultural economy imposed its limits on the population by the social mechanism just explained. And peasant society guaranteed its own poverty by subdividing its land according to the probable number of people it would feed in normal conditions, so ensuring the starvation of many whenever crops failed or other disasters occurred. Taxes, tithes, seigneurial dues, and rents were no doubt disastrous burdens for many families; but they were seldom unexpected, and their removal could only have made room for even greater numbers of poor peasants. When all is said and done, Thomas Malthus still seems to be sound in his view that a rural population had a tendency to maintain its own poverty and misery by multiplying to the limits of its food production.* Whether the population of Bourbon France was restricted by periodic plagues nourished by wars or by periodic famines caused by crop failures and compounded by disease, the

---

* Four-fifths of the *habitants* of French Canada were not insecure tenants on fixed plots but *censitaires* with as much land as they could clear and cultivate, paying light seigneurial dues, no taxes, and only a modest ecclesiastical tithe of one-thirteenth, yet they contrived to generate poverty and misery in a very few generations by multiplying in a Malthusian manner until the land of the Saint Lawrence Valley and its tributaries could not support them all. In the eighteenth century the Canadian population doubled every thirty years.

agricultural economy imposed its own limits by a Malthusian social mechanism.

These observations do not justify the behavior of the ruling classes in Bourbon France, but they suggest that the rural masses were victim to tragic circumstances even more than to oppressive landlords and governments. Furthermore, viewed in this light, the peasant masses improved their lot over the long term of the next two centuries not by destroying their oppressors in the French Revolution—a short-term benefit—but by adopting the many improvements of the civilization those oppressors gradually developed: easier and cheaper travel, bigger and better markets, cheaper and better implements, birth control, sanitary and medical care, and all of the rest. A large proportion of the landowners were, after all, middle-class city dwellers. All classes of society, not only nobles, bought seigneuries.

There is a further objection to the conventional picture of a peasant mass oppressed by landlords. To view the peasants as a mass—they were not in any useful sense a class—is to see them locked in the tragic poverty that historical studies have recently depicted so well. But to single out one peasant family is to see that luck, good times, friends, cunning, determination, and hard work might bring prosperity and even security. After all, something between a quarter and two-thirds of them, depending upon the region and the times, lived above the poverty line, and some were modestly well-off. If we distinguish the prosperous few from the miserable many, we see that several possibilities were open to those who could seize them.

In most regions peasant families learned to supplement their agriculture with spinning and weaving partly for home use and partly for sale. This was not a way to wealth but a way for industrious peasants to get by. During the winter and at any idle time of the year women spun and men wove, sometimes with local wool or with hemp or flax from their own gardens. Hemp, which grew nearly anywhere, was useful but too rough to be of much commercial value. Flax, which stands the cold even of Quebec but suffers from dry heat, grew well in the Channel and Atlantic coastal regions and in the Massif Central, providing thread for linen cloth in Brittany, the northwest, and the central highlands.

Lacemaking *(passementerie)* went on throughout northern France and in the highlands. Production of linen cloth in quantity for merchants who bleached and exported it occurred mainly in a smaller northern region centered on the town of Saint-Quentin and including Hainaut, Cambrésis, and parts of Flanders, Artois, and Picardy. Woolen cloth was produced nearly everywhere. Woolens and canvas from the cottage industries of Languedoc, and even of such remote parts as the southern Massif Central, were widely exported, as far as Canada (until 1763). But the greatest and most profitable cloth industries were in the north (excluding Brittany and coastal Normandy) and in Champagne.[12] In this we see once again how the economy of the north and northwest supported so many more peasants than did other regions. But in general, rural manufacturing flourished north of the Loire, where rotational grain growing left many idle times in the year, and in the highlands of the Massif Central and of Dauphiné.

In the great wine-growing regions peasants had different but no less profitable ways of earning money to supplement subsistence crops. Planting, hoeing, fertilizing, pruning, tying and otherwise tending the vines occupied the countryfolk of Burgundy, Alsace, and much of the south and southwest nearly all the year round and left little time for spinning and weaving.[13] Vineyards flourished in southern sunshine and produced wine of the highest quality on infertile, gravel slopes and terraces where grain would not grow. The France of grapes and olives, of wine and oil had a different economy from the France of wheat and woolens, but both offered age-old possibilities for peasant families to sell their produce and their labor. There were central regions of mixed economy, such as Aunis and Saintonge, where vineyards for brandy were interspersed with wheat fields, pasturelands and salt flats.

Tenant farming, estate management, producing and trading wine, grain, woolens, and linens were among the occupations that enabled some peasants to be better off than the rest. "There were in the countryside both rich and poor," Paul Bois writes of Upper Maine, but it was true of most provinces.[14] To study the tenant farmers of the eighteenth century on the three huge Burgundy estates of the Duc de Saulx-Tavanes, for instance,

France, Provinces and Provincial Capitals

- – · – · – France's borders in 1789
- ·············· Province boundaries
- • Provincial capitals

0   40   80   120   160   200 Miles

is to discover a mixed society of farmer-trader-managers who rose above the peasant masses. Everywhere in France historians discover *les riches laboureurs* or *les grands fermiers et les cultivateurs aisés*, who owned their own land. Even more leased land from seigneurs, sublet most of it to peasant subtenants, farmed some of it themselves, sold their crops, collected rents and feudal dues, and, if they could manage to pay their own rents and dues, would not lose their farms before the nine-year leases expired. They worked hard and saved and saved.[15] Many were like Robert Forster's "middling cultivators, wine growers, artisans and even day-laborers before the Revolution who were not desperately miserable," the future "active citizens" who were to be allowed to vote and take part in politics. Those who farmed their own land independently were fewer and poorer, it seems, than those who managed estates for absent landlords.[16]

Where at this level of society is the line between the managing farmer, in the English sense of the term, who hired tenants and day laborers but who might put his own hand to the plow and go to market, and the *fermier,* in the French sense, who merely ran someone else's estate, lived nobly, and must be described in English terms not as a farmer but as a bailiff, a manager, or a business agent? Joseph Moniotte of Beaumont in Burgundy, for instance, farmed land, sold grain, subleased tithes, ovens, gardens, and vineyards, ran a local cabaret, and lent money.[17] Was there a big social step between him and Alexandre Barangier de la Vergne, who leased La Pouplinière in Poitou from the Marquis de Chillean from 1756 to 1774, lived in the château, occupied the seigneurial church pew, cut wood in the forests, fished in the pond, and collected rents and seigneurial dues from the sharecroppers to whom he sublet the nineteen *métairies* composing the estate?[18] How many peasants began, like Claude Dumesnil in the Beauvaisis, by leasing land and went on to lease the entire estate as the principal tenant *fermier,* still describing himself as a *laboureur,* but collecting rents and seigneurial dues from his subtenants, enjoying livestock of every kind, a respectable income, and a "modest library that would not have been out of place in many bourgeois houses"?[19]

These questions, unanswerable in our present state of knowledge, are well worth considering. They are vital questions, not only in distinguishing rich from poor, "haves" from "have-nots," rulers from ruled, but also in sorting out the relations of town and country. When Jean Meyer writes of the *agents seigneuriaux* on the noble estates of Brittany and when Pierre de Saint Jacob writes of Burgundy, "It is tempting to think that one of the greatest events in the agrarian and social history of the 18th century was the appointment of the *fermier* in the heart of the fief," they are describing a type of intendant or manager from the city, a merchant or attorney or notary with business experience and legal training.[20]

Town met country on the seigneurial estate. Some of the seigneurial agents were capable, literate peasants; others higher up were lawyers or notaries from nearby towns, like Arnault Bonnet hired for a salary in 1775 to administer the family estates of the rich merchant Depont de Grange in Aunis.[21] Bonnet lived in a town house in La Rochelle and was himself referred to as a merchant *(négociant)* and a high court attorney *(procureur du parlement)*. All over France, townsmen like Bonnet in Aunis and countrymen like Dumesnil in Beauvaisis managed big estates either as salaried employees or as *fermiers* with leases. Here was one way—though not the only way—in which rural society met urban society. The two were different and largely separate, almost two opposed civilizations. The Revolution when it came was a movement of townsmen for townsmen: "[T]he Revolution was for city people."[22] Some peasants profited by it; others revolted against it.

II. *The Townspeople*

Only one-fifth or one-sixth of the population, 4 or 5 million, lived in towns, and most of them in country towns of fewer than 20,000 people. The big cities were growing at the expense of the smaller towns in the eighteenth century, but even so, on the eve of the Revolution the seven biggest cities held altogether only about 1.25 million: Nantes (60,000), Lille (70,000), Rouen (75,000), Marseilles (100,000), Bordeaux (110,000), Lyons (150,000), and Paris (650,000). Geography and history had made each town unique, as the traveller may still see for himself, but the towns had much in common to distinguish them from the countryside. Five principal realms of activity kept townsfolk busy and formed their urban character: government, the Church, the lawcourts, trade, and manufacturing. In varying proportions, then, every town was inhabited by officials, clergy, magistrates, merchants, and tradesmen or artisans. To these must be added at least four peripheral groups: the idle rich, both nobles and commoners; the much larger groups of idle beggars and wandering poor; soldiers and sailors in ports and frontier towns; and, last but not least, the domestic servants who formed at least 8 percent or 10 percent of urban populations, sometimes more— 12 percent in Toulouse, 16 percent in Paris, 17 percent in Caen, 20 percent in Lyons, and perhaps 25 percent in Angers. In Lyons about 13 percent of all families employed servants, more women than men, and mostly from the country. Nearly all the manual work was done by people who were either domestic servants or tradesmen with recognized occupations. Servants were often employed to help with family shops, with workshops, or (in the country) with farming, and the long list of guilds included many humble working groups.[23]

The five basic urban groups varied enormously in size and by their variety gave each town a different character. Every town had at least one government—its own—but thirty-two towns were also the seats of royal intendants with their clerks, many had governors and their staffs, and some of the capitals of the semi-independent *pays d'état* held provincial governments of sorts: Rennes for Brittany, Arras for Artois, Montpellier for Languedoc, and so on. Marseilles was administered by a governor and a council of sixty businessmen with a considerable subordinate staff. It was ruled mainly by its *négociants*, its merchants, who filled the council and the incidental offices. Bordeaux was governed by a council (*jurade*) of six *jurats*—that is, two noblemen, two barristers (*avocats*), and two merchants, headed by a mayor, who was usually a nobleman. The *jurats* were chosen by a twenty-four-member council of notables originally elected by heads of households paying a *capitation* tax of not less than ten livres. In all cities the royal government continually interfered, through its intendants, with elections and appointments in order to strengthen its own influence.

The governors, intendants, and bishops were distributed through the provincial towns without reference to each other, and when they inhabited the same towns, this was accidental. It should be added that the position of governor in a town was largely honorific, whereas the governors of provinces, especially frontier provinces, were still powerful military commanders. A few royal provincial capitals, such as Moulins in Bourbonnais, Pau in Béarn, and Lille in Flanders, had both governors and intendants, but no bishops. Some towns had governors but neither intendants nor bishops: Boulogne (Boulonais), Saumur (Touraine), Foix (Foix), Sedan (Lorraine), and Le Havre (Normandy). A few had intendants but neither governors nor bishops: Valenciennes (Cambrésis), Caen (Normandy), and Riom (Auvergne). But there were many ecclesiastical capitals, such as Beauvais (Picardy), Saintes (Saintonge), Saint-Flour (Auvergne), or Valence (Dauphiné), where bishops and ecclesiastical courts sat but where there were no governors or intendants. Even some archbishops sat alone, at Reims (Champagne), Narbonne and Albi (Languedoc), and Vienne (Dauphiné).

The really great provincial capitals, with archbishops, governors, intendants, and parlements, all four, were few and famous: Bordeaux (Guienne), Toulouse (Languedoc), Aix (Provence), Besançon (Franche-Comté), and Rouen (Normandy), but not far behind were Rennes (Brittany), Nancy (Lorraine), Dijon (Burgundy), Amiens (Picardy), and Grenoble (Dauphiné) with everything except archbishops. Of course, certain bishops were richer than certain archbishops, for the wealth did not always fit the rank. Colmar was the judicial capital of Alsace, for it had the sovereign council for the province, with its thirty presidents and councillors, but most other governing bodies were in Strasbourg. Not all great cities were regional capitals: Lyons was only a large crossroads, a point of transshipment for the traffic of the upper and lower Rhine, the Saône, and (by overland routes) the upper reaches of the Loire. The Lyonnais was not a province in the full sense of the word; it had never in its history formed a state like Savoy or Burgundy or a nation like Brittany.[24]

Most towns manufactured a little of everything, but many were known for the volume and quality of one or two particular product: Lyons for its silk, Rouen and Valenciennes for their calico *(toiles peintes)* and linen, Marseilles for its soap, Montpellier and Troyes for their cotton goods, Clermont-Ferrand and Limoges for their paper, Montauban, Reims, and Rouen for their woolens, Saint-Étienne for its iron, and so on. The trade guilds were characteristically urban and municipal rather than provincial or kingdom-wide. Each town had its own guilds, but there were none in the countryside. Paris had no less than 133 guilds, the greatest of which were the six *grands corps des marchands* for the drapers, grocers, mercers, skinners, hosiers, and goldsmiths, and no less than 127 other guilds in four classes. Besides all the building, printing, textile, and food trades, there were, for instance, the midwives, the lemonade makers, the painters and sculptors, the scribes and letter writers for hire, the wigmakers, the various makers of religious articles (e.g., *patenôtriers en bois et corne),* and the various criers. In Beauvais, which Paris might have swallowed up forty times over, the guilds numbered several scores, many of them for the various woolen trades in which about half the population made a living. Even small towns that were not industrial and not mentioned in reference books of the time for their manufacturing, such as Bayeux in Normandy, an ecclesiastical town of 10,000 people, or Vannes in Brittany, a port of 9,000, had their complement of guilds.

For guilds were tradesmen's way of cooperating to promote their own security and dignity. Organized by the masters, a guild set standards and examined candidates for the mastership, had a place in the municipal government, belonged to a certain parish, had a patron saint, and wore traditional regalia in the parades and ceremonies of the town. Guilds are politically interesting as part of the corporate structure of every eighteenth-century town, listed with the corporations of professional men, the ecclesiastical bodies, the magistrates, and the municipal officials. Economically they are interesting as unions not of wage-earning journeymen but of self-employed master craftsmen, from whose ranks were to come most of the *sans-culottes* of the French Revolution in its violent phase. The *sans-culottes* of 1792–94 are now well understood as a political and social force, but the elements of the prerevolutionary society, the masters and their guilds, are still little known, having been too long dismissed in historical studies as incomprehensible and outmoded monopolies.[25]

The magistrate or judge in a French court of law was not easily distinguishable from a high royal official, then described also as a *magistrat,* and their social and economic positions were similar. All towns had judges. There were perhaps 6,000 judges in France in 1730, one observer estimated, attended in court by an even greater number of attorneys, barristers, bailiffs, clerks, and other officers.[26] Nearly half of the judges, some 2,700, were in the 373 *bailliage* courts which had long been taking over the work of the declining seigneurial courts in the king's name. Angers, a provincial capital with a mere 34,000 people, had no less than 53 full-scale courts or tribunals dispensing royal, ecclesiastical, or feudal justice, each with its magistrates, barristers, chaplains, bailiffs, and other employees. At Toulouse nearly one-tenth of the population "was tied by function or family to the various tribunals," and court personnel heavily outnumbered merchants on all governing councils and administrative bodies of the city.[27] We neglect the lawyers and magistrates at our peril, for one-quarter of the men elected to the revolutionary National Assembly were lawyers, and another 43 percent were officials of one sort or another.

Our age has a tendency to underestimate the clergy in eighteenth-century France as part of the outmoded regime about to be pulled down by the Revolution. This is a result of revolutionary or left-wing dogmatism. In fact, the Roman Catholic clergy was a strong presence, for good or ill, in French society at all social levels, urban as well as rural, and had its place among the governing classes, among the property owners and employers, among the tax collectors, and among the corporate groups that managed institutions, not only churches and cathedrals but schools, hospitals, orphanages, poorhouses, and communities of monks and nuns, some dependent on charity and others self-supporting. It totaled altogether about 130,000, some 2 percent of the population. In any serious analysis of French society it will not do to dismiss the clergy as merely one of the privileged orders, for that is to stress its juridical status and to neglect its economic and social positions. According to the best estimates, the clergy owned something between 6 percent and 10 percent of the land of France, more in the north near Catholic Belgium, less in parts of the south.[28] The 14 archbishops and 117 bishops were, indeed, noblemen with full noble privileges and wealthy livings.

Many towns were dominated by their clergy. The Norman town of Bayeux, for instance, with only 9,000 people, had no less than fourteen parish churches, three orders of monks, and four of nuns. The Christian Brothers ran a boys' school; the Ursulines, a girls' school. Sisters ran a home for gentlewomen in distress, an orphanage, and a hospital. Altogether the clergy employed about 120 domestic servants, several hundred women and girls in a lacemaking establishment, an archivist, a legal specialist in feudal law, 2 bailiffs, 8 tax collectors, 2 auditors, several clerks, bell ringers, gravediggers, sacristans, clockmakers, bookbinders, jewelers, and craftsmen (for making furniture, wax candles, and the wherewithal for processions, church assemblies, and dinners).[29] The clergy was, in short, the mainstay and the backbone of that small Norman town, and its dispersal was widely regretted during the French Revolution.

To take another example, the town of Angers, the provincial capital of Anjou, on the lower Loire River, with its 34,000 people, had a cathedral, seventeen parish churches, fourteen chapels attached to cemeteries, seven houses of mendicant orders, an abbey of canon regulars, the abbey of Ronceray, houses for the priests of the Oratory, the Lazarists, and the Frères des Écoles chrétiennes, four Benedictine abbeys, a Benedictine house for women, and fourteen other religious communities for women, including three hospitals. In 1789 there were, all told, over 300 nuns, 100 monks and friars, 72 cathedral canons, 17 curates, 22 vicars, and 14 priests employed by hospitals and hospices. That is, about one-sixtieth of the people of Angers were members of the clergy, and there were scores of underlings, students, choirboys, and employees. In Caen on the eve of the Revolution the clergy, including 45 primary-school teachers, was about 6 percent of the population, more numerous than the merchants and their clerks.[30] Not all towns were as clerical as Bayeux and Angers, but all were ecclesiastical centers to some degree, if only because French law required all people to be Roman Catholic. Beauvais, a clothmaking town in Picardy of about 13,000 people, and not noted for being particularly clerical, had in the seventeenth century an ecclesiastical population of 460, or one twenty-fifth of the total, and the bishop dominated the society of the town.

The merchants in French towns were a complicated social hierarchy and no easier to classify than any other large occupational group. The peddler with a pack on his back or the retail merchant with a market stall or a small shop, had little in common with the rich Lyons silk merchant or the shipowning importer of colonial produce at one of the ports. They all had buying and selling in common, but at one end of the scale was the spectacle of poverty and desperate shifts to avoid destitution and beggary; at the other end was a spacious life of country properties with noble neighbors and the prospect of noble marriages and royal offices. Most merchants were somewhere in between, toiling early and late with clerks in a countinghouse (comptoir) with adjoining storerooms, writing letters daily to all parts of the civilized world, hurrying down to the docks or to the bourse or to the chamber of commerce, or to the notary's office, their fortunes rising and falling.

For three or four generations the bigger merchants, mainly bankers, wholesalers, and shipowners dealing in any and all commodities, including money, had been called négociants to distinguish them from the marchands, who were the shopkeepers, peddlers, and other retailers specializing in one type of commodity. This distinction was sharply drawn in the files prepared by merchant candidates for royal offices such as secrétaire du roi or trésorier de France, files in which letters attested to the fact that the candidates had not worked on a petty scale as retailers but always on a grand scale as négociants.[31] It was négociants rather than marchands who were mentioned in royal decrees pronouncing the merchant class worthy of noble rank and in writings on the much debated question of the noblesse commerçante—that is, of noblemen engaged in trade. The economic reality behind this social distinction was that overseas and other wholesale trade had grown by leaps and bounds in the eighteenth century.

The growth of trade was one of the great economic events of eighteenth-century France, for it stimulated the economy as a whole, though not in all aspects, or in all regions, or at all periods. Certainly no agricultural "revolution" occurred, as was once believed, but only a substantial, though uneven, regional growth.[32] Anjou, Maine, much of Normandy, and no doubt other provinces remained economically static during the second half of the century. Yet in spite of these limits, the growth and essential prosperity of the economy over the century are shown by long-term price rises and by a substantial growth in foreign trade.[33] By the time of the French Revolution there were many wealthy trading families, especially in the bigger seaports. The greatest fortunes in overseas trade were made during the Thirty Years' Peace of 1713–43, and the first half of the century was generally more expansive than the second half, which began with the disasters of the Seven Years' War and went on to the terrible crises of 1768–71 and 1786–89, when bad harvests cut down the production of wine, food, and textiles. The most novel and spectacular growth was in the imports of West Indian sugar, cotton, indigo, and coffee, their reexport to northern Europe, and the trade in West African slaves. The greatest commercial fortunes were made at Bordeaux, Nantes, and Marseilles in these commodities. The sugar trade gave rise to hundreds of refineries in France, the cotton trades to manufacturing in a hundred inland towns from Lille to Carcassonne, and the trade in dyestuffs to the expansion of various branches of textilemaking. More and more textiles were exported. "In the 17th and 18th centuries," T. J. Markovitch does not hesitate to write, "France was the greatest industrial power in the world."[34] At the same time grain, wine, brandy, salt, and other foodstuffs were being exported and agricultural markets abroad were growing.

Internal markets also grew in the eighteenth century as millions of new people had to be fed, clothed, and housed and as more people acquired a taste for sugar, coffee, tea, tobacco, and cotton clothing. French merchants supplied all these commodities except tobacco, which was purchased from British firms. The staple foodstuffs, too, were French. The ups and downs of the French economy seem to have domestic rather than foreign origins. When sales of wine abroad dropped off in the crisis of 1768–71, when the old textile industries in town and country went into decline, when other industries and vineyards, too, suffered by the prerevolutionary economic crisis of 1786–89, the producing and trading of food grains became vital, as hard times drove more and more people to worry about the barest necessities of life.

The grain trade was reliably profitable in hard times when

prices rose. Many a family fortune was built on successful speculations in grain, like the fortune of Nicolas Beaujon (1718–86),
court banker to Louis XV, whose father had supplied grain to
Bordeaux at moments of shortage in the early eighteenth century. Supplying army, navy, and colonies could be extremely
profitable for merchants in the victualing companies. The grain
trade, even more than the woolen and linen trades, was a mighty
link between town and country. No love was lost between the
rural producers of grain and the urban buyers, whether they
were the capitalists of the Bourbon governments or the officials
and soldiers of the revolutionary republic. Beneath all variations
in the marketing process lay the economic fact that towns and
townsmen were the principal customers for surpluses of country
produce, whether food and drink, textiles and timber, or fuel
and oil.

French towns were fundamentally markets or centers of local,
regional, and sometimes international trade. When French
authorities established a new town in North America, such as
Quebec, Montreal, Trois Rivières, New Orleans, or Louisbourg,
they provided for a market square where rural and suburban
folk might sell their produce two or three times a week. Montreal not long after its founding in 1642 had a market square
which did double duty as a parade square *(place d'armes)*, and the
market was held every Tuesday and Friday according to an ordinance of the royal bailiff *(baillis)* dating from 1676.[35] The population of 1681 was only 1,350, of whom 39 called themselves
merchants, but a big fur fair held annually in the fall attracted
people from Quebec and hundreds of Indians from far and near.
If a French center did not have a market, it was, almost by definition, not a town but a village or hamlet, not urban but rural,
for it also lacked the taxing, administering, judging, and notar-
izing authorities normally present in a market town. As well as
local markets, district cattle and other livestock markets were held
weekly, fortnightly, or monthly and listed near the end of the
Almanach royal for each year. For instance, the market town of
Lassay in Lower Maine, where a feudal castle still stands, held
frequent fairs, one in May lasting six days and noted for livestock, and "goods of thread, wool and feathers"*(marchandises de
fil, laine et plume)*.[36] Biggest of all were the annual or seasonal

fairs combined with carnivals and festivals in the regional capitals and in certain small centers: an international fair at Beaucaire on the Rhône River (21–28 July), others at Guibray (near Falaise) (16–31 August) and Caen in Normandy (a fortnight beginning on the Sunday after Easter [Quasimodo]), two at Rouen at Whitsuntide and at Candlemas, four at Lyons around Epiphany, Easter, August, and All Saints, and others.

At Bordeaux, to take another example, fairs held during the first fortnight in March and the second fortnight in October played a regional and perhaps even a national part in the French economy. The textiles to be exported in Bordeaux ships were brought in by the linen merchants of Brittany and the merchant drapers of Languedoc, Limousin, Lyonnais, and Poitou. Leather merchants came from Périgueux, Tours, and Orléans; ironware merchants from Saint-Étienne in Auvergne. Most of the merchandise was brought from the adjoining regions of the Garonne Valley, Languedoc, and the central highlands (Massif Central), and it was at such fairs as these that regional trade met international trade. Over and above these trades, however, local merchants carried on the sale of Bordeaux wines, and it was the wine trade, domestic and foreign, that provided the incomes needed to move the entire regional economy of the southwest.[37]

How were payments made, and in what media of exchange? Fairs had traditionally been occasions for settling accounts in regional economies based on barter or on current accounts. In the eighteenth century more and more coin flowed into western Europe, and in France Spanish silver was minted in the south and Portuguese gold in the north. But coin was still rare enough to be hoarded for dowries, family savings, and unavoidable cash payments, such as the advances of wages to ship's crews before they sailed. For paying large sums between distant towns, coin and specie were awkward, expensive, and risky. Therefore, in France as elsewhere, for internal as well as foreign transactions, the bill of exchange had become the principal means of payment. The practice of endorsement allowed it to circulate from hand to hand, endorsed at each transaction until it was finally submitted to the drawee at its maturity, usually stated as three, four, or more months. Its value depended on mutual trust or credit among merchants, who stood to gain by honoring their commitments and so winning the trust of others.

Bills of exchange, silver, gold, and other media of exchange, such as the notes of government financiers, sustained a growing number of merchant bankers in French towns. Forty-nine "bankers for bills and remittances from place to place" were listed for Paris in the *Almanach royal* in 1787 and 1788, fifty-one in 1789, and there were some in every town, trading in currency, credit notes, bills, marine insurance, and merchandise. Meanwhile, notaries in most towns were entering the realm of business by managing landed estates, sales of real estate and annuities *(rentes)*, private and government loans, family inheritances, investments, and the like. Families of notaries and merchant bankers carried on through the French Revolution and the nineteenth century with only brief political interruptions in their lives. But a third group of capitalists, the government financiers, were deliberately brought down by the revolutionary governments in a grand series of reforms.

Only one small group of financiers (the term referred to government financiers in Bourbon France) has appeared in most history books: the 40 farmers general of taxes, who collected the customs and excise duties and managed the state salt and tobacco monopolies. There were also, however, about 50 receivers general of finances, more than 400 receivers collecting the *tailles* and other taxes on land and persons; more than 50 treasurers general and untold numbers of treasurers managing the spending of government funds; several score payers managing the government loans and the payments to sovereign courts and others in receipt of royal stipends; hundreds of *intéressés aux affaires du roi* victualing and supplying the army, the navy, and the colonies and doing all kinds of business for the royal government and the royal family.

All of these worked for profit like private businessmen, and to describe them as officials or bureaucrats is misleading.[38] Even those with official status, like the many treasurers and receivers, were really private businessmen who had purchased their offices, just as high-court magistrates had purchased theirs and just as military officers had purchased their commissions. All these venal groups—magistrates, army officers, and financiers—dabbled in business for private profit as opportunities came their way, and

used their considerable credit to make money at public expense
and to enter the ranks of the nobility. They were a characteristic
part of Bourbon government, as they had been of Stuart government in seventeenth-century England, and from 1789 the
revolutionary governments were very much against them, just
as the English revolutionary governments had been from 1689.
Before 1789 they played a part in the eighteenth-century French
economy and society, but how big a part no one yet knows.

To describe the resident population of officials, magistrates,
clergy, merchants, and tradesmen is to suggest that townspeople
were stable, but in fact, many of them were not. Contrary to
popular myth, there were always large numbers of people moving in from the countryside or migrating from one town to
another. The city of Lyons, which had about 110,000 people in
the year 1700, received over the next ninety years about 120,000
immigrants, men and women in more or less equal numbers
seeking work, about one-third of the men and one-fifth of the
women coming from farther afield than the neighboring provinces of Lyonnais, Dauphiné, and Bugey. As a result, 40 percent
of the Lyons silk workers on the even of the Revolution had not
been born there. At the town of Meulan half of the men who
married in the later eighteenth century were immigrants, and
the figures for Marseilles were similar. At Vannes between a third
and a half of the people were no longer there after five years
and had been replaced by immigrants. At Bordeaux one-third
of the people who married between 1737 and 1791 had come
from somewhere else. Most of them came from nearby towns
and villages, but a handful of Protestant merchants from Holland, Germany, and the British Isles, and a few Jewish merchants from Portugal, had turned the town into a prosperous
international trading center. Without them, writes Jean-Pierre
Poussou, Bordeaux "would have remained, like Toulouse, a noble
old regional capital well away from the economic and urban
growth which marked the century."[39] Migration is worth mentioning, though not yet well understood, because most of the
revolutionaries in Paris and Versailles, high and low, beginning
with those in the Estates General of 1789, were not local people
but came from somewhere else.

In conclusion, it must be stressed that none of the social

groups and classes in eighteenth-century France were revolutionary.[40] The downtrodden peasantry and poor townsfolk had
always been poor and downtrodden, always more or less rebellious. There was no rising capitalist middle class that can be
identified as revolutionary, no class of rich families seeking political power by revolution, no class of frustrated or impatient
professional men, no particularly revolutionary occupations, no
satisfactory correlations between economic groups and revolutionary groups. It has proven to be almost impossible to explain
in purely economic and social terms why some men joined in
revolutionary movements and others opposed them, why some
men became radical Jacobins and others moderate Girondins.
For Frenchmen at every social level were able to think as well as
to work and eat. Explanations are incomplete without reference
to politics, political ideas, traditions, and loyalties. At the same
time their thoughts and traditions were much affected by their
circumstances, rich or poor, urban or rural, as property owners
or as tenants.

T W O   *The Social Hierarchy*

THE differences in wealth and sources of income summarized in the last chapter help explain the immense variety of people living in eighteenth-century France, and so do the geographical differences: whether people lived in one province or another, in town or country, in the mountains or on the plains. To these factors, which do not offer a full explanation of the social system, must be added varieties of upbringing, occupation, religion, and tradition. French people, like others in that age, stressed their social differences and lived in a hierarchy of superiors and inferiors, all sensitive to the insignia of rank, forms of speech, dress and address, order of precedence, and signs of association. Social differences did not disappear even in households which held highest and lowest, in easy intimacy, like the Comte de Mirabeau and his *valet de chambre*, Legrain, from a peasant family of Picardy.[1] A world of marked inequalities was just as natural to the lower classes as to the highest in that age; inequalities were not yet muted by any theory of equality.

The society of Bourbon France was divided by ill-defined gradations and by nothing so simple as a "class system" with clear distinctions. A peer like the Duc de Saulx-Tavanes (1769–1820), who lived a fashionable life in Paris, owned estates in Burgundy and Normandy, and enjoyed various court honors and pensions, was generally admitted to be socially superior to a noble magistrate in the Paris Parlement, such as Étienne-François, Marquis d'Aligre (1727–98), who was equally rich and had bought the Marquis de la Galaisière's huge estates in 1775.[2] They were both well above a noble farmer general of taxes, such as Jean-Baptiste le Gendre de Luçay, even though he was richer and his estates in Champagne were larger.[3]

In the middle ranks of society the hierarchy was no less complex. Shipping merchants at Marseilles, Bordeaux, Nantes, and other ports were a different social group from the bourgeois, who had no particular occupation but lived carefully on income from various sources, and both were socially above the retail shopkeepers, however rich and successful. These three social groups were then regarded as different and separate. Other middling occupations, too, formed professional groups, each with its place in society: lawyers, doctors, architects, notaries, royal officials, and magistrates from the *présidiaux, sénéchaussées,* and other lower courts. But all of these middling groups wore breeches and periwigs, which distinguished them from the lower classes, who wore working trousers, blouses, and their own hair. The picture is confused still further by family and religious groups that tended to cut across the occupations by commanding the loyal association of their members. Examples are the Goupy clan of Paris architects, master masons, bankers, and officials and the Depont de Grange family of merchants, landlords, and magistrates.[4] Large clans of Huguenots or "New Converts," such as the Garesché, Balguerie, and Hugues families, stayed together and married other Huguenots.[5] Although the Roman Catholic clergy did not marry, the priesthood and the religious orders drew together members from nearly every occupation except the lowest, forming collectively a distinct "order" or "estate," of some 130,000 clergy. The clergy was not a class, yet it cannot sensibly be ignored as a social group in any analysis of French society.

Among the many social differences in France, the most universal and enduring was the one between all these middling and upper groups taken together, whom we may call the "public," and the classes whom they regarded as inferior and called collectively *la foule,* or *le peuple*—that is, the "masses" or the "populace." Differences between the middling and upper groups seem insignificant in comparison with this great gulf. It was not a precise frontier, but the differences between the public and the populace were clear, constant, and tangible in the eighteenth-century mind. The philosophes and other writers and pamphleteers shared one view of the populace and condemned them, as students of the Enlightenment tell us, "to hopeless indigence and permanent exclusion from the political public." The general public assumed that "the vulgar were, and would doubtless forever be, prey to passion and superstition; reason was beyond them."[6] The principal exception, the writer Jean-Jacques Rousseau, only escaped the prevailing views of his time by dwelling upon a utopian and utterly imaginary notion of the French peasant and his life. Even those who took a charitable or humane view of the populace tended to see it as a social element with common characteristics. Peasants, laborers, tradesmen, shopkeepers, domestic servants, common soldiers, and the wandering poor seemed to be one undifferentiated pool of humanity to the middling and upper classes.

Whatever the reasons for it, there was a profound difference in behavior and mentality between the public and the populace, as the philosophes observed. Some description of it is a useful introduction to the history of the French Revolution because, in George V. Taylor's words, "The revolution began with a vast gulf of misunderstanding . . . between the mentality of the leadership and those of the popular classes."[7] That gulf remained throughout the Revolution even when political leaders developed a democratic ideology and promoted a widespread belief in social equality and even when a changing vocabulary blurred other social distinctions. During 1793 and 1794 the urban populace referred self-consciously to itself as *sansculottes* and to the public as *aristocrates*. This last term referred to all those of the middle and upper classes who thought of themselves as above the populace. In the minds of popular leaders there were only two opposed classes.[8]

It is characteristic of the gulf between them that in those years, the Marquis de Condorcet (1743–94), an intellectual statesman who had devoted much thought and effort to the welfare of the populace, began to see his hopes for it as mere illusions and to denounce those in it as ignorant and confused, a source of anarchy and tyranny, the dupes of "audacious hypocrites."[9] Already, a year earlier, on 1 August 1792, the more forthright ambassador of the United States, Gouverneur Morris, had written home to Thomas Jefferson, "Thank God we have no Populace in America, and I hope the Education and Manners will long prevent that evil."[10] The social conflict visible in such remarks as these was founded not only on differences in wealth but also on cultural differences between the public and the populace. These differences remained fundamental before, during, and after the French Revolution and were scarcely affected by the democratic theory by which revolutionaries tried to remove them.

I. The Populace

An age-old struggle for survival had created a way of life, a mentality, and a common "civilization" that marked popular behavior. No doubt the misery caused by overcrowding, limited shelter, and scarce food had a brutalizing effect. There had always been much poverty, but in the second half of the eighteenth century a substantial rise in the population of France increased the poor and wretched part of the nation. The brutality of their lives was therefore intensified. This has been described and interpreted in various ways, but most agree on its effects. Riots became more and more evident.[11]

The vital fact, however, is that there had always been riots among the populace, in France as in other countries. People who know only of those on the eve of the French Revolution are likely to see them as revolutionary, whereas a little study of the *ancien régime* will show them to be more or less normal and not revolutionary at all. In the first place, hunger and fear of hunger, not political ideas, were the strongest forces moving the populace. Most hungry people starved meekly as they had done for centuries, but occasionally a village, a city neighborhood, or a crowd in a marketplace rose in revolt against the rich or the authorities. Famine and hardship did not always take the same form. A family might lack food by reason of sudden poverty if the breadwinner lost his work or his land, his health or his life. This insecurity was a permanent feature of the popular condition. Insecurity, vulnerability, an absence of reserves, as Condorcet observed at the time, was the main characteristic of the poor.[12] To help the poor at such moments was the purpose of charity or Church provision, but it was seldom enough.

Food shortages of a different kind occurred when an entire

parish or even an entire region suffered from a crop failure resulting from bad weather or from crop diseases or pests. Similarly, at certain times of the year, usually just before crops were harvested, stocks of food might be low. In either case, it was always possible to blame the wealthy or the people in authority, and this for several reasons. First, the governing authorities and the upper classes generally—mayors, intendants, bishops, magistrates, ministers, or even the royal family—appeared to be in charge of markets and food supplies as of most things, and their very prestige laid them open to blame for famine in the eyes of the populace. The paternal image of an absolute monarch, of a bishop, of a magistrate might make the populace look to them for relief and turn against them when relief was not forthcoming. Such authorities unwittingly courted resentment by regulating markets and grain supplies and by trying to provide grain to prevent or to relieve famine. They thereby made themselves appear responsible for scarcities and high prices even when they were capable, honest, and well disposed.

A third form of disaster might occur when prices rose in hard times, and in the eighteenth century the prices of grain and bread were sensitive to supply and demand in a way that economic thinkers were only then beginning to analyze. It was hard to see why a producer of grain should profit in a famine—this seemed as immoral then as it does now—and only such economic theorists as the French Physiocrats and their friends, such as Turgot (1727–81), controller general of finances (1774–76), argued that immoral profits might eventually bring economic benefits.[13] The royal government had long been following the practice of regulating prices to protect consumers, but Turgot freed grain from price regulations on 13 September 1774 and gave the grain markets free play. The result was a series of popular uprisings to fix prices on the markets—*la taxation populaire*, as the French called it—widespread crowds doing for themselves what the government was failing to do for them. Turgot made the Crown seem more than ever responsible for inaccessible food. The Revolution did little to overcome this difficulty. Price-fixing crowds confronted municipal authorities again and again and sometimes became extremely violent, as at Étampes on 3 March 1792, when the populace killed the mayor in the marketplace.[14]

A fourth provocation resulted from efforts to provide grain to cities in times of scarcity. Royal and municipal authorities engaged certain merchants to buy grain wherever they could, and as a result, hungry or anxious folk might witness large-scale purchases and large cargoes of grain moving across the country. A popular legend easily gained credence to the effect that governments and merchants were conspiring to buy up grain, create artificial scarcities, and so drive up prices and profits. Known cases of profiteering by rapacious merchants, landowners, and dishonest officials led the populace to believe that famine was the result of a general official conspiracy, a *pacte de famine* for which there was no evidence. Economic or agricultural causes of the food shortage were harder to understand because they were complicated and impersonal. "Never did the populace admit," writes Georges Lefebvre, "that nature was alone responsible for their misery."[15]

All these suspicions provoked hostility and violence between different social groups. Much of the insurrection in the streets of Paris and other towns during the French Revolution was due to anxiety about food stocks and food prices. It was as consumers, and often from the markets, that neighborhood crowds surged out into the streets, protesting and demonstrating. Even when other motives were present, the principal driving force was an underlying anxiety over rising prices and dwindling stocks of food. The townsfolk or their *sans-culotte* armed forces in search of food clashed with peasant producers and thus aggravated the social conflicts of the revolutionary years. In the southwestern regions, as in many other parts of the country, food riots in spring 1789 rapidly grew into "a general assault of the poor on the wealthy, a movement in which the anti-landlord and anti-seigneurial disturbances of the countryside were echoed by anti-oligarchic movements in the towns."[16] But this is looking ahead to the Revolution.

The populace was itself—it cannot be said too often—a social hierarchy of differing fortunes and occupations. A wide variety appears in historical studies, but the populace can be grouped in categories. A century before the Revolution, Daniel Defoe had distinguished three groups of urban folk in London: first and highest, the tradesmen and shopkeepers; secondly, the unskilled workers, including porters, water carriers, day laborers, and domestic servants; and thirdly, the homeless beggars, vagrants, criminals, prostitutes, and other destitute folk—the urban proletariat.[17] Similar types inhabited Paris, and it was mainly from the first of them that the politically active *sans-culottes* of the revolutionary years were drawn. They and Defoe's second group, the unskilled workers, could usually get by in life if entire families, men, women, and children, worked long days and nights. But in hard times many of them were driven to join the indigent or destitute class engaged in beggary, theft, smuggling, prostitution, continual migration, and all the desperate efforts of an economy of makeshifts. Many crossed that tragic frontier between poverty and indigence during the last quarter of the eighteenth century.[18]

The hierarchy of the rural populace has often been described with all its many variations.[19] Collective or communal living was encouraged by poverty and offered a way of coping with the normal shortages of food, clothing, and shelter, as monastic religious orders had shown. The collective life of a rural community was a similar response to material problems. So was the development of the family unit in which husbands, wives, and children all needed one another for their very survival. Bands and banditry were partly a result of poverty, a collective solution to the problems of survival in poor regions and hard times. The governments of the revolutionary period studied the problems of poverty and made many plans to solve them, and it was not for lack of plans, reports, and debates that poverty survived the French Revolution and, indeed, was scarcely affected by it.[20]

To most common folk, rural or urban, revolutionary or counterrevolutionary, the governing classes were alien. Suspicion, fear, and hostility, marked the popular attitude to outsiders and the outside world, especially in the countryside. This attitude was generally combined with strong loyalty to the local community, to the village, to the guild, or to the family. Wandering strangers, vagabonds, and armed bands were age-old causes of alarm in the French countryside, where it was all too easy to steal fruit, tools, and livestock. Worst of all were the armed bands, often masked, banging at a farmhouse door, threatening to set fire to house and barn, stealing, sometimes killing, a threat to countryfolk as well as to travelers, especially in borderlands, in highlands, and in forested regions. In such districts, too, wolves still lay in wait for shepherds, children, and lonely travelers, especially in the forests of the Pyrenees, Perche, upper Maine, Anjou, Angoumois, and Périgueux, and they killed dozens of people each year until they were exterminated in the nineteenth century. In the *élection** of Anjou, not the wildest or most isolated part of the kingdom, over 250 wolves were killed in the five years 1774 to 1778.[21] The ancient dangers from wolves and strange men had left their mark on the popular mind.

The mass of the townsfolk were not so different in mentality from the peasantry as might be imagined. This was because of the continual influx of peasants into the towns as domestic servants and laborers of different kinds. All historians of towns tell the same story of urban populations constantly absorbing the surplus members of large peasant families in search of livelihoods. Once established in a certain occupation in a city, a provincial family tended to attract others from home. In Paris water carriers came from one district of the Auvergne, horse dealers and stonemasons from Normandy, building laborers from the Limousin, market porters from Picardy, coal heavers and rabbitskin dealers from the Auvergne, and hired servants from Gascony. About two-thirds of the population of the fauxbourgs Saint-Antoine and Saint-Marcel in the French Revolution had come from outside Paris. More than half of the 800 or 900 *vainqueurs de la Bastille* on 14 July 1789 had been born in the provinces.[22] The crowds of vagrant poor continually pressed upon the towns, and many took root in them.

Urban life changed people's minds in certain ways, but suspicion, fear, hostility, and anger were close to the surface of the popular mind in town as well as in the country and flared up quickly in response to rumors or suggestions. In town or coun-

---

*An *élection* was a fiscal district, and in earlier times it had been also a court of magistrates (*élus*) with jurisdiction over the *élection*. By the eighteenth century most functions of the *élus* had been assumed by the intendants and the magistrates of the *bureaux des finances*, but they continued to use the *élection* as a district. In 1789 there were 178 *élections* in the provinces where the crown collected the *taille*, the *capitation*, and the *vingtième*—that is, in the *pays d'élection*. There were no *élections* in the *pays d'état*, where the provincial estates collected the property taxes.

try, north or south, the populace in that age was easily aroused against something or someone seen as a threat. The same was true in England and elsewhere; when roused, people often rioted. "The riot," writes George Rude, "is the characteristic and ever-recurring form of popular protest which, on occasion, turns into rebellion or revolution."[23] Here was the element of truth in eighteenth-century public opinion about the populace, the inspiration for the English Riot Act passed by Parliament in 1715 because (read the act) "of late many rebellious riots and tumults have been in divers parts of this kingdom, to the disturbance of the publick peace. . . ."[24] Violent and destructive crowds of people disturbed the public peace often enough in France, too, as much detailed research has shown.

One of the characteristics of the populace was violent behavior and a general indifference to cruelty. Historians are agreed on the prevalence of popular violence, the pitched battles between villages at fetes and fairs, the journeymen's cruel rituals, the knifing, beating, and brawling in cabarets and houses, the brutality shown to women and children. This behavior, writes Arlette Farge, a specialist in the study of the populace, was normal in city streets. Another historian, Daniel Roche, describes in detail "the permanence of violence and the prestige of force" in popular behavior. "The French farm labourer and apprentice indulged in gratuitous, meaningless violence," writes Olwen Hufton, and François Lebrun writes of continual "brigandage and assassination on the roads, armed robberies, fights between peasants, insults, blows . . . and infanticide."[25]

Let us add at once that the common people had long been schooled in violence and cruelty by noblemen who led the royal armies into battle and who defended their honor with sword duels; by magistrates who used to burn witches to death publicly as recently as the age of Louis XIV; and by magistrates who regularly ordered public floggings and the torture of criminal suspects to wring confessions from them and then, having got confessions, tortured them to death in public executions. An immense crowd assembled in Paris on 28 March 1757 to watch Robert-François Damiens, who had stabbed Louis XV, slowly tortured to death by the most painful process the authorities could devise. Strapped down naked before a huge crowd, Damiens lay shrieking with his right hand fixed in a fire of burning sulfur (which set alight the straw under his head), while boiling liquid was poured into holes cut in his flesh (ten minutes). Then his four limbs were attached to horses (twenty minutes), and he was slowly pulled to pieces; but he proved exceptionally strong so the hangmen had to loosen his joints with a knife (four minutes). Damiens watched his arms being pulled off and then died. There had been one interruption of this process while two confessors, Guéret, curé of Saint-Paul's Church, and de Marsilly, doctor at the Sorbonne, sang the appropriate canticle, Le Salvé (eight minutes) and exhorted Damiens to repent.[26] On 10 March 1762 a Protestant merchant, Jean Calas (1698–1762), was similarly tortured to death at Toulouse.[27] Such diabolical cruelty in public, justified by Church and State, went far beyond the rough justice of a hanging or a beheading. Its effects on the nation are difficult to assess.

In addition, daily life in that age brought the populace close to death in various forms. At least three features of the agricultural economy tended to breed popular violence in eighteenth-century France. First, common folk, particularly peasants, were inured to wringing the necks of domestic birds and cutting the throats of livestock; the annual pig killing, with the pig squealing and struggling as it bled to death, was a joyous public event. Secondly, in a society with no knowledge of modern medicine, anesthetics, disinfectants, or obstetric care, pain and hopeless suffering were a feature of daily life. Thirdly, death like pain was close and visible: not only public executions by hanging, beheading, garroting, or burning—more or less normal in pre-Enlightenment societies—but frequent deaths in every family, watched anxiously by the survivors and accepted as normal and inevitable. Inasmuch as about half the children died before reaching adulthood, the deaths of little children were so common that many parents did not bother to attend burial ceremonies.[28]

Death and violence naturally affected the middling and upper classes, too, but their mentality and behavior had begun to change in the eighteenth century. Many influential writers like Voltaire (1694–1778), Rousseau (1712–78), and the Encyclopedists (the authors of the first French encyclopedia, published in the 1750s and 1760s), denounced cruelty and intolerance and began to teach the thinking public to do the same.[29] A host of lesser writers took up the cause, and it became a fashionable enthusiasm. This movement in favor of humanity and tolerance, a major part of the eighteenth-century Enlightenment, affected the reading, writing, and ruling classes, but it had little effect on the populace. There is plenty of evidence that they remained, in general, as rough and cruel as before. Human suffering and death, André Corvisier tells us, aroused much regret and even horror in the public, but not among the populace. "The popular classes seem to have been late in following the progress of sensitivity."[30] The brawling and bullying so common in the people's cabarets were rare in middle-class cafés. Again, the primary or rural *cahiers de doléances** taken to the Estates General in 1789 show no sign of the hope and reforming ideas of the Enlightenment, whereas the urban middle- and upper-class *cahiers* of the *bailliages* do reflect the Enlightenment among the clergy and nobles as well as the Third Estate.

The populace was notoriously violent in the years of the French Revolution. This was true in southern France, where vendettas and a long tradition of fighting and killing, especially in mountainous regions, led to a murderous series of events during the Revolution.[31] It was true also in many other parts of France. Detailed studies have undermined the theory that the massacres and widespread killings were the work of brigands, criminals, or the dregs of society. In fact, crowds of ordinary lower-class people did most of the killing or stood about while some of their number did it.† On a typical occasion, on 2 August

---

Cahiers de doléances, often translated as "registers of grievances," were lists of recommendations and complaints brought to the meeting of the Estates General in 1789 by the elected deputies. Each *cahier* had been drawn up by a deputy's own electorate and was a statement of electoral opinion. Many hundreds of these interesting documents survive in the archives, and many have been published.

† The story of the Russian Revolution in 1917 gives evidence of a similar bloodthirsty populace, "and as in the France of 1789–93," writes Marc Ferro, "the rapid political and cultural upheaval allowed men to wrap a cloak of theory around the violence, and to identify or suppress as enemies of the people whoever opposed the new leaders, i.e. the Bolsheviks as they were collectively known." (Marc Ferro, *October 1917: A Social History of the Russian Revolution*, London, 1985, p. 264. I owe this interesting comparison to Dr. John Hutchinson, Simon Fraser University.)

1789, a group of tradesmen at Saint-Denis, north of Paris, indignant about the high price of food, beat and stabbed the mayor's lieutenant to death. Then they cut off his head and mutilated his body.

On another typical occasion, on 19 August 1792, soon after the populace had been admitted to the National Guard, a crowd of them at the village of Bellesme (Orne) surrounded a retired priest's house, struck his mother, dragged him out of the attic, and tried to force him to take the required oath to the nation. When he refused, they beat him to death, cut off his head, and paraded it about on a stick, while a crowd of village children dragged his body along in the procession. Then for several hours the crowd went looking for other victims.[32] The popular violence of which these are only examples was particularly common after 1791 because the old restraints of Church and State were gone; because certain politicians—Marat and Hébert, for example—urged the common folk to mete out the rough-and-ready "justice" of the sovereign people; and because threats of invasion, counterrevolution, and starvation caused popular hysteria. The same factors explain the killing of more than 1,000 prisoners in nine Paris jails during the first week in September 1792.

True, the journalists who incited the populace to violence were not men of the people. The terror, red and white, the wholesale executions by guillotine in Paris, the wholesale repression by shooting, hanging, and drowning in western and southeastern districts were usually directed by middle-class leaders. They were leaders who adopted the attitudes and methods of the populace and were ready to sacrifice the liberal attitudes and methods of the public. After all, a leader of the populace could hardly do otherwise. The angry violence of the people went hand in hand with egalitarian dress and vocabulary. For thinking people who adopted them, social democracy became a religion based on the principle of popular sovereignty. Opposition seemed an evil to be stamped out. A popular democracy in eighteenth-century Europe, like a "people's democracy" in twentieth-century Europe, was likely to maintain itself by terror and death. Humanity, tolerance, and justice could be imposed only by a public imbued with the liberal causes of the Enlightenment, the causes promoted by such thinkers as Locke, Montesquieu, Beccaria,

Voltaire, and the Encyclopedists. Members of the public who joined the populace made an ideology of its cause and justified terror and death on ideological grounds.

Some historians of our own day shrug off all the killing or leave it out of account for the same reasons. They seem to think that the democratic revolution of 1792–94, like a war, could not be waged without victims, and these were unfortunate but almost irrelevant. The populace could do no wrong, runs the theory, for its cause was just. Such is the attitude toward mob, murder, massacre, and mutilation in many history books of our time. Even George Rude, the gentlest of men and better acquainted with popular violence than most, passes over it in his book *The Crowd in the French Revolution* (1959) almost without comment, leaving his readers with the impression that it was normal and necessary.[33] Another historian of the revolutionary populace, Albert Soboul, devotes no more than 5 pages to violence in his 1,168-page study, *Les sans-culottes parisiens en l'an II* (1958), suggesting that it was temperamental, perhaps biological, and merely "the weapon which aristocratic resistance forced the *sans-culottes* to adopt."[34] Even so thorough a scholar as Pierre Caron subsides into the incantations by which historians commonly dismiss popular violence: ". . . it was an act of the masses, resulting . . . from collective mental preparation . . . ," merely the sovereign people exercising their sovereign right and duty.[35] Charles Tilly has expressed a similar view of French popular violence: "By actions that authorities call disorder, ordinary people fight injustice, challenge exploitation, and claim their own place in the structure of power."[36] These and other historians like them persist in overlooking the injustice, cruelty, and destruction of mob violence, preferring to see the violence as a political necessity. Are they a prey to ideological obsessions? Do they believe, as Olwen Hufton suggests, that to examine popular violence too closely might in some way "detract from the essential worthiness of those [the common people] predestined to win the ultimate political crown?"[37]

The superstitious and credulous tendency in the popular mentality has been faced more frankly. Even that small fraction of the Paris folk that rejected authority and became popular leaders in the French Revolution were relatively simpleminded.[38] And most ordinary folk subscribed to a mosaic of inherited beliefs and superstitions. A universe full of anthropomorphic forces gave meaning to death, violence, and suffering and cleared the survivors' minds of anxieties that might otherwise have proved unbearable. For many centuries these forces had been crowned by the tradition of the Roman Catholic faith. The Roman Catholic Church, which had founded the primary schools of France in the seventeenth century, had evolved a socially beneficial belief to explain the miseries of life: "[S]uffering and sickness are sent by God to punish men for their sins and to warn them to repent while there is yet time. As for death, it is also a punishment ordered by God and a reckoning at once unforeseeable and inevitable, it is the passing from this vale of tears to eternal life, an infinitely dreadful passing, for only a small number will be chosen for salvation from the punishment that awaits the great majority of people, and no one can predict the sentence of the Sovereign Judge."[39] The clergy preached in every parish, especially since the Counterreformation of the seventeenth century, the message of obedience to the laws of God as interpreted by the Church. It was in some of its parts a harsh and oppressive teaching, for priests were only men and the Roman Catholic Church received from the ambient society as much as it gave to it.

Under the pressures of the official faith, many folk turned to sorcery, witchcraft, and astrology, which blended with Christianity among the populace in general and even in many educated minds. An elaborate system linked saints with the hope of curing diseases: Saint Sébastien for the plague; Saint Méen in Brittany for leprosy; Saint Avertin in Touraine and nearby for ears, eyes, nose, and throat; Saint Apolline at Armollé for toothache; Saint Lazare at Saint-Christophe-du-Bois for skin diseases; Saint Hubert for rabies; and so on.[40] Ancient rites for winning the attention and intercession of the saints, some public, others private and secret, were passed from generation to generation and prescribed in popular almanacs: processions, prayers, vigils, candles, magic words, gestures, incantations, pilgrimages to shrines, fountains, collections of relics, and divinely inspired individuals. What Lebrun writes of Anjou was true for France in general: "Christianity remained for many, on the eve of the

Revolution, what it had been in the 17th century and before: one of the elements of a popular religion in which faith and superstition were inextricably mixed."[41] Peace of mind won by simple faith is no small thing to be sneered at by a twentieth-century intellectual, but certainly popular credulity in Bourbon France was a factor in the French Revolution.

Canny and practical in some matters, peasants were the most ignorant and simpleminded of people in others. In the "silent, laborious solitude" of rural Maine, Paul Bois tells us, "new ideas penetrated to the peasant with difficulty and were received with the defiance of a slow, obstinate mind."[42] Even those who could read—and Voltaire believed that nearly two-thirds of the French of his time could not so much as sign their names—had scant access to the Enlightenment of the age.[43] To read is not necessarily to imbibe reason or sense, and there was little enlightenment and much fantasy in the books read by simple folk in Bourbon France, mostly booklets published in blue paper covers by about 150 printers and hawked about the countryside by peddlers.[44] Folk almanacs, filled with astrology, homily, scandal, predictions of all sorts, and much fanciful history, took second place immediately after religious writings, in their volume and diffusion. Newspapers and journals were only beginning to appear in French towns in the reign of Louis XVI and did not reach the mass of rural folk. Rumor was therefore a strong current in the popular mind, a substitute for news. The gossip of innkeepers, domestic servants traveling with their masters, of priests and schoolmasters, of the notaries and barristers and their clerks with whom humbler folk had occasional business, of landowners and bailiffs and tax collectors—all these fed the popular imagination with rumors.[45]

In the adopting of a social category for the "populace" there is danger of homogenizing many varieties of French folk as certain writers have done. Twenty million people can scarcely be reduced to a united social force and labeled *le peuple*, as Jules Michelet (1798–1874) did, or lumped together as the "mob," the "rabble," *la canaille*, etc., in the terms of Hippolyte Taine (1828–93), Edmund Burke (1729–97), and others of the past.[46] These terms conceal the many differences between people of the lowest social classes. What, after all, did a Breton sailor or a Flemish weaver have in common with a Roussillon shepherd, or an Alsatian vineyard laborer with a Bayonne housemaid? In addition to all other differences, these five might speak little French and much Breton, Flemish, Catalan, German, or Basque. How, then, could they discuss the brotherhood of man with one another, or with a Lyons silk weaver or a Norman plowboy? Even those who spoke one language were divided in innumerable ways. The southeastern regions were in popular culture not much affected by northern influences, nor vice versa.

Here, in fact, is the strongest trait of members of the populace, and what marks them off most clearly from the public: an inability to rise above their differences, or to see public issues, or to discuss projects for improvement, or to collaborate with others for the common good. The popular movement in Paris was interested only in immediate local matters and indifferent to national and international issues. Among the peasantry the idea of self-government by discussion and instruction was never grasped, and the civic or public life of the village made little progress.[47] The populace in general was hostile to strange men and new ideas. There were, of course, excellent reasons for these shortcomings, and poor working folk are not to be reproached for what they are, at least not by people blessed with education, leisure, and enough to eat. The search for historical truth bids us avoid hostile caricatures of the common people as well as sentimental portrayals. The same effort is required to arrive at a fair estimate of the middle and upper classes, to which we must now turn.

II. The Public

Very few of the populace played leading parts in the French Revolution. Very few were elected to the National Assembly in any of the forms it took during the French Revolution. Who then filled the ruling assemblies and played the leading roles? For the most part, the Revolution was led and put into effect by government officials, lawyers, and other members of the public, including a certain number of clergymen and noblemen. Nearly all of the leading groups in the French Revolution were part of a vigorous and expanding French public, comprising people from the upper and middle classes, which developed in the eighteenth century. The growth and liveliness of the public—that is, of the literate, observant, responsive part of the nation—were remarkable. During the eighteenth century the public was unwittingly preparing to govern France by election and debate, by assembly and committee, by pamphlet and journal, by legislation and organization. This development was more easily seen in after-years, when Talleyrand, for example, wrote in retrospect, "An entirely new power sprang up in France, that of opinion . . . the opinion of an impetuous and inexperienced people."[48]

The liberal process of self-government calls for a long apprenticeship, as third world countries are discovering in our own age, and the French nation began its apprenticeship in the Age of the Enlightenment. Never in the history of France had there been so much observing, thinking, writing, meeting, and conversing about public matters. In this complicated field many activities grew together, and no single impulse can be traced as a cause.

The numbers of printed books, pamphlets, and journals grew prodigiously during the second half of the century. The censorship services of the Crown and the Church were still active, but more and more relaxed as a result of liberal views among the governing classes. The Crown's censorship bureau (the *librairie*) paid about a hundred censors to read everything before it was printed or imported for French readers, with a view to censoring religious heresy and liberal political ideas, but during the years 1751 to 1762 the director, Chrétien-Guillaume de Lamoignon de Malesherbes, tended to sympathize with imaginative writers and to allow much publishing that would earlier have been prevented.[49] Very little of what was printed could be called revolutionary, certainly not the famous *Encyclopédie* of Diderot and d'Alembert or the writings of Voltaire and Rousseau, but much of it was stimulating to a public unaccustomed to discussing the nature of man, society, morality, and government. About the time Louis XVI came to the throne in 1774, more and more writers began to take up political subjects. The vast collections of so-called revolutionary pamphlets now preserved in the libraries of Europe and America go back well before the Revolution.[50]

The origins of the Revolution are often sought in revolutionary ideas that must, it seems, have grown out of the ferment of the eighteenth-century Enlightenment. But where in the prerevolutionary years are the ideas of nationalism, of republicanism, of national sovereignty, of democracy, of government by terror and guillotine and the other guiding ideas of the Revolution? Most of them can scarcely be found at all, and certainly not in any strong or widespread form. There was no revolutionary literature, no revolutionary thought, no plan, and certainly no revolutionary class or group. "For," as William Doyle concludes, "the French Revolution had not been made by revolutionaries. It would be truer to say that the revolutionaries had been created by the revolution."[51]

If the pamphlets and books of the prerevolutionary years say little or nothing about the ideas of the coming Revolution, what, then, is in them? For one thing, they show strong classical influences, the effects of education in the Greek and Latin classics. The schools attended by the generation of the French Revolution taught Virgil's *Aeneid,* Cicero's orations, Horace's odes, Sallust's *Conspiracy of Catiline,* Ovid's *Metamorphoses*, and passages of Tacitus and Livy. They must have touched young minds with ideas from the Rome, Sparta, and Athens of ancient times.[52] Here were seeds of liberal, republican, and even democratic ideas. More than that, here was a vision of public life and statesmanship, a fund of imagery and eloquence, and a certain view of law and order. Orators of the revolutionary assemblies, with the exception of a few like Georges-Jacques Danton, often referred to classical events or heroes and were understood by their hearers. Here was a public of nobles and commoners alike with a classical education and vocabulary that set them apart from the populace. This difference was visible during the French Revolution in, for example, the revolutionary festivals, imposed by representatives from Paris, which showed classical influences and had little in common with the age-old popular festivals.

Academies increased in the eighteenth century until there were thirty-two academic towns with a total of some 2,500 academicians.[53] Most of these were in place thirty years before the Revolution, and their collective influence was considerable. Jean-Jacques Rousseau's fame began when he won a prize offered by the Academy of Dijon. Various academicians later became revolutionary leaders, such as Brissot of the Academy of Châlons-sur-Marne and Robespierre of the Academy of Arras. One response to the academies was a movement in the 1780s to bring learning to a wider public in the so-called *musées*. The *musées* of Paris, Bordeaux, Amiens, and other towns were cultural centers for "free public instruction in the sciences and the arts," larger and less exclusive, than academies. Wives and friends were admitted, and there were frequent musical and social events. The Bordeaux *musée* founded in 1783 soon had 150 members.

Among the most celebrated intellectual groups of the pre-revolutionary generation was one of some 200 contributors to the *Encyclopédie* directed by Denis Diderot and Jean le Rond d'Alembert. This great work, which they published between 1751 and 1772 in seventeen volumes of articles and eleven volumes of engraved illustrations, was not revolutionary and could be interpreted as such only by people who believe informed and independent thought to be revolutionary. One of Diderot's three main purposes was to work out a natural morality as an alternative to the prevailing Christian morality, a common endeavor in the eighteenth century which some historians have seen as revolutionary, but on that view nearly all modern philosophy must be included in a vast and meaningless indictment.[54] A second purpose expressed in much of the *Encyclopédie* was to reflect on the history of thought, the progress of the human mind through the ages. A third purpose was to impart practical, useful, often technical information. A great number of the articles are about subjects in medicine, manufacturing, farming, natural science, and engineering which were characteristic of the age. Much writing then was in the form of manuals and theoretical treatises on many different subjects and intended to encourage practical improvements or to inform and to enlighten the reading public.

The contributors to the *Encyclopédie,* and the editors, were educated people, both noblemen and commoners, most of them professional, technical, or administrative men with practical experience, most with some property and income. It would be meaningless to describe them as "bourgeois," however, because a far greater number of the middle classes were counted among their enemies and because the characteristic of those in the group was not their social origins but their common devotion to the public well-being, *le bien public,* their effort to be useful to society. It has been established, too, that no fewer than 125 of them were employed in one or another of the government services.

To take one of the fourteen technicians as an example, Jean-Rodolphe Perronet (1708–94) told Diderot about the newly invented steam-driven water pump.[55] The son of a poor widow, he became a civil engineer by joining the army at sixteen, then the Paris city architect's office, then the *généralité* of Alençon, where he became the head civil engineer. With a prominent administrator, Daniel-Charles Trudaine (1703–69), he helped found the official civil engineering school in 1747 and 1748 and headed it for the next forty-seven years, while also working as chief engineer in the royal service and general inspector of the saltworks *(salines)*. In 1763 the king gave Perronet letters of nobility, and by 1789 he had been elected to the royal academies of sciences and architecture, the royal society of agriculture, the British Royal Society, and the academies of Stockholm, Berlin, and other European capitals. He invented several machines, planned and built thirteen elegant bridges in France, including the Pont de la Concorde in central Paris, and in 1778 Catherine II of Russia asked him to design a bridge over the Neva River. An example of the twenty-two medical men was Chevalier Louis de Jaucourt (1704–79), a Protestant with no fortune, who had been trained as a medical doctor at the University of Leiden; by his impressive learning he was elected to the academies of Berlin, Bordeaux, and Stockholm and the British Royal Society.

Another movement characteristic of the century was Freemasonry, with English liberal origins, philanthropic purposes, and a tradition of secrecy. It spread rapidly in France from the 1730s and soon had many more adherents, high and low, than did the academies. Though often suspected after the Revolution of revolutionary influence, the Masonic lodges seem in fact to have had no political programs or policies at all, and at the time they were not generally seen as a threat to the nobility, the clergy, or the monarchy.[56] A certain fraternal spirit of equality, of benevolence, tolerance, and humanity characterized the movement, and it was therefore a good school of liberal citizenship for its tens of thousands of members, who, by 1789, were organized in more than 900 lodges in France.

Many of the public were attracted to another novelty of the time, the investigation of political economy. The leading group in this field, the Physiocrats, who often called themselves the "Economists," were led by François Quesnay (1694–1774), one of Louis XV's court physicians, and the Marquis de Mirabeau, father of the revolutionary Comte de Mirabeau. Beginning with Mirabeau's first book, *L'ami des hommes, ou traité de la population* (1756), and Quesnay's two articles in the *Encyclopédie,* on *grains* and *fermiers,* they worked out a controversial economic theory.[57] Sometimes described as the theory of laissez-faire, this was based on the idea that the wealth of a country is produced by its agriculture, and the best way to promote agriculture would be to leave trade and industry, which produce nothing but only sell or transform agricultural products, entirely free from regulations and restraints. Quesnay and Mirabeau gathered a few devoted followers, notably Mercier de la Rivière (1720–94), du Pont de Nemours (1739–1817), Le Trosne, and two priests, Abbé Baudaud and Abbé Roubaud, and in the next twenty years they wrote two periodicals and hundreds of books, pamphlets, and letters to promote their theories. Whether these writings deserve any more respect than what earlier or later economists wrote is debatable, but the Physiocrats provoked much thought and discussion among the European public. Closely related to their movement were many practical efforts to improve French agriculture. Between 1761 and 1763 royal societies of agriculture were formed in at least sixteen provincial towns, and a literature of agricultural science sprang up, partly published in new journals such as *Le journal économique* (1751–72), and the Physiocrats' *Le journal de l'agriculture* (1765–83).[58]

A movement of a different kind began when Franz Anton Mesmer (1734–1815) arrived in Paris in 1778, the year Voltaire and Rousseau died, and found a large and receptive public for his entertaining cures by "animal magnetism" or mesmerism. Mesmerism "probably inspired more interest than any other topic or fashion during the decade before the edict of 5 July 1788 concerning the convocation of the Estates General initiated a free-for-all of political pamphleteering."[59] The modern discoveries of gravity, magnetism, and electricity lent Mesmer's invisible forces in the human body a certain plausibility, and by 1789 his Society of Harmony had 430 members in Paris, despite the fee of 100 louis, and branches in the major provincial towns. Among the most devoted enthusiasts were some of the future revolutionary leaders, Jean-Paul Marat, Jacques-Pierre Brissot, Jean-Louis Carra, and the Marquis de Lafayette, who lectured the American Philosophical Society at Philadelphia on mesmerism in 1784.

All these literary and intellectual circles were only the colorful parts of a larger French public that read, wrote, conversed, and attended the theater more than ever before. "The literary salons are wrongly considered to be the essence of social life at the end of the *ancien régime*," writes a historian of the Paris Parlement who finds the ordinary social life of the nobility just as lively and more influential.[60] The public grew in provincial towns as well as in Paris. The splendid new theater which opened at Bordeaux in 1780 played mostly light comedies before the Revolution but nevertheless created a theater-going public. The Comédie française de Strasbourg languished in neglect for half a century after its founding in the 1690s but drew large crowds in the prerevolutionary decades.[61] This was a period in which many French towns built their first theaters. Metropolitan contempt for provincial society, itself a kind of provincialism, is seldom justified, and a detailed investigation of people living even hundreds of miles from Paris often turns up respectable libraries and scientific equipment such as those assembled at La Rochelle in the 1760s by a Huguenot merchant from Quebec, Jean-Mathieu Mounier.[62]

At the little naval port of Rochefort a clerk of the naval treasurers general was in close touch with one of his colleagues in Paris concerning the writings of the 1760s. "Several days ago a book entitled *L'Anti Créancier* appeared," the Paris clerk wrote on 17 December 1763. "It is extremely well written, but forbidden [by government], hard to find and expensive. Nevertheless, if you are curious to have it I shall find it for you as cheaply as possible."[63] Merchants at provincial towns lived in close-knit groups, met continually at the bourses and in the street, and exchanged news from town to town in their busy correspondence. In the 1770s and 1780s there were even reading rooms and book clubs. The English traveler Arthur Young commented on "an institution common in the great commercial towns of France, but particularly flourishing in Nantes . . . a *chambre de lecture* or what we should call a book club . . ." where there was a library, a reading room, and a conversation room.[64] There was usually a price to pay—four sous a day at the *cabinet littéraire* in Metz, where Young went to read newspapers and journals on 14 July 1789—but these reading rooms were used by more and more townspeople with an interest in national and provincial affairs.

In the organized outlying provinces, the *pays d'état* with their own estates, the ancient spirit of independence found expression in patriotic societies. In the southeast, up the Rhône Valley and in eastern Languedoc, fierce provincial loyalties were expressed in the Estates of Gévaudan, the Vivarais, and the Velay, and fierce local loyalties in towns like Marseilles, Aix, Arles, Nîmes, and Lyons, which had traditional liberties and self-government. "All the major issues that were to characterize the national debate in 1789 were already present here in early 1788. These issues undoubtedly primed the pump of revolutionary politics earlier in the Midi than elsewhere."[65] In Brittany permanent officials of the Estates became a sort of leading patriotic society, as did the Parlement at Rennes, both of them so hostile to the monarchy that the role of the royal intendant more and more resembled a painful diplomatic mission to an enemy power.[66] After the election of deputies to the Estates General early in 1789, the Breton deputies met in the basement of a Paris café to found a club which later became the famous Jacobin Club. The Jacobin debates of 1793, however, would have been bewildering and horrifying to the Breton Club of 1789.

Even in provincial capitals where the ancient Estates had long been suppressed, the public was stimulated by provincial patriotism in 1788 and 1789. Cultivated provincial noblemen such as the Comte d'Antraigues, born in the Vivarais in 1753, nourished a hatred of monarchical despotism in a tradition inherited from the Middle Ages.[67] A strong movement of nobles and commoners at Grenoble, led by Barnave and Jean-Joseph Mounier, the son of a merchant draper, began to campaign for the restoration of the Parlement of Grenoble and went on to campaign also for the restoration of the Estates of Dauphiné suspended in

1639. These Estates eventually did meet from 1 December 1788 to 16 January 1789, when public interest began to turn to the forthcoming assembly of the Estates General at Versailles.[68] The Estates of Provence had been suspended since 1639; but late in 1787 it was decided to revive them, and in 1789 a project for a reformed Provençal constitution sprang up.

The pattern of provincial politics was not everywhere the same, but a vigorous political life grew up. Provincial patriotism was one of the great moving forces in the public of the prerevolutionary years 1787 and 1788, for the general public rallied to the cause of the parlements against the Crown. The public had for centuries been legally divided into three orders or estates (*états*). The First Estate was the clergy, the Second Estate the nobles, and the Third Estate the substantial or taxpaying commoners from the towns. These were legal categories but not coherent or distinct social classes. This is obvious in the case of the clergy, the First Estate, which could not form a social class because its members did not marry or have families and which was drawn from every social level. Less obvious is the wide variety of noblemen, a social class only in the loosest sense of the term. Grand families of ancient lineage had little in common with rising families recently ennobled; military men of the so-called *noblesse d'épée* were quite different from magistrates of the *noblesse de robe;* proud, poor families on seigneurial estates in outlying provinces were scarcely in the same class with families of courtiers at Versailles.

It is therefore misleading to divide the public of those years into clergy, nobles, and bourgeoisie and to search for some underlying class struggle as though there were social and economic differences more powerful than the general public opposition to the royal government. Noblemen were, after all, no less interested than commoners in the progressive, reforming projects of the age, as the registers of grievances were to show in 1789. "The noble *cahiers,* as enlightened and often more so, than those of the third estate, attest to the favorable welcome given by the second estate to reforming ideas."[69] Indeed, the uprisings of that period, such as the *journée des tuiles* in Grenoble on 7 June 1788, in which workers, fishwives, and visiting peasants threw stones and roof tiles at the garrison in protest at the exiling of the provincial Parlement, brought out people from every social level in a public revolt against royal power represented by the intendant, the governor, their troops and staffs.[70]

Provincial loyalties remained strong at Grenoble, at Toulouse, at Rennes, at Pau, and at most other provincial capitals, partly because of isolation. But towns were slowly being brought together by improved postal and transport services. Travel in France became much easier in the eighteenth century. The royal engineering service, the Ponts et Chaussées founded in 1599, made a general plan for a road system in 1738 and built many new roads and bridges during the next forty years, especially north of the Loire River.[71] Postal services improved as a result. The postal service for the Norman town of Caen, for instance, had 48 horses in 1741, 63 in 1760, and 117 by 1789, and by then there was a reliable daily coach service from Caen to Paris, Rouen, Alençon, and Cherbourg. Although a good deal of mail and freight moved along these roads, the public did not travel much, as Arthur Young observed with astonishment. French towns were farther apart than Dutch or English towns and were only beginning to overcome the age-old habits of isolation. But already there was much more movement on the Atlantic and Channel coasts, linked by coastwise shipping as well as roads. Small inland towns and such regions as the southern Massif Central were the most isolated.

Travel in the grand style of noblemen with coaches and servants was much more common than before, but not yet for ordinary provincial magistrates. Royal service in the colonies, at sea, or in the army took men abroad, as did wholesale trade and religious missions. There was no lack of French clergy, soldiers, and merchants abroad in the eighteenth century. "Trade heals destructive prejudices," Montesquieu wrote in 1748, "and it is almost a general rule that everywhere where there are gentle manners there is trade, and everywhere there is trade there are gentle manners."[72] The same could scarcely be said of war or Roman Catholic missions, but colonial and diplomatic officials also traveled. At least five of the last French officials at Quebec, all humbly born, returned after the Seven Years' War to settle in small French manor houses as country gentlemen with books and social circles.[73] The long list of officials, magistrates, and

technical experts who traveled to England, attracted by its wealth
and success, includes many inspectors of manufactures, such as
Morel in 1738, Jubié about 1747, Jean-Marie Roland in 1771,
1778, and 1784, and also Charles de Biencourt (1747–1824), a
future deputy to the Estates General of 1789, who went to England
in 1784, Louis-Sébastien Mercier, a writer, in 1781, F. I. de Wen-
del, inspector general of artillery, in 1775 and 1784, Jean-Sam-
uel Depont, an intendant, and his son, Charles-François Depont,
a *parlementaire* from Metz, whom Edmund Burke befriended in
1785.[74]

The influence of English civilization on the French public
can hardly be exaggerated, whether directly from the British
Isles or indirectly through the American colonies. Swiss influence was also strong through Jean-Jacques Rousseau (1712–78),
Jacques Necker (1732–1804), Jean-Jacques Burlamaqui (1694–
1748) and others, and Dutch influence through the great publishing and trading centers of Holland, but the rising world of
the Protestant Atlantic was more and more centered on Great
Britain and its American colonies. The pockets and periods of
anglophobia that have been so carefully chronicled were merely
a descant to an infinitely greater anglophilia lasting into the early
years of the Revolution.

"You are always quoting the English to us," Voltaire has a
priest say to one of the contributors to the *Encyclopédie.* "You are
determined to praise that ferocious, impious and heretical nation;
you would like to have, like them, the privilege of examining, of
thinking for yourselves, and you would snatch from the clergy
the immemorial right to think for you and to direct you."[75]
Whether we think of the Paris physician La Coste returning from
England in 1723 to publish an influential account of new methods of inoculation against smallpox, or the progressive magistrate Malesherbes praising the freedom of the press in England
and predicting in 1771 that France would soon follow the English
example, or the paradoxical Mercier predicting that in the year
2440 the English would still be "the first people of Europe . . .
with the ancient glory of having shown their neighbours the government which suits men jealous of their rights and of their happiness," or the rich receiver general of finances Claude-Henri
Watelet (1718–96) creating an English garden and writing about

it in 1774, or John Holker, John Kay, and dozens of other English manufacturers introducing new methods into France, or Benjamin Franklin (1706–90) charming the French public, we see everywhere the imprint of the English and English-American example.[76] "Everything is in English fashion," the American businessman and future ambassador Gouverneur Morris wrote to George Washington from Paris on 3 March 1789. "The desire to imitate the English is visible no less in the proposed form of the constitution than in the cut of men's suits." Such key words in the revolutionary vocabulary as *esprit public, budget, suffrage universel,* and *convention* came from English. At the end of 1791 the Jacobin Club of Marseilles solemnly unfurled the Union Jack in its assembly hall and sang odes in its honor.[77]

While English liberal and progressive influences grew, Roman Catholic authoritarian influences waned. In the years 1762 to 1764 the monks of the Society of Jesus, the best defenders of Roman Catholic hierarchical authority, were driven out of France. Until then they had been the greatest teaching order in the kingdom, with about 105 colleges and schools employing perhaps 15,000 teaching Jesuits. Their nearest rivals, the Oratorians, were running only 29 colleges in 1789. The Jesuits had been learned and capable teachers, lacking neither in devotion nor in preparation, but they had taught obedience to the papacy and had opposed the Gallican or national tendencies of the French Church. The followers of Edmond Richer (1559–1631) and of Cornelis Jansen (1585–1638) joined with an older Gallican tradition to denounce the Jesuits through the parlements.[78] Meanwhile, during the two mid-century wars three rising anti-Catholic powers, Great Britain, Brandenburg-Prussia, and Russia, proved powerful enough to impose themselves on the declining Roman Catholic empires which had threatened the Protestant countries for two centuries.

The French public and the governing elites were, of course, divided in their religious loyalties but turned more and more against Roman Catholic forces. Writers like Condorcet or like Cesare Beccaria (1738–94), author of the influential *Of Crimes and Punishments* (1764; French edition, 1766), despised the "fanatical education" they had had in Jesuit colleges, and distinguished French champions of law reform likened the cruel criminal code to the Roman Catholic Inquisition.[79] Vadier, the future chairman of the Committee of General Security during the Terror, grew up hating the Church in Pamiers, his hometown in the Pyrenees. Even the elementary schools, the *petites écoles* taught by orders less rigorous than the Jesuits, were challenged in the middle eighteenth century by municipal training schools and charitable trade schools.[80] Among the rural populace the clergy lost little influence, and many a peasant community was ready to defend its priests against the hostile forces of the French Revolution, but among the public there was such a ferment of new ideas that even the clergy itself was affected.

It is hard to assess those few radical thinkers among the clergy, such as the abbé Gabriel Bonnot Mably (1709–85), the curé Jean Meslier (1664–1729), and the Benedictine dom Léger-Marie Deschamps (1716–74), or the revolutionary leader the curé Jacques Roux (1752–94), who went so far as to work out utopian social systems. Much clearer is the liberal movement among the members of the clergy, at least 700 of whom joined the Freemasons, 300 of them in the Paris lodges alone. Several hundred joined the academies and made up between 15 percent and 35 percent of the total academic membership.[81] At least nine abbots wrote articles for the *Encyclopédie*. Such affiliations help explain why the clergy elected to the Estates General in 1789 was ready to support the Third Estate in its campaign for a national assembly and a constitution. When three priests from Poitou had the courage to join the Third Estate on 13 June, they were the very first to do so, and one of them, Jacques Jallet, then announced ". . . we come, Messieurs, preceded by the torch of reason, led by the love of public good *[le bien public]* to take our places beside our fellow Citizens. . . ."[82]

These three curés did not think of themselves as revolutionaries then, they appear so only in retrospect. Writing to their bishops to explain their actions, they reproached the bishops with having gloomy revolutionary forebodings, "the property of the clergy despoiled and dissipated, the very Throne shaken. Who would not tremble at the mere idea of such an upheaval!" As Jallet had said in his speech to the First Estate on 12 June, these curés thought of themselves as representatives of the nation with a primary duty to join in the movement for "public utility" and with only a secondary duty to represent the special interests of their own estate or order. There was a constitution to be drawn up, and many public improvements to be made. "Our criminal code," Jallet wrote, "is in general one of the most barbarous imaginable. . . . [A] man owes his fellow citizens every care of humanity and benevolence."[83] It was such fashionable ideas as these, liberal rather than revolutionary, that moved the clergy on 19 June to vote 148 to 136 in favor of joining the Third Estate.

The liberal curés of the majority, living on their tiny *portions congrues* of the tithe, had less at stake than the conservative bishops and abbots of the minority, but the curés' gesture can scarcely be interpreted as a movement of the poor against the rich. After all, rich bishops had ruled over poor curés for a thousand years. And priests like Jallet can hardly be accused of cunning self-interest in joining the Third Estate. Their own words show them to have been inspired by a naïve liberal idealism from which most bishops were preserved by their practical responsibilities and their political experience. Even the bishops and other higher clergy engaged in a spirited struggle together with the parlements against the monarchy from 1787 to 1789, a struggle against what looked to the clergy like royal tyranny.[84] Had the curés and their allies among the higher clergy foreseen the revolutionary events of the next five years, or even of the next twelve months, they would most certainly not have voted to join the Third Estate. The fearful bishops were, as it turned out, quite right. Their forebodings were soon to be realized, and the bright hopes of the curés dashed. Even Abbé Sieyès, author of the famous pamphlet *What Is the Third Estate?*, who went further than most clergy in a revolutionary direction, veered around in 1789 to wage a desperate defense of the tithe and of Church property in general against the National Assembly.[85]

The events of the French Revolution led the clergy, like the public in general, along unfamiliar paths and in directions they had not intended to take. What, after all, was revolutionary in the thinking of the eighteenth-century Enlightenment? "The philosophy characteristic of the 18th century," Robert Mauzi concludes from his deep study of the subject, "consisted in drawing all the consequences from a fundamental fact: the natural sociability of man."[86] The key words in the curé Jallet's vocabulary, *humanité et bienfaisance, utilité publique, le flambeau de la raison,* expressed the ideas of the public in that age. Montesquieu described his *De l'esprit des lois* (1748) as something he had done *"pour l'utilité publique."*[87]

Sometimes the newfangled benevolence and philanthropy seem to be nothing more than old-fashioned charity and patronage, as, for instance, among the noble magistrates of the Paris Parlement. Yet the causes championed in the Enlightenment—tolerance, humanity, practical common sense, education, improvement, and reform—came to be widely supported in the public of that age. An assembly of the clergy wrote rhetorically to Louis XVI in 1785 that "the lessons of the new philosophy echo even in the workshops of the artisan and under the humble roof of the farmer."[88] Strong though the impulses of the Enlightenment were, they had in fact little effect on the lower classes, and they were not revolutionary. Malesherbes was not revolutionary when, as government supervisor of the book trade in the 1750s, he tempered the censorship of books and treated such authors as Rousseau and Diderot with indulgence. Nor was Condorcet when he "sacrificed the hope of private wealth to his passion for the public good" or tried to work out a science of citizenship.[89] Nor was Rousseau when in 1762 he published an abstract academic treatise on the idea of the social contract. There is good reason to beware of the temptation to assume that the French Revolution must somehow have been thought out in the Enlightenment that preceded it. After all, the Enlightenment also preceded the great civilizing movements of the nineteenth century, and its basic notions of tolerance, humanity, and social utility are with us to this day.

THREE *The Monarchy of*
Louis XVI

T HE political history of the French Revolution, reduced to two sentences, is that in summer 1788 Louis XVI gave in to public pressure for a meeting of the Estates General, in June and July 1789 he lost the initiative in government to the Estates General turned National Assembly, and thereafter he suffered a series of reverses, ending with his execution on 21 January 1793. Already the monarchy had been officially suspended, with Louis's arrest on 10 August 1792, and converted to a republic on 22 September. These elementary facts are easy to verify but difficult to interpret.

The very first interpretation, expressed by the republicans of the revolutionary assemblies and their public, was that an indignant nation had at last risen up against a tyrannical king, the last of a long line of kings who had ruled by the force and cunning of a corrupt regime. In one form or another, this interpretation has satisfied many citizens of republics inclined to believe that monarchy is intrinsically a bad and outdated form of government maintained only by repression and tyranny. Careful study of Louis XVI's reign shows, however, that for the eighteenth century he was a relatively benign and enlightened ruler whose regime, corrupt though it was in many ways, hardly abused the nation any more than did the First Republic (1792–99) or the Second (1848–51). Furthermore, beyond the court circles of Paris and Versailles, Louis XVI was generally a well-beloved monarch who did not share in the unpopularity of his Austrian queen, Marie-Antoinette. He was everywhere welcomed and respected when traveling across Normandy to Cherbourg in June 1786.[1] Republican feeling can hardly be found in France before 1791, and the *cahiers de doléances* showed little hatred of the king or of monarchy in general. The republican views expressed at the trial and execution of the king had developed during the revolutionary years, not earlier. Republicanism in France was a result of the Revolution, not a cause of it.

Royalist interpretations of the monarchy's decline and fall have meanwhile been founded on the unsatisfactory belief that seditious and heretical forces conspired against the Crown and the Church. This belief is unsatisfactory because there is not much evidence of conspiracy as a moving force in the Revolution and because too many loyal monarchists and Roman Catholics in France have been perversely inclined to see all opposition as seditious and heretical. No doubt royalist or counterrevolutionary interpretations might seem more convincing if they had had the benefit of as much scholarly labor as has been devoted to revolutionary interpretations during the past 100 years. There is still much to be discovered about political leadership and organization.[2] Yet it seems likely that detailed research will merely fill out the picture of an eighteenth-century French public educating itself to play a part in the liberal process of government by debate, as the American, British, and Dutch publics were already doing.

A more fashionable and widespread interpretation of the Bourbon monarchy holds that it was the instrument of the ruling class, the feudal nobles, and fell with that class. On this interpretation the Revolution was essentially a social event and the political changes it brought about were secondary. First, the nobility, led by the parlements, challenged the monarch as it had often done in the past; then the rising urban middle class, the capitalist bourgeoisie, led the nation in a struggle against the noble landowning class, which had traditionally staffed the monarchy, supported it, and benefited by it and which seemed to dominate it in August 1788. The bourgeoisie, triumphant in the ensuing struggle, pulled down the monarchy with the nobility and replaced it with a republican regime of its own. This plausible theory has inspired the work of many twentieth-century historians, notably Jean Jaurès, Albert Mathiez, Georges Lefebvre, and Albert Soboul.[3] "The Legislative Assembly [of 1791–92] saw itself as the master of the State," writes Georges Lefebvre, "and that Assembly was the *bourgeoisie*. . . . That constitutional monarchy was a bourgeois republic."[4] Whatever the merits of this theory in explaining the events of 1791 and 1792, some other explanation must be found for the events of the previous years, in which the king lost the political initiative and the monarchy became subservient to the revolutionary National Assembly. The revolutionary events of 1787, 1788, and 1789 cannot yet be ascribed to a "reactionary nobility" vanquished in its turn by a "triumphant bourgeoisie" because research does not show the political struggles of those years to have been between any such social classes. It seems, indeed, doubtful whether these terms have any validity at all in the history of those years and doubtful whether there was a social revolution at all, at least before 1791. The monarchy declined and fell in a series of political struggles; these certainly dispersed the nobility and removed the monarchy, but the ruling groups left in command of the state were in no sense capitalists. Furthermore, they were hardly even a distinguishable social class, bourgeois or otherwise, during the political struggles of 1787–91.

Why then did the monarchy collapse during the struggles of those years? If it was not so oppressive or tyrannical as the revolutionaries later painted it, if it was not so widely hated, if there was no early republican conspiracy to pull it down, and if it did not fall victim to a struggle of social classes, then why did it not surmount the difficulties of the time as it had so often surmounted those of times past? Much of the answer to this question is to be found in a study of the strengths and weaknesses of the monarchy under Louis XVI. This is a neglected subject in histories of the Revolution by writers who, knowing that the monarchy fell, assume that it necessarily had to fall as if by some law of history.

A study of the monarchy makes its fall seem astonishing, a great wonder—truly revolutionary, in fact. There had been kings of France for well over 1,000 years, and the monarchical tradition had never been broken as it had during the civil wars in Britain and the Netherlands. Louis XVI was the thirty-second in the third dynasty of kings that began with the crowning of Hugh

Capet in the year 987. By the time the Bourbon branch* of the
Capetian line began in 1589, French kingship was deeply rooted
in what one specialist identifies as seven kinds of law: divine law,
canon law, feudal law, customary law, Salic law, Roman law, and
fundamental law.[5] The first made the monarchy divine by the
anointing of each king with a holy oil brought from heaven in
496 by a dove for the first king, Clovis, and the second gave the
Church's blessing to the rules of succession and anchored the
ruling dynasty in the Roman Catholic Church. The many feudal
and customary law codes established the king's position as over-
lord with a measure of authority over noble lands and their noble
owners. Salic, Roman, and fundamental law were late-medieval
and early-modern systems which defined and redefined the
monarchy. They were partly revivals and partly inventions worked
out by magistrates in the sovereign courts established in the
fourteenth and fifteenth centuries. Much myth and little history
went into the making of all these bodies of law, but even in the
enlightened age of the eighteenth century the ancient mysteries
of monarchy and Church were venerated by all but a few intellectuals.

The effect of all this law was to give the monarchy a constitution—that is, a body of principles and practices recognized by
the lawcourts and by the king and his ministers. This constitution was not a single tidy document of the modern republican
type, for it had not been born in a revolution and had never
needed defining, justifying, or public intoning. The unbroken
succession of kings as personal embodiments of the monarchy
gave the constitution a living continuity which put abstract written documents in the shade. The age-old view of the monarchy
as a living organism, a body politic, with a head (the king), organs

*The Bourbon dynasty of French kings were the following:

Henri IV (1589–1610), heir to the throne when the Valois dynasty died out
    with Henri III
Louis XIII (1610–43), son of Henri IV
Louis XIV (1643–1715), son of Louis XIII
Louis XV (1715–74), great-grandson of Louis XIV
Louis XVI (1774–93), grandson of Louis XV
Louis XVII, son of Louis XVI, lived 1785–95 and never ruled
Louis XVIII (1814–24), brother of Louis XVI
Charles X (1824–39), youngest brother of Louis XVI

(the councils, courts, etc.), and limbs (the intendants, the armed forces, the clergy, etc.), was different from the eighteenth-century view of the State as a rational, ordered system with mechanical properties, a view no doubt recently derived from the cosmologies of Descartes and Newton. The king's authority was vague and had never been defined. Indeed, as the historian Lavisse writes, "Royal authority was so formidable only because it could not be defined."[6] On this crucial issue the constitution left room for infinite disagreement, not because constitutional lawyers had been muddleheaded or negligent but because the politics of the monarchy's growth and development had often left room for dissent in sovereign and ecclesiastical courts and in provincial estates.

The monarchy had grown from the twelfth century with the gradual addition of feudal principalities to the royal domains around Paris. These had been acquired one by one by inheritance, conquest, or marriage, and each one had joined the monarchy on different terms and preserved certain ancient rights and immunities in the process: lawcourts and codes, customs duties, provincial estates, weights and measures, and so on. Meanwhile, the papacy had never ceded all authority over the Roman Catholic Church in France, and ultramontane bishops were always ready to challenge Gallican claims or pretensions. When, therefore, a king declared (as all the Bourbons did) that he was responsible only before God, was above the nation, and was the only source of temporal authority in France, many voices were ready to remind him that France had a constitution that was above the royal will, a constitution made of historic customs, contracts, and decrees. This is why the Bourbon monarchy was described as absolute but neither tyrannical nor despotic, and in modern terms it may be thought of as authoritarian but neither totalitarian nor dictatorial. The king had the last word in ordinary matters of government, he could make final decisions, and so could put an end to otherwise endless wrangling in the kingdom; but his every word was not law. The evident danger of arousing too much opposition obliged him and his officials to be wary in dealing with provincial, municipal, ecclesiastical, and corporate powers. Political good sense imposed limits on his authority in many matters great and small.

In the hearts and minds of the people, as well as in law, Louis XVI was as firmly established as many of his forebears had been. When he was crowned at Reims on 11 June 1775, he fulfilled one of the ancient royal duties of blessing some 2,400 scrofulous pilgrims* who had come in the belief that the Lord's anointed could heal them by his divine touch. Louis XV had touched more than 2,000 scrofulous subjects at the time of his crowning in October 1722.[7] Victims of scrofula sought the king's supernatural healing powers just as the victims of toothache in Anjou sought the help of Saint Apolline, just as people bitten by wolves, dogs, or horses went to the "relatives" of Saint Hubert d'Ardennes.

An informal political system reinforced the king's authority among the public and, indirectly, among the populace. All offices, appointments, military and ecclesiastical ranks, pensions, new noble titles, and even minor employment were in the king's gift, and so he commanded the gratitude of an army of his subjects beholden to him for his grace and favor. Much royal patronage was exercised indirectly through courtiers, officials, and favorites but was no less effective for that. The mere hope of royal favor kept many people attentive to the royal court, and there was sharp competition for each post, office, or honor. The pages of the annual *Almanach royal*—714 pages in 1789—list the names of all the archbishops, bishops, abbots and abbesses, cashiers, receivers, controllers, payers, chaplains, canons, almoners, governors, magistrates, bailiffs, attorneys, presidents, administrators, commissioners, directors, intendants, secretaries, clerks, treasurers, councillors, marshals, brigadiers, generals, colonels, ambassadors, consuls, officers of the knightly orders of the Holy Spirit, of Military Merit, of Saint Michel, of the Golden Fleece and of Saint Louis, notaries, censors, academicians, doctors, engineers, etc.[8] The rank and file of domestic servants employed by these and by the royal family can only be imagined, and the purchasing power of the monarchy in equipment, food, clothing, textiles, and military supplies was certainly a great force for loyalty, though it has never been carefully calculated.

Loyalty was required by the king's soldiers and sailors, and

*Scrofula, "the king's evil," old names for tuberculosis of the bones and lymphatic glands.

after 1763 recruiting was a royal prerogative. Soldiers scattered in hundreds of thousands throughout the populace of town and country, especially in the north and east, during their eight years of voluntary enlistment and after retirement. By June 1789 the loyalty of the 156,000 men then in the army was no doubt strained by too much police duty, by revolutionary propaganda, and by the political confusion in the kingdom, but even then they might have responded to vigorous and decisive royal leadership. There is no evidence that the soldiers in general were committed to the Revolution during the critical months of June and July 1789.[9] Through the army, the Church, and the officialdom, then, a vast pyramid of royal patronage reinforced the ancient religious and customary hold of kingship on French hearts.

The king acted most directly and vigorously through his ministers, his councils, and their agents, the intendants of the generalities posted out in provincial capitals. In constitutional theory, the controller general of finances and the four secretaries of state, for war, marine and colonies, foreign affairs, and the royal households, were merely royal executive agents, not a cabinet; but in fact, they had policies of their own, and the king consulted them. There were four main councils in 1788 and 1789, after some changes in previous years: the Conseil d'état, sometimes called the Conseil d'en-haut, for discussion of the greatest matters of state including foreign affairs, the Conseil des dépêches for the internal affairs of the realm, the Conseil royal des finances et de commerce, and the Comité intime de la guerre, a small ad hoc committee to deal with military contingencies.[10] In constitutional theory they did not exist apart from the king's person; they were held to be all one and the same council, no matter which councillors were present; they were supposed to keep affairs of state secret; and they were supposed to do no more than advise the king and execute his commands.

In practice councils were essential cogs in the machinery of state and imposed considerable limits on the king's will. The *commissaires départis du conseil*, better known as the intendants of the generalities and provinces, numbered thirty-three in 1789. They were the principal representatives of the king out in the provincial capitals, almost viceroys in the range of their duties, famous as experienced administrators, and the monarchy depended on them to stand up to the parlements, the provincial Estates, the big municipal governments, and various privileged social groups. Faced with daunting political tasks such as their postrevolutionary successors, the prefects, were not to meet, the intendants maneuvered among provincial forces with much tact; but they did not turn away from the monarchy and become provincial leaders, as some historians have mistakenly believed. Even out in the semi-independent *pays d'états*, Provence, Brittany, Burgundy, and Languedoc, the intendants at the end of the *ancien régime* remained king's men.[11]

The intendants were remarkably capable, as were many of the officials serving the king in Paris and Versailles. And well they might be, for Louis XVI (1754–93) was a thoughtful, informed, and devoted ruler, not strong or determined but not the pitiful dullard of the historical legend, either. Until his father died in 1765, Louis was not the heir apparent, and because he was reserved and self-possessed in childhood, his father, who did not understand him, used to compare him unfavorably with his more talkative brothers, the future kings Louis XVIII and Charles X. Later others at court also misunderstood him and disliked him, notably some of the Duc de Choiseul's friends in the pro-Austrian "party," and the Austrian ambassador, Mercy d'Argenteau, whose letters have too often been read uncritically. Louis XVI has suffered in the history books from unfair judgments lifted out of the court gossip of the time. As he wrote in one of his schoolbooks, "The French are anxious grumblers; the reins of government are never directed to their taste. They shout, they complain, they grumble eternally; it might be said that complaining and murmuring are part of their essential character."[12] Scholars who reach beyond the court gossip of the reign discover a serious, hardworking, conscientious ruler very different from the conventional descriptions of him.

In some circles Louis has been misunderstood for the same reasons that his confessor, Abbé Placide Soldini, his tutor, Quélen, Comte de La Vauguyon, and his minister, Jacques Necker, have been misunderstood: They all were affected by the amiable spirit of humanity abroad in their time. They encouraged Louis XVI to be a sincere Christian with a benevolent and humane attitude toward his fellowmen. As often happens, Louis's goodness and simple virtues were interpreted in sophisticated circles as weakness and pious hypocrisy. He was taught from childhood that all men are equal before God, and a reading of Montesquieu and the Encyclopedists reinforced his inclination to be tolerant, peaceable, and devoted to the general well-being of his servants and his subjects. "Sovereignty is essentially benevolent," he wrote in his youth. "The confidence of the nation is the government's due, but it is up to the sovereign and his ministers to work continually to deserve it and to maintain it."[13]

Little wonder that Louis XVI employed ministers and intendants who busied themselves with the poor and unfortunate, who tried to improve agriculture, to see to food supplies, to inoculate against smallpox, to train midwives, to improve the lot of the Protestants, to remove torture from the legal procedure, to shift the burden of taxation onto the richer classes, and, in short, to make the type of improvements that we rightly associate with that age of the Enlightenment. Louis XVI was quite at home with the projects of such enlightened ministers as Turgot, who in 1776 tried to abolish the *corvées,* forced labor on road building; Necker, who founded the Paris hospital that still bears his name; Malesherbes, who did so much to end official persecution of Protestants; and Lamoignon so busy with legal reforms, and of such intendants as Depont at Metz, Sénac de Meilhan at Valenciennes, Caze de la Bove at Grenoble, and Bertrand de Molleville at Rennes. In his vocabulary, as in theirs, the Enlightenment echoed in terms like *raison, humanité, sensibilité, citoyen, patriote, amour de l'humanité,* and *amour de la liberté.* Louis XVI and Jacques Necker formally abolished serfdom on Crown lands in 1779 by a decree "which reads as if it had been drawn up by Voltaire."[14] A practical concern for public well-being or happiness *(le bien public, le bonheur public)* easily led to a tolerance of public opinion and an unwillingness to stifle public debate in the manner of Louis XIV and previous kings.

Through his natural decency, Louis XVI was a sort of liberal, like his enlightened ministers. Herein lay the fatal weakness of his rule. Absolute authority had to be exercised or it would atrophy like an unused muscle. A Bourbon king who did not resort to force, bribery, political cunning, and charisma ran the risk of challenge to his government. Jean-Joseph Mounier, a

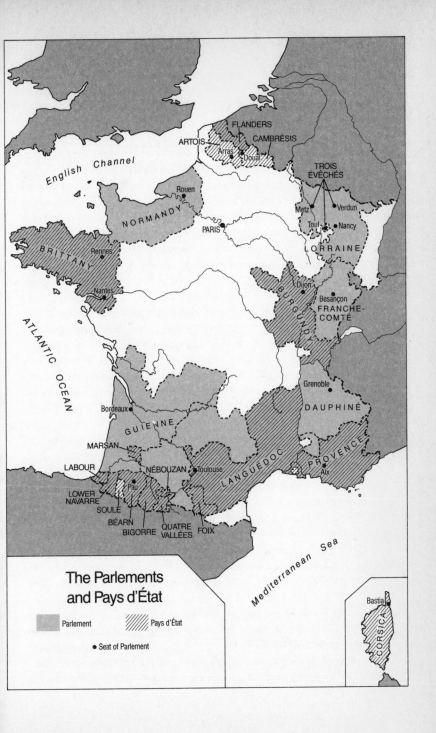

English Channel

FLANDERS
ARTOIS
CAMBRÉSIS
Arras • Douai
TROIS
ÉVÊCHÉS

Rouen

Metz • Verdun

NORMANDY

PARIS

Toul • Nancy

LORRAINE

BRITTANY
Rennes

Dijon

Nantes

BURGUNDY

Besançon
FRANCHE-
COMTÉ

ATLANTIC OCEAN

Grenoble

DAUPHINÉ

Bordeaux

GUIENNE

MARSAN

NÉBOUZAN • Toulouse

PROVENCE

LABOUR

Pau

Aix

LANGUEDOC

LOWER
NAVARRE
SOULE
BÉARN
BIGORRE
QUATRE
VALLÉES
FOIX

Mediterranean Sea

The Parlements
and Pays d'État

Parlement //// Pays d'État

• Seat of Parlement

Bastia •
CORSICA

lawyer from Grenoble, deputy to the Estates General in 1789, reflected just after Louis XVI was deposed and imprisoned in 1792: "It is frightful to think that with a less benevolent soul, another prince might perhaps have found the means to maintain his power."[15] This paradox is one of the clues to the outbreak of the French Revolution, as also to the many revolutions that brought down European rulers in 1848. Like Louis-Philippe of France, Charles Albert of Piedmont, Pope Pius IX, and other rulers in the 1840s, Louis XVI in his time tolerated public debate and political organization because he and some of his ministers were sympathetic with the prevailing liberal fashion and did not foresee where it might lead. The sovereign courts were allowed to debate and resist royal policy in full view of the general public for years before being stopped by royal decree, something Louis XIV had not tolerated.

The financial difficulties of the government were revealed in detail to the public as never before, in pamphlets, printed remonstrances, journals, and books, some of them published even by the ministers of finance. Frank and informed writings like Necker's *Compte rendu au roi* (1781) and *De l'administration des finances de la France* (1784, three volumes), or Calonne's *Réponse de Monsieur Calonne à l'écrit de Monsieur Necker* (1788), were without precedent in French history and became best sellers in their time. Necker appealed to the general public as no one had before him. "Yes, generous nation, it is to you that I consecrate this work," he wrote in the introduction to *De l'administration des finances*, and went on for sixty-two chapters, based on his five years as minister of finance, as though he were taking the public into his confidence. In 1786 the government decided to put its financial projects before an Assembly of Notables and did so in spring 1787. The public followed its proceedings with keen interest, observing that opposition to the government's projects grew and flourished unmolested until the crisis of the following summer.[16]

At the assembly one of the first reforms to be proposed by the Crown and approved by the Notables was the election of provincial assemblies in which the traditional distinctions between clergy, nobles, and commoners were preserved only after much debate. As announced by the liberal minister Loménie de Brienne in June 1787, these assemblies were part of a larger hierarchy of assemblies within each generality, including municipal assemblies, which implied great changes in the established city governments. During those same prerevolutionary years provincial Estates were allowed to revive briefly in Dauphiné, Franche-Comté, and Provence.[17] The ancient traditional secrecy of criminal trials and the exclusion of the public from the courts were being challenged by such progressive magistrates as Mercier-Dupaty of Bordeaux.[18] The censorship of publications was no longer rigorous under directors like the liberal intellectual Malesherbes, and matters of state were discussed with impunity in private clubs and meetings. "Of course," we may say to all this, "why not?" The answer is that the Bourbon monarchy had never before tolerated such a generous measure of public debate and political freedom. A quiet liberal revolution was in the making under the leadership of the king and his ministers.

It is a mistake to imagine that in these matters the royal government was the unwilling victim of public pressure. Before 1788, at least, liberal reforming zeal came from the government more than from the public. The public emotions of 1788 and 1789 were results of the Crown's reforming policies, not the victorious climax of a long public campaign. Public opinion was divided, as it nearly always is, and every reform aroused support in some quarters and opposition in others. Some of the most liberal reforms stirred up the strongest opposition. For instance, an edict intended to give Protestants a civil status in the realm was prepared in official circles and sent to the Paris Parlement for registration on 19 November 1787. Most of Paris was opposed to it, and it provoked a crisis in the Parlement.[19] Even in the modified form in which the Parlement registered it two months later the parlements of Bordeaux, Besançon, and Douai refused it, and the clergy, which had not been consulted when the edict was drafted, firmly opposed it.

Another liberal and humane reform that aroused more public opposition than support was the criminal law which the keeper of the seals (the chief legal officer of the realm), Lamoignon de Basville, imposed on all the sovereign courts in an authoritarian declaration of 1 May 1788.[20] This abolished the last vestiges of torture in the judicial process, provided legal counsel for the accused, tried in other ways to make criminal trials fairer, mitigated the harsh terms of the death penalty, and reorganized the criminal courts, but these worthy reforms won the sympathy of only a small enlightened minority of the magistrates and the public. The reforms were preceded by some notorious cases, such as that of Victoire Salmon, a servant girl sentenced by the *bailliage* of Caen on 18 April 1782, then again by the Parlement of Rouen, to be put to the *question ordinaire et extraordinaire* (i.e., tortured) and then burned alive for allegedly poisoning her eighty-eight-year-old master to death.[21] The then keeper of the seals, Miromesnil, passing through Rouen, took up the case and observed that there was no proof of her guilt. He had the Council of State overrule the Parlement, and after much altercation the Parlement of Paris acquitted her on 2 March 1786. Such was the public interest in her case that a subscription was opened for her; she was presented to the king, the queen, and the court and soon married at Saint-Séverin before a large crowd. This was not an isolated case. After various parlements had denounced Lally-Tollendal, the French commander in chief at the Indian colony of Pondicherry, lost to British forces, he was executed. His son tried to have him declared posthumously innocent, but the parlements would not hear of this. However, on 4 September 1786 the Royal Council overruled the Parlement of Dijon, and Louis XVI cleared his name.[22]

Nor was the public generally in favor of the Crown's proposed unification of the customs duties and the salt and tobacco monopolies, which caused great hardship in their unreformed state because they varied from province to province according to old agreements.[23] In encouraging or tolerating public debate on these and other matters, the monarchy was following the inclination of the large liberal or enlightened element within its own ranks and also hoping for public support for its reforms against the opposition of the sovereign courts. Louis XVI sought political solutions for the political problems his government faced and resorted to force only when hard pressed.

Was he merely weak and vacillating as is usually said? Or did he reflect that 100 years of political opposition in England and Holland had not brought down the reigning monarchs of the Hanoverian and Orange lines but only limited their power?

Or did the liberal ideals of the Revolution in America reinforce his own inclination to give a freer rein to French public opinion? Did he imagine that his subjects might learn to use gifts of liberty no less well than the Americans used the liberty they had seized from George III? The point of these speculations is that Louis XVI might have used military means instead of political means to pursue his policies.

The monarchy fell mainly because the monarch chose not to defend it in the traditional manner. In 1774, when Louis XVI came to the throne, he inherited all the authority, power, and precedent needed for authoritarian rule. As recently as January 1771 the rebellious sovereign courts had been silenced by the authority of Louis XV and his hardheaded chancellor, Maupeou (1714–92); the parlements had been dissolved, and the magistrates in them banished or appointed to a new set of courts. That put an end to half a century of their resistance to royal decrees and their criticism of government policies on taxation and finance. No rebellion threatened anywhere in France, but had any broken out, Louis XVI commanded armed forces of no less than 150,000 regular troops, 75,000 militiamen, and a large territorial police force (maréchaussée). The troops of the royal households alone numbered more than 7,000. No ominous revolutionary clouds, no inevitable fate hung over the kingdom; those in the history books were invented ex post facto by historians wise after the events of 1788–93. A Louis XIV or even a Louis XV might have gone on ruling firmly into the nineteenth century. "The ancien régime," writes Georges Lefebvre in his study of the Orléans district, "was not ready to defend itself."[24] The militia had not assembled for thirty years; the troops were not properly applied, as they might have been to the problems of civil disorder.

Louis XVI did not organize any defense because he reigned as he had been reared, a Christian gentleman of the siècle des lumières, enlightened but not despotic, modest and humane, tolerant of politics, reluctant to punish, and inclined to appoint men like himself as ministers. In the circumstances of the 1780s these very qualities were his undoing. The ancient habit of secrecy had been essential to the mystery of royal government, the king moving like God in a mysterious way his wonders to perform.

But now a new practice of publicity came to be recognized in some circles, partly because publicity prevailed in England, Holland, and America and partly because the swelling French public cried out for knowledge of public life. Secrecy with its twin, propaganda, breeds tyranny and is, indeed, one of the rules of despotism, for it lends respectability to false rumor, to the use of scapegoats, and to the sudden arrests and arbitrary imprisonments by which despotic governments defend themselves. Louis XVI tolerated public initiatives in matters which more despotic rulers or their ministers were accustomed to directing themselves. He let vital matters of state become public issues, and the public eventually overwhelmed him.

The royal ministers and the public debated the financial difficulties of the reign so vigorously that they soon blew them up into insoluble problems. The original difficulties were not new, after all, but had faced nearly every French ruler. When had there not been a shortage of funds? Which king had not been plagued with mounting debts? Which had not faced political opposition in the sovereign courts? The difficulties Louis XVI faced were old perennials, albeit deep-rooted ones, but the problems he made of them were new and complex. Problems, like beauty, are in the eye of the beholder, and Louis XVI and most of his ministers tended to see their major difficulties as public issues—that is, issues on which opinions might be openly expressed by any magistrate, financier, official, or other citizen who could dash off a pamphlet. "The things of the State had long concerned only the State," Daniel Mornet writes, "and the State had done everything it could to surround them with a dreadful mystery and to punish the desecrators. But the seven seals were broken, and about 1780, anyone might enter the sanctuary."[25] The censorship of the period was light by the standards of earlier kings, extremely light by the authoritarian standards of the Roman Catholic Church or the Communist dictatorships of later times or, indeed, of the despots who ruled most of eighteenth-century Europe. The Crown made only halfhearted efforts to stifle or to direct public debate.

The financial difficulties were in large part inherent in the financial system. This was a system of venal, independent financiers who managed the collecting and spending of all government funds partly on commission, partly for fees, and partly in the hope of social advancement.[26] All these receivers, treasurers, paymasters, and tax farmers, several hundred of them, bought their offices and remained free to carry on all manner of private business so long as they avoided bankruptcy and seemed to be managing their royal accounts honestly. Like private business-men, they were not part of a bureaucratic hierarchy, not answer-able to supervisors or inspectors, and for their royal business they were accountable only to the magistrates in the Chamber of Accounts. This chamber, being one of the sovereign courts, worked by its own customs and standards, indifferent to the finance minister's policies and suspicious of ministerial plans for reform.

Such a system offered opportunities for graft, embezzle-ment, or profiteering, especially in wartime, and the rulers of the sixteenth and seventeenth centuries had from time to time set up a temporary tribunal, a so-called Chambre de justice, to discover and punish dishonest financiers or merely to frighten rich ones with the threat of prosecution. The Chambre de jus-tice—Louis XIII held one in 1624, Louis XIV in the 1660s, the regency in 1716 and 1717—served several purposes, not the least of them being a canceling of government debts to the financial capitalists. In 1717 the regency reduced its debts enormously by fining about 4,000 rich financiers in this way. The harsh but sal-utary institution of the Chambre de justice was never used again, except on a small scale in the *affaire du Canada*,* and so the financiers waxed ever richer and stronger in the kingdom until their demise in the French Revolution. As a result, the govern-ment could neither supervise nor control its own financial pro-cesses but waged a vain day-to-day struggle with its own financiers, who became its masters by lending it money. The debt to these financial capitalists, in the purchase price of their venal offices and in short-term loans, is incalculable now, just as it was then,

*The *affaire du Canada* began in 1761 when the government arrested about fifty of its officers and officials who had just arrived back from Canada after its loss to Great Britain in the Seven Years' War. They were charged with defrauding the Crown and the public, tried by a special tribunal, and fined huge sums, and the greatest of them, François Bigot, intendant of New France, was banished for life. (See J. F. Bosher, "The French Government's Motives in the *Affaire du Can-ada*, 1761–63," *English Historical Review*, vol. XCVI [1981], pp. 59–78.)

but in August 1790 the revolutionary Comité des finances reckoned it at nearly 2 billion livres.[27] Whatever their total, these debts dwarfed the more famous *rentes* or government bonds, the funded debt, too long regarded as the main burden. With a reformed financial administration, France could have coped with a funded debt of that size just as Great Britain was coping with it. But how could the financial system be reformed?

Louis XVI and his ministers, from Turgot's ministry (1774–76) to Necker's second ministry (1788–90), attempted many reforms of the system. The old method of the Chambre de justice seems never to have appealed to them, perhaps because they judged it politically impossible, the financiers having intermarried with the ruling classes.[28] Rather than attempt a frontal attack on his financiers, Louis XVI and his governments chose to shoulder the state debts in the hope of paying them by raising taxes, cutting costs, and rationalizing the financial administration.

The usual financial strains on the government were aggravated in the reign of Louis XVI by hard times. The previous reign had benefited by good times, especially in the twenty years after about 1750, but during the years around 1770, earlier in some regions, later in others, a severe depression occurred throughout much of the kingdom.[29] Crops failed, food was scarce and dear, textile manufacturing declined, much wine was of poor quality, and exports declined. The economy began to revive after the crisis of 1769–71 but never fully recovered; hard times continued, and in the late 1780s the population, which had been growing, faced unemployment and a threat of starvation. In the Lyons silk industry the depression in the winter of 1786–87 was the most serious period of stagnation in the industry's history.[30] Trade languished, agriculture failed, and a general crisis in the revolutionary years 1788 and 1789 struck twenty-seven of the thirty-two generalities.

Only the big Atlantic ports continued to flourish. The monarchy was hard pressed to cope with all the distress in town and country, and its efforts earned little applause. By its very efforts to provide grain for starving provinces, the Crown incurred popular suspicion. The widespread legend of the "pact of famine" taught that big profiteers were managing the grain trade in the king's name and exploiting consumers in hard times. Like other authoritarian governments, it found that its own paternal habits aroused expectations it could not hope to meet. A government which claims universal authority may attract universal blame. The trade treaty with Great Britain signed in 1786 was blamed rightly or wrongly for much distress in the textile and hardware industries. Inflation was slight by later standards, but it prompted claims for higher pay. The taxed classes were less and less able to pay taxes, but the revenues from them were needed more than ever.

The monarchy in its foreign policy never recovered the prestige it had lost in the Seven Years' War. Foreign influence was seen on all sides. A fall in the sale of French textiles and other manufactures in Spain and the Levant during the 1770s and 1780s was known to be due to English and German competition.[31] The victory in the American War of Independence, the only French success in the reign of Louis XVI, seemed to bear no fruit, and the hoped-for flourishing of trade with the United States never materialized because American businessmen found French regulations tiresome and preferred to trade with their old partners in Great Britain.[32] France was unable to prevent Russia, Prussia, and Austria from partitioning Poland in 1772 and could regard the restoration of Gustavus III in Sweden that year as a victory only by ignoring the decisive roles of Frederick II of Prussia, Gustavus's uncle, and of Great Britain, an opponent of Russian power in the Baltic region. In 1787 the foreign minister, Vergennes, threw French support behind the pro-French Patriot Party in the Dutch Republic, only to find himself defeated when the Prussians sent a force to destroy the Patriot Party.[33]

Great Britain, a Prussian ally in that struggle and an antagonist of France for the best part of 100 years, seemed ever more prosperous and powerful, an even greater obstacle to French hegemony in Europe than the traditional Habsburg enemies. Two principal foreign ministers, Choiseul and Vergennes, pursued a determined anti-British foreign policy which could hardly be described as a success, notwithstanding the victory in the American War. For one thing, the French and Americans had won a victory for a liberal republican movement over a monarchy, a dangerous and morally dubious cause for the Bourbon monarchy to espouse, as events in France swiftly proved. A good number of the court nobles who joined the troublesome and dangerous Company of Thirty, which met in Paris to discuss public issues in 1788, including Lafayette and the Lameth brothers, had served in the American War.[34] For another, British imperial power had merely been driven over the border to Canada by the Treaty of Versailles (1783), whereas French imperial power had been driven out of North America altogether by the Treaty of Paris (1763). The many attempts to invade England, Scotland, and Ireland had all failed,* as had all efforts to expel the British from Gibraltar and the Mediterranean. The Mediterranean mind of Napoleon betrayed an almost neurotic exaggeration of the British threat when he declared, a few years later, "Truly, to overthrow England we must occupy Egypt."[35] The diplomatic situation of France was surely not as bad as that, yet no one on the eve of the French Revolution would have attributed supremacy in Europe, or even some preponderance, to the kingdom of France. "Public opinion in France," writes Albert Sorel, "unanimously desired the restoration of French prestige abroad."[36] Here was a major source of political weakness in the monarchy of Louis XVI.

*In 1692 Louis XIV had an invasion army ready near La Hogue on the coast of Normandy, but in May the invasion fleet under Admiral Anne de Cotentin, Comte de Tourville (1642–1701) was defeated by Anglo-Dutch forces. In July 1715 a French fleet at Le Havre was preparing to assist a Jacobite rising in Britain. In February 1744 Marshal Maurice, Comte de Saxe (1696–1750) assembled an invasion army and transport ships at Dunkirk to assist Charles Edward, the Stuart pretender to the British throne, but it gave up in the face of gales and opposition in the English Channel. Late in 1745, 15,000 troops were assembled again at Dunkirk for an invasion attempt, but British forces outmaneuvered it and the supporting Brest fleet. Early in 1759 special invasion barges were being built at several Atlantic and Channel ports, and in the fall a large invasion force assembled with the Brest fleet under Admiral Hubert de Brienne, Comte de Conflans, in Quiberon Bay in southern Brittany, where it was defeated and dispersed on 20 November by Admiral Edward Hawke (1710–81). In 1779 a combined Franco-Spanish fleet set off under Admiral Louis d'Orvilliers (1708–92) to invade England near Plymouth but was deterred by bad weather, disease and the superior forces of Admiral Charles Hardy (1716–80). French attempts to invade the British Isles are chronicled in many books, but summarized in J. A. Williamson, *The English Channel: A History*, London, 1961, ch. 14. On the most recent attempt, see J. R. Dull, *The French Navy and American Independence*, Princeton, 1975, pp. 143–59. On subsequent attempts, Édouard Desbrière, *Projets et tentatives de débarquement aux Isles Britanniques, 1793–1805*, Paris, 1900–02, 5 vols.

Within the kingdom there had always been forces of provincial independence opposed to the central authority of the monarchy. This is not surprising in view of the long struggle, since the fifteenth century, to impose the royal government on ancient cities and feudal principalities that might otherwise have remained as independent as the principalities and free cities of Germany or Italy. The ancient ruling families of certain provinces had resisted the monarchy until well into the seventeenth century, and some never acquired a firm loyalty to the Crown. Cardinal Richelieu had had much success in destroying their power during his long ministry (1624–42), but the revolt called the Fronde (1648–53), in which several princes and other high noblemen revolted against the Crown, had shown how much power they still had after his death. In the reign of Louis XIV the Breton nobility acquired the habit of a permanent and systematic political obstruction, directed mainly against the royal intendants and the bureaucracy at Rennes and Versailles.[37] Everywhere in the ancient feudal principalities there were provincial noblemen opposed to divine-right monarchy.[38] Thousands of seigneurial courts—about 2,500 in Brittany alone—were ready to defend themselves against reform. From the beginning of Louis XVI's reign the Breton Estates were left to choose their own *commission intermédiaire,* and the royal government gave up trying to control the appointments. The powers of these commissions were very great indeed, for they were answerable only to the Estates. An extension of their power might have excluded royal officials altogether and created the most decentralized of regimes.

More aggressive than the ancient feudal families, however, were the parlements, those provincial high courts, a dozen of them, composed of noble magistrates who had been collectively resisting royal policies in matters of finance ever since the Seven Years' War. They had, indeed, a long tradition of resistance; it was their hostility to the royal government that had set off the civil wars of the Fronde in 1648. In the reign of Louis XVI the parlements proved to be the monarchy's most dangerous enemies, able to lead other provincial forces against Louis XVI in 1787 and 1788. Those other forces included considerable sections of the public resentful of the closed circle of local notables controlling the towns as petty agents of the bureaucracy.[39] Commercial centers like Bordeaux, Marseilles, Lyons, and Nantes manifested local feeling which could on occasion turn against the monarchy. Bordeaux had a traditional assembly, the *cent-trente*, to be convoked by the *jurats* of the town whenever the ancient municipal rights and privileges were in peril. In July 1789 there were strong elements in all but two of the thirty biggest towns ready to challenge the old subservient municipal governments and to replace them with revolutionary committees.[40] These have usually been interpreted as middle-class elements challenging the nobility in a class struggle, but in many towns there were mixed nobles and commoners together challenging the monarchy. All this occurred in towns where the royal agents had taken root like garrisons; in rural communities no royal rule, indeed, no rule of any kind, had ever been established.[41]

One of the great props of the monarchy was the Roman Catholic Church, to which the Bourbons had firmly committed it. Protestants had been persecuted from Cardinal Richelieu's ministry (1624–42) in spite of the Edict of Nantes (1598), and when His Most Christian Majesty Louis XIV repealed the edict in October 1685, there remained no legal impediments to a war of extermination on Protestants. Subsequently such heretics as Jansenists and Richerists were also outlawed. Louis XIV committed France to promote the Roman Catholic cause in opposition to the Protestant Dutch and English, and religious hatreds played a big part in his many wars. The French court harbored the Catholic Jacobite pretenders to the English throne and joined in the Jacobite rebellions in 1715 and 1745 which seemed deadly serious at the time.[42] During the later eighteenth century, after two lost wars against Protestant powers and the rise of anti-Catholic countries in general, Catholicism weakened among the French ruling classes. A Jansenist and Gallican movement in the parlements succeeded in bringing the powerful Society of Jesus into disrepute, and it was driven out of France from 1762 to 1764.[43]

To denounce and destroy the greatest teaching order in the kingdom was to undermine what it had been teaching. The Oratorians and secular clergy that took over the confiscated Jesuit secondary schools were not commandos of the Counterreformation as the Jesuits were; besides, the Enlightenment of the

eighteenth century inclined many of the clergy toward tolerant
and humane views repugnant to the Church of that day and
incompatible with official religious policy. Abbé Morellet, Abbé
Véri, Abbé de Ponçol, Abbé Rémy, the mysterious Abbé Morelly,
Abbé Mably, Abbé de Condillac, Abbé de Marsy, and how many
more, broke with the old policies of the Counterreformation.
They did not need to become atheists and communists like the
curé Jean Meslier or even utopians like the Benedictine dom
Léger-Marie Deschamps to break with the official Catholic religion, but only liberal intellectuals. In the intellectual atmosphere
of the later eighteenth century many of the clergy could no longer
be counted on to oppose the liberal and Protestant heresies which
Louis XIII, XIV, and XV had committed the monarchy to destroy.
Even the principal tutors to Louis XVI and to the younger princes,
La Vauguyon and Soldini, taught a tolerant, humane brand of
religion. Louis XVI became a benevolent Christian, the despair
of orthodox Roman Catholic clergy, and his younger brother,
the Comte de Provence, the future Louis XVIII (king from 1814
to 1824), became a skeptical Voltairean.[44] In their time there
were even a few who, like the bishop of Autun Talleyrand, were
ready as early as 1789 to nationalize all church property, and a
few who, like the curé Jacques Roux and the Oratorian Joseph
Fouché, were ready in 1793 to become violent revolutionaries.
These were by no means typical, but they show how the French
Church, one of the pillars of the absolute monarchy, was no longer
the staunch bulwark of orthodoxy it had been a century earlier.

The monarchy collapsed, finally, because it had no organized defense. Those who ought to have been its defenders, the
bishops and clergy of the realm, the court nobility, the great
officers and magistrates, the military and naval chiefs of staff, in
short the ruling classes, did not foresee where events were leading them until too late. The ruling classes in general made a
serious error of judgment: They did not realize that the public
was ready to rule and the populace to revolt. They lacked leadership, it is true, for Louis XVI was hesitant, tolerant, "always
dominated by a great mistrust of himself," as Mollien, a royal
official, afterward recalled. "I reproach myself (I and so many
others) with not having been able to defend him better."[45] Louis
XVI needed a strong minister to take charge at court, as Riche-

lieu had done for Louis XIII, and as Cardinal Fleury and Choiseul had in turn done for Louis XV. The problem for Louis
XVI was the ever-present problem of moving with the times,
keeping abreast of basic changes in the kingdom without losing
the initiative necessary for royal leadership. Louis XVI characteristically chose to be a reforming monarch, like most other
European kings in that age, and by his reforms he divided the
ruling classes and demoralized them.

Even before the reign Louis XV had allowed an old religious antagonism, that between the Jesuit and Jansenist sympathizers within the Church, to blossom into a major political crisis
in which the observing public took sides for or against the Jesuits.
The Crown's handling of this affair showed indecision, compromise, and even weakness. Already the enlightened Malesherbes
during his term of office as director of the censorship office
(*librairie*) had established a tolerant policy that could scarcely be
reversed.[46] A mounting flood of pamphlets, addressed to every
conceivable public issue, could not be stopped by a ruling class
with so many officials and magistrates who enjoyed reading and
writing pamphlets themselves! The proposed reforms of the
criminal courts pleased enlightened admirers of Voltaire, who
had publicly championed Calas, La Barre, Sirven, Lally-Tollendal, and other victims of injustice, but antagonized most of the
magistrates in the parlements.* The choice of Turgot (1774–76)
and then Necker (1776–81) as controller general of finances
divided the ruling classes into the supporters of doctrinaire eco-

*These were the most notorious of the cases of injustice Voltaire publicized.
Jean Calas (1698–1762), a Protestant merchant at Toulouse with an English wife
of Huguenot extraction, was judged guilty of his son's murder, sentenced by the
Parlement of Toulouse, and publicly tortured and executed on 10 March 1762.
Pierre-Paul Sirven (1709–64) and his wife, Toinette Léger, Protestants living
near Castres (Tarn), were sentenced to death in 1764 by a magistrate at the
village of Mazamet for the supposed murder of their daughter, who had, Voltaire believed, been driven mad and perhaps murdered at a convent where she
had been imprisoned; they fled to Switzerland. François Le Fèvre, Chevalier de
La Barre (1747–64), arrested for blasphemy and desecrating a cross, was tortured and executed at Abbeville (Somme) on 1 July 1766. The sentence had been
upheld by the Parlement of Paris. Thomas-Arthur, Comte de Lally, Baron de
Tollendal (1702–66), son of an Irish Jacobite and a French noblewoman, was
sentenced to death and beheaded in the Place de Grève on 9 May 1766 on
trumped-up charges arising out of French defeats in India where he had been
the commander in chief.

nomic liberty, supporters of practical administrative reform, and opponents of change. Calonne's reforming measures put before the Assembly of Notables in spring 1787 shattered the public into conflicting factions. In all this political activity the defense of the monarchy was largely forgotten until too late.

A king who wished to rule his kingdom had first to rule his court, the political center of the kingdom, where factions struggled and maneuvered. The problem was complex, for the factions were more or less temporary coalitions of people with mixed motives. Pensions, stipends, offices, lucrative marriages, and other financial rewards obsessed some courtiers; titles, honors, and other marks of esteem were uppermost in the minds of others; some sought useful service as makers of policy or royal administrators; other such as the Roman Catholic *dévots* and certain provincial noblemen pressed the cause of the Church or of a particular province.

Whatever their predominant motive, most factions were alliances of ambitious and self-seeking families bent on influencing the king through his trusted advisers and friends, his family, his mistresses, or his confessor. Obscure though they are, these factions usually had influence, as a close study of any reign will show, but in the reigns of Louis XV and Louis XVI they became excessively powerful. Louis XVI lost the respect and support of a large number of courtiers by failing to understand and to manage politics at his court. For one thing, he appointed too many provincial noblemen and too many outsiders, such as the philosopher intendant Turgot, the Swiss Protestant banker Necker, and the relatively obscure Comte de Vergennes to high ministerial posts. For another, he let his young, frivolous queen, Marie-Antoinette, dispense too much patronage among the circles of her friends, the Polignac family, the Princess de Lamballe, and the Comte de Vaudreuil, thereby neglecting many families of court nobles.

In 1788 and 1789 many disgruntled court nobles, including the powerful house of Noailles that had been neglected since the accession of Louis XVI, were leading the Patriot Party, which triumphed in the elections to the Estates General. Nearly half the identifiable members of the politically progressive Company of Thirty—twenty-three out of fifty-five—belonged to noble families traditionally attached to the court at Versailles.[47] These were not conspiring to bring down the monarchy but merely expressing resentment at being kept in the shade at court. Great was their alarm when, in the course of 1789 or later, they realized they had helped open a Pandora's box of revolutionary forces ready to destroy the monarchy, the Church, the nobility, and the entire civilization they knew.

As he lost the support of many noble factions and faced the rebellious wrath of the sovereign courts, Louis turned to the Third Estate as other kings had done before him. In 1788 and 1789 some of his councillors, notably Jacques Necker and those who supported him, were similarly inclined. So while the parlements called for a meeting of the Estates General as a step in their own program, Louis XVI and his advisers granted this meeting in the opposite hope of finding support for the royal cause. "I have nothing to reply to my Parlement," Louis told the magistrates in Paris on 9 December 1788. "It is with the assembled Nation that I shall make arrangements to consolidate public order and the prosperity of the State forever."[48]

FOUR *Divine-Right Monarchy Undermined, 1774–88*

WHEN Louis XV died in 1774, he left the kingdom in the hands of some firm and capable ministers. Only a few years before, royal authority had been challenged and defended as in times past. In 1771 the royal government had faced the rebellious parlements with a determination worthy of the reign of Louis XIV; they had abolished these troublesome courts and banished their magistrates to small towns. This masterful stroke had been carried out in 1771 by the chancellor, Maupeou, assisted by the controller general of finances, Abbé Terray, and by such staunch royal servants as the old secretary of state, Louis Phélypeaux, Duc de La Vrillière (1705–77), and his relative, the military commander in chief in Brittany, the Duc d'Aiguillon, made secretary of state for foreign affairs on 6 June 1771. Whatever we may think ex post facto, the future revolution had not yet undermined the monarchy Louis XVI inherited on 10 May 1774. Its future depended not on some inevitable destiny, some inexorable working of historical laws, but on the king, his ministers, and his people.

I. Reforms and Court Politics to 1786

Louis XV's ministers, particularly Maupeou and Terray, had affirmed royal authority, but at the price of antagonizing more than 1,000 higher magistrates discharged and exiled to small towns. The observing public, including the fashionable writers of the day, were divided in their sympathies, some joining the magistrates in denouncing "royal despotism," others joining the Crown in denouncing the stubborn disobedience of the vanquished sovereign courts. In general, the clergy and its following among the ruling classes, described as *dévots,* opposed the magistrates because in the early 1760s the parlements had destroyed the powerful Society of Jesus and confiscated its colleges and houses. Among these *dévots* were to be found the powerful Noailles, Rohan, and Polignac families; the king's nearest brother, the Comte de Provence; and the royal aunts, Adélaïde and Louise. In general, too, the farmers general and receivers general of taxes and all the venal financiers of the monarchy opposed the magistrates, who were among their most vociferous critics. Some fashionable writers, such as Voltaire, the Physiocrats, Abbé Joseph-Alphonse de Véri, and other such believers in "enlightened despotism," also sided with the Crown.

Opposing them were the many friends and clients of the vanquished parlements, and a mixed element of "patriots," so called, who shared the parlements' ideas about the "rights of the nation" and the "general will." Such distinguished figures as Malesherbes, a son of the former chancellor Lamoignon, sided with the sovereign courts on principle.[1] But the Crown had other opponents guided in this matter more by politics than principles. Most of the peers and the royal princes of the blood (*les princes du sang*), the king's relatives, protested against Maupeou's coup because they had traditionally had seats in the special sessions of the Parlement of Paris called the Court of Peers (La cour des pairs).[2] Besides, every reign had its troublesome princes likely to side with the Crown's political opponents. A few years later, in the early stages of the French Revolution, the king's younger brother, the Comte d'Artois, and a cousin, the Duc d'Orléans, were still working against the king in various ways. Already, at the beginning of the reign, Orléans sided with the parlements, partly because he was under the influence of the attractive Marquise de Montesson* and the Montesson family was related to

*Charlotte-Jeanne Béraud de Lahaie du Riou, the Marquise de Montesson (1737–1806), was born in Paris into a noble Breton family, married at seventeen to an old general, and left a widow in 1769. Refined, literate (she wrote plays), attrac-

the du Prat family of *parlementaires*.

Court politics also impelled the Duc de Choiseul to take sides with the parlements. After twelve years as the most powerful minister at court, he had been disgraced on 24 December 1770 during Maupeou's coup and so regarded Maupeou as an enemy. Among his many supporters were the Duc d'Orléans, the Prince de Conti, the Duc de Chartres, Madame du Deffand, whose salon was something of a Choiseulist center, and the Rohan-Soubise-Guéménée clan, which was influential until the Prince de Rohan-Guémenée went bankrupt in September 1782. These and all the "patriots" hoped to restore Choiseul to favor at court. They were not an organized political party, any more than the *dévots* were, and they were often rent by personal rivalries and differences of opinion over particular issues. Court politics were always more complicated than a brief account will convey.

What would Louis XVI do when he came to the throne in 1774, not yet twenty years of age? To whom would he turn for advice? He went first, it seems, to his aunts, Adélaïde and Louise, who advised him to call upon the old Comte de Maurepas, a member of the distinguished Phélypeaux family that had served the royal family at court for generations. Maurepas had been in charge of the navy and colonies from 1723 to 24 April 1749, when Louis XV dismissed him and exiled him from court. Since then Maurepas had been only an observer of events, but remarkably well informed, with a prodigious memory and many relations in high places. He had family connections with Maupeou and with many other great families. When Louis XVI recalled him to court on 20 May 1774, Maurepas's nephew the Duc d'Aiguillon was secretary of state for foreign affairs, and his wife's brother (also a cousin) the Duc de La Vrillière was secretary of state for the royal households. Maurepas at seventy-two was wily, conciliatory, conservative, and without ambition for himself. He took no formal post at court but moved with his wife into an apartment at the palace next to the king's own, and the king trusted his advice, though not exclusively, until his death on 9 November 1781. Much depended on that advice.

tive and fairly rich, she secretly married the Duc d'Orléans in 1773 and had some influence on him. She survived an imprisonment during the Terror.

SOVEREIGN COURTS IN THE REIGN OF LOUIS XVI

Provinces	Parlements (In order of seniority)	Number of Bailliages	Chambres des Comptes	Cours des Aides	Cours des Monnaies (Mints)[c]
Many and different for each court	Paris	143	Paris Blois (abolished July 1775)	Paris Clermont-Ferrand (for Auvergne, etc.)	Paris (for nearly the entire kingdom)
Languedoc	Toulouse	24	Montpellier	[b]Montpellier	
Dauphiné	Grenoble	12	Grenoble	[a]Grenoble	
Guienne	Bordeaux	25	(under Paris)	Bordeaux Montauban	
Burgundy	Dijon	20	Dijon	[a]Dijon	
Normandy	Rouen	37	Rouen	[b]Rouen	
Provence	Aix	12	Aix	[b]Aix	
Béarn	Pau	7	[a]Pau	[a]Pau	[d]—
Brittany	Rennes	27	Nantes	[a]Rennes	
Trois Evêchés	Metz	15	[a]Metz	[a]Metz	[d]—
Franche-Comté	Besançon	13	Besançon	[a]Besançon	
Flanders	Douai	6	(under Paris)		
Lorraine	Nancy	32	Nancy Bar-le-Duc		
Nivernais	(still feudal and independent)		Nevers		
Total	13	373	14	13	1

SOURCES: *Almanach royal*; Léon and Albert Mirot, *Manuel de géographie historique de la France*, 2 vols. (Paris, 1948).

NOTE: There were Conseils supérieurs at Colmar (for Alsace), Perpignan (for Roussillon), and Bastia (for Corsica) and a Conseil provincial at Arras for Artois. Counting these there was a total of thirty-three separate sovereign courts; but this is only an approximate figure, as there is not perfect agreement on which courts to include as sovereign.

[a] Combined with the parlement.

[b] Combined with the Chambre des Comptes.

[c] A Cour des Monnaies sat at Lyon from 1704 to 1771. In 1789 coins were officially being minted in eighteen towns.

[d] Duties performed by the provincial parlement.

THE PROVINCIAL ESTATES IN THE EIGHTEENTH CENTURY

Estates	Clergy	Nobility	Third
Artois	2 bishops 18 abbots 14 chapter deputies	All gentlemen of century-old nobility	12 councillors of Arras 9 town deputies
Béarn	2 bishops 4 abbots	12 barons and the holders of the 500 seigneuries	Deputies from 4 towns, 3 valleys, and 34 guilds
Bigorre	1 bishop 4 abbots 2 priors 1 commander of Malta	The holders of the 12 baronies and the 70 seigneuries	29 deputies from guilds
Brittany	9 bishops 9 chapter deputies 40 abbots	All the gentlemen (about 3,000) 500 or 600 usually	Deputies from 42 towns
Burgundy	5 bishops 20 abbots 22 deans of chapters 72 priors	All the gentlemen with fiefs and four degrees of nobility	Deputies from 55 towns
Cambrésis	The archbishop Chapter deputies Abbots	12 gentlemen	Magistrates from Cambrai
Corsica	5 bishops 18 curates	23 deputies	23 deputies
Foix	The bishop and clergy	70 gentlemen	120 deputies from guilds
Labourd	——	——	Deputies from 40 guilds
Languedoc	23 bishops	23 barons	68 deputies
Lower Navarre	2 bishops 1 curate 2 priors	60 gentlemen	28 deputies from guilds
Marsan	——	——	Deputies from 23 guilds

THE PROVINCIAL ESTATES IN THE EIGHTEENTH CENTURY
(*Continued*)

Estates	Clergy	Nobility	Third
Nébouzan	3 abbots 1 syndic	24 gentlemen	Deputies from the guilds
Provence	2 *procureurs* And a general assembly of 37 guilds	2 *procureurs*	
Quatre Vallées	———	———	10 deputies
Soule	———	———	Deputies elected since 1733
Walloon Flanders	A special assembly	A special assembly	4 seigneurial bailiffs Deputies from Douai and Orchies A Lille magistrate

(Based on: Maurice Bordes, *L'administration provinciale et municipale en France au XVIIIe siècle*, Paris, 1972.)

Maurepas took the classical kingly view that Louis XVI, *le grand arbitre,* should favor no political group but should reign above politics and choose ministers without regard to political affiliations. On the major political issue of the time, Maurepas thought it best for the king to revive the old sovereign courts, recall the banished magistrates, and sacrifice Maupeou and his policy to a fresh beginning. Louis XVI acted accordingly, replacing most of his ministers over the next few months, removing Maupeou on 24 August, and announcing the parlements' recall on 27 September. These were conciliatory steps intended to mollify opposition to the Crown and to recover the political initiative for Louis XVI, but in retrospect they appear as political blunders, indeed, among the fateful steps toward revolution. When in 1787 and 1788 Louis XVI's government decided at last upon harsh measures like Maupeou's, it was too late. Already, at the beginning of the reign, the magistrates who returned to Paris on 9 November, and to the provincial capitals, far from chastened by their years of banishment, viewed their recall with the self-righteous triumph of men secure in the knowledge that their traditional resistance to the Crown was drawing support among the observing public. The Choiseul party and the "Patriots," far from mollified by Maupeou's and Terray's disgrace, continued to intrigue in the circles around the king and queen and to work in opposition along with the magistrates.

Worse still, the Choiseulists and the Austrian ambassador, Mercy d'Argenteau, created a strong pro-Austrian faction to influence the king through Marie-Antoinette, the Austrian emperor's sister. Choiseul had arranged Louis's marriage to this Habsburg princess on 19 April 1770 as the greatest in a series of Franco-Austrian marriages intended to unite these traditional enemies in a new foreign policy. Marie-Antoinette was regarded as a political agent for the manipulation of Louis XVI by her mother and brother, who ruled the Habsburg empire jointly, until 1780. (The brother ruled alone thereafter.) Louis soon learned to be suspicious of the Austrian faction, as his grandfather had before him.

I must admit [the queen wrote to Joseph II on 22 September 1784] that policy matters are those on which I have the least grip. The natural suspiciousness of the king was first strengthened by his tutor. Monsieur de la Vauguyon had frightened him even before my marriage about the influence his wife would want to have over him, and Vauguyon's black soul amused itself frightening his pupil by all the ghosts invented against the house of Austria. M. de Maurepas thought it useful for his own credit to maintain the king in the same beliefs, although with less force and wickedness. M. de Vergennes follows the same plan. . . .[3]

What Louis XVI could not cope with was the effect on public opinion of the sneers and jokes about him whispered by many of Choiseul's allies, by Mercy d'Argenteau, and even by the queen when they found they could not influence him as they had hoped. The habit of belittling and disparaging the king spread through various disgruntled circles in and out of court, and the king, decent, modest soul that he was, merely carried on, hoping for the best. "The king is despised," a German observer wrote as early as 1774. "The nation regards him as a [stupid] beast."[4] This was exaggerated, and for "the nation" in that sentence we should read "some circles in Paris"; but it caught the atmosphere created by political factions which helped undermine the authority of a conscientious and well-meaning, though rather weak, ruler.

All these factions and forces hampered the new ministers in their reforming policies. Not all these ministers were reformers, it is true. Maurepas's rather inept relative Miromesnil, who as keeper of the seals took Maupeou's place, and Vergennes, a diplomat who replaced La Vrillière as foreign secretary in 1775, were neither reformers nor members of strong political factions. But Sartine, appointed naval secretary on 24 August 1774, and his successor, Castries, went on building up the navy that Choiseul had begun to reform after the Seven Years' War. When Malesherbes reluctantly joined the ministry on 21 July 1775 as secretary of state for the royal households, and the capable Saint-Germain as war secretary on 27 October 1775, reforms were already beginning under Turgot, the intellectual and highly principled intendant at Limoges, brought to Versailles as naval secretary on 20 July 1774 and then as controller general of finances on 24 August. He had the most far-reaching plans for improving the French economy and its management as well as the financial system of the Crown.

A friend of du Pont de Nemours and his Physiocratic circle, a believer in free trade, market prices, and large-scale agriculture, Turgot freed the vital grain trade from government controls on 13 September 1774. On 12 March 1776 he had Louis XVI force the Parlement of Paris to register six edicts that would have abolished the guilds throughout the kingdom, replaced the age-old *corvée,* or obligatory feudal labor, with a tax on landowners, suppressed duties on grain and flour in Paris, discharged the corrupt officials of the Paris markets and docks, suppressed the *caisse de Poissy* tax on cattle and meat and other duties on suet. He also began to abolish financial offices and to make other economies. These changes were only an hors d'oeuvre to Turgot's more sweeping plans, but they aroused antagonisms among the ruling classes, especially the sovereign courts, and revolt among the populace, which rioted in the Paris region from 27 April to 10 May 1775. The queen never liked Turgot. No politician, he was incapable of marshaling support for his reforms except in his own intellectual circles. Louis XVI and Maurepas, ever sensitive to expressions of hostile opinion, thought it politic to retract these measures and to dismiss the minister, as they did on 12 May 1776.[5]

Maneuvering yet again among the various political factions, they eventually chose Jacques Necker, who represented a successful Genevan bank in Paris and already had a reputation as an independent and statesmanlike thinker in the field of political economy.[6] Madame Necker, née Suzanne Curchod, the cultivated daughter of a Swiss Calvinist minister, had once been courted by Edward Gibbon, the English historian of the Roman Empire, and in Paris she presided over a salon which helped make her husband's reputation. The appointment of a foreigner was not so outlandish as it may seem; after all, the queen was a foreigner, as were nearly all French queens; Saint-Germain, the war minister, had once served the king of Denmark; and the king of Prussia had employed a French farmer general of taxes to manage his finances. As a Protestant, a banker, and a commoner, however, Necker was a daring choice reminiscent of the notorious Scottish banker John Law (1671–1729), who had taken charge of French finances in the troubled years 1715 to 1720 after the long wars of Louis XIV and had left hurriedly under a cloud when his ingenious central bank had failed on 17 July 1720. But Necker seemed even worse in some circles because Law had at least turned Roman Catholic.

Necker has been harshly judged by historians of the French Revolution, most of whom have not bothered to work out what he was trying to achieve, but he was the most outstanding finance minister of the reign, experienced in money matters and business management, with credit in France and abroad, especially among the rich Protestant bankers of that age, shrewd enough to see the real faults of the financial system and the political obstacles to reform. He developed a brilliant policy of winning a public following by philanthropy and by the unprecedented candor of his books and decrees on the problems facing the French government. The public that Necker thus informed and aroused was the same public that swept enthusiastically into revolution in 1789. But this is looking ahead.

During his first ministry (1776–81) Necker won the esteem

of many other statesmen as well as a large part of the French public. He won the hatred of the financiers and of all venal officeholders by abolishing scores of venal offices, including even those of the fifty powerful receivers general of finances, and by trying to rationalize the management of government funds. Faced with the obstinate disobedience of the six noble intendants of finance in his ministry, he dismissed them and abolished their venal offices. Meanwhile, he provoked the hostility of Maurepas and Vergennes by gaining enough influence at court to have the naval minister, Sartine, replaced by his own ally Castries (13 October 1780), and the war minister, Montbarey, by his ally Ségur (23 December). When his clever *Compte rendu au roi par Monsieur Necker,* published on 19 February 1781, explained his policies to a fascinated public without mentioning Maurepas, Necker was brought down at last by the intrigues of a coalition that included the jealous Maurepas, the ambitious future minister Calonne, the indignant Vergennes, soon to succeed Maurepas as principal royal adviser, and many anxious financiers and angry higher officials. Much of his work was undone at his fall on 19 May 1781, but his public esteem was unimpaired, so strong, in fact, that it was to bring him back into power again in August 1788 and yet again in July 1789.

Necker fell during the American Revolution, in which France meddled secretly from 1776 and joined openly in a treaty of trade, friendship, and alliance on 6 February 1778. The British ambassador left Paris on 15 March. For all its victories, the War of American Independence brought scarcely any benefit to the French monarchy except the immediate satisfaction of revenge on Great Britain for earlier humiliations. The French government apparently had no intention of trying to recover Canada from Great Britain or Louisiana from Spain or of otherwise extending French influence in North America.[7] The war tended to undermine the monarchy by its enormous cost and by the republican and liberal ideas it taught a part of the French public. Since the monarchy was already burdened with a large debt and a large political opposition, the American war had the effect of increasing them both to a point of crisis. Vergennes is not perhaps to blame for failing to anticipate the crisis, but he is to blame as foreign secretary for the decision to intervene in the war and as chief of the Council on Finances for much of the weakness in financial policy during the critical years 1783–87, when Calonne as controller general of finances was undoing Necker's reforms and patronizing expensive and wasteful financiers.[8]

The fatal anti-British policy of that time had originated with Choiseul in the 1750s, perhaps even earlier, but Vergennes adopted and developed it in the reign of Louis XVI. Aggressively hostile like Choiseul toward this *"peuple inquiet, calculateur, égoïste,"* which refused to recognize French supremacy, Vergennes began immediately in 1774 to build up the navy with an energy equal to Choiseul's, and Sartine collaborated.[9] The American Revolution offered them a heaven-sent opportunity. When Vergennes sent Achard de Bonvouloir to make contact with the American rebels in 1775, and soon afterward helped send aid to the rebellious colonies, this was only the first unofficial phase of a war he had long planned against England as a formidable obstacle to Louis XVI's becoming the arbiter of Europe. Again and again Vergennes urged war in memoranda to the reluctant Louis XVI.[10] Among the royal advisers, Sartine and Maurepas soon shared Vergennes's aggressive policy. Turgot's firm but futile opposition was swept aside, and by 1780, when the pacific Necker, not a member of the Conseil d'état or even of the Conseil des finances, gathered enough political strength to take peace initiatives, the harm had already been done. The war soon added a large sum to an already large debt, perhaps 1 billion livres. The total debt would be difficult, perhaps impossible, to calculate because the officials of that day could not agree on a figure. Necker reckoned it in 1784 at something over 3.4 billion livres, on which the annual charges were about 207 million. The best scholarly study of our time puts the debt at about 5 billion livres by 1787, with annual charges of more than 318 million.[11]

Even this was not a crippling debt for a wealthy country of 27 or 28 million people. Great Britain with only one-third the territory and one-third the population had a similar debt, which it never failed to manage well enough for its own political purposes. By determined reforms of the administrative system such as Turgot and Necker proposed or by the time-honored methods used by Louis XV after the Seven Years' War and by Louis XIV after the Thirty Years' War and the War of the Spanish Succession, an enlightened government like that of Louis XVI might have managed its debt satisfactorily. The debt could not, in itself, have brought the monarchy to its knees.

Under Louis XVI, however, public opposition nearly always brought a halt to financial reforms and soon began to shake public confidence in the finances—that is, to discredit the Crown. Opposition was reinforced by public admiration for the British Parliament with its organized and vocal opposition and then by the American alliance, which put the Crown in the anomalous position of helping rebellious people to resist their king in one of the great opposition movements of modern history. The French alliance with the Dutch patriots in November 1785 had a similar effect. The monarchy of Louis XVI was brought low not by a large debt but by a political opposition that included liberal "patriots," factious noblemen, truculent *parlementaires,* dispossessed pensioners, and anxious financiers with venal offices such as those Necker had tried to abolish.

During the six years after Necker's fall on 19 May 1781, the Crown tried to satisfy parts of the opposition by appointing ministers of finance with suitable connections and policies. The financiers recovered a measure of influence. The General Farm of Taxes raised its head again only after 1781, in the time of Joly de Fleury, of Lefèvre d'Ormesson, and of Calonne.[12] Jean-François Joly de Fleury (1718–82), appointed on 21 May 1781, was a councillor of state from a family of *parlementaires* with many financial relatives, including a treasurer general for war (Mégret de Sérilly), and at least three farmers general (Douet, Desvieux, and Jogues). His policy was to restore all the financial offices abolished by Necker and to rely upon the financiers for loans and services according to the age-old system. He trusted the advice of at least two other farmers general (de la Perrière and de Saint-Amand) and of a powerful purveyor of army foodstuffs (Marquet de Bourgade). Henry IV-François de Paule Lefèvre, Marquis d'Ormesson (1751–1808), appointed on 29 March 1783, one of the noble intendants of finance whom Necker had dismissed in 1777, was not in the financiers' camp and was driven out of office after only five months for trying to transform the General Farm into a *régie*.*

With Calonne, who held office from 3 November 1783 to 8 April 1787, the financiers were more fully reassured than they had been for many years. He was their man in both his social connections and his policies.[13] Although he came from a family of *parlementaires* in the Parlement of Flanders at Douai, his wife, a Marquet, had brothers, sisters, and uncles who included a farmer general, receivers general of Finances for Orléans and Guyenne, a financial adviser to Joly de Fleury, the wife of a great banker, Laborde, a treasurer for the Royal Corps of Artillery at Metz, and two cousins one of whom was a receiver General of Finances for Rouen and the other the wife of a farmer general. Calonne's mistress and future wife was the daughter of the great Habsburg and Belgian banker, Mathias Nettine and presently the wife of a keeper of the royal treasury, Micault d'Harvelay. As we might expect, Calonne in no way threatened the royal financiers during his term of office, but he even went as far as to encourage spending and speculation. This was something new at a court where most finance ministers had been urging thrift and economy.

It was court nobles, however, who put Calonne into office and supported him. For Calonne had sufficient charm and poise to cultivate a wide circle of nobles: the rich Prince de Robecq,† the Prince de Condé and his son the Duc de Bourbon, Comte Esterhazy, and others. He had a certain friendship with the Choiseul family: The Duc de Choiseul took an interest in Calonne when he served as intendant at Metz (1766–78); the duc's brother, archbishop of Cambrai, married Calonne and his first wife on 12 April 1769. At court Calonne's candidature for the post of controller general of finances was supported by the Comte d'Artois, the Comte de Vaudreuil, and the Polignac and Luyne

---

* A *régie*, defined in the eighteenth century as the opposite of a *ferme* (e.g., tax farm), was composed of government officials rather than profit-making businessmen. *Régisseurs* did not take the profits from their *régie; fermiers* did take the profits from their *ferme*. Making a *régie* of the General Farm was, in twentieth-century terms, to nationalize it. For the implications of this difference, see Bosher, *French Finances, 1770–1795*, p. 121.

† Anne-Louis-Alexandre de Montmorency, Prince de Robecq (born 1724); for the others see Who's Who in the French Revolution above.

families as well as by the queen, who befriended these patrons. Vergennes, too, spoke in his favor.

Reigning quietly over these three finance ministers, informally at first and then, from 20 February 1783, as chief of the Royal Council of Finances, was Vergennes. Under him and them the traditional system of royal finance carried on unchallenged and unreformed in postwar years that called for reforms or for authoritarian measures like those used from 1769 to 1771, from 1715 to 1722, and in the 1660s. At last, in August 1786, at Calonne's request the Crown decided to consult a select body of the public at an Assembly of Notables to be convened the following spring. Such assemblies had been held in 1525, 1526, 1527, 1529, 1557, 1596 (at Rouen), 1617, and 1626 but had not been part of the governing process since early in the reign of Louis XIII (1617–43).

II. Reforms and the Assembly of Notables, 1787–88

Why did king and Council agree to have an Assembly of Notables? At first, it appears, Louis XVI had great doubts about the wisdom of it, and Vergennes and Miromesnil thought it dangerous. They proposed, instead, the usual method of compelling the parlements to register royal decrees, but Calonne argued that an Assembly of Notables might be easier to convince than the parlements and, once convinced, might strengthen the king's hand in dealing with the parlements.[14] It is not clear why Louis XVI had come around to Calonne's view by 29 December 1786, when he announced an impending Assembly of Notables to the Conseil des dépêches, but the queen and other ministers such as Castries, Ségur, Breteuil, and Ossun do not seem to have been influential or even, in some cases, consulted at all. Whom, besides Vergennes and Miromesnil, did Louis XVI talk things over with in 1786? His friend the discreet and judicious Comte de Montmorin whom he made foreign secretary on 14 February 1787 at Vergennes's death and trusted thereafter as a sort of confidant and messenger to other ministers? One of the aunts whose opinion he asked from time to time, or his confessor, Jean-Jacques Poupart, the curé at Saint-Eustache, to whom he had confessed regularly since 1778? Or was he speaking the simple truth when he told Malesherbes on 5 November 1788 that Miromesnil, more than any other, had convinced him to call the Assembly of Notables? Louis XVI then claimed to have dismissed Miromesnil on 8 April 1787 for opposing Calonne's projects in the Assembly after recommending them so strongly. That Miromesnil, an intriguer with mediocre ability and mainly personal concerns, should have had a decisive voice in persuading Louis XVI to call the Assembly seems unlikely, for Louis XVI must have taken his measure during his twelve years as keeper of the seals. The king may have been still under the influence of Vergennes, the principal adviser since Maurepas's death in 1781, for Vergennes' death on 13 February 1787 filled him with anguish.

There were several reasons or motives for the Assembly. Both Calonne and the king seem to have been anxious to break out of the scheming rivalries and jealousies of court circles, Calonne because he was particularly beset by hidden opposition, the king because he was genuinely seeking the good of his subjects. Calonne's reform projects appealed to Louis XVI for the relief they might bring to the poor as well as to his own finances. In particular, he liked the proportional tax in kind to be imposed on all land, even the estates of the privileged orders, a sort of state tithe but levied variously according to the productivity of the land. This was intended to replace the *vingtième* taxes and so to remove many inequities and to shift the burden somewhat from the small peasants to the large landowners. He also liked the old plan to remove the internal customs barriers at which duties were collected on salt (the *gabelles*), on tobacco (the *tabac*), and on wine and spirits (the *aides*) as well as on general merchandise, for these had always been a burden on the provinces. Calonne convinced Louis XVI that these two reforms, among others, would cut down costs, increase revenues, and at the same time ease the burdens of ordinary folk. Such projects were easy enough to plan and had, indeed, been drafted and redrafted for generations; the main problem was to win the support needed to put them into effect. The parlements and the provincial Estates in the *pays d'état* were certain to reject them. An assembly of prominent citizens, carefully selected from the politically active groups or bodies, might be persuaded to endorse them and to give the Crown enough political support in the kingdom to take reforming initiatives.

Much depended on the choice of *notables,* and it was made with care. There were to be 25 mayors and other municipal dignitaries; 33 leading magistrates of the parlements, 2 from the chambers of accounts, and 2 from the courts of the *aides,* which were also sovereign courts; the lieutenant civil from the Châtelet criminal court; 12 representatives from the *pays d'état;* 7 bishops and 7 archbishops; 12 councillors of state; 28 great nobles, including 6 peers and 6 other dukes; 8 marshals; and 7 royal princes of the blood—a total of one hundred and forty-four members. Differently analyzed, the membership included 37 municipal and provincial dignitaries, 37 sovereign court magistrates, 14 clergymen, 36 great noblemen, and 20 people from the royal court, including 7 members of the royal family, who were to serve as chairmen of the committees. Most were noblemen, and most, both noblemen and commoners, were from provincial towns; but a simple analysis by geography or social status might be misleading because of the complexity of the selection process.

It was reasonable to suppose that a gathering of such various groups would be incapable of any common view or firm purpose such as each unified corps of bishops or magistrates was used to expressing in its own meetings. The various groups, divided as they were among the seven committees *(bureaux)* that were intended to discuss Calonne's projects, would be discouraged from forming coalitions. Furthermore, the sense of social rank and the habit of deference toward men of higher standing could be counted on to give the princes, peers, marshals, and other courtiers some weight, and they were loyally enthusiastic about the royal reform projects. Each of the seven committees was chaired by one of the seven royal princes: the Comte de Provence, the Comte d'Artois, the Duc d'Orléans, the Prince de Condé, the Duc de Bourbon, the Prince de Conti, and the Duc de Penthièvre.* Many of the mayors, the first presidents of the parlements, and the sword nobles owed their posts to royal nomination, as, of course, did the bishops, councillors of state, and

---

*Louis-Jean-Marie de Bourbon, Duc de Penthièvre (1725–93), grand admiral of France; for the others see Who's Who in the French Revolution above.

marshals who were personally beholden to the king and committed to his service.

The twelve councillors of state and masters of requests, key
figures in the Assembly as *rapporteurs* to the committees, were
the Crown's own officials enjoying royal confidence enough to
be invited to serve as ministers; indeed, at least five of them were
asked at one time or another to take the post of controller general of finances. It is usual to point out Calonne's many enemies
and rivals in the Assembly, but he also had allies and personal
friends, such as the councillor of state Le Noir, the Prince de
Montmorency-Robecq, the Comte d'Artois, and the two representatives from the Estates of Artois, d'Estournel, and Duques-
noy. Many others shared the not unreasonable hopes of Calonne
and Louis XVI, but they all were to be disappointed. During the
Assembly's brief life, from 22 February to 25 May 1787, it studied, debated, and finally dismissed Calonne's reform projects.
Louis XVI then dismissed Calonne and Miromesnil on 8 April
and appointed a new controller general, a new keeper of the
seals, and a new chief of the Royal Council of Finances (to replace
the late Vergennes). Almost immediately these new ministers
began to implement a new set of reforms by royal decree and to
meet the ensuing political crisis with force.

Why and by whom had Calonne been defeated? The usual
answer to this question is that the Notables turned out to be noble
landowners bent on defending the privileges of their class against
the taxes Calonne was proposing. This may be true, but if so, it
is so small a part of the truth that it would not have satisfied
historical opinion if it had not happened to fit the prevailing
revolutionary and postrevolutionary theory of an underlying class
struggle. At least three other truths must be added to do justice
to the history of 1787. First, the Assembly of Notables behaved
much like a parliament, an inexperienced parliament conscious
of being consulted by an authoritarian government for the first
time in well over a century.[15] The Bourbons had not consulted
an Assembly of Notables since 1626, an Estates General since
1615. By so doing in 1787, Louis XVI gave vent to a body of
public opinion, both noble and common, that had been growing
for many years, expressing itself in clubs, pamphlets, journals,
and remonstrances. It was remarked in Britain that the French

troubles resembled political life at home.

The king and some of his ministers were themselves imbued with certain liberal principles or they would not have called an Assembly in those circumstances and asked its opinion. Louis XVI was already seeking public support for his ministers and their policies, as he continued to do when he dismissed Calonne and appointed Loménie de Brienne, an "opposition" leader in the Assembly, and the popular Necker a few months later. These steps have usually been explained as being due to the king's weakness, personal and financial. Whatever the truth in that, he certainly engaged in national politics from the first, deferring to public opinion as he saw it, appointing and dismissing ministers to satisfy opinion, as Louis XIV would never have done. There was no essential difference between Calonne's fall and the falls of Turgot, Necker, Joly de Fleury, and d'Ormesson; but the parliamentary process in the Assembly makes Calonne's fall clearer than the usual secret processes at the royal court.

Why then did Calonne fall? The Assembly opposed him as a member of the class of financiers who, with their noble friends at court, were growing fat collecting, spending, and managing government funds. Here is a second truth easily overlooked. Calonne's new land tax, the *subvention territoriale*, appeared to the Notables as another subsidy for the royal receivers general, treasurers general, farmers general, payers of the *rentes*, and their noble patrons. Pressed upon the king by a coalition of nobles and financiers, Calonne had used government funds to pay 28 million livres of the Comte d'Artois's debts and large sums to sustain the Comte de Provence, and even the Prince de Rohan-Guéménée, *grand chambellan de France*, who had gone bankrupt in a great scandal that began in September 1782.[16] Others in the circles of the Comte d'Artois had borrowed large sums: Comte Rigaud de Vaudreuil owed the Crown 900,000 livres and Loménie de Brienne commented on this, "[I]t is absurd for the king to lend; this is surely to dissipate."[17] Then Calonne arranged to support various great noble houses by the device of buying their lands and forests: 200,000 livres a year to be paid to the heirs of the Duc de Choiseul, 86,000 to the creditors of the Prince de Rohan-Guéménée, 200,000 to the Duc de Liancourt, 100,000 to the heirs of the Maréchal de Soubise (for the estate of Viviers in

Lorraine), and so on. In 1784 a certain Baron d'Espagnac, a cavalry and royal guards officer, had been awarded 1 million livres in an apparently fraudulent exchange of properties with the Crown.[18] The Assembly of Notables discussed these and other such cases with indignation on 1 April, and from time to time thereafter, when Lafayette, de la Luzerne (bishop of Langres), and others denounced them roundly.[19]

Calonne also promoted financial companies on a grand scale, especially at the Paris money market *(bourse)*, where he arranged to float the shares of his Compagnie des Indes founded on 14 April 1785, of the Paris Water Company, and of the Bank of Saint Charles linked with the Spanish Banco Nacional de San Carlos directed by François Cabarrús in a profitable scheme to import Spanish pieces of eight. To maintain the rising value of all these stocks on the money market, Calonne then used government funds to promote financial syndicates speculating in company stocks, notably a group directed by Abbé d'Espagnac, whose inordinate profits were denounced to the Assembly of Notables by Mirabeau in a sensational pamphlet which circulated even more widely when Calonne had Mirabeau arrested on 18 March.[20] Meanwhile, in April 1786, Calonne engaged a banker, Giacomo Campi, to sustain the shares of the Paris Water Company by judicious purchases; when Campi went bankrupt in November 1787, he laid claim to large sums from the royal treasury, which the Crown eventually settled at nearly 1.5 million livres.

This was only the last of a series of spectacular bankruptcies in financial circles during that disastrous year: a receiver general of finances who fled to Belgium on 20 January, a treasurer general for the navy who interned himself in the Bastille on 2 February to escape from his creditors, a *régisseur des economats* (Church properties) who went bankrupt on 17 February, the treasurer for the Comte d'Artois who fled to England on 5 March, and a treasurer general for war who declared bankruptcy on 1 June. Bankruptcies had occurred among the royal financiers from time to time throughout history, but 1787 was truly a year of crisis. So many great failures reflected a waning public confidence which compounded with each disaster. By 5 April other great financiers, even the keepers of the royal treasury, were threatened with failure. The Assembly of Notables learned that stocks were falling sharply at the bourse on 13 April, again on 14 April, even more on 20 April, worse on 21 April, 26 and 27 April. On 29 April there was a general consternation that reached even the royal family, who were informed that there was scarcely enough cash or credit for another week. The *Gazette de Leyde* reported imminent disaster in its issue of 29 April.[21] Meanwhile, each new bankruptcy confirmed the magistrates in the Chamber of Accounts and the parlements in their view that the financiers in general ought to be prosecuted. In the Assembly such prominent magistrates as Aymard-Charles-Marie de Nicolay (1747–94), first president of the Chamber of Accounts, and such army officers as the Duc de Châtelet and the Marquis de Contades denounced the financiers and the minister who supported them.[22]

In this atmosphere the Assembly of Notables began very early in its proceedings to question the government in a parliamentary spirit. A group of forty-two members, six from each committee, met Calonne at the Comte de Provence's house on 2 March and began to ask for details of the deficit, which Calonne reluctantly admitted to be at least 112 million livres for the current year. After the royal session of 23 April, on Loménie de Brienne's recommendation, the Notables were given a statement of receipts and expenditures, the bases for the estimated balance sheet for 1787. But none of the seven committees could make a convincing estimate of the deficit, though they all put it higher than Calonne had—their estimates ranged from 133 million to 145 million. Their efforts in this matter were only a part of their parliamentary pressure on the king and his ministers in, for instance, their resolution of 5 May that the finances should be controlled by a five-man committee of "citizens from the different Orders" which would supervise financial accounting. "The desire to put the king under tutelage was unmistakable," writes Jean Egret.[23] In trying to establish figures, Calonne foolishly embroiled himself in a public argument with Necker over receipts and expenditures in the American War of Independence, thereby raising a general inquiry about the notorious *acquits de comptant*, payments to hundreds of people in a form not accountable to the Chamber of Accounts.

As the days went by, opposition to Calonne's projects grew,

led by the clergy, resentful of the new taxes they would have to pay by the proposed *subvention territoriale* and still smarting from Calonne's efforts to press them at their general assemblies in 1785 and 1786.[24] Managing large personal and ecclesiastical properties had made some of the bishops into experienced business managers. Many were in any case from noble families of statesmen. The bishop of Langres, César-Guillaume de la Luzerne, was Malesherbes's nephew and a future cardinal; the future bishop of Autun, Talleyrand-Périgord, was to become one of the remarkable statesmen in French history; and the archbishops of Aix (Boisgelin de Cucé), Bordeaux (Champion de Cicé), and Narbonne (Dillon) were prominent public figures of the day. These began to oppose Calonne vigorously, and Boisgelin de Cucé went so far as to argue on 2 and 3 April that the financial system needed a sweeping reform to cut out the harmful powers of the financiers and to create a consolidated revenue fund.

Outside the Assembly other bishops opposed Calonne: for instance, the bishop of Arras (Louis-François-Marc-Hilaire de Conzié), who turned the Duc de Nivernais, one of the notables, against Calonne, and the bishop of Montauban (Anne-François-Victor le Tonnelier-Breteuil), a close relative of Calonne's rival the minister Breteuil. The leader of the clerical party in the Assembly, however, was the archbishop of Toulouse, Loménie de Brienne, who in the 1760s had presided over an ecclesiastical commission that had closed about 500 monasteries. He had such a grasp of public affairs and spoke with such authority that he was able to enter into a discreet correspondence with Louis XVI beginning about 12 April, to win the support of the queen and several ministers, and so to be appointed chief of the Royal Council of Finances on 1 May and principal minister on 26 August. The leader of the opposition thus became, in effect, the next finance minister, and technically the successor to Vergennes with authority over Calonne's successor, whoever he might be. Loménie de Brienne asked for Necker; but the king refused, and they fell back on an official, Pierre-Charles Laurent de Villedeuil (1742–1828), as controller general.

With Calonne fell his "party" and his policy. Loménie de Brienne headed a government differently composed and drawing on different public support. At ministerial level, his first allies were the three ministers who had advanced his candidature at court: Lamoignon (keeper of the seals), Breteuil (secretary for royal households), and Montmorin (foreign secretary). To these were soon added two secretaries of state without portfolio, Malesherbes and a diplomat, Nivernais, who was a friend of Necker, named on 7 June 1787. At the end of August the war and naval secretaries (Castries and Ségur) resigned and were replaced in December by close supporters, Loménie de Brienne's brother the Comte de Brienne and Malesherbes's nephew the Comte de la Luzerne, a brother of the Duc de la Luzerne, bishop of Langres. As for the Contrôle général des finances, it was headed first by Laurent de Villedeuil, then from September 1787 to August 1788 by Claude Lambert, both very much subject to Loménie de Brienne, who himself set financial policy as chief of the Royal Council of Finances. Here was a comparatively unified ministry under a principal minister to whom the king had delegated a certain authority to act in his name.

Loménie de Brienne's financial policy, first worked out among the bishops in the Assembly of Notables, was intended to appease that body of opinion that had risen up against Calonne's financial policy. Quickly put into effect were several projects, the most obvious and urgent of which was the cutting down of expenses by a series of regulations. Many millions were saved by dismissing officers of the royal households, selling a number of châteaus and other royal properties, reducing the pension list, and ordering economies in the financial, postal and military services. Less obvious but more fundamental was the creation of an organized central treasury to collect, manage, and pay out government funds that had hitherto been held in many separate *caisses* by independent financiers. This reorganization—obvious to the many Frenchmen acquainted with British administration—had been proposed to the Assembly of Notables early in April 1787 by Archbishop Boisgelin de Cucé in a memorandum that excited general approval, and Loménie promptly began to implement it. It gave the government a greater measure of control over public funds and thereby made a budget possible. Loménie published the first French budget on 27 April 1788.[25]

These praiseworthy reforms helped undermine the monarchy from 1787 to 1789 by arousing hostility among the magistrates of the Chamber of Accounts, the pensioners, the financiers, and all other beneficiaries of the old financial system. At court the Comte d'Artois, the Polignac and Vaudreuil families, the Calonne faction, and (in Loménie de Brienne's words) "that class of favorites who regarded the public treasury as an inexhaustible source of funds on which they were entitled to draw" led the opposition to Loménie de Brienne.[26] When at last Louis XVI accepted his resignation on 25 August 1788, the immediate reason was a general discrediting of government paper on the Paris money market owing in part to uneasiness caused by Loménie de Brienne's reforms and by the resistance to them. The Assembly of French Clergy had just voted a very small subsidy *(don gratuit)* of 1.8 livres, when 8 million had been expected. In part, too, the public reluctance to take government notes was due to an economic recession in the years 1785–89 that had contributed to the notorious bankruptcies of 1787. Whatever the causes, Loménie de Brienne found himself unable to find the 240 million livres in short-term advances budgeted for 1788, and on 16 August he took a momentous step toward modern public financing by announcing that the treasury would make payments in paper notes backed by royal decree or government fiat, somewhat like our present-day paper money.[27] This was a logical corollary to his treasury reforms, a step the National Assembly was to take with success less than three years later, but in 1788 Loménie de Brienne did not have sufficient political support to implement such a reform. The uproar in Paris brought down his ministry, and he retired to what he hoped would be a quiet life at his château of Brienne. Louis XVI had lost the political initiative. He could no longer resist the pressure of public opinion, at least not by political means, and he gave way to it by appointing Jacques Necker, for the second time, on 25 August 1788. The French public now had a decisive voice in the government of France.

The End of Divine-Right Monarchy

IT WAS NOT only Loménie de Brienne's reforms which caused a public uproar leading to his dismissal. Other ministers with other reform plans fell with him. His brother the Comte de Brienne, who was the secretary of state for war, formed a nine-man war council on 9 October 1787 under the chairmanship of the Comte de Guibert, a brigadier with experience in the War Ministry, much admired for his *General Essay on Tactics* (1772), and a member of the French Academy. This council proceeded to retire 359 brigadiers, 6 marshals, 5 colonel generals, 300 men of the royal bodyguard, the 900 men of the Gendarmerie de France, and a large number of lieutenant colonels. It also confirmed the policy set on 22 May 1781 of restricting military commissions largely to sword nobles from old families, not as part of a "noble reaction," but in the belief that the best officers were made by family tradition, the noble code of honor, the habit of command, and the superiority conferred by a favorable environment.[1] This policy, inspired by the example of the successful Prussian officer corps, was not unreasonable, but in 1788 it added to the uncertainties and discontents that were undermining the monarchy.

Even more unsettling than the Brienne brothers' changes were the sweeping reforms of the keeper of the seals, Lamoignon. These, like nearly all the reforms of this period, had been discussed by public-spirited officials for many years, lately at the Assembly of Notables, and Lamoignon was determined to implement them. On 19 November 1787 he asked the king to put an edict before the Paris Parlement granting civil status to Protestants so that their marriages, baptisms, and deaths might be registered and that they might take up trades and professions. The toleration in this edict did not go very far, for it reaffirmed the monopoly of the Roman Catholic Church in public worship, forbade Protestants to form any society or community, denied them judicial, municipal, and teaching posts, and granted no rights or powers to their pastors; but even so, the Parlement debated it hotly for two months before registering it at last on 29 January 1788.

Roman Catholic opinion—i.e., nearly all public opinion—saw the edict as a grievance. Most people in Paris, and clergy throughout the country, were opposed to it. Miromesnil, Madame de Noailles, and the archbishop of Paris worked against it. The parlements of Besançon, Douai, and Bordeaux refused to register it. The Assembly of the Clergy that met in 1788 voted only a small sum to the Crown *(don gratuit)* as a result of it and of the proposed taxing of Church property. This modest edict of toleration aroused hostility toward Lamoignon, Loménie de Brienne, Malesherbes, Breteuil, and their elite of liberal noblemen and commoners who had prepared and promoted the reform. Evidently the anticlerical attitude, a large component of religious tolerance, so prevalent in the French Revolution, did not begin to sweep through the public until 1789, any more than did the new ideas of nationalism and equality. In 1787 and 1788 these were still only the ideas of small minorities.

Lamoignon, the keeper of the seals, also had plans to reform the criminal laws and procedures. The laws set forth in the Criminal Ordinance of 1670 had already been amended by a Declaration of 24 August 1780 which had abolished the *question préparatoire*, the legal torture to make prisoners confess. Lamoignon went a step further on 12 February 1788, when he sent the Paris Parlement a declaration to abolish the *question préalable* by which prisoners were tortured to make them reveal the names of their accomplices. Other reforms of criminal law, too, were embodied in the declaration, but jealous of its prerogatives, the Parlement moved with such reluctance that Lamoignon withdrew his declaration at the end of March. Faced with so much resistance in the sovereign courts, he was already planning a coup d'etat against them, somewhat like Maupeou's coup but more thorough. Here was the most ambitious and provocative of Lamoignon's reforms, more provocative even than Loménie de Brienne's financial reforms, for to many people it smacked of tyranny.

Lamoignon's coup had two aspects. In part, it followed quite simply from his plan for judicial reform. The sovereign courts were to be swept away to make room for a new set of courts. He planned to have most legal cases, civil and criminal, judged by intermediate courts at two levels. At the lower level the présidial courts were to have final jurisdiction in civil suits up to 4,000 livres and appellate jurisdiction in criminal cases. Above them, forty-seven *grands bailliages* courts were to have final jurisdiction in cases of under 20,000 livres and in criminal cases not involving clergymen or noblemen. By simplifying procedures, these reforms would remove many cases from the parlements and abolish the twenty-six *bureaux des finances* (financial courts), the *élections* (tax courts), the *cours des traites* (customs judges), the seigneurial courts, and others. A *cour plenière* was to assume the political functions of the Parlements—that is, to register royal laws—and was to have no fewer than 142 members drawn from various courts, plus noblemen, councillors of state, and masters of requests.

Suppressing the parlements was a logical development of Lamoignon's judicial reforms, but it was also a political maneuver in a struggle with the parlements that had flared up during the Assembly of Notables. The proposed new stamp and land taxes had been the main provocation for this trouble; the Paris Parlement had refused to register them. But the struggle quickly embraced other issues: The Paris Parlement in its Court of Peers indicted Calonne for alleged fraud on 10 August 1787 and would have put him on trial if he had not fled to England. Tempers rose when the Crown arrested some leading magistrates by issuing royal *lettres de cachet*, warrants for arrest which a French king could issue on his own absolute authority. On 15 August 1787 the Crown went as far as to transfer the Paris Parlement to the town of Troyes, about 100 miles southeast of Paris, each magistrate being ordered to move there immediately. The Chambre des comptes and the Cour des aides were not banished or molested, though they had sent remonstrances to the Crown in support of the Parlement's cause.

Meanwhile, the provincial parlements rallied support for the Paris Parlement and, acting on the principle of a common cause adopted in 1756, each sent the Crown remonstrances on behalf of the others. They refused to register the new stamp and land taxes. They all protested against the arbitrary arrests of sovereign-court magistrates, and the parlements of Metz, Dijon, Grenoble, Toulouse, and Rennes denounced the very principle of the royal *lettre de cachet* used for the arrests. They all cried out for a meeting of clergy, nobles, and commoners in the traditional Estates General of the realm. How Louis XVI and his ministers must have regretted the decision to reverse Maupeou's coup of 1770–71! How Maupeou must have shaken his head when the news reached him in his rural Norman retreat! In the face of such opposition, the Crown prudently decided on 20 September 1787 to give way, to bring home the banished Paris magistrates, and even to drop the proposed new taxes.

But these concessions were only part of a tactical maneuver. The struggle was not over yet. It was in these circumstances that Lamoignon's coup against the sovereign courts was planned. Lamoignon's plan to reform the courts was a blow at the parlements even more radical than Maupeou's reform of 1771. When he sent six companies of the French Guards regiment to Paris to invade the Parlement chamber on 5 May 1788, to arrest two of the leading magistrates, Duval d'Epremesnil and Goislard de Monsabert, imposed sweeping reforms by a *lit de justice* on 8 May and a month later exiled most of the *parlementaires*, Parisian and provincial, he was having Louis XVI behave like an absolute monarch and a Bourbon. Why did this royal coup fail? Why did Louis XVI discharge Lamoignon on 14 September 1788 and why, on 23 September, did he give up the May edicts and restore all of the parlements?

The answer is that Louis XVI decided to bow before a storm of hostile public opinion which blew up during the Lamoignon-Loménie de Brienne ministry. Whatever may be said ex post facto about Louis's judgment, any ruler might have found the protests of these months daunting. They came from every direction and seemed to be growing. There were opponents even

among the highest nobility. Some of the seven clerical peers of
the realm and the twenty-seven lay peers attended sessions of
the Parlement of Paris from 22 June 1787 until the coup of
5 May 1788, as they were entitled to do whenever it sat as a
Court of Peers. Some of them joined actively in the opposition
to the Crown's policies. Indeed, the Duc d'Orléans and a dozen
peers, the dukes of Aiguillon, Aumont, Bethune-Charost, Fron-
sac, La Rochefoucauld, Lauzan (or Biron), Luxembourg, Luynes,
Praslin, Talleyrand-Périgord, and Uzès, were openly hostile to
the royal government, some since the Assembly of Notables, and
by the end of 1788 most of them had joined a political club of
liberal "patriots" called the Société des trentes (Company of
Thirty), which, notwithstanding its name, did not limit its membership to thirty. Provincial noblemen opposed to divine-right
monarchy, such as the Comte d'Antraigues, also agitated for a
meeting of the Estates General.[2] Meanwhile, an Assembly of
French Clergy, which met in Paris from 5 May to 5 August 1788,
as it happened, brought together sixty-four members, including
thirty bishops and archbishops, and after drawing up a firm
remonstrance on their own account, they broke a long tradition
of loyalty to the Crown and disappointed their colleague Loménie
de Brienne by joining in the general clamor on behalf of the
banished sovereign courts. Some of the magistrates working for
Lamoignon, such as C.-M.-J. Dupaty, an advocate general from
Bordeaux on the Law Reform Commission, resigned in protest
at his policy. Crowds of common folk, too, made their characteristic demonstrations at critical moments, moved partly by public
support for the parlements and partly by rising prices. Troops
patrolled the streets of Paris from 21 August to 7 September
1787 and again in August and September 1788, when a rise in
the price of bread, adding economic strains to the political
excitement of the time, caused sporadic riots.[3] A hostile crowd
had gathered to watch the guards occupy the Parlement chambers on 4–5 May 1788.

In some of the provincial capitals as well, six in particular,
rebellion flared up sporadically in 1787 and 1788. At Rennes,
home of the Breton provincial Estates since 1732 and of the
Parlement of Brittany (but not the Chamber of Accounts, which
sat in Nantes), a fierce national loyalty, akin to Welsh or Scottish

loyalty, prompted quick resistance to Lamoignon's reforms as it had to Maupeou's earlier. Trouble grew from 10 May 1788, crowds began to take up the cause of the parlements early in June, and on 9 July the royal intendant, Bertrand de Molleville, fled to Paris. Already there was political activity that was to give rise a year later to the Breton Club, forerunner of the Jacobin Club. At Bordeaux the Parlement of Guyenne was exiled to Libourne, by a *lettre de cachet* dated 12 August 1787, for opposing the proposed provincial assemblies, and there it remained until a formal reading of Lamoignon's decrees on 9 May 1788 ended the Parlement's session as well as its exile, pending the announced reform of the judicial system. But the Parlement of Bordeaux remained at Libourne during the ensuing crisis, while it rallied support among the magistrates of the lower courts. The public in the province, indifferent until then, rallied behind the Parlement at last and so lent its weight to a movement that brought the Parlement back to Bordeaux in triumph on 20 October.[4] At Pau the populace and the public rose up in a body on 19 June 1788 in defense of the Parlement of Béarn; the intendant and the governor were powerless until troops arrived.

These were movements of provincial resistance to the central government, but such resistance was even stronger in certain provinces where the king's forebears had done away with the provincial Estates. A vigorous movement grew up in Dauphiné for the revival of the provincial Estates, which had been suspended since 1628, and the Crown decided to revive them in August 1788. Similar movements broke out in Provence, where the Estates, suspended since 1639, were eventually revived from 30 December 1787 to 1 February 1788; and in Franche-Comté, where the Estates, suspended since 1674, were revived in January 1789. The Estates in other provinces, too, stirred by these examples, began to hope for such meetings: the Normandy Estates, suspended since 1666; the Auvergne Estates, suspended since about 1680, and others. These movements went hand in hand with the movements of defense for the provincial parlements against Lamoignon's coup.

In the provinces, as in Paris, noblemen led these political activities. By no means all the nobility opposed the Crown, many of the rebellious magistrates and others were commoners, but it would be hard to see the movements of 1787–88 as anything but aristocratic revolts. The court at Versailles saw them as such and turned to the old alliance between king and Third Estate which had served the monarchy many times in its struggles with intractable nobles.[5] This seemed politically sound because in all provinces except Dauphiné the Third Estate gave the Second Estate only halfhearted support. At Grenoble, the Dauphiné capital, it is true, a general uprising on 7 June 1788, called the *journée des tuiles* because angry townsfolk threw roof tiles at the troops, was followed a fortnight later by an assembly of 150 clergy, 165 nobles, and 276 of the Third Estate in which the lawyer Mounier took a leading part in drawing up a formal request for the restoration of the Parlement and Estates and for meetings of the Estates General. But elsewhere the Third Estate tended to be grateful for Lamoignon's reforms and less interested than the upper orders in reviving parlements and provincial Estates. A majority of the magistrates in the forty presidial courts and five *bailliage* courts chosen to be *grands bailliages* were commoners, and most were pleased at their promotions.[6] In some provinces, especially Brittany, the Third Estate was soon in bitter opposition to the upper orders over reforms of the Estates meetings and believed itself to be in alliance with the Crown. In Provence and Dauphiné the Third Estate won a representation equal in numbers to the upper Estates combined and a system of voting in a general assembly—i.e., by head *(par tête)*—rather than in separate Estates. With such events as these, it seemed in 1788 as though the Crown in alliance with the Third Estate might defeat the rebellious nobles and clergy.

For Louis XVI, however, this informal alliance may have been more than merely a political maneuver. He seems to have developed almost a liberal view of the public or nation and of its representation. A study of his speeches of 22 February, 17 April, and 19 November 1787, of 8 May, of 5 and 15 June, and of 6 July 1788 shows a willingness to end the arbitrary royal rule and the "ministerial despotism" to which the "patriots" of the time objected. He said to the clergy on 6 July 1788: "I want to entrust the nation again with the exercise of their rights. I have said I will assemble them not once but as many times as the needs of state require. My words are neither vague nor fanciful. It is in the midst of the Estates that I wish, in order to assure forever the liberty and happiness of my people, to consummate the great work I have begun of regenerating the kingdom and restoring order in all its parts."[7]

In such speeches as these, the king was speaking to his people over the heads of the rebellious sovereign courts. These, whatever they liked to pretend, were not the only bodies which could represent the French nation. From early in his reign Louis XVI had known of projects for representative provincial assemblies championed by Malesherbes in 1775 in the Cour des aides, by Turgot and Necker during their first ministries, by Calonne, and by others. He had approved of Necker's experimental assemblies set up in Berry (1778) and Haute-Guienne (1779) and also of Calonne's more ambitious projects that were put before the Assembly of Notables, developed in Loménie de Brienne's edict of June 1787, and launched in a series of regulations that summer. According to this project, provincial assemblies were to be elected in twenty-three of the twenty-six generalities of the *pays d'élections*, but not for the *pays d'état*, or for the generalities of Bourges and Montauban, where Necker's assemblies still met. They were intended to meet without the traditional division into three Estates. Many liberal-minded nobles and noble clergy were active in them, as they were later in the National Assembly of 1789–91, and the Paris Parlement registered the founding edict by a huge majority. In spite of hostility in some provincial parlements, the Crown intended to have these assemblies debate and approve tax reforms—hardly the autocratic intention to be expected of an absolute monarch.

Beneath some of the provincial assemblies were municipal and other local assemblies, and to crown this hierarchy, the Estates General seemed natural and inevitable. Loménie de Brienne, like many others, considered the Estates General an extension of provincial assemblies and delayed calling it for the political purpose of maintaining royal initiative. A meeting of the Estates General had been suggested during the Maupeou coup in 1771; a *parlementaire*, Jean-François-André Le Blanc de Castillon, had mentioned them early in the Assembly of Notables; and on 21 May 1787 Lafayette boldly asked the king to convoke "a truly national assembly."[8] The rebellious parlements and then the public in general took up the cry for the Estates General during that year. The Court of Peers clamored for it on 2, 9, and 26 July. On 19 November Loménie de Brienne advised the king to announce a meeting of it for an indefinite date not later than 1792, by which time the financial difficulties might be overcome. This did not appease the faction of the rebellious Duc d'Orléans or the *parlementaire* leaders in Paris and most of the provincial capitals, especially Rennes, Grenoble, Bordeaux, and Besançon. Months later, early in the crisis in which Louis XVI dismissed Loménie de Brienne and Lamoignon, the ministers advised him to announce the Estates General for 1789, and on 8 August 1788 Loménie announced it for 1 May 1789.

This sequence of events shows that the Estates General was forced on a reluctant government, but it is well to remember that the Crown chose to respond to the political force of public opinion. There were few arrests, few interventions by soldiers, no executions, no mass murders, no terrors, none of the brutal acts of tyranny such as a Napoleon or a Robespierre used to maintain his authority. Louis XVI and his ministers were already recognizing public opinion, already taking part in national politics. On 15 June 1788 the king told the assembled clergy: "[N]o court [such as the proposed Cour plenière] can represent the Nation, which can only be represented by the Estates General. I cannot tolerate the usurping of my rights and its rights [i.e., the nation's] by any private body."[9] A king who could appoint so many liberal statesmen to his councils—Turgot, Necker, Malesherbes, Lamoignon, and Loménie de Brienne, to mention only the best known—could not be implacably hostile to the Estates General. Nor could a king who was sponsoring so many great reforms and reformers. Court policy was to choose its own moment for a meeting of the Estates General with a view to keeping the initiative in it. The royal government followed public opinion with the intention of leading it, not crushing it.

A less civilized ruler, even an "enlightened despot" such as ruled elsewhere in continental Europe, might have dispatched forces to arrest Adrien Duport, Lafayette, the Duc d'Orléans, Mounier in Grenoble, and the rest in order to deal with them summarily. He would have found plenty of support in the ranks of his officials, in the great silent majority of his nobles, who were soon to emigrate, and in the observing public of business-men, professionals, shopkeepers, and tradesmen. The mass of peasantry would have rallied to him, as they rallied later to Napoleon and to other determined leaders. Even the *cahiers de doléance* of 1789 show scarcely any revolutionary feeling, scarcely any enmity between the three political orders, scarcely any evidence of class warfare. There was general hostility to the financiers, as there had always been, and the king could have whipped up public hatred of them in a noisy trial, as Louis XV had done from 1761 to 1763, the regent prince in 1716 and 1717, and Louis XIV in the 1660s. The truth is that Louis XVI faced a liberal opposition of "patriots" who were only a congeries of minorities taking advantage of his hesitant, liberal instincts.[10] After all, Louis and many of his ministers shared their premises about peaceful political process.

The liberal political elements remained no more than minorities but grew larger and clearer during the ten months between the announcement of the Estates General in August 1788 and its first meeting on 5 May 1789. This was partly an effect of deliberate political campaigns, the most notorious of which had long been led and paid for by the Duc d'Orléans, a rich royal cousin, at the Palais Royal in Paris and on his immense estates in various parts of the kingdom. Though not so influential as royalists later alleged, he and his many friends and employees deliberately opposed Louis XVI and his government throughout the 1780s, unwittingly undermining the monarchy itself by the "massive use of wealth, research and propaganda" for the purpose of forming public opinion and swaying public policy in liberal directions.[11] From about November 1788, however, an even more influential group of leaders began to gather three times a week in Paris. This was the Company of Thirty (Société des trentes) numbering, despite its title, about threescore within a few months. This was "a loose coalition of like-minded men drawn from all three estates."[12]

More than a score of them were *nobles de race* from the feudal families of the Middle Ages, of which ten were peers, belonging to families traditionally attached to the court at Versailles and prominent in the highest circles of Paris society.[13] Many of them were hostile to the court because they had not been favored with court offices, pensions, or honors and had been passed over in the choice of *maîtres des requêtes*, intendants, army officers, royal councillors, and ministers. Only three of the thirty-six ministers who served Louis XVI had been chosen from old feudal families, though all except Necker were noblemen. Some, like the Vicomte de Noailles and his relative Latour Maubourg and his friends Castellane and Destutt de Tracy had become angry enemies of Marie-Antoinette and her favorites, the Polignac family. Others, like Lafayette, related to the Noailles family, the Duc de Lauzun, and the three Lameth brothers, had been among the chiefs of the French expeditionary force to America, where they had picked up American political ideas about liberty, national sovereignty, and written constitutions. Others again, such as the Marquis de Condorcet and the Marquis de Mirabeau, were intellectual liberals already known for their writings on political matters. Most were influential noblemen with considerable followings.

The Company of Thirty included, besides these sword nobles, more than a score of robe nobles from the Parlement of Paris.[14] Among these were the two whom Lamoignon had arrested on 6 May 1788, Duval d'Espremesnil and Perrotin de Barmond, but the leader—and, indeed, the founder—was Adrien Duport, twenty-nine-year-old son of a rich family of *parlementaires*. About 1785 he had become active in the mesmerist sect which met at the house of a financier, Guillaume Kornmann, and included Lafayette, Jacques-Pierre Brissot, and many other educated men who turned their attention to politics in the years 1787–89.[15] Among the Thirty, too, was the distinguished Paris lawyer Guy-Jean-Baptiste Target, a leader in the revolt of 1788, in the Third Estate during 1789, and in legal reforms. These were soon in the forefront of the opposition to Lamoignon's reforms and of the support for the Estates General, for a declaration of rights, and for a constitution.

The Company of Thirty was far from single-minded and certainly not a conspiratorial revolutionary cell. The members had many differences, notwithstanding their common tendencies, and met only to discuss, to debate, and to promote liberal thinking in France. They helped disseminate pamphlets written in Paris by their colleague Abbé Sieyès and others sent from Languedoc by the Comte d'Antraigues, the Huguenot pastor

Rabaut Saint-Étienne and the lawyer Albisson, from Dauphiné by Mounier, from Brittany by the writer Chasseboeuf de Volney, and from Provence by Servan. They were aware of various political clubs, salons, and cafés such as the Club des Enragés, which met at Massé's restaurant under the arcade of the Palais Royal; Abbé Morellet's Sunday-morning debating society; the secret Société de Virofly; the Club de Valois, to which Sieyès, Talleyrand, Lafayette, Biron, Bougainville, Chamfort, Condorcet, and the Lameths belonged; and an unknown number of provincial clubs.

In the provincial towns, indeed, the public discussed political issues in many groups much like the Parisian groups. More than any other, however, the Company of Thirty stimulated and tried to steer the protest movement for doubling the Third Estate and the electoral campaign for the Estates General, as it was later to try to steer the transformation of the Estates General into a National Assembly. Its causes were taken up in the provinces by like-minded "patriots" such as the Baron de Wimpffen, who had fought on the battlefields of America and who tried to persuade the nobles at the *bailliage* of Caen to give up their pecuniary privileges. By the end of 1788 the Thirty had abandoned the cause of the parlements, which had come to seem conservative, narrow, and selfish, in favor of a liberal constitution, a declaration of rights, and a limited monarchy of the English type.

The role of the Company of Thirty is easily exaggerated. The political scene during the period from September 1788 to May 1789 is difficult to interpret. Certain it is that on 25 September, soon after the Estates General had been decreed for 1 May 1789, the Parlement of Paris provoked a conflict between the Third Estate and the upper orders by registering the decree with the stipulation that the meeting be held according to the rules applied in the meeting of 1614–15. Those rules would have made the clergy and the nobles preponderant and reduced the Third Estate to subservience. To interpret the ensuing political conflict as a phase in the struggle of two warring social classes, the nobles and the bourgeoisie, is attractively simple but no longer seems tenable except to dogmatic Marxists. The nobles who joined the parlements in defending their privileged status and political leadership were a juridical category, not a social class. A large number of nobles sided with the Third Estate in the struggle for a liberal constitutional monarchy; many were relegated to the Third Estate by an old-fashioned and rigorous definition of nobility. The Comte de Provence firmly and cleverly stood up for the principle of doubling the Third Estate; even the king and queen were incensed by the nobility and soon agreed to double the numbers of the Third Estate in the forthcoming meeting of the Estates General.[16] And there is no evidence of a general desire in the Third Estate to destroy the nobles or to dispossess them of their fortunes or their landed estates.

Behind the rhetoric about the "nation" and the "citizens" lay a firm and clear intention to guarantee property by organizing the political rule of the propertied classes in general. The Third Estate seems to have wanted legal or juridical changes to create a unified ruling class of property owners. This was the purpose of even such radical pamphlets as the famous *What Is the Third Estate?*, by Abbé Sieyès, which appeared in January 1789. Sieyès was himself associated, after all, with the noblemen in the Company of Thirty, in the salons of Condorcet, Madame Helvétius, and Madame Necker, and with the Duc d'Orléans. The attack on the privileged orders in 1788 and 1789 was apparently an attack only on those parts of the nobility and clergy that stood by their ancient legal prerogatives. These opposed doubling the Third Estate in the Estates General and any other advancement of the Third. Their views were expressed, for instance, in the *Mémoire au roi* submitted to Louis XVI on 12 December by five princes of the blood: the Prince de Conti and the counts d'Artois, de Condé, de Bourbon, and d'Enghien. On that day, too, a second Assembly of Notables, 147 of them, ended a session convened on 6 November at Necker's request to establish rules for the Estates General, and this Assembly voted equal numbers for each of the three estates, thus enraging the Company of Thirty and the entire "National Party of Patriots."* Petitions on behalf of the Third Estate rained down upon the royal government.

---

*The terms *patriotes* and *parti national* were adopted informally and loosely from 1787 to 1789 to designate those who opposed royal "tyranny," stood for national consultation and representation, and called for a meeting of the Estates General. These terms were not clearly defined and did not always take the same form. Political groups in England, America, and the Dutch Republic had already called themselves "Patriots," though sometimes not with quite the same meaning.

But the Patriots or National Party did not represent any one social class.[17]

On 27 December 1788 the Royal Council announced a decision to double the numbers of the Third Estate in the forthcoming meeting of the Estates General, thus making the Third equal in numbers to the other orders combined. This was followed on 24 January 1789 by regulations for the election of deputies to the Estates General, which duly provided for 600 Third Estate deputies and 300 for each of the other orders. To elect these deputies, the three orders were to meet separately in 490 constituencies, which were, in fact, a selection of the old *bailliages* and *sénéchaussées*. In many constituencies, elections were to be held in two stages, secondary *bailliages* electing delegates to attend the meetings of the principal *bailliages* where the deputies were to be elected for the Estates General. The regulations took care to establish representation for towns roughly proportional to their populations. Thus, the seven industrial cities—Bordeaux, Bourges, Lyons, Nîmes, Rouen, Tours, and Toulouse—were each to have 16 deputies, and Paris 40 deputies and 28 for its suburbs.[18] In the electoral process the numbers were small enough in the upper Estates to present no problem. Meetings of the First Estate could be attended by all members of the clergy with benefices, provided they could find people to do their work during their absences. Monasteries and cathedral chapters were to send delegates; convents, to be represented by proxy. Nobles holding land by feudal tenure could attend the meetings of the Second Estate; noblewomen and minors were to be represented by proxy. Nobles could be represented by proxy in all constituencies in which they held property.

Numbers were a problem in the Third Estate, however, as every Frenchman on the tax rolls twenty-five years of age or older who was not an actor, a domestic servant, or a bankrupt was to have a voice in the election. Convenient bodies were therefore established as primary electoral assemblies: Each professional, industrial, and commercial guild was to meet to choose a delegate for each 200 voters; townsmen not in guilds were to choose a delegate for each 200 voters; villagers, to choose a delegate for 200 households or less and another for each 100 households above the first 200. Paris, an awkward exception in both size and composition, was divided into twenty *quartiers*, in which resident noblemen chose a delegate to the general election for every 20 voters, and divided into sixty districts, in which the resident Third Estate chose a delegate for every 100 voters. Unbeneficed clergy met in a single meeting to choose a delegate for every 20 voters, and beneficed clergy could vote directly (with the delegates of the unbeneficed clergy) at the general meeting of the Paris First Estate. At the general meetings of each Estate in Paris, the delegates chosen in the primary process elected the appointed number of deputies to the Estates General.

What were the results of the elections in the spring of 1789? The First Estate sent to Versailles only 51 of the 147 bishops and archbishops, only 44 other ecclesiastical functionaries of the kingdom, and 16 monks or abbots, but no fewer than 192 curés.[19] The electoral arrangements had given the rural clergy a preponderant voice in the elections, and so the lower clergy was in a large majority. Only a few were politically radical, but those few paralyzed the First Estate by giving voice to its doubts, hesitations, and internal conflicts. Although the French clergy in general was neither decadent nor rebellious, it was troubled by great variations in wealth and social standing between rich bishops such as Rohan-Guéménée, archbishop of Cambrai, with revenues of 200,000 livres reported in the *Almanach royal* (1789, p. 68), and poor parish priests living on 200 livres a year. It was believed that less than one-sixth of the French Church's revenues were assigned to the lower clergy. Resentment among the lower clergy had been fed for more than a century by the Richerist movement of Catholic presbyterianism, which taught that diocesan synods of parish priests should share the bishops' authority. Parish priests in Provence and Dauphiné had already organized in a kind of guild. In addition, the clergy being literate by profession had read deeply in the writings of the time and so were divided, some sympathizing with the National or Patriot Party, others with the more conservative groups that feared (rightly, as it turned out) that the Patriots would put the Church, its property, and the very throne in jeopardy. Some agreed with the official toleration of Protestants; most did not. The clergy that gathered at Versailles in May 1789 was, in short, far from united.

If the clergy was a divided estate, so were the 282 noblemen who came to Versailles in May 1789.[20] About 46 liberal nobles were immediately ready to join the Third Estate in a common assembly and so voted on 6 May, whereas 188 voted against this. A further 30 noblemen were generally sympathetic with the liberal ideas of the time. When the Dauphiné representation of 11 arrived with other late delegations, there were altogether perhaps 90 or 100 liberal nobles. They were not inclined to sacrifice the noble order, any more than the liberal clergy was inclined to sacrifice its order, but they were ready to collaborate with the Third Estate in a movement to reform and regenerate the kingdom. The conservative wing, for its part, was also divided into moderate and intransigent groups. These were political, not social, groups. The liberal nobles were not the poor nobles or the lower ones, nor were they drawn from any particular part of the nobility. On the other hand, liberal nobles did tend to be younger, more urbane, more cosmopolitan, often traveled in England or the United States. Finally, in the noble delegation to the Estates General as a whole, there were eight times as many military men as magistrates, and there was a disproportionately large number of court noblemen.

The Third Estate, largely peasants and artisans, did not come to Versailles themselves but sent 648 literate, educated deputies to represent them. Nearly half these deputies—that is, something between 278 and 315—were officeholders and officials of various kinds, including a large group of magistrates from the *bailliage* and *sénéchaussée* courts. A quarter of the Third Estate deputies (151 to 166) were lawyers or notaries; about 13 percent (85 or 90) were businessmen, including about 75 merchants; and another 5 percent (30 to 35) were doctors (18 to 21), teachers, professors, clergymen, literary men, or scientists. There were a few manufacturers and big farmers *(cultivateurs, fermiers, laboureurs)* but no artisans or peasants.[21] At least 70 percent of these deputies (463) came from 261 towns and cities with populations of 2,000 or more; about 25 percent of them (163) from the 42 cities of more than 15,000. More than two-thirds of them came from the 121 *bailliages* in the northern half of France; less than one-third from the 53 *bailliages* in the southern regions where certain cities—Montpellier, Avignon, Nice, Saint-Étienne, and Bayonne—sent none of their residents to the Estates General.

Two-thirds of the deputies were between thirty-five and fifty-four years of age in 1789, and only 3 percent were under thirty. They were loyal subjects of Louis XVI, not revolutionaries in any sense of the term, and would have been amazed to learn what was going to happen in the next two years. A few, particularly those from Paris, wanted a written constitution, permanent representative institutions, and other radical changes, but most were thinking only of local grievances and reforms of the taxes or of parts of the administration. A revolution was by no means a foregone conclusion when the Estates General first assembled on 5 May 1789.

Hard times in 1788 and 1789 aggravated the political crises by increasing hunger, unemployment, and anxiety among the populace, urban and rural. Hard times were common enough in that preindustrial economy, but 1788 and 1789 were extraordinarily bad years as a result partly of stagnation over one or two decades and partly of a sudden violent crisis. The eighteenth century had been relatively prosperous until about 1770, when most regions of France had been affected by a first sharp crisis from which they had not entirely recovered. There is no simple explanation for it.[22] The production and sale of wine stagnated throughout the 1780s. The textile trades, on which many towns depended and in which so many peasants supplemented their small farming incomes, languished. The harsh winter of 1786–87 destroyed most of the mulberry plantations in Italy that were the primary source of Lyons's raw silk, and by 1788 production was declining and there were nearly 22,000 unemployed. The year 1789 brought no relief. In northern regions severe frost in the winter of 1788–89 had been followed by prolonged cold rains, which destroyed many vineyards by July. Manufacturing suffered; bankruptcies increased; unemployment spread.

Rural indebtedness and rents in arrears grew throughout the 1780s. By 1786 and 1787 a business depression was affecting government revenues as well as private incomes. Only the international trade of the large seaports continued to flourish. Meanwhile, the earlier good times had caused a growth in the population which now came to seem a burden, and the wandering poor were alarmingly numerous. Thousands crowded into the towns in search of work and food. Poverty, crime, illegitimacy, and abandoned children were on the increase in many towns. A sudden shortage of food in such times was bound to result in social and political unrest, especially because the government's usual policy of trying to maintain supplies of cheap food had "accustomed the populace to hold the Government responsible for dearth and high prices."[23] There was even a widespread popular myth that capitalists and government officials were conspiring to cause artificial grain shortages for profit. When, therefore, a hailstorm ravaged the grain harvest on 13 July 1788 in the Paris region, in the Beauce, Soissonais, and Picardy, and prices on the Paris markets rose from the usual eight or nine sous for a five-pound loaf to over fourteen sous by February 1789 and remained high until July, riots and demonstrations were only to be expected. In April mobs wrecked the large wallpaper-manufacturing business of a certain Reveillon for suggesting that workers ought to manage on fifteen sous a day. In Orléans a crowd gathered on 24 April 1789 to wreak vengeance on the hoarders and profiteers whom they believed responsible for the shortage and high price of food.[24] Such incidents were common in most regions.

The elections to the Estates General and the meetings themselves took place in the tense atmosphere of these hard times, not only in Paris but throughout much of the kingdom. At Lyons, more than 3,300 angry silk weavers took command of the main primary assembly of the Third Estate, overwhelmed the silk merchants in the guild, and elected 34 of their own whom royal officials regarded as troublemakers.[25] The silk weavers wanted government control of their industry rather than the economic freedom that favored the merchants. In country districts and in most towns there was not so direct a connection between the depression and the elections. The usual trouble was pillaging of granaries, rioting in markets, bakeries, and town halls, assaulting farmers and grain dealers, enforcing price controls, and destroying property in various ways. From December 1788 to the end of July 1789 such troubles were reported in most of the French provinces. These were mainly spontaneous outbursts, not politically organized. North of Paris, bands of country folk began to roam through the big estates of the royal family, the Prince de Conti, and others, poaching deer and rabbits partly for food and partly to protect crops.[26] In Franche-Comté, Dauphiné, Provence, Languedoc, Picardy, Hainaut, and Cambrésis, peasants rose up at various times that spring against seigneurial and royal tax gatherers. Hunger riots occurred in many towns.

We must remember, however, that the suffering and protesting of the populace in those hard months had little direct influence on the elections or on political events in general. On the one hand, the political classes of that age, whom we call the "public," did not analyze social and economic problems as we do and did not see unrest as the result of rising populations in the throes of economic depression. On the other hand, the subpolitical masses, urban and rural, whom we call the "populace," could not appreciate the liberal principles of self-government, tolerance, humanity, freedom, and the rights of the citizen. The populace was not entirely indifferent to politics, of course, but a great gulf of misunderstanding separated the officials and lawyers who met at Versailles in May and June 1789 and the anxious, unemployed, or hungry crowds who watched their carriages drive by.[27] The French Revolution was not a result of the hunger and misery that had forever been the lot of the masses, nor were the revolutionaries thinking of hunger and misery when they revolted against royal government and the upper Estates in May and June 1789. The populace was to intrude directly in the political process but only occasionally; most of the time they watched and waited, anxious, ignorant, and violent.*

During the nine months between the announcement of the Estates General and its opening on 5 May 1789, the court and the government hoped like the nation that political and financial relief might be found at the Estates General. Immediate difficulties therefore took their attention. Under the sway of public opinion the court reluctantly brought Necker back as director general of finances on 25 August 1788. The government's credit, or power to borrow, strengthened at once because of public confidence in Necker. The same public that had clamored against Loménie de Brienne for trying to find cash by giving forced currency to the notes of the *caisse d'escompte* by a decree of 18 August quietly accepted 15 million livres' worth of these notes by Neck-

---

*For a discussion of the populace, its life, motivation, and behavior and its relation to the public, see Chapter 2.

er's arrangement of 4 September, another 15 million on 16 October, and yet another 10 million on 6 April 1789. Meanwhile, *anticipations,* or the assigning of current payments to future revenues, proceeded at an even faster pace: When the Estates General met on 5 May 1789, Necker told it that 172 million had been spent in advance on the revenues of the remaining eight months of the years, and about 90 million on the revenues of 1790. These sums were owing mainly to the receivers general, the farmers general, and other big financiers, the Crown's age-old short-term bankers. By this time, however, the finance minister had a better command of the spending and accounting processes through the royal treasury that Loménie de Brienne had begun to organize early in 1788. With his old assistant, Bertrand Dufresne, at its head, Necker was at last able to control many of the royal financiers as he had tried to do during his first ministry.

A large sum—at least 25 million by 1 July 1789—Necker spent on foreign grain he thought necessary to help feed the populace in that depressed year.[28] The ruined crops, the rising prices, and the threat of starvation worried him more than any other matter during his second ministry. Reversing Loménie de Brienne's policy of free trade in grain, decreed on 17 June 1787, Necker forbade exports of grain (7 September 1788), ordered all grain to be sold only at public markets (23 November 1788), and authorized intendants and other magistrates to take steps to provision the markets (23 April 1789). In this way Necker did what he could to feed the populace but revived the enmity of grain producers and of that part of the public that had been taught by Turgot and the Physiocrats to believe in a right to dispose of grain freely whatever the social consequences.

A third major preoccupation, after the financial and food problems, was the planning of the promised Estates General and the arranging of the elections with their many details and difficulties. In this Necker's ultimate goal was a political constitution on the English model, which he had long studied and admired, with an upper legislative chamber of noblemen, a lower chamber of mixed social background, and an executive cabinet chosen by the king from the legislature and directed by him.[29] Necker's intention was neither arrogant nor even unreasonable in that period, for his immense popularity and prestige seemed to give him command of the future as well as of the royal government. Even Maximilien Robespierre, the future Jacobin leader during the Terror of 1793–94, admired Necker in 1789. "And thou, generous citizen," he apostrophized Necker in February, "take care not to despair of the French and to abandon, on a stormy sea, the helm of this superb vessel bearing the destinies of a great empire that thou must bring into port."[30]

A limited monarchy of some kind did not seem unreasonable to Robespierre then, or to Jean-Paul Marat, another of Necker's admirers who was soon to be a terrorist, or even to Malesherbes, who resigned from the royal councils when Necker returned to power, or to some of the statesmen who remained on the councils.[31] Louis XVI could scarcely have been hoping to preserve the absolute monarchy when he chose such councillors as Necker, Malesherbes, Malesherbes's nephew Luzerne, Necker's ally Montmorin, or the liberal and enlightened Duc de Nivernais. The king and his councils as well as the public appear to have been ready for some kind of liberal constitution, though they did not all share Necker's enthusiasm for the English kind. It was in that liberal frame of mind that on 27 December 1788 the Royal Council decided, under Necker's leadership, to double the numbers of Third Estate deputies in the Estates General. It was in that frame of mind that they drew up the electoral regulations of 24 January 1789, providing for a wide suffrage.

When the Estates General met on 5 May 1789, the French Revolution was neither inevitable nor indeed foreseen, but at Versailles there was certainly a general expectation of political change. What exactly was to be changed, how, and by whom were far from clear. In this respect the assembled deputies were already in the same uncertainty as every French founding, or constituent, assembly from that day to this. A majority of them, even many nobles and clergy, certainly Louis XVI, had already embraced the republican idea that the assembled deputies represented the French nation, even though they and the nation still loved their sovereign king.[32]

Many were the misunderstandings and the differences at Versailles in May and June 1789, but the ideas of the National or Patriot Party soon prevailed among the Third Estate. The effect of bringing together 1,000 educated men from all over the kingdom was exhilarating for politically prepared orators or leaders and stimulating for the rest. The deputies who gathered at Versailles, meeting in cafés, in lodgings, in the Breton Club founded there during May 1789, and in other clubs, soon formed their own collective mentality. What they did, the Third Estate in particular, was determined not by the *cahiers de doléance* they brought with them, much less by any conspiracy or prearranged revolutionary inclinations, but by their collective response to events at Versailles. The king, his councils and his ministers, did not foresee what was about to happen; hardly anyone else did, either.

After a grand procession on 4 May, the deputies met all together for the opening ceremonies with addresses by the king and the chief ministers. They met in the large hall hastily prepared for the purpose at the Hôtel des menus plaisirs, rue des Chantiers, and then the nobles and clergy retired to two smaller rooms reserved for them nearby in the same building. At the very next stage of the proceedings, the formal convocation and roll call of each separate estate, the Third Estate heard arguments by the deputations from Dauphiné, especially Barnave, and Brittany, fresh from the political struggles in their provinces, to the effect that it would be a mistake to organize and proceed as a separate estate. Most delegates of the Third Estate were ready to be persuaded that the First and Second Estates represented only the clergy and the nobles, whereas they themselves represented the French nation, and they straightway began to call themselves the "Commons" *(les communes)* in imitation of the British House of Commons.

Already someone had suggested they behave as an Assemblée nationale, a term Necker had used in his project for provincial assemblies in 1778, and on 17 June they adopted this title by 491 votes to 89. Such liberal enthusiasts as Mounier, Sieyès, Malouet, Target, Mirabeau, Duport, and Le Chapelier had already worked out various republican thoughts. "A people who has no constitution and who wants one," Mounier had written earlier that spring, "must meet in a body as a nation, through its representatives at least, in order to make one."[33] Many others had the same idea, and during the next ten days the Third Estate decided to behave like a "National Assembly." In the circumstances, after so many tense political conflicts, this seemed a small step, and the future lay hidden, as it always does. The king and the two upper Estates gave way, with the result that on 9 July the Third Estate was able to change its name to the National Constituent Assembly and set about drafting a constitution with the collaboration of many nobles and clergy and the grudging complicity of king and council. Such was the climax of the famous revolution of the Third Estate.

King, councillors, nobles, and clergy might have been expected to overpower the rebellious Third Estate. They did not because they were far from united, because many of them were either in sympathy with the Third Estate or else filled with uncertainty, and because in the hurly-burly of each day's events few of them saw where those events were leading. On 12 June the Third Estate invited the two upper orders to join them in forming a National Assembly, and the next day 3 village curés, Jallet, Ballard, and Le Cesve, all from the province of Poitou, joined the Third Estate because, as they explained to their bish-ops, "Reason tells us that good can only be done by the meeting of minds *[la réunion des esprits],* and that minds will never be united so long as the three Orders are separated. . . . [You, my lords, foresee terrible disasters,] the Clergy's property despoiled and dissipated, even the Throne itself shaken. Who would not trem-ble at the very idea of such an upheaval!"[34] Those apprehensive bishops were quite right, as it turned out later, but in June 1789 other bishops and many curés were carried away by an effusion of hope and goodwill. Six more curés joined the Third Estate on 14 June, more each day thereafter, and on 17 June no fewer than 149 voted to join the Third in a body. Meanwhile, the noblemen of the Second Estate, who on 6 May had voted 188 to 46 to refuse to join the Third Estate, still counted no more than about 60 liberal deputies on 27 June, when the king suddenly sided with the minority and gave the command to join the Third. A large number of noblemen obeyed.

Why did Louis XVI and his Council give way to the Third Estate? At first he, like most people at court, thought the Third Estate should be stopped in its rebellious course, and on 19 June he decided to impose his will at a royal session of the Estates

General, a sort of *lit de justice,* to be held on 23 June. Until then the meeting hall of the Third Estate was to be kept closed, ostensibly for repairs, and so the deputies found it when they arrived on the morning of 20 June. The general feeling among them was an indignant desire to carry on notwithstanding, and at the suggestion of Dr. Guillotin they went to the nearby hall of the Jeu de Paume (tennis court), where 577 of them, including 7 clergy, soon signed Mounier's famous oath "never to disperse; and to foregather wherever circumstances require until the kingdom's constitution be established and fixed on sound foundations. . . ." Only one refused to sign without the king's approval.

At this point it would have been easy to disperse the Third Estate with a small body of troops. After all, ten years later the Bonaparte brothers had no trouble in driving out the Five Hundred elected deputies assembled at Saint-Cloud. Neither Louis XVI nor any of his ministers took such a resolute step in June 1789 partly because Louis was as usual restrained by his own decent, liberal inclinations, partly because he was very much upset by the death of his eldest son on 14 June, and partly because his councillors were divided in their views. Four of them, Necker, Montmorin, Saint-Priest, and de la Luzerne, urged the king to be flexible and to adopt a compromise. In the Council meetings of 19, 21 and 22 June and at the royal session of the Estates General on 23 June, Louis adopted the firm conservative views of the other three councillors, Barentin, Villedeuil, and Puységur, and of the royal family, but when he was informed that the Third Estate refused to disperse even after his disciplinary speech at the royal session, he suddenly gave way, as he had so often given way before. *"Eh bien, foutre! qu'ils restent!"* he said wearily, oblivious of where such weakness might lead the kingdom.

In the next two days most of the clergy and forty-seven nobles joined the Third Estate, whose prestige was growing. King and Council turned the king's unexpected moral collapse into a tactical defeat when they decided, on 26 June, to lie low until more troops could be assembled. The next day, Louis formally invited the reluctant nobles and clergy to join the Third Estate, which immediately turned to the business of drafting a constitution for the kingdom. Although nobody then knew what the future held, Louis XVI and his ministers were destined never to recover the authority they had just lost. The king of France was to reign for three more years, but his rule had come to an end.

SIX *A Liberal Interlude,*

1789–91

ONCE the king's consent had been given on 27 June, grudging and hesitant though it was, the Third Estate received all comers from the upper Estates and began to organize itself as a National Assembly. It was soon named the National Constituent Assembly because the members agreed at once to draw up a constitution for the kingdom, as many of them had sworn to do in the Tennis Court Oath of 20 June. For this purpose they decided on 6 July to appoint a committee to draft the constitution for debate, clause by clause, and to make whatever other preparations seemed necessary. Twenty-seven months were to elapse before the constitution was at last adopted on 3 September 1791 and sanctioned by the king on 14 September. The Assembly was not to disband until then, after it had provided for the general elections to the Legislative Assembly its new constitution had provided for.

During those months the Assembly did much else besides write a constitution: it inquired into the structure and workings of the kingdom as it was, pushed through many changes, and took control of more and more functions of government. All this work can be understood more easily if considered apart from the political struggles of those years. The politics was not, in fact, separate but was complicated enough to warrant explaining as a separate subject. The Constituent Assembly itself, moreover, tried to keep politics out of its constitutional arrangements.

I. *The Work of the Constituent Assembly,*
June 1789–September 1791

Rules of procedure adopted by the Assembly on 29 July, and practices that grew up over the years, made French assemblies different from Parliament in England and Congress in the United States. In the name of national unity, which ranked in its members' minds with liberty, equality, and fraternity, the Assembly viewed political parties as corrupt private groups deserving of no place in the new constitutional arrangements. The votes cast for and against motions in the Assembly were deemed to represent the conscientious opinions of citizens elected as *députés*, not the tendencies of conflicting parties, much less the interests of warring social classes. The majority vote behind every piece of legislation was regarded as the General Will of the French nation, not the victory of a political party or coalition. Accordingly, the seats in the chamber were arranged in the semicircular shape of an amphitheater, all facing the chairman *(président)* down at the front, quite different from the House of Commons, where two separate bodies, government and opposition, face each other from opposite sides of the hall like two teams in a debate or a football game.

Political differences soon crept into the Assembly in the choice of seats, however, for the deputies were not assigned seat numbers as in a theater but left to sit where they wished. As the radical deputies with democratic republican opinions tended to sit on the extreme left of the chamber, and the conservatives and royalists on the extreme right, people soon began to use the terms "left" and "right" to denote political tendencies. Here began the modern image of the political "spectrum," a device by which all opinions, principles, interests, and those who hold them may be classified on a scale from left to right. To this day the entire field of French politics, including the National Assembly, is customarily analyzed in the newspapers by means of a semicircle divided into various wedge-shaped sections. The beguiling simplicity of this device has never blinded discerning politicians and historians to the complex realities that it conceals, such as the capacity of any conscientious or intelligent citizen to be radical, moder-

ate, and conservative by turns, depending on the subject under
discussion.

So thought the Constituent Assembly. Whatever political
divisions crept into it were never formally recognized or provided for in the rules of procedure. Assuming that their own
lofty ideals of citizenship and public spirit would inspire elected
deputies in general, the Constituents arranged an apolitical system of subdivisions. On 30 July they divided themselves into thirty
bureaux to discuss the reports of the Constitution Committee
before the debates and votes in the Assembly as a whole. This
was a traditional French subdivision by which, shortly before,
the Assembly of Notables had been divided into seven *bureaux*
for preliminary debate. Every major subject was treated thereafter in similar stages: first, in a special committee which drafted
a report and proposals; secondly, in the thirty *bureaux;* and finally,
in the whole Assembly. But the Constituent Assembly thought
of its own committees and sections as ad hoc arrangements necessary only for its own special tasks and did not write them, or
anything like them, into the constitution. The only committee it
provided for the National Legislative Assembly was a committee
of the whole *(comité général)* that could be called into being by not
less than fifty deputies (section II, article 2).[1] In general, legislation was to be read and debated three times at intervals of a
week or more (section II, articles 3–6) by a quorum of not less
than 200 deputies (section II, article 7) and then, if passed, sent
to the king for his sanction (section III, articles 1–8). The legislative processes of the Constituent Assembly were not so orderly
as those it laid down for its constitutional successor, but they
produced tidy results on paper concerning a score of major issues.

Declarations and decrees are not worth the paper they are
written on unless they are enforced, and justly enforced. Many
in the Constituent Assembly, for all their high-minded rhetoric,
soon saw the need for organized executive ministries and independent courts of justice. The king, his ministers, and ministries, being already in place, so to speak, could scarcely be denied
the executive functions of government. They were, moreover, a
natural executive power, experienced, capable, and eager for
reforms that would render the process of government more efficient. Some in the first generation of revolutionaries were bent

on implementing administrative reforms planned under Louis XVI and earlier: plans for uniform and equitable taxes, for a single tariff of customs duties at the frontiers to replace the congeries of internal duties, for uniform weights and measures, for a central treasury with a consolidated revenue fund, and others. Reforms like these were what officials like Bertrand Dufresne, Charles-François Lebrun, and Mahy de Cormeré thought the Revolution had been for. The Assembly had no qualms about adopting the monarchy's old projects but had misgivings about royal executive authorities that might use their power to influence or even to corrupt the lawmakers of the legislature and the magistrates of the lawcourts.

They were aware, of course, that French kings and their ministers had always governed by an elaborate system of patronage and that British kings and ministers influenced the House of Commons by patronage. And the position of legislature which they had usurped in June 1789 rendered them vulnerable to any counterrevolutionary steps the king's court might take. Pressed by its own political position, encouraged by the American example, and inspired by various currents of Enlightenment thinking, the Assembly hoped to preserve the independence of the legislature and the judiciary by a system of divided powers, legislative, executive, and judicial. The constitution (*titre* III) expressed that division with admirable brevity under the title *Des pouvoirs publics.* "The government is monarchical," reads article 4. "The executive power is delegated to the king, to be exercised under his authority by ministers and other responsible agents in a manner that shall be determined hereafter." It remained to be seen whether Louis XVI and his ministers and loyal supporters would be content with restricted powers delegated by an upstart assembly they had called into being to aid them in their struggle with the rebellious parlements. On 28 March 1791 the Assembly went as far as to decree that "the King, the first civil servant [*premier fonctionnaire public*], must have his residence no farther than twenty leagues away from the Assembly when it is in session."[2]

This form of government contained the seeds of future conflict, but in 1789 and 1790 Louis XVI and some of his ministers were, as we have seen, in sympathy with the National

Assembly's fundamental principles. King, ministers, and a majority of deputies shared the enlightened principle of social utility they had learned from philosophes of their generation. The deputies were assembled to do what they could for French citizens and the French nation. One of their first acts was to draw up a statement of general principles. This was the Declaration of the Rights of Man and the Citizen discussed by the Assembly from time to time through the summer of 1789, adopted on 26 August, sanctioned by the king the next month, and included in the constitution as part of the preamble. In the many preliminary drafts and debates this Assembly of "country attorneys and obscure curates," as Burke called them, indulged in so much repetition of their own abstractions that they bored each other and began to stay away from the sessions. After all, liberty, property, security, and national sovereignty were scarcely more than poetry when expressed as "natural rights": "[G]overnment is not made in virtue of natural rights," as Burke remarked.[3] Yet their solemn formulation was a first step toward their establishment as *civil* rights. Some fundamentals were at stake, and some practical results followed. For the seventeen articles of this declaration contained, like seeds, the formative principles of the fully grown constitution of 3 September 1791, which ran to 207 articles.[4]

One of the classic statements of liberal thinking, the Declaration of the Rights of Man and the Citizen affirms that men are born and remain free and equal in their rights (article 1), which are liberty, property, security, and resistance to oppression (article 2). Liberty has no limits except those necessary to protect the equal rights of other people, and those limits are to be determined by the law (article 3). Therefore, no one should be arrested, detained, or punished except under the terms of the law (articles 7 and 8), and no one should be presumed guilty until judged so according to the law (article 9). Everyone may think, speak, and write whatever he wishes, even on religion, so long as he does not disturb the public peace as laid down in law (articles 10 and 11). The citizen holds his property as an inviolable and sacred right and cannot be deprived of it except for public necessity as laid down in law, and then only if just compensation is paid in advance (article 17). The law mentioned in the above clauses may prohibit only what is harmful to society (article 5); the forces carrying out the law must work for the advantage of all citizens and not for their own advantage (article 12), for the purpose of government is to maintain the citizen's rights (article 2). The law is the expression of the General Will, and every citizen may take part in its formation (article 7), for the nation is sovereign and the only source of legitimate authority (article 3). The taxation necessary to pay for the government and its policies must be imposed equally on all citizens according to their capacity to pay (article 13). The citizen must be fully informed of taxes, and his consent is necessary for their collection and expenditure (article 14). Wherever the citizen's rights are not guaranteed, there is no constitution and he has a right to resist (article 16).

So defined, a citizen was first and foremost a member of the French nation and only secondarily a subject of the king. To mark the change, the king was defined in the constitution as *roi des français*, no longer *roi de France* (*titre* III, article 4). Nationality suddenly became vital and exclusive, its terms laid down in the constitution (*titre* II, articles 2–6): "The status of French citizen may be lost," (reads *titre* II, article 6), "1° by naturalization in a foreign country, 2° by sentence to punishments implying civic degradation, 3° by sentence *in absentia* until it is annulled, 4° by affiliation with any foreign order of chivalry or any foreign body which requires either proofs of nobility, or distinctions of birth, or religious vows." Under the monarchy the Chamber of Accounts had issued papers of naturalization, but nationality had been of no special importance. After all, nearly all French queens and many nobles had come from abroad, maids and gardeners often came from England, the famous Swiss Guards at court were not French, and there were entire regiments of other foreign soldiers. It was not necessary for Jacques Necker, when he became Louis XVI's controller general of finances, to take out French nationality. France had always harbored many foreigners and would continue to do so, but their position became more and more precarious during the Revolution as nationalism became intense.

To strengthen national unity, the National Constituent Assembly decided almost at once to replace the historic local and provincial divisions of the kingdom with a logical system of divisions. In this, the euphoria of the delegates' own revolutionary

English Channel

MANCHE
St.Lô•
Caen•
CALVADOS
EURE
Évreux•
Versailles•
SEINE-
ET-
OISE
PAS-
DE-CALAIS
Arras•
Lille•
NORD
SOMME
Amiens•
SEINE-
INFÉRIEURE
Rouen•
•Beauvais
OISE
SEINE•
PARIS•
Melun•
SEINE-
ET-
MARNE
AISNE
Laon•
Châlons-
-s.-M.•
MARNE
Mézières•
ARDENNES
MEUSE
Bar-le-
Duc•
MOSELLE
Metz•
MEURTHE
Nancy•
BAS-
RHIN
Strasbourg•

FINISTÈRE
Quimper•
St.Brieuc•
CÔTES-DU-NORD
ILLE-
ET-VILAINE
Rennes•
MORBIHAN
Vannes•
ORNE
Alençon•
MAYENNE
Laval•
SARTHE
Le Mans•
Chartres•
EURE-ET-
LOIR
Orléans•
LOIRET
Troyes•
AUBE
Chaumont•
HAUTE-
MARNE
VOSGES
Épinal•
Colmar•
HAUT-
RHIN
HAUTE-
SAÔNE
Vesoul•
Besançon•
DOUBS

LOIRE-
INFÉRIEURE
Nantes•
MAINE-
ET-
LOIRE
Angers•
Tours•
INDRE-
ET-LOIRE
Blois•
LOIR-
ET-CHER
CHER
Bourges•
Auxerre•
YONNE
CÔTE-D'OR
Dijon•
NIÈVRE
Nevers•
SAÔNE
-ET-LOIRE
Mâcon•
JURA
Lons-
le-Saunier•

VENDÉE
La-Roche-
sur-Yon•
DEUX-
SÈVRES
Niort•
Poitiers•
VIENNE
Châteauroux•
INDRE
CREUSE
Guéret•
ALLIER
Moulins•
Bourg•
AIN
RHÔNE
Lyon•

ATLANTIC OCEAN
La Rochelle•
CHARENTE-
INFÉRIEURE
Angoulême•
CHARENTE
HAUTE-VIENNE
Limoges•
PUY-DE-DÔME
Clermont-
Ferrand•
LOIRE
ISÈRE
Grenoble•

Bordeaux•
GIRONDE
Périgueux•
DORDOGNE
CORRÈZE
Tulle•
CANTAL
Aurillac•
HAUTE-LOIRE
Le Puy•
ARDÈCHE
Privas•
Valence•
DRÔME
HAUTES-ALPES
Gap•

LANDES
Mont-de-Marsan•
LOT-ET-
GARONNE
Agen•
LOT
Cahors•
Rodez•
AVEYRON
LOZÈRE
Mende•
GARD
Nîmes•
BOUCHES-
DU-
RHÔNE
Aix•
BASSES-
ALPES
Digne•
Draguignan•
VAR

BASSES-
PYRÉNÉES
Pau•
Tarbes•
GERS
Auch•
HAUTE-
GARONNE
Toulouse•
TARN
Albi•
Montpellier•
HÉRAULT

HAUTES-
PYRÉNÉES
Foix•
ARIÈGE
Carcassonne•
AUDE
Perpignan•
PYRÉNÉES-
ORIENTALES

Mediterranean Sea

France, Departments 1790

.... Department boundary

• Department capital

0   40   80   120   160   200 Miles

Bastia•
CORSE

gathering overcame their loyalties to the provinces and towns that had elected them to the Estates General, and they declared on the night of 4–5 August 1789: "A national constitution and public liberty are more advantageous to the provinces than the privileges some of them enjoy and whose sacrifice is necessary to the close union of all parts of the empire. All special privileges of the provinces, principalities, *pays*, cantons, cities and communities of people, whether pecuniary or of any other kind, are abolished forever and will remain fused in the common rights of all Frenchmen."[5] By 15 February 1790, after much debate on many drafts, of which Jacques-Guillaume Thouret's was perhaps the most influential, France was divided into eighty-three more or less equal *départements* that have remained the basis of the administration to this day. The elected assemblies and the district and canton subdivisions which they worked out, were replaced in 1800, under Napoleon Bonaparte, by the present prefects *(préfets)* who took charge of departmental administration in the capital *(chef-lieu)* of each department.[6]

To be a French citizen was to have equal civil rights—that is, natural rights guaranteed by law—and these worsened the lot of a few but improved the lot of a great many. On 4 August 1789 the Assembly decided to abolish the three Estates of clergy, nobles, and commoners, and this was followed with a decree on 19 June 1790 suppressing all ranks and distinctions of nobility, and another on 12 July removing the special status of the clergy. About 1.5 million serfs were freed and declared citizens by a vote in the Assembly on 4 August 1789 and a decree of 15 March 1790 abolishing mortmain.*[7] These had been still unable to will or inherit property and legally bound to feudal landlords, mainly in central and eastern regions, who had not followed the king's example when he had freed the serfs on the royal estates in 1779.

Applying its liberal principles in another direction, the Constituent Assembly abolished the old practice of attainder by a law of 21 January 1790. On the principle of attainder, or "corrup-

---

*Mortmain (*mainmorte* in French) was the feudal law by which a serf could not inherit or will property; a serf's property escheated automatically to his lord. This was one of three legal conditions of servitude, the other two being *formariage,* or the obligation to marry within the serf's own community, and various feudal dues and services.

tion of blood," common to most of Europe in the Middle Ages, a person convicted of a crime had not been punished simply as an individual: His kith and kin had also been disgraced, his family exiled or imprisoned, and his property confiscated. This had happened, for instance, to Jean Calas, the Protestant executed at Toulouse in 1762. His family had been destroyed, his daughters imprisoned in Roman Catholic convents, and his wife and sons exiled. Following ideas developed in the Enlightenment, the Constituent Assembly now declared punishment for crime to be a precise and personal matter. Madame Calas, who lived until 1792, was in Paris when this reform was made, and four plays about the Calas case were then written and played there.[8]

The Calas case had developed on the basis of discrimination against Protestants. For more than a century more than 1 million Huguenots in the east, in the southwest, and in Normandy had been legally held to be outlaws. Louis XVI had recently granted them a certain legal status and permitted them to marry by an edict of 19 November 1787, but that had done little more than legitimize Protestant children, hitherto legally treated as bastards. The Crown had been able to include Protestants, however, in the elections to the Estates General, to which about fifteen had been elected. The Roman Catholic authorities that had prevented further emancipation were now broken by the Assembly, and a decree of 24 December 1789 gave Protestants the right to hold public office. Laws of 10 July and 10 December 1790 even voted compensation to the descendants of families that had lost property after Louis XIV had repealed the Edict of Nantes in October 1685.

The opposition to granting full citizenship to the 40,000 Jews in France, of whom the biggest community were some 25,000 Ashkenazim in Alsace, was even stronger than that to Protestants, and Louis XVI's efforts on their behalf had come to little. They had not been allowed to take part in the elections to the Estates General, but Necker had granted them the right to submit *cahiers de doléance*. In the Constituent Assembly a pro-Jewish campaign, led by Abbé Grégoire with the support of Archbishop Talleyrand, Robespierre, Mirabeau, the Paris municipal authorities *(la commune)*, and other strange bedfellows, divided the various political and social groups. The most anti-Jewish views of all occurred among some of the members of the extreme left, especially Jean-François Reubell.[9] There was a long, thorny debate before the Assembly decided on 27 September 1791, three days before breaking up, to admit Jews as equal citizens.

Opposition to emancipating African slaves and granting them citizenship was even stronger. Hardly a score of the *cahiers de doléance*, brought by the elected deputies to the Estates General, had called for emancipation, and the campaign waged by the Société des amis des noirs—Brissot, Condorcet, Lafayette, Mirabeau, Sieyès, and others—was wrecked by the big colonial planters, shipping interests, and administrators in the Club Massiac. The public was generally indifferent because slavery was already illegal in France itself and the hundreds of thousands of West Indian slaves seemed so remote. Slaves were valuable property, furthermore, and a commodity French merchants and planters would have continued trading in until the emancipation laws of the Second Republic (1848–50) had they not been checked by the slave revolt of Toussaint l'Ouverture (1743–1803) in Haiti and, from January 1793, by the British navy, which posted an antislavery patrol off the West African coast well before the end of the Napoleonic Wars.[10] The revolutionary assemblies did, it is true, publish decrees against slavery, notably those of the Legislative Assembly in April 1792, but before they were properly enforced, Napoleon restored slavery by a law of 10 May 1802 that was written into the Civil Code of 1807.

The rights of property were attended to by taking care to secure or repay the many government debts, a care so scrupulous that Barnave, one of the deputies, began to see the Assembly as a body of shareholders in the national debt committed to their own interests. Burke in 1790 remarked on "the great care which, contrary to their pretended principles, has been taken, of a monied interest originating from the authority of the Crown."[11] He was referring to the financiers with venal offices. As the venal offices were suppressed, their owners were reimbursed in paper *assignats,* which did not lose much of their purchasing power until their inflationary use in the war beginning in April 1792. From 1793 to 1798 much debt was recorded in the *Grand livre de la dette publique,* a monument to the revolutionary government's concern for the rights of property, carried on into the nineteenth century.[12] The deep concern for family property reflected in the Civil Code of 1807 went back to the first years of the Revolution, when, to cite another example, the National Assembly refused to emancipate West Indian slaves, partly because they were valuable property, bought and paid for.[13]

In its political arrangements, too, the Assembly provided for a distinction between "passive" citizens, who, in Sieyès's words, "have the right to protection of their persons, their liberty and their property," and "active" citizens, "who contribute to the public establishment and are the true shareholders in the great public enterprise."[14] Thus, to vote or to be elected to the Legislative Assembly, a person had to be an "active" citizen' aged twenty-five or more, a Frenchman born or naturalized who had taken the oath, not employed as a domestic servant, established in some locality as a member of the National Guard, and a taxpayer paying at least three days' wages annually, the value of a day's wages to be set every six years by the Legislative Assembly and the administrators of each *département*. About 4.3 million men qualified as "active" citizens out of a total population of 27.4 million. In Paris about 80,000 qualified out of 650,000, or about half the men, and in some districts this disenfranchised men who had once qualified as voters under the electoral act of 24 January 1789.[15]

That was a distinction based on wealth, but not all property was deemed sacred. The National Assembly and its committees spent much time debating what was legitimate property and what illegitimate. The rights of property did not extend, in the view of the majority, to seigneurial rights, and it proceeded to abolish them, though not all at once. Responding to widespread unrest in the countryside, the Assembly remained in session late into the night on 4 August 1789 while the deputies, noble and common, vied with one another to give up seigneurial rights. They gathered up the results of that euphoric night's work in a decree of 11 August abolishing the nobility's hunting rights, the ecclesiastical tithe, and the seigneurial monopolies of dovecotes and rabbit warrens. The Crown hesitated to approve this decree but finally did so on 3 November. Four months later a decree of 15 March 1790 went on to abolish the seigneurial rights and monopolies over fairs and markets, tolls (*péages*), fishing, hunting, and the mill and bread-oven *banalités*. At the same time seigneurial dues were not abolished but declared open for purchase by those who paid them. They were a major source of revenue for many landowners and not to be lightly sacrificed. The procedure for this (a contract between landlord and tenant) and the price (twenty or twenty-five times the annual sum of the dues) were laid down in another decree dated 3–9 May 1790. Such a high price made the purchase impossible for most peasants, as the next legislature, the Legislative Assembly, began to realize, and on 17 July 1793 the third legislature, the National Convention, ended the matter by suppressing all seigneurial dues without compensation. Only rents, pure and simple, were left.

These changes were not made in clean legislative strokes; landlords and peasants struggled, appealed, and petitioned all over the country. Some landlords, like Philippe-Égalité, Duc d'Orléans, understood the issues and were sometimes ready to act in a spirit of social justice, the spirit of 4 August. But for him the seigneurial dues became a secondary issue, as the National Assembly was bent on confiscating his entire royal *apanage*—that is, the huge *domaines*, the equivalent of six *départements* near Paris, which Louis XIV had granted his family in 1661.[16] Most landlords struggled against the loss of their revenues or, like the Duc de Saulx-Tavanes who could not see why the bailiffs and farmers on his estates in the Saône Valley sent him less and less revenue, simply did not understand what was happening.[17] In legislating on landlord and tenant struggles, the National Assembly seems to have acted with moderation, in an equitable manner, as an enlightened legislature imbued with the principles of its Declaration of the Rights of Man and the Citizen.

In much of the countryside, including the huge estates of the ducs d'Orléans and de Saulx-Tavanes, the peasants had been in a state of ferment ever since the preparations for the elections to the Estates General early in 1789. Peasants' purposes were, on the whole, neither liberal nor democratic; specialists agree on this.[18] But they knew how to struggle against seigneurial burdens. They also knew how to struggle for collective advantage. The collapse of absolute monarchy in 1789 left towns and villages free to act for themselves. Some rural communities tried to win official recognition of a communal status they had not yet acquired. Some sprawling suburbs tried to win independence by seceding. Established villages and *bourgs* competed for the honor of being the seat of a lawcourt or the center of a new jurisdiction. By a momentous decree of 14 December 1789, the National Assembly declared that a new municipal government would be formed in each town, *bourg*, parish, or community. Also, having swept away the old courts and administrative structures, the Assembly based the new ones on systems of election which kept the countryside in a ferment of activity.[19]

The greatest changes in provincial France followed upon the National Assembly's ecclesiastical policy. It decided to confiscate, or "nationalize," all the French property of the Roman Catholic Church. It should be added at once that other confiscations were also in the wind; for instance, the three huge properties called *apanages*, amounting to whole provinces, granted to three royal princes, the Duc d'Orléans (granted in 1661), the Comte de Provence (1771), and the Comte d'Artois (1773), were "nationalized" with effect from 1 January 1791. But the confiscation of Church properties had a much greater political effect on the country. This policy was adopted in principle as early as 2 November 1789 by a vote of 568 to 336 with 40 absent or abstaining. The idea had been in the air since 4 August, when the ecclesiastical tithe had been abolished with certain seigneurial rights, at least in principle, but it must be admitted that the monarchy had already pointed the way by confiscating the property of Huguenots after 1685, Jansenists after 1709, and Jesuits after 1764. After much debate the Assembly decided to dispose of the property—worth about 2.5 billion livres, according to the Finance Committee[20]—and to apply its value to the debt by printing paper notes *(assignats)* for use in paying off the government's creditors.

The sale of Church property made reform of the clergy and its relations with the State seem urgent. The clergy suffered several incidental knocks in 1789, such as the abolition of the tithe in principal, the release of all monks and nuns from their vows by a decree of 28 October 1789, and the dissolution of the monasteries and convents (though not of schools and charitable houses). The National Assembly's Ecclesiastical Committee, created on 20 August 1789 and re-formed on 7 February 1790, eventually drafted what came to be called the Civil Constitution of the Clergy. The Assembly approved this, after much debate, in a decree of 12 July 1790, and the king sanctioned it after much hesitation on 24 August. This was fated to divide the nation more than any other single measure. Reorganizing the dioceses and parishes to fit the new departments, and removing the cathedral chapters of canons, were not excessively disturbing, nor was the decision to lodge and pay the clergy out of public funds according to graduated salary scales that bettered the lot of the lower clergy and amounted to 100 million livres. But the new system of electing bishops to dioceses and priests to parishes, which would give the laity a strong voice, raised the ancient problem of papal and ecclesiastical authority that had been one of the principal issues in the Protestant Reformation of the sixteenth century. The National Assembly seldom gave a thought to what the papacy might think. The clergy in general objected to a reorganization on which the Church had not been consulted.

Even more, the oath clergymen were now supposed to take, "to be loyal to the nation, the law and the king, and to uphold . . . the constitution," aroused the determined hostility of at least half the French clergy and of the entire Church establishment abroad. Impatient with the resistance of the clergy, and the delays and silences of Pius VI, the Assembly pointedly imposed the oath on priests holding public office, by a decree of 27 November, which Louis XVI sanctioned a month later.[21] Within the Assembly only about one-third of the clerical deputies (110) took the oath before the end of the prescribed week of grace, and no more than 7 or 8 bishops (including Talleyrand) out of 160 in the kingdom ever took it. When on 4 May 1791 the pope published his brief, *Caritas quae*, denouncing the Civil Constitution of the Clergy, many who had taken the oath retracted it. "We spoke to God," said Pius VI, "and ordered public prayers to obtain for these new legislators a disposition which will recall them from the precepts of the philosophy of this age back to the laws of our religion and their practice."[22] It was scarcely a united nation that elected the Legislative Assembly under the terms of the constitution of 3 September 1791.

II. *Political Struggles, 1789–91*

For about a year after the revolutionary events of June 1789, the Assembly depended for its work and its very existence upon the acquiescence of the king. Louis XVI chose to defend the monarchy by political means, but he might easily have used the army. He may, indeed, have thought of doing so, as troops were moved from the frontiers to Paris in April and May 1789, and in one week of early July the Paris forces increased from 4,000 to 17,000. Some units, like the Gardes françaises and the Royal-Cravates felt uneasy dealing with riots, and in various provincial towns troops began to fraternize with the people. Two detachments of Gardes françaises with five cannons played a decisive part in the taking of the Bastille on 14 July 1789.[23] But most regiments remained firm and obedient. The rate of desertion rose from 1.87 percent in 1788 to only 3.62 percent in 1789 and 4.88 percent in 1790, and in general the army remained loyal and serviceable until well into 1790.[24] Nine-tenths of the officers were noblemen. There were more officers in the French army than in all the others put together, and in the *Almanach royal* the lieutenants general and *maréchaux de camp* together outnumbered the National Assembly, as did the colonels alone, as well as the sublieutenants.

To take military command of Paris, all that was needed was firm leadership, and it is romantic nonsense to imagine that the army was cowed by the sovereign people led by valiant revolutionaries. A few years later an army under General Menou paralyzed and disarmed the insurgents of the Paris sections on 20–24 May 1795, and Paris was again subdued on 5–6 October, this time by about 5,000 troops with artillery under half a dozen generals (including Bonaparte), directed by Barras. On 19 Brumaire 1799, Lucien and Napoleon Bonaparte dispersed the legislative councils assembled at Saint-Cloud, the Ancients and the Five Hundred, with nothing more than their own guard.[25] The army was to take Paris by force again in June 1848 and yet again in May 1871. The Paris police, it may be added, never ceased to deal with civil disturbances throughout the revolutionary years and to go through their usual process of arresting and interrogating the leaders, keeping all the while those careful records that have proved so useful to the historians of riots.[26]

With quite enough forces at their disposal, Louis XVI and his ministers did not oppose the Assembly firmly because they were not military leaders; they were semiphilosophes, liberal to some extent, almost won over to the revolutionary cause. Unlike his forebears, Louis XVI usually dressed as a civilian rather than a military officer. On 4 February 1790 he appeared in the Assembly to express quite revolutionary ideas in support of constitutional monarchy.[27] The letter he had Montmorin send out to French ambassadors abroad was an admirable summary of the constitutional monarchy: "The sovereign nation now has only citizens equal in rights, no other despot but the law, no agents but public servants *(fonctionnaires publics);* and the King is the first of them. Such is the French Revolution."[28] In the *Almanach royal* for 1790, the National Assembly, and the names of its officers, committees, and members, filled the twenty-four pages immediately after the clergy (pp. 125–49) which in 1789 had been taken up with the officers of a dozen royal households. The royal households were not listed because, according to a notice, the king intended to reorganize them, but they were not included in the volumes for 1791 and 1792 either. Louis XVI, by his complicity and hesitations, may almost be said to have abdicated.

The cause which gave the National Assembly its moral victory over the monarchy from 1789 to 1791 was not the republican democratic cause of 1792–94. Hardly anybody in 1789 thought of abolishing the monarchy or the nobility. In the early years the monarchy and royal authority had scarcely any opponents in the country at large, and as of old the National Assembly's opponents were thought to be the king's entourage, not the king himself.[29] The National Assembly's intention was "to settle the constitution of the kingdom, effect the regeneration of public order, and maintain the true principles of the monarchy," in the words of the Tennis Court Oath on 20 June. "The kingdom is one and indivisible," the Assembly declared in its constitution of 3 September 1791 (*titre* II, article 1). "I swear to be faithful to the Nation, to the Law and to the King . . ." began the oath required of all French citizens by that constitution (*titre* II, article 5). "The government is monarchical," began its article 4, *titre* III.

Its second chapter guaranteed and defined the monarchy in forty-five clauses under four heads: "Of Royalty and the King," "Of the Regency," "Of the King's Family," and "Of the Ministers." It began: "*La Royauté* is indivisible and hereditarily delegated to the reigning dynasty (race) from male to male by order of primogeniture, to the perpetual exclusion of women and their descendants. The king's person is inviolable and sacred; his only title is 'King of the French.' " The Assembly at Versailles, including hundreds of noblemen and clergymen, was disobedient but not disloyal.

They were, moreover, on the side of monarchy, law, and order when armed gangs burned down forty of the fifty-four customs posts at the Paris city gates on 11 and 13 July. These gangs were led, as Roger Dion's close historical study of the documents makes clear, by smugglers and wine merchants who stood to gain by the removal of the duties on wine entering the capital.* Other crowds with other motives began to roam about the city in violent mood. The National Assembly immediately drew up detailed plans for a citizens' militia and on 14 July was spurred on by the disturbing news, which it greeted "with a mournful silence," that a crowd of 800 or 900 civilians and soldiers had invaded the Invalides and then captured the Bastille. On 16 July it named its militia the National Guard and put it under the command of General Lafayette, the veteran of the American War, whereupon Louis XVI ordered the regiments of soldiers away from Paris and Versailles.

The mob that captured the Bastille had been moved by fear of troop movements rumored, perhaps rightly, to be against Paris, by anxiety over food shortages and unemployment, and by a characteristic angry violence that made it first seek weapons and then murder the governor and half a dozen guards of the Bastille, the chief of the provisional city government, and on 22 July

---

* These duties, the *droits d'entrée*, had been collected since 1785 at gates in a new wall the farmers general of taxes had been building around Paris. As each section of the wall was built, it became harder to smuggle wine and other goods into the city. Two smugglers, Monnier and Darbon, found it easy to whip up popular hostility against the duties, the clerks who collected them, and the wall. "At last we are going to drink wine at three sous," cried a typical workman. "We have been paying twelve sous for quite a long time!" (Roger Dion, *Histoire de la vigne et du vin en France des origines au XIXe siècle*, Paris, 1959, pp. 518–27.)

the royal minister Foulon and his son-in-law Berthier, the intendant of Paris. Rumors of these doings and of the troop movements reached peasants in the countryside a few days later and helped set off riots of panic and violence. These, collectively known as the "Great Fear," spread from village to village across the countryside in eight huge waves from about 20 July to about 6 August.[30] Seigneurial records were destroyed, some châteaus burned, a few landlords and their agents murdered. We know from the work of Georges Lefebvre (1874–1959) and George Rude (1910–) that these were spontaneous uprisings that sprang, like earlier peasant riots, from the nervous tension of a rural populace beset by hardship, anxiety, and rumors of brigands. But the National Assembly, the king, and the ministers all thought of them as the result of political agitation. A committee of investigation appointed by the Assembly on 28 July concluded that all this unrest was a result of royalist conspiracy.

Uprisings of the populace in town and country seemed to threaten the Assembly as well as the king. Two months later the crowds that went out to Versailles on the afternoon of 5 October burst into the Assembly chamber with hostile shouts at the clergy in particular.[31] Lafayette's 20,000 national guardsmen, with companies of soldiers and volunteers, who arrived late that night, were bent on fetching the Assembly as well as the royal family to Paris. Once again the royal guards and the Flanders Regiment stationed at Versailles to cope with such disorders might have been reinforced and firmly led, but Louis XVI still saw his predicament as a political one that did not call for a military solution.

The king and his ministers were not faced with a revolution that could be simply identified and put down. They were maneuvering amid a welter of different forces and parties. Those within the Assembly were the least dangerous and troublesome because their purposes were openly expressed in parliamentary debate. From late August until the move to Paris in early October, a committee of fifteen led by Malouet, Mounier, Lally-Tollendal, the bishop of Langres, and the Comte de Virieu drew together about half of the Third Estate deputies in a conservative group called first the *impartiaux* and then the *monarchiens*.[32] They shared a desire to establish a moderate constitutional monarchy. In the face of less conservative opposition, more than two dozen of them withdrew from the Assembly on 7 October and organized a political club early the next year.

Even the king had come to share the widespread faith in that philanthropic, liberal idealist Lafayette, "our Washington," as some called him. Louis XVI was pleased with the National Guard, which he inspected on 18 October at Lafayette's request. Lafayette remained loyal to the king as well as the Assembly and refused to use the national guardsmen, who all swore loyalty to him on 24 October, to achieve political objectives of his own or to destroy his opponents in the Assembly.[33] He was to be seen in such civic exercises as reviewing the National Guard on 25 April 1790 with the veteran Corsican patriot General Paoli and show- ing Paoli the Bastille in the course of demolition on 5 May. Lafayette was criticized by some of the more reform-minded deputies such as Mirabeau, Barnave, Pétion, Robespierre, Sieyès, Grègoire, and the Lameth brothers, Charles and Alexandre. But in 1789 and 1790 their activities were parliamentary and no threat to the monarchy.

The monarchy was to be undermined by activities of groups outside the Assembly, though the danger was scarcely visible in the early years. Lafayette kept abreast of conspiracies through a large and well-paid intelligence service but treated them with moderation. For governing authorities, the problem was to determine what was merely a normal part of the parliamentary process and what was subversive. There seemed little danger from the left-wing deputies who remained in the Breton Club after the move to Paris when it became the Society of the Friends of the Revolution and finally, in the course of 1790, the Jacobin Club. But the Jacobins became a party and even a movement by the constitution they adopted on 8 February 1790. That is, they began to form branches all over the kingdom by affiliating with a variety of literary, philanthropic, and fraternal societies turned political under the pressure of recent events. By the end of 1791 they were corresponding with more than 400 affiliated Jacobin clubs, and there were another 500 towns with unaffiliated clubs.[34] Long before then, in summer 1790, they had begun to respond to more radical leaders and to criticize and undermine more moderate clubs, such as the Société de 1789 formed in January by Lafayette, Sieyès, Mirabeau, Talleyrand, Brissot, Condorcet, and Le Chapelier.[35]

In 1789 and 1790 many elements in Paris were more radical than the Jacobin Club—that is, more hostile to the National Assembly, the Church, the monarchy, and authority in general. The 407 electors in the sixty electoral districts of Paris maintained a political activity never intended by the electoral law of 24 January 1789. Nor was political activity reduced by the law of 21 May 1790 that reorganized Paris in forty-eight sections. The assemblies of these sections, which first met on 1 July, were intended to elect the 148 members of the new municipal council, but they soon developed into centers of left-wing political activity. Already in January 1790 Danton was a leader in the Cordeliers district on the left bank and able to prevent the National Guard from arresting Marat on 7 January. Here the Cordeliers Club of the rue Dauphine was soon formed and rapidly assumed the leadership of Lafayette's opponents in July. In October 1790 Abbé Claude Fauchet opened another democratic club, Le cercle social, which attracted several thousand members.

Other dangers threatened from other quarters. Among them was the busy disruptive pressure of the king's cousin Philippe, Duc d'Orléans and his friends, who were using massive wealth, research, and propaganda for the purpose of forming public opinion and swaying public policy against Louis XVI.[36] Counterrevolutionary groups of noblemen more royalist than the king were meanwhile forming within and without the kingdom. Mounier, appalled at the power of the left once the Assembly moved to Paris, withdrew in autumn 1789 and began to organize opposition to the Assembly out in Dauphiné. Such counterrevolutionary activity was soon growing rapidly in defense of the Church, which was threatened earlier than the monarchy. A motion in the Assembly on 12 April 1790 to the effect that "it neither has, nor can have, any power over conscience or over religious opinion," which should remain free, was opposed by about one-quarter of the deputies (297 to 903), who thought the Roman Catholic Church should be declared the official state church.[37] Nearly 300 royalist and Catholic deputies assembled at the Capuchin Convent to declare their religion in danger. In the Vivarais, Catholic forces began to organize counterrevolution during the summer of 1790.

In Paris and all over France conflicts were flaring up in the absence of clear, firm political authority. Before the uneasy marriage of king and assembly could establish a united government, men all over France began fighting in the name of the one or the other.[38] First, in summer 1789 groups of men in all but two of the thirty biggest towns drove out the municipal governments and formed governing committees and branches of the National Guard.[39] Then the National Guard everywhere organized "federations" during the first half of 1790 and a great national celebration in Paris on 14 July. Part of the public supported these new authorities in the name of the revolutionary Third Estate, but another part stood by the old municipal authorities in the king's name. The army and even the National Guard were more and more paralyzed by uncertainty about who was their master.

Meanwhile, various groups began to graft their own immediate struggles onto this conflict. Soldiers in various regiments, thinking equality meant insubordination, began to work up a revolutionary cause against their officers, and at Nancy a noisy mutiny was crushed in August 1790 by a force under General Bouillé, Lafayette's cousin, in what Marat described as a "massacre." The Catholic municipal authorities in Montauban, Nîmes and Uzès organized a counterrevolutionary resistance to the national guardsmen who were mainly Protestants, now equal citizens very much in favor of the revolutionary expropriation of Church property and the Civil Constitution of the Clergy. Hundreds died in pitched battles on two Sundays, 2 May and 13 June 1790. In various country districts peasants rose up from time to time against seigneurial courts not really removed until after a decree of 16 August 1790 and payments not finally done away with until as late as 17 July 1793.[40] It was one thing, after all, for the National Assembly to abolish seigneurial dues in principle on 4 August 1789, but quite another to enforce that revolutionary principle across the kingdom. Most threatening of all, sections of the urban populace began to see a revolutionary cause of their own, a cause that some educated men, including a few deputies to the Assembly, found easy to idealize.

First in the Constituent Assembly to espouse the cause of the populace was Maximilien Robespierre, deputy for Arras, who in 1789 and early 1790 spoke with eloquence against the proposed royal veto of legislative decrees, against taxpaying as a qualification for political life, and against the use of military force to put down peasant uprisings in Quercy, Rouergue, Périgord, Bas-Limousin, and Basse-Bretagne.[41] On 1 July 1790 he spoke in favor of admitting a deputation of the Paris sections, on 23 October about the political rights of the poor, and on 5 December he tried to speak in favor of admitting all citizens, not merely the better off, to the National Guard. When silenced in the Assembly, he expressed his democratic principles in speeches to the Jacobin Club. Robespierre's courage and idealism found admirers on all sides, but the Assembly was against him in great majority. It was outside the Assembly that he gathered support, among the popular leaders in the forty-eight sections of Paris and among men of democratic principles in some of the clubs. The popular journalist Jean-Paul Marat declared him to be "the only deputy who appears aware of the great principles, and perhaps the only true patriot sitting in the Assembly."[42] Hébert, who long admired Mirabeau, Danton, and other radical leaders, later decided that Robespierre "alone remained in the breach to defend the rights of the people before the Constituent Assembly."[43] A few other rigorous democrats, notably Jérôme Pétion de Villeneuve, seconded Robespierre in delivering "the shocks of public spirit against private interests, of reason against prejudice, of modern truths against old practices."[44] Robespierre and his few friends in the Assembly were the idealistic parliamentary tip of a revolutionary movement growing among the Paris populace.

Here was the most dangerous of the forces that grew up in the benevolent, moderate atmosphere of a liberal Assembly. The driving force in it was politically active minorities in the Paris populace, which tended to be fitfully anxious, hungry, envious, violent, and vengeful. They were also gullible and easily led. And they had their press, as did all other groups in that tolerant, liberal kingdom. Jean-Paul Marat (1743–93), a medical doctor and writer who had traveled a good deal and lived in London as a young man, began to publish a popular journal, *L'ami du peu-*

ple, in September 1789. At first he wrote as a liberal monarch-ist.[45] Then, growing weary of parliamentary processes, Marat soon expressed a bitter, bloodthirsty violence against nearly all in authority and the ruling classes in general. His influential journal ran to 242 numbers and did not end until 14 July 1793, the day after he had been stabbed to death in his bathtub by an enterprising royalist girl, Charlotte Corday. From September 1790 Marat's journalism was matched in regular, bloodthirsty vio-lence by another popular journal, *Le Père Duchesne,* chiefly by Hébert and his collaborators. Hébert, in the guise of *le père* Duchesne, amused his readers with the bluff vulgarity of the ordinary workingman with his pipe, his bottle of wine, his fam-ily, and his anecdotes and obscene comments, often from the gallery of the National Assembly or the Jacobin Club. "My blood boils," he wrote on 28 November 1790, for instance. "Tell me, Frenchmen, is it possible? If that man you call the Holy Father takes it into his head to oppose your laws, do you dare, are you stupid and base enough, to give them up? What do you expect from a Pope? Screw the Pope, believe me; it is your turn at last; for ten centuries the Pope has screwed you" etc., etc.[46] These are only examples of the many left-wing journals and pamphlets of the time.

During 1790 and 1791 what might have been a moderate compromise developed into a deeper conflict. In February 1790 five *gabelle* collectors were lynched at Bèziers, and a military con-voy in Paris was pillaged and burned. On 30 April and 1 May 1790 rioters seized royal strongholds in Marseilles, killing a com-mander in the action. A mob nearly set fire to the conservative Salon français on 14 May 1790, and the police drove it under-ground by closing it down the next day.[47] On 28 February 1791, 1,000 workingmen from the faubourg Saint-Antoine under Antoine-Joseph Santerre tried to demolish the Château de Vin-cennes before it could be turned into a prison but were stopped by 1,200 troops under Lafayette. Violent crime, traditional and eternal among the populace, was more and more being justified by invoking revolutionary motives.

Ideological excuses for violence, which lie at the roots of modern terrorism, were already tending to demoralize the forces of law and order in 1790 and 1791. In a demonstration at the place Vendôme, on 24 June 1791, there were calls for a republic. The victorious Third Estate was breaking down in internal quarrels. The constitutional monarchists and the revolutionary democrats were drawing farther apart, and this antagonism became an open conflict in the course of 1791. Unemployment rose in 1791 until by June there were as many as 31,000 in the public workshops (*ateliers de charité*) where a subsistence wage of twenty sous a day was paid.[48] But in mid-June the Assembly decided to close these workshops because they seemed to concentrate the unemployed dangerously. Petitions to the Assembly were drafted: one on 28 June; another on 3 July drawn up by Camille Desmoulins in the name of the Bastille Workers; another by the Cordeliers Club on the fateful 17 July. Journeymen in various trades, encouraged by revolutionary democrats, were pressing for higher wages. Tension mounted.

Meanwhile, on 11 March and 13 April 1791, Pope Pius VI denounced the revolution in general and the Civil Constitution of the Clergy in particular, and he naturally stood behind the hostile Declaration of Pillnitz issued by the Habsburg emperor on 27 August. Two months earlier, on the night of 20–21 June, the royal family had set out secretly in a coach toward the northeastern frontier. They were recognized the next day by a postmaster in the small town of Varennes and brought back ignominiously by local national guardsmen. After that the revolutionary republican movement grew very quickly, and the constitutional monarchists were more and more demoralized. The regime defended itself, however, long enough to finish and implement the new constitution in September. On 16 July the 2,400 members of the Paris Jacobin Club split when about 1,000 constitutional monarchists, the so-called Feuillants, including more than 300 deputies, left to join Lafayette and the remains of the old Society of 1789.[49] The tensions of 1791 reached a climax the next day, on 17 July.

The Feuillants had quit the Jacobin Club in protest against the majority's sympathy for the revolutionary democratic cause and its hostility to the monarchy. So apprehensive were the constitutional monarchists that on the following day about 10,000 national guardsmen clashed with a relatively peaceful demonstration of 50,000 people who gathered on the Champ-de-Mars to sign a petition under the leadership of revolutionary clubs and societies. Many of the crowd were arrested, about 50 were killed, and a dozen wounded in what was later called the "massacre of the Champ-de-Mars." During the months before and after this event, the police arrested another 250 people in the various Paris sections for incendiary remarks about the regime or men in it.[50] Thus did the regime maintain law and order in the capital, in the short term at least. Calm reigned on 3 September, when the Assembly approved the final draft of the new constitution, and on 14 September, when Louis XVI approved it. In the elections for the new Legislative Assembly, none of the Constituents stood for election, according to a self-denying decree of 16 May 1791, but a body of very similar men was elected. A constitutional monarchy had been established before the National Constituent Assembly disbanded on 30 September. It might have endured like the Constitution of the United States, but it did not. A second wave of revolutionary force swept it away in less than a year.

SEVEN *1792: War and the Monarchy's Fall*

MORE than two and a half years of liberal government followed the revolution of the Third Estate in June 1789. A majority of the men in the Constituent and Legislative assemblies believed in government by free debate in public meetings, and they were not inclined to silence criticism or to censure heretical opinions expressed in the journals and club meetings of their enemies. People were punished for violent acts but seldom for violent views. Louis XVI and his ministers, falling easily into step with this moderate form of government, rarely banished the writers of inflammatory or threatening tracts. An atmosphere of political and religious tolerance prevailed. The principal threats to it came from counter-revolutionary nobles and clergy, who would have liked to restore absolute monarchy and established Church, and from groups of the populace that had little regard for freedom as it provided neither food nor employment. Nor did the government even remove feudal dues and other tax burdens at first.

The National Assembly did not speak for all Frenchmen but only for a certain public. Its gospel did not appeal to the dispossessed noblemen and clergy, some of whom schemed to destroy the Assembly and to restore the old order of things. For example, agents of Lafayette and the Comité des recherches at the Hôtel de Ville discovered in December 1789 that a certain minor nobleman, Thomas de Mahy, Marquis de Favras, was raising large sums in Paris for the Comte de Provence and (they concluded) was plotting to murder Necker, Bailly, and Lafayette and to have

troops take the king away from Paris.[1] The agitation in Paris that
resulted from this discovery was not calmed by the Comte de
Provence's efforts to clear himself in a special meeting of the
municipal council at the end of December. The Châtelet criminal court on 17 February 1790 declared Favras guilty of counterrevolutionary conspiracy and had him publicly hanged two
days later. Nor did the gospel of the Third Estate appeal to the
masses, rural or urban, which were inevitably sunk in poverty,
insecurity, and anxiety. Many enemies took advantage of the new
liberty to threaten the government that stood behind it. Radical
leaders and inflammatory journalists like Marat, Danton, and
others in the Cordeliers Section of Paris soon learned to manip-
ulate a popular following hostile to the regime. During the year
1792 the government fell victim to violent crowds of the populace, but not before it had gone to war against the powers that
seemed to threaten it from abroad.

I. A Revolutionary Crusade

When on 20 April 1792 the king and the Legislative Assembly
declared war on the Habsburg emperor supported by the King
of Prussia, they were acting contrary to the spirit of the constitution, if not to its letter. In the constitution the National Assembly and the king, summarizing a decree of 22 May 1790, had
declared, "The French Nation will undertake no war for conquest and will never use its forces against the liberty of any people." The government repeated this principle in its declaration
of war and went on to explain that "the war which it is obliged
to wage is not a war of nation against nation, but the just defense
of a free people against the unjust aggression of a king."[2] To
this, the leader of the war party in the Assembly, Jacques-Pierre
Brissot de Warville, added in a major speech, "The moment has
come for a new crusade, a crusade for universal liberty."[3] The
ambiguity in these doctrinaire phrases was part and parcel of
the French Revolution. "Hate war; it is the greatest crime of
mankind, and the most fearful scourge of mankind," Pierre-Victurnien Vergniaud said to the Assembly in one of his bellicose
speeches.[4] "It was in detesting war that I voted for its declara-

tion," Condorcet afterward declared.[5] Twenty years later, after France had conquered all of continental Europe, the "first representative of the nation" was still praising peace and liberty. "Nobody loves peace more than I do," Napoleon wrote to Cambacérès in 1813.[6] Behind their ideological mask, Brissot and his friends in the Legislative Assembly were just as aggressive in 1792 as Napoleon in 1813. Even that lover of mankind, the friend of black slaves, Abbé Henri-Baptiste Grégoire, recommended the annexation of Savoy and helped to carry it out there as a representative of the National Convention.[7]

The warlike policy of the Brissotins is not easy to account for. Its first and strongest proponents were Brissot himself, a clever but shallow journalist from a humble family of Chartres, who had traveled a good deal and in 1791 secured his election in Paris; the voluble and emotional Henri-Maximin Isnard, from a prosperous merchant family, elected for the Var Department in the extreme southeast; and Jean-Louis Carra, editor of *Les annales patriotiques et littéraire,* formerly a librarian and archivist. Brissot and Carra had a record of fascination with novel causes: mesmerism and attacks on the academic establishment in the early 1780s; the antislavery movement in 1788 when they founded the Amis des noirs with Abbé Grégoire, Étienne Clavière, and a few others, and the causes of foreign political exiles.[8] Clavière was one of these, from Geneva, anxious to attack the regime that had driven him from his homeland, and another was the cosmopolitan banker Anacharsis Cloots from the Prussian Rhineland, who dreamed of a universal republic. Dutch exiles, too, who came to France in thousands, influenced Brissot and his friends. They were steeped in the humane and democratic ideals of literary circles, such as the salon of Madame Roland, wife of the inspector of manufactures who was to serve in 1791 and 1792 as minister of the interior with Brissot in support.

When they first began to make bellicose speeches, in September and October 1791, they were anxious to assume the leadership of the newly elected Legislative Assembly and to undermine the political influence of rival groups. The strongest of these in the Assembly were the Feuillant constitutional monarchists, some 300 in number then, and the strongest outside the Assembly were such radical groups as those led by Robespierre and Pétion de

Villeneuve in the Jacobin Club and by Danton, Marat, and the more obscure leaders of the Cordeliers Club. A war might draw such groups into a common cause. Most of all, Brissot, Carra, and Isnard were able to persuade more cautious men in Paris and in provincial Jacobin clubs that only an aggressive foreign policy would destroy counterrevolutionary forces in France and abroad. Vergniaud, a captain in a National Guard regiment at Bordeaux, Gensonné, a lieutenant in another, Condorcet, Guadet, Fauchet, and others little by little came around to the war party.[9] Many did so, like Condorcet, out of indignation at the king's flight to Varennes.[10]

They were also responding to the threat of hostile forces abroad.[11] Being inexperienced in foreign affairs, they misjudged these forces and exaggerated their threatening aspect. Being revolutionary idealists, they were filled with self-righteous fury. That the papacy might resent the confiscation of Church property, the Civil Constitution of the Clergy, the occupation of Avignon and Venaissin on 12 July 1790, their formal annexation on 13 September 1791, and the massacre of sixty "counterrevolutionaries" in one of the towers of the papal palace there on 17 October did not trouble them. That German princes might resent losing their domains in France on the principle of the "sacred and inalienable rights of nations" did not interest them. That the Belgian people might not care to be liberated, even though a "United Belgian Estates" declared itself on 7 January 1790, was a possibility that occurred only to Robespierre and a few others. That Emperor Leopold II (1790–92) of Austria and King Frederick William II (1786–97) of Prussia might not act upon their joint Declaration of Pillnitz (27 August 1791) against France did not occur to the Brissotins. But in fact, Prussian policy was focused on Poland at the time, and Prussian armies made a poor showing in the eventual war with France. Leopold was naturally concerned for his sister Marie-Antoinette but was content with a passive "concert of observation" once Louis XVI had accepted the constitution on 27 September 1791. The Austro-Prussian alliance of 7 February 1792 was merely defensive, because Leopold and his minister, Prince Kaunitz, would not interfere in France unless all the major powers joined them first. By the time Leopold died on 1 March 1792, and the less cautious

Francis II (1792–1806) ascended the imperial throne, the French government had already decided upon a war. The British government had meanwhile remained firmly neutral, steadfastly ignoring all the efforts of Calonne, Dillon, and other émigrés to draw them into conflict with the French government. There were no British efforts at this time to rouse counterrevolutionary forces in France, but war was encouraged by a general belief in France, among royalists and revolutionaries alike, that the British government was spending money on a large scale for the purpose of stirring up revolt.[12]

The war when it came was as much against French émigrés as against the rulers who gave them shelter. At every stage in the Revolution Frenchmen fled abroad for various reasons. Much the greatest number of them were commoners, as might be expected, many of them quite humble folk, but it is the noble and clerical émigrés who have always been remembered for their counterrevolutionary activities.[13] The controller general of finances Calonne had fled to England as early as 1787 to escape prosecution by the Parlement of Paris. When the king's younger brother, the Comte d'Artois, the future Charles X (1824–30), fled to Vienna in 1789, Calonne, having failed to influence the British government, became his political adviser, and these two were at Pillnitz when the famous declaration was signed there.[14] Meanwhile, the Duc de Condé had begun as early as 1789 to raise an émigré force at Turin, where he was joined by the Comte de Maillebois in March 1790. The fascinating Comte d'Antraigues had emigrated on 2 February 1790 to Switzerland, where he soon began to preside over an extensive intelligence network more hostile to Louis XVI than to the émigré princes.[15]

Waves of emigration followed the dramatic fetching of the royal family to Paris on 5–6 October 1789 and their forced return there from Varennes on 21 June 1791. Another wave followed the king's endorsement of the constitution on 27 September 1791. Already many bishops and clergy had emigrated, especially after the election of new bishops in spring 1791 to replace the 135 who had refused the oath. At Coblenz the royal princes set up their headquarters and began to organize their propaganda, their forces, and their intelligence services. At Venice, Vienna, and London émigrés gathered and plotted. They were divided into various conflicting groups but had certain policies in common. Most were opposed to the Franco-Austrian alliance that since 1756 had interrupted the traditional struggle of Bourbons and Habsburgs, brought Marie-Antoinette to the French court, and led (in their view) to many of the kingdom's ills.[16] Most wanted war in the expectation that the European powers would defeat the French forces and end the revolutionary episode. Similar expectations induced royalist forces within France to promote war also.

Among these were counterrevolutionary movements such as the Salon français, which worked openly in 1789 and 1790, and then secretly, to gather information and to plan royalist uprisings, escape routes for the royal family, and the coordination of forces at home and abroad. In a gathering at the Château de Jalès in the Vivarais on 18 August 1790, some 20,000 national guardsmen pledged themselves to restore the monarchy and the Church. In January 1792 royalist insurrection broke out in the Massif Central, in the Ardèche, in Roussillon, in Provence, and near Lyons.[17] Many conspirators glimpsed, half known or half suspected, in revolutionary circles seemed more numerous and dangerous than in fact they were. The royal family, more and more suspected of collaborating with counterrevolutionaries at home and abroad, seemed to justify such suspicions by its efforts to leave the country in June 1791. An "Austrian Committee" led by Baron de Breteuil was said to be calling on the queen's many crowned relatives for assistance. The Brissotins, or Girondins as they came to be called, persuaded a large following that war would unite the country and force king and court to come out into the open and declare themselves. The Assembly struck at the émigrés with more and more decrees: that those who joined in conspiracies would be condemned to death and their property confiscated (3 October 1791); that the king ask the princes of the empire to put an end to émigré armies and gatherings (29 November 1791); and suchlike.

The radical clubs, especially the Jacobins, were divided on the issue of war. Robespierre was by no means alone there in his antiwar campaign. Only three of the forty-eight Paris sections were in favor of it. Hébert's *Le Père Duchesne* and Marat's *L'ami du peuple* treated the prospect of a war with much less belliger-

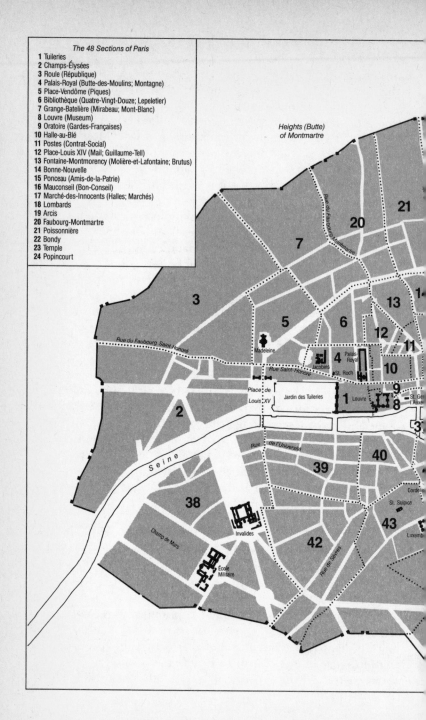

The 48 Sections of Paris
1 Tuileries
2 Champs-Élysées
3 Roule (République)
4 Palais-Royal (Butte-des-Moulins; Montagne)
5 Place-Vendôme (Piques)
6 Bibliothèque (Quatre-Vingt-Douze; Lepeletier)
7 Grange-Batelière (Mirabeau; Mont-Blanc)
8 Louvre (Museum)
9 Oratoire (Gardes-Françaises)
10 Halle-au-Blé
11 Postes (Contrat-Social)
12 Place-Louis XIV (Mail; Guillaume-Tell)
13 Fontaine-Montmorency (Molière-et-Lafontaine; Brutus)
14 Bonne-Nouvelle
15 Ponceau (Amis-de-la-Patrie)
16 Mauconseil (Bon-Conseil)
17 Marché-des-Innocents (Halles; Marchés)
18 Lombards
19 Arcis
20 Faubourg-Montmartre
21 Poissonnière
22 Bondy
23 Temple
24 Popincourt

Heights (Butte) of Montmartre

The 48 Sections of Paris (continued)

25 Montreuil
26 Quinze-Vingts
27 Gravilliers
28 Faubourg-Saint-Denis (Faubourg-du-Nord)
29 Beaubourg (Réunion)
30 Enfants-Rouges (Marais; Homme-Armé)
31 Roi-de-Sicile (Droits-de-l'Homme)
32 Hôtel-de-Ville (Maison-Commune; Fidelité)
33 Place-Royale (Fédérés; Indivisibilité)
34 Arsenal
35 Île-Saint-Louis (Fraternité)
36 Notre-Dame (Île; Cité; Raison)
37 Henri-IV (Pont-Neuf; Révolutionnaire)
38 Invalides
39 Fontaine-de-Grenelle
40 Quatre-Nations (Unité)
41 Théâtre-Français (Marseille-et-Marat; Marat)
42 Croix-Rouge (Bonnet-Rouge; Bonnet-de-la-Liberté; Ouest)
43 Luxembourg (Mutius-Scoevola)
44 Thermes-de-Julien (Beaurepaire; Chalier)
45 Sainte-Geneviève (Panthéon-Français)
46 Observatoire
47 Jardin-des-Plantes (Sans-Culottes)
48 Gobelins (Finistère)

Heights (Butte) of Belleville

The Forty-Eight
Sections of Paris

For details of changes in the sections, see Albert Soboul,
Les sans-culottes en l'an II, Paris, 1958, pp. 1067–76.

ence than they were accustomed to treating most other events.[18] Once war was declared, however, it was not long before these elements—even Robespierre—came to see it as a crusade against enemies of the Revolution within and without.

King, court, and ministers for their part hoped, even expected to recover their authority either at the hands of victorious foreign armies or at the head of victorious French ones. Accordingly, Louis XVI went along with the majority led by the Brissotin war party. He appointed Louis, Comte de Narbonne-Lara minister of war on 7 December 1791 to make preparations for a spring campaign. By the time Narbonne was dismissed early in March 1792 all seemed ready and three generals were put in charge of the armies; two of them, Rochambeau and Lafayette, were heroes of the American War of Independence. War was declared in April by a ministry composed of Dumouriez, an excellent general whose victories late in 1792 are usually forgotten because of his defection on 5 April 1793, Jean-Marie Roland at the Ministry of the Interior, Étienne Clavière, and other Brissotins.

The professional French Army was only a remnant, having lost most of its officers and its foreign regiments.[19] As it crumbled, however, the National Constituent Assembly had called for volunteers for the nation's defense on much the same principle that had given rise to the National Guard, and to include, indeed, a proportion of national guardsmen. Decrees of June 1791 provided for "battalions of national volunteers" to be raised in each department, equipped and employed as part of the regular army, but commanded by their own elected officers. More than 100,000 of these in 169 battalions had been provided for by the time the Declaration of Pillnitz was made on 27 August 1791. The obvious faults of these volunteers—inexperience, lax discipline, an inclination to go home at every opportunity—were matched by some qualities that were unexpected by eighteenth-century Europeans, who were accustomed to mercenary armies of poor or foreign soldiers indifferent to the cause for which they were fighting. Dressed in uniforms of red, white, and blue, the *tricolore* adopted by the National Assembly in 1789, and drawn from the active citizens of the public, these volunteers were easily inspired by the national cause. Even when volunteers were raised among the passive citizens after the war had begun, their quality was excellent compared with the usual rabble of the eighteenth-century army.

Vast numbers of them could be raised in a country as populous as France. After a little trial and error the generals found them useful as a mass advancing over the battlefield with fixed bayonets. They made a reputation at the Battle of Valmy (20 September 1792) where thirty of their battalions proved themselves in service with forty-four battalions of professional troops.[20] They tended, furthermore, to undermine enemy morale by preaching a revolutionary cause that appealed to any group that could interpret its own desires as rights to be claimed in the name of liberty and equality from whatever "tyrants" were denying them. Once volunteer battalions had been integrated into the army as a regular part of it, by decrees of 21 February 1793 and the efforts of Saint-Just, France was equipped with the first national army in Europe. From this army's first invasion of the Austrian Netherlands in April 1792, it served as the instrument of a revolutionary crusade to impose French ideas and French authority on the rest of the world.

The war was seen from the first as a crusade against enemies within and without and a way of unmasking traitors. As a result, treachery was suspected in every authority, plots behind every setback. The day before war was declared, Lazare Carnot, then a young career officer, predicted treason among the generals. Before the victories of autumn 1792, several months of defeat provoked fear, anger, and revenge, particularly among the active revolutionary minorities. Almost immediately on 28 March 1792 Théodore Dillon, an officer in charge of a detachment sent from Lille to retake Tournai, was slaughtered and mutilated by his own troops while they were trampling one another to death in a retreating panic.[21] Biron at Mons, Riccé at Tiercelet, also suffered defeat and the hostility of their own troops. Émigré groups abroad and counterrevolutionary journals at home did not conceal their satisfaction at French reverses. Other newspapers denounced treachery everywhere, but especially an "Austrian conspiracy" at court that was said to embrace ministers, moderates, deputies, noblemen, and the royal family. Robespierre at the Jacobin Club denounced Lafayette and the ministers as traitors.[22]

At the end of June, when the country seemed threatened, Carnot urged the Assembly to issue pikes to the Paris populace for national defense, and on 1 August municipalities were authorized to see to their manufacture and distribution. On 5 July the Assembly had issued a decree of general mobilization with the famous words *"Citoyens, la patrie est en danger,"* and the next day a British embassy dispatch to London reported, "We are on the eve of a great crisis. . . ."[23] On 9 and 11 July Robespierre made alarming speeches, echoing earlier reports from Rouen, about *la patrie en danger* not only from foreign enemies but from conspiracies at court and among the generals. The Assembly published a decree calling for emergency measures. On 28 July Louis XVI received a manifesto from the Duke of Brunswick, commander in chief of the Austro-Prussian forces, threatening Paris and Parisians with savage punishments; the king published this on 3 August. Prussian forces crossed into France on 16 August, Austrian forces on 19 August. The fortress of Longwy fell to them on 20 August, Verdun on 2 September. Only feeble defenses on the Aisne and Marne rivers stood between the invaders and Paris. Already, on 10 August, a coalition of the Paris sections and the *fédérés* from the provinces had invaded the Tuileries, arrested the royal family, and proclaimed France a republic. It was the republic that was to turn defeat into victory and to proceed to the conquest and annexation of Savoy, Belgium, the Rhineland, and the county of Nice, before the end of the year.

II. The End of Liberal Government

The revolution of 10 August 1792, which brought down the constitutional monarchy, was not merely an advanced stage of the Revolution that had broken out in June 1789. It was quite different and brought changes as profound in their way as those of June 1789. Small groups of radical leaders came to the fore with the vigorous support of the populace. Their intention was to found a democratic republic that would express the revolutionary principles of unity, liberty, equality, and fraternity and would mobilize the nation to fight its enemies at home and abroad. To the democratic leaders the constitutional regime was failing in these tasks because it represented the social hierarchy of those loyal to the monarchy rather than to the nation. And the monarchy seemed ready to betray the nation for the sake of ancient dynastic links with foreign rulers. Accordingly, the new regime launched campaigns to destroy a wide range of enemies and suspects: monarchists, constitutionalists, members of the Feuillant Club, moderates, and nonjuring priests. The climate of fear, suspicion, and violent death created by the men of 10 August and their popular support was fundamentally different from the political climate of the constitutional monarchy. The republic continued to live, as it was born, by fear and violence. It succeeded in turning back the foreign armies and bringing victory out of defeat, but only at great cost. The liberal government for which the men of 1789 had struggled died a violent death.

The constitutional monarchy when it fell was in part a victim of its own benevolent weakness, like the absolute monarchy before it. As every military officer knows, a habit of impunity is fatal to law and order. General Lafayette knew this, of course. When in October 1789 a mob took Denis François, a baker and national guardsman of the Notre-Dame district, hanged him for hoarding, and paraded his head about on a pike, Lafayette proposed a law against riots and a tribunal to judge cases of *lèse majesté*—that is, of people taking the law into their own hands.[24] The Assembly passed a new riot act on 21 October, and the next day martial law was declared, the man who had hacked off François's head was banished for nine years, 2 men who had incited the riot and led in the killing were hanged, and later nearly 200 officers and men of the National Guard were dismissed for not protecting François.

Unfortunately the constitutional regime did not maintain this vigorous defense of law and order. On 21–24 May 1790 the National Guard rescued a man whom a mob was trying to lynch for trampling on a *tricolore* flag but failed to rescue two others, who were consequently lynched, and a third, who was stoned to death. On 25 May another mob overwhelmed the National Guard on the quai de la Feraille and lynched someone they called a "hoarder." Early in the events at the Champ-de-Mars on 17 July 1791 bystanders lynched two men before the National Guard could intervene.[25] There were many other such incidents. After the *journée* of 20 June 1792, Lafayette rode back to Paris from his frontier command and pleaded with the Assembly to seize and punish the leaders for their violent invasion of the Tuileries, but no will to do this remained. As the American ambassador observed, the municipal and departmental authorities whose business it was to defend the civil order were "too weak to resist the demonstrators."[26] Meanwhile, the National Assembly had likewise failed to maintain discipline and morale in the army, the principal force for law and order. The army had already fallen a prey to ideological quarrels between officers loyal to the monarchy and groups of men won over to the republican democratic cause.[27]

A small measure of popular democratic ruthlessness might have sufficed to defend the monarchy against the left-wing movement its own ideals obliged it to tolerate. Did not this very thought, indeed, occur to later generations of liberals, the men of the Second Republic when they crushed a similar movement in June 1848 and the men of the future Third Republic when they ruthlessly crushed another in May 1871?[28] But the men of 1789–92 had a different past. They had no history of law and order to guide them except the history of the "tyrannical" absolute monarchy they had just overthrown. They saw the threat of popular tyranny through a haze of their own revolutionary sentiments. In July 1791, when the National Guard, not yet well trained in crowd control, killed or wounded 50 people in its efforts to control some 50,000 on the Champ-de-Mars, the government that let itself be shamed by this "massacre" could not foresee a republican-democratic massacre of hundreds on 10 August 1792, of more than 1,000 the following September, and of many thousands in 1793 and 1794.[29] The mayor and the police did try to maintain order in 1791 by evicting the Cordeliers Club on 11 May and arresting 200 or 300 demonstrators that spring. But the National Assembly that released them in a general amnesty on 13 September 1791 could not foresee that after 10 August 1792 there would be no amnesty for the hundreds of their own

members being hunted down as Feuillants, moderates, or royalists. The insurgents of 10 August were free to prepare their
revolution in a liberal atmosphere which they destroyed the
moment they seized power.

The constitutional monarchy was compromised, too, by the
equivocation of the royal family and then by its outright treachery.[30] Louis XVI might have survived public hostility toward
ministers at court, such as Breteuil, Montmorin, and Bertrand
de Molleville, for opposing the constitution out of a desire to
return to absolute monarchy. In 1790 even the Jacobin clubs still
held to the ancient principle that bad ministers were to blame
for bad royal policies, and the king, forever good, might be a
victim no less than the nation.[31] The Constituent Assembly sang
frequent Te Deums for the king's health. Louis XVI might even
have survived public hostility to the queen's foolish intrigues with
Mirabeau, Mercy d'Argenteau, and the Austrian court and her
intrigues against Lafayette, the émigré princes, and many more.
"Foreign queens have always favored the people of their native
lands," the Jacobins of Marseilles reflected in January 1791, and
in future kings should be required to marry Frenchwomen.[32]
What Louis XVI could not survive was public knowledge of his
own intrigues with national enemies, especially Leopold II of
Austria, and his sympathy with emigrant nobles and nonjuring
priests. He did the monarchy no good when he vetoed a legislative decree of 31 October 1791 against émigrés and another of
29 November enforcing the Civil Constitution of the Clergy.[33]
By then he had already shocked public opinion in general and
demoralized constitutional monarchists in particular by trying to
emigrate in secret with other members of the royal family on the
fatal night of 20–21 June 1791.

French history might have turned out differently if they had
not been recognized in their coach by the postmaster at the little
town of Varennes, a few miles from the frontier, and escorted
back to Paris by local battalions of the National Guard.[34] They
were caught only by chance; on the same night Louis's eldest
brother, the Comte de Provence, the future Louis XVIII, got
away to Belgium with his family under an assumed name. As it
turned out, the "flight to Varennes" did incalculable harm to the
constitution by losing many of its supporters and discouraging

others. The general public was, like Condorcet, thunderstruck. Jacobin clubs all over France were shocked and dismayed. The National Assembly formally pardoned Louis XVI on 15–16 July, but when he appeared in the chamber on 14 September, the deputies remained seated and did not remove their hats. The compromise on which the constitution was being based had suddenly crumbled. The monarchy had lost its great binding force, and the Patriots of 1789 soon felt more and more driven to choose between the old absolute regime dear to the royalists and the republic which now, suddenly, appeared on the scene as a real possibility. Faced with this prospect, about 300 monarchists, *monarchiens,* and constitutionalists formally withdrew from the Jacobin Club on 16 July 1791 to form their own Feuillant Club. In the Constituent Assembly and its successor, the Legislative Assembly, elected in September, the same group drew together to form a conservative right wing. The king went on trying to behave like a constitutional monarch, but no one was reassured by tactical statements such as his description of himself, in sanctioning a decree on the military emergency (*la patrie en danger,* 11 July 1792), as "a king proud to command a free people."[35] The flight to Varennes was a political turning point. To it more than to any other single event may be traced the developments leading to the revolution of 10 August 1792 and the king's execution on 21 January 1793.

The republican movement, as distinct from a few scattered republican thinkers, began after the flight to Varennes, but the democratic movement on which it was grafted had begun earlier. In Paris—and it was the Paris movement that counted—a vigorous political life had sprung up in the sixty electoral districts created for the primary elections to the Third Estate in April 1789.[36] Independent of central control from the first, these districts refused to dissolve after the elections, and some of them continued to take an interest in public events under middle-class leaders with democratic ideas. Here is where George-Jacques Danton, Jean-Paul Marat, Camille Desmoulins, François Robert, and many other leaders and journalists got their start in politics. Even the future communist from Picardy François-Noel ("Gracchus") Babeuf, in jail as usual, played a part through his *Journal de la confédération,* which Marat smuggled out of jail for him.

Some of these leaders were also members of the Jacobin Club, which became a revolutionary democratic center under Robespierre and Pétion after the Feuillant moderates left in July 1791. Their following before 10 August 1792 was relatively small, not more than 2,000 or 3,000 in all, but among them were a good many shopkeepers and tradesmen, the future *sans-culottes*. In spring 1790 they agitated and petitioned in favor of a system of democratic local self-government for Paris. On 21 May 1790 the National Assembly adopted instead a representative system with a restricted franchise, the famous distinction between active and passive citizens, and abolished the sixty districts in favor of forty-eight sections. In response to this challenge, the democratic leaders were able to adapt their political life by organizing popular societies. In April the Cordeliers district on the left bank, now absorbed into the Théâtre-français Section formed the Cordeliers Club, which was to be a center of democratic revolutionary activity during the next few years. More than a score of other popular societies had formed by the summer of 1792 and had infiltrated about one-third of the forty-eight sections.

The flight to Varennes made this movement republican as well as democratic, revolutionary on both counts. To this movement the war brought popular support in several ways. Government spending in the form of the paper *assignats* was already causing inflation in the winter of 1791–92, and the war made it worse.[37] Food became scarcer and more expensive. Hoarding and speculating, denounced in sermons and at section meetings (often in churches) by such men as the *enragé* priest Jacques Roux, aroused much popular indignation. Soldiers for the battlefronts were levied among the passive citizens, who were thereby drawn into the arena of public affairs. In the summer a fear of invasion by the Austrian and Prussian armies had a tonic effect on popular opinion. One popular society began to agitate as early as January 1792 for the arming of all citizens with pikes, and by the summer the feminists Anne-Pauline Léon and Théroigne de Méricourt were talking of arming contingents of women volunteers.[38] Most of all, the struggle against foreign enemies without led directly to a struggle against enemy sympathizers within. The war abroad was soon matched by a civil war in which the urban populace mobilized by democratic leaders did not always distinguish its political opponents from enemy sympathizers.

Republican democratic groups began to press the regime in summer 1792 with petitions and demonstrations on various issues. On 20 June, the third anniversary of the Tennis Court Oath, some 10,000 citizens from the Gobelins, Quinze-vingts, and Popincourt sections gathered under such leaders as the brewer Santerre, the postal clerk Varlet, the butcher Legendre, the journalist Robert, and others from the Cordeliers Club to submit a petition to the Legislative Assembly for the recall of Clavière, Roland, and Servan, the radical ministers whom the court had dismissed. In the afternoon and evening a large number broke into the Tuileries Palace and filed through the royal apartments, shouting slogans and jostling the king and queen. "The constitution has this day, I think, given its last groan," the American ambassador wrote to Lord George Gordon.[39] An official inquiry seemed to show that the mayor, Pétion, and his chief officer, Manuel, had not done their duty in keeping order, but when the Paris Department suspended them on 7 July, this was an excuse for another agitation.

Events followed in quick succession.[40] On 27 July a Central Correspondence Bureau was set up to unite the forty-eight sections. On 30 July the radical Théâtre-français Section published a manifesto, drafted by Danton, the journalist Chaumette, and the printer Momoro, abolishing the distinction between active and passive citizens. Other sections soon followed suit. A sudden massive influx of passive citizens began to overcome the moderating influence of cautious majorities in some sections. Meanwhile, during that month hundreds of *fédérés* volunteers had come to the capital for celebrations planned for 14 July. Notable were a large contingent from Brest and about 500 from Marseilles who arrived singing their new war song, "La Marseillaise," too late for the celebrations but in time for the struggle that followed the Mauconseil Section's resolution of 31 July calling for the removal of the king. On 5 August Varlet put before the Assembly a petition, covered with signatures and the X marks of the illiterate. Its twelve points nicely drew together the objectives of the coming revolution: a democratic republic for the purpose of making a more vigorous war effort, of impeaching Lafayette, of replacing all nobles in civil or military posts, and of suppressing speculators, hoarders, and counterrevolutionaries.

Although the summer of 1792 was filled with anxiety and tension, the revolution of 10 August was no spontaneous upsurge of an indignant people. An attack on the governing authorities, the court, and the Legislative Assembly was planned and openly prepared by leaders of the clubs, the popular societies, the Paris sections, and the visiting *fédérés*. A secret directory of the Jacobin Club, with sixteen members, including leaders later to be cast out as "Girondins," worked to bring down the constitutional monarchy. They counted on the support of the *fédérés* from the provinces invited for the 14 July celebrations. Robespierre harangued them on 11 July in a famous speech about *la patrie en danger* and persuaded them to stay for revolutionary purposes. In a room at the Jacobin Club on rue Saint-Honoré, the *fédérés* formed a central committee of forty-three with a five-man secret directory that was preparing an insurrection by 4 August, if not earlier.

On the night of 5 August the Marseillais took up billets in the Théâtre-français Section near the Cordeliers Club, with which they already had an understanding. The police administrators, Danton's friends Étienne-Jean Panis and François Sergent, were already giving out weapons and ammunition to the *fédérés* and the sections. The Théâtre-français Section thought of calling for an uprising as early as 8 August. Already the Quinze-vingts Section had resolved on 4 and 7 August that if the Legislative Assembly did not suspend the king by Thursday, 9 August, it would call for collective action, and it had invited other sections to send representatives for this purpose. About 11:00 P.M. on 9 August, the Quinze-vingts resolved that each section should name three delegates to meet at the Hôtel de Ville to take measures *sauver la patrie*. At least thirteen other sections agreed to this immediately, and by midnight a total of thirty were collaborating. As a result, a revolutionary municipal assembly was formed on 10 August by these section delegates together with such members of the former Assembly as remained. The 288 men of this commune were destined to have decisive influence in the government of France until 1 December. And the men who then took office after the election of November were no different in character or influence.

The Quinze-vingts plan in early August 1792 was soon supported by large contingents of the *fédérés* and the National Guard. On 10 August a retired military officer from Alsace, François-Joseph Westermann (1751–94), who had come to Paris in May and joined Danton, put himself at the head of the *fédérés* from Brest to lead the attack on the Tuileries together with the colonial planter, Claude Fournier *l'américain* (1745–1825) and various leaders from the sections such as Charles-Alexis Alexandre, a former *agent de change*. The National Guard was ostensibly one of the principal forces for law and order, but it appears that many of its battalions had lately been won over to the revolutionary cause by propaganda and an influx of passive citizens. The National Guard had originally been organized in battalions based on the forty-eight sections but was soon removed from section control by the strong central command organized by Lafayette. At the same time it had been restricted to active citizens. This arrangement changed in July and early August 1792, when the democratic movement to admit passive citizens to the sections led to a similar effort to democratize the National Guard and to recover section control of its battalions. No one knew in early August how many national guardsmen or how many *fédérés* would join in the insurrection. When the time for action came, however, the commander of the battalion for the Enfants-trouvés Section, Antoine-Joseph Santerre, a Paris brewer's son, led a large body of national guardsmen against the Tuileries. His part in the battle may be judged by the fact that as soon as the monarchy had fallen, the triumphant republican authorities were to appoint him general commander of the Paris National Guard. With these forces came unknown but certainly large numbers of the Paris populace, the shopkeepers, tradesmen, and wage earners who were beginning to describe themselves as *sans-culottes*.

The numbers, ferocity, and determination of these forces caught the government by surprise. An uprising had been expected and about 4,000 men with cavalry and artillery had been on the alert from the beginning of the month. These comprised 200 or 300 loyal gentlemen, about 1,000 Swiss Guards, including the 300 ordinarily at the palace and another 300 recently brought in from the country, about 900 mounted gendarmes, and about fifteen battalions numbering just more than 2,000

national guardsmen. They did not include the so-called Constitutional Guard, which the Assembly had abolished by a decree
of 29 May 1792, or the grenadiers, elite troops of the National
Guard, withdrawn on 30 July. Worst of all, the national guardsmen and the 900 men of the territorial gendarmerie, the old
mounted constabulary (maréchaussée), were of uncertain loyalty
at the time. Nevertheless, the government seems to have believed
itself capable of withstanding a revolutionary attack. It was well
aware of the hostile intentions of the Cordeliers and Jacobins;
on 7 August royal officials even considered arresting such leaders as Robespierre, Danton, Marat, Panis, Sergent, and Santerre.
Three things the authorities seem to have been unprepared for:
the treachery of the national guardsmen at the Tuileries; the
assault by masses of the populace as fédérés, national guardsmen,
and common citizens; and the strategic use of the municipal government, in which revolutionaries were already entrenched.

The victorious attack on the Tuileries, described in most
histories of the French Revolution, left the new municipal
assembly in command of the central government. Its new president, Sulpice Huguenin of the Quinze-vingts Section, a former
customs clerk, immediately addressed the Legislative Assembly
and secured its collaboration. This was not difficult because
Feuillants, moderates, and monarchists of every description had
disappeared, leaving no trace even in most history books, and
there remained fewer than 300 deputies, all republican democrats.[41] These promptly suspended royal power and replaced it
with a provisional executive committee of the king's ministers:
Jean-Marie Roland (Interior), Étienne Clavière (Public Contributions), Joseph Servan (War), Gaspard Monge (Marine), and
P.-H.-H.-M. Tondu called Lebrun (Foreign Affairs), to whom
they added Danton as minister of Justice to satisfy the democratic forces. This executive committee was to rule instead of the
king and in collaboration with various municipal and legislative
committees. As for the legislature, the rump of the Legislative
Assembly decreed its own replacement by a democratic National
Convention, to be elected in a few weeks by all men aged twenty-
one or more, except domestic servants.

The National Convention, comprising 749 elected members, was a second Constituent Assembly elected for the purpose

of drawing up a new constitution. It began by unanimously abolishing the monarchy and announcing that 21 September 1792, the date of its own first meeting, was the last day of the monarchical era, the *ancien régime*, and 22 September the first day of a new era, Year I of the republic. When Year II began twelve months later, there had been devised a republican calendar that was destined to be the legal measure of time until Napoleon restored the Gregorian calendar beginning on 1 January 1806. A constitution committee that included Danton, Pétion, Brissot, Vergniaud, Gensonné, Condorcet, and Thomas Paine had a new constitution, the so-called Girondin constitution, ready by 15 February 1793. By then, however, the wartime emergency, the warlike Jacobins, and their ally the Paris Commune stood in the way of a liberal constitution. Committees of the Convention were already in command. Government by terror was the order of the day.

The Terror was based on the violence of the populace, led mainly by educated leaders who approved of popular violence on ideological grounds. It began on Friday, 10 August 1792, from which day sudden death or the threat of it came from these two groups in slightly different forms but leading to the same political result. After the collapse of the defenders at the Tuileries on 10 August, the populace murdered several hundred men in the Swiss Guards, the palace domestic service, and the groups of loyal gentlemen. Those Feuillants and other political moderates who did not hide, as did Pierre-Louis Roederer, du Pont de Nemours, and hundreds of others, were murdered along with the rest, their bodies plundered, stripped, mutilated, and their heads hacked off and paraded about on pikes.[42]

One brief spell of vengeance in the heat of battle? Not at all. This event was a characteristic expression of popular violence forshadowed by much scattered killing earlier and soon to be followed by even bigger massacres. Such killings were reported all over the country, not only in Paris. On 15 July, for instance, a mob at Limoges murdered Jacques Chabrol, a priest of the local Church of Saint-Michel-des-Lions. Sixty-five similar incidents in the provinces from July to October—not a complete list—have been chronicled by a historian, Pierre Caron, all showing the same characteristic behavior of *le menu peuple*.[43] For instance, at Reims a crowd of local folk and passing Parisians killed ten people on 3–4 September 1792.

In many rural districts the violence of this period was no doubt due to the factors mentioned in the curé Pierre Dolivier's petition concerning the Seine-et-Oise Department: "[T]he riot had no other cause than the alarm of the people concerning *subsistances;* their only purpose was to bring down the price of grain."[44] But it is hard to see any such motive in incidents like the massacre at Meaux of 14 prisoners in the courtyard of the prison by a mob in full view of a crowd of several hundred men, women, children, and national guardsmen. In the five days 2 to 7 September the Paris populace visited seven prisons and massacred more than 1,000 people. At Versailles 44 prisoners were massacred on 9 September. At Lorient a mob broke into the prison on 15 September 1792 and murdered a merchant it suspected of treason. Not all this killing was done in sudden, thoughtless passion. Indeed, the notorious September massacres were being discussed in some quarters as early as 11 August. Furthermore, the killing was done not by criminals or hotheads, Caron concludes, but by ordinary folk sharing one collective mentality.[45]

Closely linked with this part of the Terror was the more carefully organized violence of democratic leaders who were not themselves men of the people. The populace "would not allow itself to be governed," writes the authority on the Commune of 1792, "but let itself be led."[46] Scholars agree that for every leader who came from the people, like the illiterate ex-sailor and cobbler Jean-Louis Vachard, who kept a beer shop in the rue de l'Enfer, there were many more like the ex-professor François Robert, editor of the *Mercure national,* and his aristocratic wife, Louise de Keralio, from Nantes; or like the ambitious adventurer Sulpice Huguenin, who was elected chairman of the new municipal council after ordering the massacre of some 50 Swiss Guards on 10 August; or like the members of the Cordeliers Club, "that nursery of democratic party chiefs"—Danton, Marat, Billaud-Varenne, Momoro, Ronsin, Legendre, Jacques Roux, etc.—whose influence and organizing efforts can be detected in most sectors of the "popular" movement; or like another of their members, Danton's lawyer friend Étienne-Jean Panis, and his colleagues on the municipal Surveillance Committee who had almost unlimited powers of arrest in August and September 1792.[47] Of 206 members of the revolutionary Paris Commune whose occupations are known, only about one-third were trades-men or shopkeepers.[48] Several were shortly to become distin-guished deputies to the Convention: Robespierre, Tallien, Fabre d'Églantine, Collot d'Herbois, Chénier the writer, and Hassen-fratz the chemist. The most influential in the conduct of the Commune's business were a score of other middle-class men, including 8 lawyers, 4 writers, and 2 priests.

Theirs was an organized violence. On 17 August they set up a *tribunal criminel extraordinaire* to hasten the trials of suspects. The next day 1,000 suspects were named in a printed *Liste des membres composant le Club des Feuillants dont d'André était président*, certified correct by eight police administrators.[49] The revolu-tionary leaders discussed other lists, such as the electors of the Saint-Chapelle Club, formed in November 1791, and the 20,000 petitioners who had protested against the events of 20 June in the name of law, order, and the king's safety. Executions began almost immediately. On 29 August a Genoese wrote to his father from Marseilles: "In the past week, a machine called the *guillo-tine* was tried out, having been erected on two Paris squares. This machine removes the heads of the condemned with greater speed and facility, and by this time who knows how many of the most distinguished people have tried it. . . ."[50] The most distinguished of all, Louis XVI, "the chief of the people's assassins," as one Jacobin described him, was brought before the National Con-vention for trial right after Christmas and executed on 21 Jan-uary 1793.[51] This was the Convention that had been elected under the shadow of 10 August, when royalists were being hunted like outlaws, and statues of kings, nobles, and saints were being pulled down. The elections had been by open voting without benefit of secret ballot, and no more than one-tenth of the 7 million eligi-ble voters had taken part.[52]

The press, an essential part of constitutional government, was soon persecuted and then muzzled. More than 500 journals of various types had been founded during the liberal interlude that began in 1789, but on 12 August 1792 the Paris Commune decided to suppress royalist journals, such as *Le mercure de France*,

L'ami du roi, La feuille du jour, L'indicateur, Le journal royalist, and
Le journal de la cour et de la ville. Their printing presses were
given to left-wing journalists; Marat obtained four of them. Soon
afterward the Commune and the popular clubs began to threaten
Girondin journals and others with moderate views, such as
Antoine-Marie Cérisier's *Gazette universelle* and Jean-Baptiste
Louvet's *Sentinelle.* The freedom of the press was more and more
curtailed, and the journalists were terrorized. On 9 March 1793
mobs destroyed the presses of Brissot's *Patriote français* and Gor-
sas's *Courrier des 83 départements.*

When on 29 March the Convention decreed punishments
for incitement to murder or destruction of property, the intent
of the decree was perverted to revolutionary ends by popular
pressure and the Revolutionary Tribunal. Incitement to murder
and destruction was daily fare in such left-wing journals as
Hébert's *Le Père Duchesne,* Marat's *L'ami du peuple,* and its successor, *Le publiciste de la république française.* The Jacobin Club's *Journal de la montagne* and later the Committee of Public Safety's *La
feuille de salut public* were not above reproach. But these were
among the few journals to survive the increasing persecution.
On the other hand, all opposition journals, even Carra's popular
Annales patriotiques et littéraires, were suppressed after 2 June 1793.
The ruling Jacobin committee would tolerate no printed criticism. Robespierre, once in power, forgot the passionate speech
on the freedom of the press he had made to the Constituent
Assembly on 11 August 1791.

The "democratic" minority kept itself in power by terrorizing the public, but it also brought a new efficiency to the war
effort. Its methods served somewhat the same purposes as the
cat-'o-nine-tails and the yardarm on a warship. Outside Paris the
nation did not support the Revolution of 10 August with the
same universal enthusiasm it had shown for the Revolution of
June 1789. By sending thirty commissioners out into the provinces on 29 August, two dozen more on 3 September, and various other agents—Chaumette and Momoro to Normandy,
Billaud-Varenne to Châlons, Ronsin to Soisson, etc.—republican
authorities raised money and new battalions of volunteers.[53] By
sending Carnot, Prieur de la Côte-d'Or, and other *représentants
en mission* to the armies at the front, they got rid of constitutional

generals such as Luckner, who fled immediately, and Lafayette, who went over to the Austrians on 20 August. "To arms! citizens!, the enemy is at our gates!" read a call for a general mobilization on 2 September, the day Verdun fell. Before the end of the month more than 20,000 volunteers had left Paris for the battlefronts. Even the *fédérés,* who had stayed in Paris on an allowance of thirty sous a day in case the Commune might need support, left for the front in mid-September. The Paris sections organized workshops, often in churches, where skilled tradesmen and volunteers could make weapons, tents, wagons, harnesses, and clothing. A dozen volunteers from the rump of the Legislative Assembly set an example in helping fortify a new army camp on the northern outskirts of Paris, including the heights of Montmartre and Belleville.[54] By such methods as these was the enemy turned back on 20 September at Valmy and a great victory won on 6 November at Jemappes.

Victories led to imperial expansion, which the Convention justified with a theory that France ought to extend to "natural frontiers": the Pyrenees, the Alps, the Vosges, and the Rhine River.[55] Brissot expressed this idea as early as November in a letter to General Dumouriez. Danton gave the Convention a clear formulation of it in a speech on 31 January 1793. Accordingly, it voted for the annexation of Savoy (on 27 November 1792), of the county of Nice (31 January 1793), of Belgium (fifteen decrees in March), of the principality of Salm in the Vosges (2 March), and of the entire region between the Rhine and the Moselle (30 March). Some Girondin leaders, encouraged by foreign refugees such as the editor of *La gazette de Leyde* and others on the Dutch Revolutionary Batavian Committee, wanted to organize "sister republics" farther afield. Shortly after the extravagant festival of victory held on 14 October 1792, Pierre-Louis Manuel had proposed worldwide conquest at the Jacobin Club. "It is not enough to affiliate [Jacobin] societies," he cried. "We must affiliate kingdoms."[56] As more farsighted Jacobins such as Robespierre warned, French expansion was to give rise to hostile foreign coalitions. Already Danton had sent a deputation to London to try to secure British neutrality in summer 1792, but which British government could remain neutral when Belgium and Holland were invaded?

The king's overthrow, and his execution even more, stirred up deep hostility abroad. Lord Gower, the British ambassador, had been recalled to London immediately after the events of 10 August. When news of Louis XVI's execution reached London, the French ambassador, Chauvelin, was asked to leave. Even so, it was the French Republic that declared war on Great Britain and the Dutch Republic on 1 February 1793. Spain joined the anti-French coalition on 7 March. The first series of French victories now came to an end. On 18 March French armies under Dumouriez were disastrously defeated at Neerwinden in the Netherlands, and Dumouriez defected to the Austrians a fortnight later. A serious revolt against the republic was breaking out meanwhile in the Vendée Department near the Atlantic coast. In the face of such opposition and disaster, the French Revolution was about to enter a new phase.

EIGHT   *The First People's*
Republic, 1793–94

T HE republic "one and indivisible" survived during its first
two years at great cost. By an immense effort and by ruthless violence, groups of capable leaders warded off every
threat to its unity. To hold together a republic of 27 or 28 million people was an extraordinary feat in the eighteenth century.
The German and Italian nations were still divided into many
small principalities and were to remain so for generations to come.
When they united at last after 1870, they did so with French
ideas in mind and the French example before them. The French
Republic inherited a united kingdom, it is true, but when the
monarchy was destroyed, the members of the royal family killed
or dispersed, the nation might have disintegrated. That was what
the observing foreign governments expected to happen.[1] France,
they thought, is no longer a threat on the international scene
because there will no longer be a unified leadership capable of
marshaling French men and money in the service of a single
policy. Great was their surprise when they found themselves facing a republic even more determined and aggressive than the
late monarchy.

The republic remained "one and indivisible" by a vigorous
use of wartime emergency powers. Only by pointing to the menace of foreign armies could successive republican governments
draw Frenchmen together and induce them to sink their differences in a common struggle. Only that common struggle lent the
ruling groups the authority they needed to defend themselves
by destroying their opponents. The tyranny of the First Repub-

lic was a tyranny of wartime powers that were not to last any
longer than the military emergency which threatened in 1793
and 1794. After the fall of the Jacobin dictatorship in July 1794
the republic was governed by other means.

The very existence of a strong executive was anathema to
republicans. Many deputies to the National Convention, including the Girondins, could not visualize a unified republic as large
and diverse as France and sometimes thought of a federation
like those of the United Provinces of the Netherlands or the
United States of America.[2] Tyranny, they thought, was an executive power maintaining itself by the bribery of the public treasury and the force of the army. The limited monarchy of 1789–
92 had been pulled down because its executive power, Louis XVI
and his ministers, had sought to establish that sort of tyranny.
Experience as well as republican principles called for a dominant legislature.

When the National Convention declared France a republic
on 21 September 1792, no strong executive existed, and none
was to appear until 2 June 1793, when renewed danger from
foreign armies and from dissenting French forces called one into
being. This change began during the month of May, when resolute extremists in the Paris sections formed a council in the
former bishop's palace (*l'évêché*) and a twenty-five-man Central
Revolutionary Committee, headed by Claude-Emmanuel Dobsen, to plan an insurrection against the moderate majority in the
Convention.[3] In response to their efforts, a force of 80,000 *sans-
culottes* with artillery, under François Hanriot, surrounded the
Convention on 2 June. With this menace and this encouragement, the Jacobin minority soon purged the Convention of its
political enemies, the Girondins, and established its own dictatorship. Until then the elected deputies might have gone on forever making action and organization wait upon debate, and their
political rivalries might have led to civil war.

I. Jacobins and Girondins

Let us now go back and examine these conflicting groups more
closely. For the first eight months after the Convention had

assembled late in September 1792, it was torn by the rivalries of
Jacobins and Girondins. Who exactly were the men in these rival
groups? The names Jacobin and Girondin, used at the time, lend
a specious clarity to the struggling groups in the Convention and
their supporters throughout France. Various historians have tried
to penetrate the clouds of propaganda, the smoke of battle, the
charges and countercharges of Jacobins and Girondins to discover what lay behind it all.[4] The Jacobin clubs, at least, are fairly
clear by their formal organization. The Jacobin leaders were at
this stage those who sat on the "Mountain"—that is, in the upper
left-hand seats of the Convention. The Girondins, somewhat more
difficult to pin down, have often been seen as the representatives
of big commercial interests like those at Bordeaux in the department of the Gironde, whence came some of the Girondin chiefs.
Bankers like Étienne Clavière and Jacques Bidermann naturally
seemed to fall in with Brissot and Roland; they all shared a belief
in free trade, a reluctance to prosecute hoarders and speculators, a hostility to the economic controls of the Jacobin wartime
economy.[5] In that view, the Jacobins appear to be less selfish,
more patriotic, and more sympathetic to the Paris populace beset
with unemployment and food shortages.

On the strength of these tendencies, it was not hard to pro-
pound a theory that Girondins and Jacobins represented conflicting social classes: The Girondins can be made to seem like
leaders of the capitalist bourgeoisie, the Jacobins, like petit-
bourgeois leaders of the working classes. This theory does not
stand up to careful examination. But like the other theories in
this field, it contains a measure of truth. In the course of the
conflict the Girondins came to seem like reactionary defenders
of the bourgeoisie, and the Jacobins like men of the people. This
was not true on either side, but the Girondins were more firmly
opposed to Paris and popular violence than the Jacobins were.
The Girondins tended to be cultivated men of broader outlook,
more intellectual and idealistic, but less empirical and less capable in practical politics than the Jacobins. On the other hand, a
close study of the Jacobin Robespierre and the Girondin Brissot
shows them to have had the same thought on many subjects.[6]

Approaching the problem from a different direction, Michael
Sydenham discovered that various lists of Girondins drawn up

at the time were not the same. On any particular occasion a different group of men were described as Girondins, and relatively few of the same men appear on different occasions. If the lists are added up, a total of about 200 deputies of the 740 in the Convention were described as Girondins at one time or another.[7] In this view, a Girondin was a deputy who opposed the Jacobins or the Paris municipal forces, and the Girondin party was a figment of Montagnard propaganda. Any moderate, independent deputy who refused to follow the Mountain was a target for Jacobin denunciations and eventually Jacobin or section violence. Thus, no Girondin party can be distinguished from the main body of moderate or uncommitted deputies, generally described at the time as *la plaine* or *le marais*. "Under examination the party disintegrates."[8] A list, discovered since Sydenham wrote, of 102 deputies whom Marat called Girondins leads a French historian to the same conclusion.[9]

This is not, however, the end of the matter. The Jacobins and Girondins could have been political elements other than organized parties. All historians find that disciplined political parties of a later type cannot be found in revolutionary France. If the "party" of Jacobins behind the Montagnards are easier to identify by virtue of their membership in Jacobin clubs, they, too, behaved in an erratic, independent manner by modern standards. The analysis of their voting behavior by Alison Patrick shows that a maximum of 302 deputies may be described as Montagnards; 219 cooperated with the Mountain fairly consistently in 1793–1794; and of these, only 87 appear to have been reliable, committed Montagnards.[10] Coalitions formed for particular purposes (as they still do, indeed, in the Fifth Republic). After all, liberal or republican theory required elected deputies to vote independently, according to conscience and conviction, and most of them did so. Groups of friends gathered around leaders like Brissot, Roland, Robespierre, and Danton. These were no doubt too unstable, too volatile, to be regarded as "parties" in the modern sense, but they were nevertheless political forces to be reckoned with, "factions" perhaps they should be called.

Seventeen deputies loyally followed Brissot, according to Sydenham's analysis of voting behavior, and including these, about sixty deputies generally voted the same way on the major issues in the Convention.[11] Some of these, notably Abbé Claude Fauchet, Lanthenas, Condorcet, Roland, Jean-Henri Bancal, and Jacques-Antoine Creuzé-Latouche, were engaged in a publishing enterprise that spread Girondin views across the country from summer 1791 to summer 1793. This was the Imprimerie du cercle social, a group of writers and printers who produced books, pamphlets, and such influential journals as *Le chronique du mois,* written for the educated public, *Le sentinelle* directed at the Paris sections, and *La feuille villageoise* for the rural population out in the provinces.[12] In their pages the Montagnards and Jacobins were treated with an unscrupulous hostility similar to that directed at the Girondins in Jacobin writings.

Girondins and Jacobins were not generally antagonistic until after 10 August 1792, not clearly so until after the September massacres. Earlier they all had been part of a common struggle against the Feuillants and other monarchists. A Girondin orator, Pierre-Victurnien Vergniaud, presided over the Paris Jacobin Club from 2 to 16 April 1792; Girondins were a majority in the club until May; and the conflict then beginning in the club was stifled in a common struggle against the constitutional monarchy. The Jacobin Club had been only a general forum, after all, not a party. But in September 1792 it split in the conflict of Brissot's friends and Robespierre's friends. The Girondins seceded from it after they had formed a new inner group by taking control of the Reunion Club, which drew up a prospectus as a club on 21 September. Earlier the Reunion Club and the Jacobin Club had had many members in common.[13] On 10 October the Montagnards, now dominant in the Jacobin Club, formally expelled Brissot, and, on 14 October, all others who would not rally to the club's Montagnard majority. This conflict was to ring through the Convention and through France even after the Girondin defeat on 2 June 1793.

One of the principal issues was the violence of the Paris sections. After the purge of the Feuillants on 10–11 August 1792, the rump of the Legislative Assembly was largely Girondin. On the other hand, the new assembly of the Paris Commune included a majority of Jacobins and Cordeliers. Before long Danton and Robespierre and others outside Girondin circles had an informal alliance with leaders of the Paris sections. In the elections to the Convention no Girondin was elected to any of the twenty-four seats of the Paris delegation. The Mountain was in place henceforth: Robespierre, Danton, Billaud-Varenne, Camille Desmoulins, Marat, Philippe-Égalité, Collot d'Herbois, the painter David, Legendre, Sergent, Manuel, a dozen of their friends in Paris, and about fifty like-minded deputies from the departments, including Couthon, Saint-Just, and Carnot. These, with the possible exceptions of Marat, Legendre, and Sergent, were probably in no way implicated in the September massacres, but Girondin leaders believed they were. This belief was encouraged by Robespierre's and Billaud's cold-blooded efforts to have Brissot and Roland massacred with the rest and by a general connivance at the massacre that is now thought to have been merely tactical. Danton cheerfully (and falsely, according to Norman Hampson) claimed responsibility for the massacres.

Whatever the truth about the massacres, Girondin leaders blamed them on the Paris Commune and the Mountain in speeches and in print. *Les buveurs de sang, anarchistes, demagogues* were among their favorite expressions in denouncing their opponents during the next few months. These denunciations were certainly exaggerated and tactless, as many a historian has pointed out. The Mountain was driven into an alliance with the Commune and the sections that was ultimately fatal to the Girondins. On the other hand, there seems to be no reason to pass lightly over the issue of popular violence. Girondin denunciations of Paris and the Jacobin rump were not merely to make political capital of the September massacres. The Girondins were also speaking out against political murders in general and the political use of popular violence. At this stage they were vociferous defenders of law and order. In September 1792 Gensonné, Kersaint, Buzot, and other Girondins tried to persuade the Legislative Assembly and the Convention to set up a departmental guard as a counterweight to Paris. In February 1793 Condorcet put before the Convention the Girondin constitution, full of safeguards for the person and property of the individual citizen. The Girondins were by no means all or always opposed to violence, but they had a much cleaner record than the Jacobins. To summarize, the Terror began on 10 August 1792, the

Jacobins compromised with it, and the Girondins were its first opponents. They fought a good fight against it until the Jacobins used the king's trial to put the leading Girondins in the wrong and, pressed hard by the Paris sections, had them purged in June 1793 and executed in October.

One of the leaders in the struggle was Jean-Marie Roland, the Girondin minister of the Interior, who had considerable prestige as a defender of persons and property and a man of political morality.[14] The Legislative Assembly voted him 100,000 livres to establish a Bureau de l'esprit public. He and the bureau's head, Lanthenas, made excellent use of this opportunity to propagate their moderate, liberal view of the Revolution. More and more they spoke out against the violent rule of Paris. And Roland also subsidized the Cercle social. When on 21 January 1793, the day of the king's execution, the Jacobins induced the Convention to abolish the Bureau de l'esprit public, this was a terrible blow to the Girondin cause. The events of 21 January prompted Roland to give up his ministerial post the next day and to retire from politics.

One of Roland's allies, the deputy from Marseilles, Charles-Jean-Marie Barbaroux, had led the twelve Marseilles deputies to denounce Robespierre and all the prominent Montagnards. He had also encouraged the Marseilles battalion of *fédérés* to be "a sort of praetorian guard for Roland."[15] But four of these deputies joined the Mountain early in January 1793 and began an attack on the Girondins for their resistance to the king's execution. The Jacobin Club of Marseilles expelled Barbaroux and all other Girondins on 23 January. In response to an appeal from Marseilles, a majority of Jacobin clubs also expelled Girondins. As the dangers of war and civil war increased in spring 1793, the moderate views of the Girondins lost influence in many parts of France and the ruthless Jacobin Terror was the order of the day.

The Girondin leaders lost many friends and followers, some trimming to the new political winds, others genuinely changing their minds. The Jacobins had been able to divide and demoralize the Girondins during the king's trial, and the events of the spring completed the process. A general indifference greeted the Girondin constitution put before the Convention on 15 and

16 February. Men long uncommitted such as Danton, conservatives such as Carnot, Barère, and Cambon went rapidly from being regicides to being enemies of the Girondins, the common Jacobin progression at the time. Danton and Barère were among the nine elected to the first Committee of Public Safety which met 117 times before 2 June, but no Girondins were elected to it. The Girondins managed on 15 March to capture the six-man committee to oversee the new Revolutionary Tribunal, but the Jacobins were soon able to have this committee abolished. By the time the Girondins were purged from the Convention by massive rallies of section activists which cowed the moderate deputies, they had lost practically all their control over administrative and executive services of the government. For more than a year the Mountain was to rule. France now had a one-party government. The change was fully recognized in some provincial circles at least: It was now that Charlotte Corday resolved to kill Marat, whom she blamed for the arrest of the Girondins, the "people's representatives," as she called them.[16]

II. *The Jacobin Dictatorship*

The regime that ruled France by terror from early June 1793 until late July 1794 was not a simple one. It was different from what went before and after, and it aroused emotions of enthusiasm or horror so strong that even two centuries later they are still likely to move the reader to take sides. The most fair-minded may stumble in seeking the truth in the works of the famous historian Albert Mathiez (1874–1932), which depict Maximilien Robespierre as a towering hero; in those of Alphonse Aulard (1849–1928), which make a martyr of Danton; and in the many famous writings of twentieth-century professors in the Sorbonne chair of the French Revolution, which conspire to make a collective hero of the populace.*

The regime as a whole is not easy to judge. On the one hand,

*In particular, Georges Lefebvre (1874–1959) and Albert Soboul (1914–82). The bias in these historians' general interpretation does not, of course, detract from the value of their many learned and original studies.

it gave a vigorous leadership that preserved the republic against the assaults of its enemies within and without; on the other, these successes were won by the terrorizing of millions of people, the arrests of hundred of thousands, the massacre of 100,000 or more in the genocidal pacification of the Vendée, and the execution of 15,000 or 16,000 after the mock trials of revolutionary tribunals. Again, on one hand, the Terror treated nobles, priests, and the rich with a rigor satisfying to many a reader's sense of social justice. On the other, no more than one-third of the victims were nobles, clergy, or rich commoners. Just over one-third were property-owning peasants or lower middle-class townsmen, and just under one-third came from the urban working class.[17] The Jacobin dictatorship was not the rule of one particular social class, however "classes" may be defined. Careful scholars in every corner of the subject resort to political rather than social explanations.

The Mountain, men from the Jacobin Club, ruled the Convention in alliance with the militants of the Paris sections. This was a dictatorship because the Mountain was a minority in the Convention—267 men, according to one scholarly list[18]—and the section militants were a minority in Paris, a tiny minority in France. Neither of these minority groups was representative of a particular social class. Their principal opponents were, after all, of similar social origin. In the convention about half the 749 deputies were lawyers (406), and the other half were also from middle-class occupations: businessmen (67); clergymen, including 9 Protestants (55); civil servants (51); medical men (46); farmers, but not peasants (38); soldiers and sailors (36); writers (30); academics (11), artisans (6); and clerks (3).[19] A disproportionately large fraction of these, some 40 percent, came from large towns. On the whole, the older men from smaller communities less exposed to national politics tended to support the Girondins, though the Girondin leaders were themselves among the youngest. The youngest men with the most political experience, usually in their late thirties or early forties, including most of the 191 from the Legislative Assembly, tended to support the Mountain. This large contingent from the Legislative Assembly is hard to identify with the rump left sitting after the purge of 10 August 1792, always thought to have been Girondin in sympathies. A large number of them may, of course, have changed with the times, like the famous Vicar of Bray in the English Revolution a century before.[20]

During the fourteen months of the Jacobin dictatorship the Mountain ruled the Convention and the nation through two committees. The first of them, the Committee of General Security (Comité de sûreté générale), had been set up as early as 2 October 1792 on the model of the Surveillance Committee in the Legislative Assembly and, before that, of the Research or Information Committee created by the Constituent Assembly on 28 July 1789. The purpose of all these committees was to deal with treason, subversion, foreign agents, counterfeiters, and all other conspirators against the State. Like any institution in a dictatorship, the Committee of General Security was soon packed with men of the ruling group. In fact, it had been reorganized on 21 January 1793 as a group of twelve Jacobins, including Chabot, Legendre, Tallien, and Jean-Baptist Drouet, and dominated by Vadier and Amar, two conspiratorial terrorists who were to play a big part in bringing down Robespierre and his colleagues in July 1794.[21]

They were assisted everywhere in France by local imitations of themselves which sprang up spontaneously here and there, notably in some of the Paris sections, but were legally set up by a decree of 23 March 1793. These were Surveillance Committees, often called Revolutionary Committees, perhaps 20,000 of them in all, which volunteered to spy on their neighbors in order to denounce royalists, traitors, Girondins, aristocrats, Feuillants, wealthy men, hoarders, and other counterrevolutionaries. The political purposes of these committees were clear from the first.

Surveillance and denunciation were one thing; arrests, trials, and sentences were another. Police and criminal courts had already been reorganized under municipal and departmental authorities. Early in March 1793 the Mountain proposed a Revolutionary Tribunal in Paris that might expedite the trial of suspects and secure rapid convictions, as Robert Lindet put it, "by all possible means." This tribunal, Danton argued, "is to replace the supreme tribunal of the people's vengeance." There would have been no massacres in September 1792, he thought, if there had been a Revolutionary Tribunal then: "[L]et us use terror so that the people will not need to! *(soyons terribles pour éviter au peuple de l'être!)*"[22] The Revolutionary Tribunal was created immediately on 10 March with five elected judges, twelve jurors, and a public prosecutor. The prosecutor, an efficient civil servant with legal training named Antoine-Quentin Fouquier-Tinville, was entitled to try anyone on his own initiative—even suspects arrested out in the provinces—except members of the Convention, executive ministers, and army generals, whom he could arrest only on orders from the Convention, usually from one of the two main committees. The property of anyone sentenced to death was to escheat to the republic.

The first trial began on 6 April, but the tribunal was hampered by a general reluctance to give up employment in order to serve as judges and jurors. In its first six months it sentenced only 70 people to death. By the end of its first year, however, it had guillotined more than 500, and by the end of July 1794, when the dictatorship was overthrown, the score was nearly 2,700. Only at Nantes and Lyons were there more victims of revolutionary "justice." In the course of 1793 and 1794 the tribunal supplanted the ordinary criminal courts, but its political complexion discouraged the barristers from pleading before it. The profession of barrister was abolished by the Convention on 24 October 1793 in favor of a system in which anyone could act as counselor in cases before the tribunal. Defendants were exploited by unscrupulous individuals who played upon their fears.

The trials were at once farces and nightmares. Fouquier-Tinville, who presided over them, acted on orders from the Convention's committees, and the judges fell into step with him. Late in the evening, after the day's work, he used to visit the committees to discuss cases with them and receive his orders. The jurymen, drawn mainly from the Paris sections and the Jacobin Club, did nothing to distinguish guilt from innocence, and could not have done so even if they had wished to. Charges were hopelessly vague, and the tribunal had neither the time nor the inclination to seek the truth in particular cases, especially after the Law of Suspects voted on 17 September 1793 to prevent delays. At least two jurors passed the time sketching the prisoners, and others made ribald jokes about them and their almost certain death.[23] For example, Clément Charles François de L'Averdy (1724–93), the controller general of finances from 1763 to 1768, now seventy years old, was tried for the crime of throwing wheat, the people's food, into a pond on a property he had not visited for years. The remarks he made in his own defense were pointed, intelligent, and utterly convincing, but he was judged guilty and executed on 23 November 1793.

Rather than face such a nightmare, many prisoners took their own lives, as Étienne Clavière did with a knife on 8 December 1793, Jacques Roux with a knife on 10 February 1794, and Condorcet probably with poison. Three Girondins—Pétion, Buzot, and Barbaroux—shot themselves in the fields near Saint-Émilion to escape the execution their friend Guadet and his family suffered there, but Barbaroux, not quite dead, was dragged off to the guillotine. Others showed transcendent courage. Charlotte Corday, the handsome twenty-five-year-old Norman girl charged with Marat's murder, answered all questions firmly and went to her death, after a two-hour ride in a tumbril through the raving crowds, with perfect self-possession.[24] She, at least, was charged with a recognizable crime and was guilty of it.

The repressive Committee of General Security and the Revolutionary Tribunal were parts of a dictatorship crowned with the principal committee of the Convention, the Committee of Public Safety (Comité de salut public). Founded on 6 April 1793, this group soon took charge of the country in the manner of an emergency wartime cabinet. Eight of the twelve men in it at its height, including a former nobleman, Hérault de Séchelles, and an arthritic cripple, Georges Couthon, had been trained in the law (Barére, Billaud-Varenne, Lindet, Prieur de la Marne, Robespierre, and Saint-Just); two were engineers and army officers (Carnot and Prieur de la Côte-d-Or); one had been an actor and playwright (Collot d'Herbois), and another a Protestant minister (Jeanbon Saint-André). All were capable and energetic, but three of them did outstanding service: Barère, prodigiously active in matters of policing, war, munitions, and the navy; Lazare Carnot, a great strategist and war leader; and Robespierre, who presided over the committee and the nation with a clear and unwavering determination, turning his hand to all sorts of tasks. They were too busy, like most cabinets, to keep minutes and were in any case supposed to be working in secret. Conse-

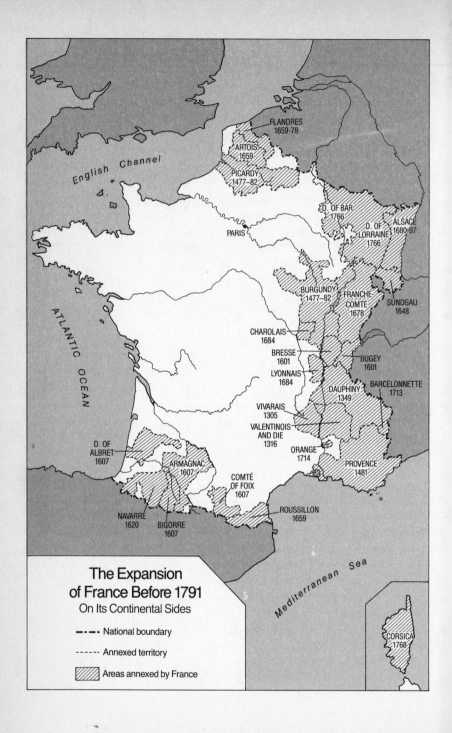

English Channel

ATLANTIC OCEAN

PARIS

FLANDRES
1659-78

ARTOIS
1659

PICARDY
1477–82

D. OF BAR
1766

D. OF
LORRAINE
1766

ALSACE
1680-97

BURGUNDY
1477–82

FRANCHE-
COMTÉ
1678

SUNDGAU
1648

CHAROLAIS
1684

BRESSE
1601

LYONNAIS
1684

BUGEY
1601

DAUPHINY
1349

BARCELONNETTE
1713

VIVARAIS
1305

VALENTINOIS
AND DIE
1316

ORANGE
1714

PROVENCE
1481

D. OF
ALBRET
1607

ARMAGNAC
1607

COMTÉ
OF FOIX
1607

NAVARRE
1620

BIGORRE
1607

ROUSSILLON
1659

Mediterranean Sea

The Expansion
of France Before 1791
On Its Continental Sides

—·—· National boundary

------ Annexed territory

▨ Areas annexed by France

CORSICA
1768

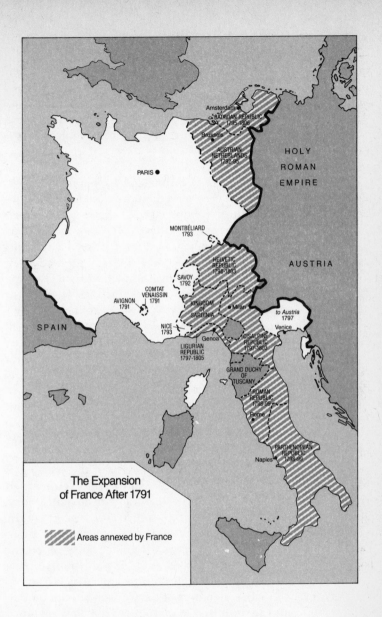

The Expansion
of France After 1791

Areas annexed by France

Labels on map:
Amsterdam
BATAVIAN REPUBLIC 1795-1806
Brussels
AUSTRIAN NETHERLANDS 1792-95
HOLY ROMAN EMPIRE
PARIS
MONTBÉLIARD 1793
HELVETIC REPUBLIC 1798-1803
AUSTRIA
SAVOY 1792
COMTAT VENAISSIN 1791
AVIGNON 1791
KINGDOM
Milan
SARDINIA
to Austria 1797
Venice
NICE 1793
Genoa
CISALPINE REPUBLIC 1797-1803
LIGURIAN REPUBLIC 1797-1805
SPAIN
GRAND DUCHY OF TUSCANY
ROMAN REPUBLIC 1798-99
Rome
PARTHENOPEAN REPUBLIC 1798-99
Naples

quently, there is some uncertainty about how they divided their many tasks among them, and the thousands of orders they penned and signed do not show specialized functions for most of them. Their headquarters was a green room in the Tuileries Palace, where they spent many hours each day around a table, but several of them went off on special missions to armies or to provinces troubled by uprising.

Eighty-two representatives on mission (*représentants en mission*), only a few of whom ever served on the Committee of Public Safety, were sent out on 9 March 1793 to raise 300,000 men for the armies on the foreign frontiers. Even more than their predecessors of August and September 1792, they served as agents of the dictatorship in Paris. A series of decrees in the weeks following their departure removed legal impediments to tyranny by terror: death for émigrés and nonjuring priests as soon as caught (18 March); death for rebels against recruiting and other war measures (19 March); the Surveillance Committees in villages and town sections to check passports and the identities of foreigners and other strangers (21 March); death for émigrés who returned to France (28 March). They were assisted in many departments by committees set up by local Jacobin clubs to organize recruiting, forced loans, and dictatorial violence. In about half the departments they were soon also assisted by "revolutionary armies," civil contingents of the populace organized to carry out revolutionary and dictatorial purposes. Robespierre proposed these as early as May, and by the end of the year about forty of them were roaming about the countryside, seizing food from peasants and hoarders and valuables from all and sundry, arresting rebels and other suspects, and trying to destroy the parish life of the church in the brief dechristianizing campaigns of the winter 1793–94. In all, perhaps 30,000 men joined the revolutionary armies. None played a bigger part in terrorizing the nation than the representatives on mission. A decree of 29 December sent 58 more members of the Convention out on missions, with unlimited authority, each to serve the dictatorship in two departments.

The most active and violent were those in provinces that rose in revolt against the Jacobin dictatorship. After 7 June 1793 a Federalist government at Lyons would take no further orders from Paris and prepared to defend the city with 10,000 volunteers under the Comte de Précy, a former member of the Garde royale. General François-Christophe Kellermann besieged Lyons from 8 August 1793 on, and when he had starved it into submission on 9 October, Collot and Fouché organized a savage repression. Their Tribunal of Seven executed about 20 people a day in November. From 4 to 7 December, some 360 men, women, and children were murdered by grapeshot from cannons near the ditches they were to be buried in, and by April 1794 almost 2,000 people had been killed. Meanwhile, other representatives were on missions at neighboring towns, Georges Couthon and Étienne-Christophe Maignet at Clermont-Ferrand, and Claude Javogues in the Loire Department, where he executed 15 people on 11 December, 21 ten days later, and 208 on 5 December. "Javogues' most constant preoccupation," Colin Lucas tells us, "was with repression."[25]

At Marseilles and Toulon, as at Lyons, resistance to the dictatorial government of Paris led to siege and repressive terror. The *fédérés* and the royalists were strong in these cities, so far from Paris and so near the counterrevolutionary centers in Italy, Savoy, and Switzerland. On 22 June 1793 a general committee of the thirty-two sections of Marseilles decided to ignore the Convention's orders and raised a force that set out to march on Paris. After taking Avignon, it was defeated by an army that then besieged Marseilles, which it took on 25 August. The repression was moderate until two of the Convention's representatives, Barras and Fréron, took command of it on 12 October. They soon executed about 500 people, renamed Marseilles Villesans-nom, and ruined its once-great trade. On 12 December they were briefly diverted to Toulon, about to fall at last to a besieging army.

Barras and Fréron were doubly keen to subdue Toulon because they had been arrested there by the insurrectionary committee when it had raised the standard of revolt on 18 July 1793. Barras and Fréron had managed to escape, but the naval officers leading the revolt had then gone as far as to call upon the British Mediterranean fleet for help. The commanding admiral, Samuel Hood, had agreed to defend Toulon if it would recognize Louis XVII as the legitimate ruler of France, and the committee, at least, had done so. With British supplies and a force of more than 16,000 men, Toulon withstood the siege until 18 December 1793. When the town fell, the British ships sailed off with thousands of French refugees, and the avenging representatives shot about 800 people, pulled down much of the town, and renamed it Port-la-Montagne.

The worst terror of all was organized at Nantes in the rebellious west of France. Prieur de la Marne set up a tribunal there, the Commission militaire Bignon, named after its chairman, and it sentenced more than 2,900 people to death. Hundreds were shot. Boatloads of men, women, and children from the counter-revolutionary armies of the Vendée were drowned in the Loire River at Nantes on the orders of a particularly cruel representative, Jean-Baptiste Carrier, who had been a Jacobin Club member and chairman of the Surveillance Committee at Aurillac in the Auvergne. Much of the killing Carrier ordered was a wild, barbarous butchery even worse than the usual execution by guillotine.[26] The explanation for such cruelty may lie partly in the character and background of the individual. The son of a prosperous peasant farmer who had originally intended him for the Church, Carrier became clerk to a lawyer *(procureur)*, then a lawyer himself, somber, taciturn, tall, a little bent, with small eyes and a vague expression. Carrier's was an extreme case, but not really exceptional, essentially no different from the rest of the representatives on mission from the Convention. And he was certainly no worse than many men lower in the hierarchy of terrorists, such as Nicolas Guenot (1754–1832), who used the opportunities of 1793–95 to wreak vengeance on personal enemies, real and imagined.[27]

The Jacobin dictatorship, like all dictatorships, defended itself by executing its political enemies on various pretexts. Vague accusations of counterrevolution, intrigue, and corruption sufficed to get rid of the Girondins, thirty-one of whom were executed on 31 October 1793, and of many others at various times. By a natural turn of events, however, the rulers soon began to denounce one another. In April 1794, for example, Robespierre, Saint-Just, and Couthon had organized a police surveillance bureau to work for the Committee of Public Safety, and this aroused the mistrust and hostility of the Committee of General Security. Soon all the members of this committee except Philippe Lebas and Jacques-Louis David were hostile to the Committee of Public Safety. Disagreements and jealousies among the Jacobins and sections led to political struggles, and these led to the guillotine.

The best example is the fate of Danton and his followers. This affair began in March 1794 with the arrest of Hérault de Séchelles, whom his colleagues on the Committee of Public Safety had never liked and had mistrusted during his mission to Alsace the previous year. He had been denounced as early as 12 October 1793 for allegedly keeping the Austrian government informed, by a certain Fabre d'Églantine, who was himself arrested in March 1794. On the night of 30 March, Robespierre, Barère, and Saint-Just ordered the arrest of Danton, of Camille Desmoulins, an old school friend of Robespierre's, and of two other deputies, Pierre Philippeaux and Jean-Michel Lacroix. These were involved, it seems, in various extortion rackets, but the committee denounced them mainly for allegedly conspiring with dangerous foreign interests. When they were executed on 5 April, it was with General Westermann, somehow tarred with the same brush as the traitor General Dumouriez, and with François Chabot, a representative on mission at Toulouse in 1793, formerly a Capuchin monk, who had married into a family of Austrian Jewish bankers. Some of the victims on this occasion were, like Danton himself, heroes of the 10 August 1792, but the Committee of Public Safety saw them as dangerous enemies. Political safety was becoming more and more uncertain.

Already less than a fortnight earlier they had inadvertently broken the alliance with the Paris sections on which their power depended. This was not the first time the Jacobin dictatorship had attacked and dispersed a group of popular leaders: In the fall of 1793 the *enragé* socialists had suffered for their criticisms of the government. Jean-François Varlet had been imprisoned on 19 September. Jacques Roux had been arrested several times by municipal police for his agitation, especially in the columns of *Le publiciste*, and he was arrested again on 26 November with his principal followers in the Gravilliers Section. In November the Revolutionary Women's Club had been closed. Claire Lacombe and Anne-Pauline Léon, with her *enragé* husband, Théophile-

Victor Leclerc, had been silenced. In March 1794 the victims were eighteen popular leaders of the Paris Commune and their friends, the so-called Hébertists, executed on 24 March. A few of these were prominent or wealthy men, like the bankers Anarcharsis Cloots and Jean-Conrad de Kock and the former governor of Pondicherry, General Michel Laumur. But most were merely activists from the sections who had fallen in with Hébert, editor of the popular journal Le Père Duchesne, "too much concerned with himself," said Robespierre; François Desfieux, a wine merchant from the Lepelletier Section; Jean-Baptiste Ancard, an artisan from the Unité Section; and the printer Antoine-François Momoro and his protégé Frédéric-Pierre Ducroquet, from the Marat Section. These also were denounced for some vague foreign conspiracy.

When the Jacobin leaders executed the Hébertists and others from the Paris sections, such as Chaumette, guillotined on 13 May, they were sawing off the branch on which they themselves were perched. The militants of the Paris sections had put them into power in the uprising of 31 May–2 June 1793 and had supported their dictatorship ever since. The moderate majority in the Convention and moderate opinion across the country in various guises—Girondins, fédérés, muscadins, and counterrevolutionaries—had been intimidated by repression organized by Jacobins and Paris sections. Stunned and confused by the execution of the Hébertists, the Paris sections lost the will to turn out the mobs that had terrorized Paris on behalf of the Jacobin dictatorship. This change was not immediately visible. But on 27 July 1794, when the Jacobin leaders were challenged in the Convention, no Paris mob appeared in their defense.

The occasion was provided by one of those bitter quarrels within the ranks of the Jacobin leaders that confused their supporters and subordinates. A plan to betray Robespierre revealed weaknesses in the ruling committees to the Convention and moved the moderate majority to turn against its dictatorial leaders. The political struggle that followed in Paris was sharp and decisive. On the same day and the next, eighty-three of the Jacobin leaders, including Robespierre himself, were guillotined in the terrifying process they had themselves devised. The remaining leaders, Barère, Billaud-Varenne, Collot d'Herbois, and Vadier, expected to carry on as before but soon found themselves swept aside in a reaction against the dictatorship of the past months. A new government came into being, the so-called Thermidorian regime named for the month of this sudden reversal, and by the end of the year it had dismantled the institutions of the Terror and even closed down the Jacobin Club.

III. The War Effort

The overriding purpose of the Terror was to destroy the nation's enemies. Whatever the purposes or unconscious motives of individual terrorists, the republic intended to raise men, equip them, and deploy them to defeat foreign armies and counterrevolutionaries. It achieved these purposes with remarkable success in 1794, as it had in 1792. The rebellious forces in France were subdued even earlier, the remnant of a Federalist army defeated just north of Marseilles on 24 August 1793, Lyons occupied on 9 October, Toulon on 19 December, and the *grande armée* of the Vendée defeated at Cholet in October 1793 and at Le Mans and Savenay before the year's end. Early in 1794 Lazare Carnot assisted by Saint-Just worked out the strategy of an offensive campaign. When the fighting season opened that spring, they deployed about two-thirds of the French forces against the Austrians, Prussians, and British from Dunkirk to Switzerland, and the remaining third against the Spaniards in the south and the Sardinians in the southeast. French troops secured the Mediterranean coastline of France in April. In the north, at Fleurus on 26 June, the first of many victories gave access to Belgium. On 9 Thermidor (27 July 1794), the day the Jacobin dictatorship fell, General Pichegru entered Antwerp and General Jourdan entered Liège. By August Belgium had been reconquered; by the end of the year the Rhineland was occupied and the conquest of the Dutch Republic was assured. Cologne fell on 6 October; Amsterdam, on 19 January 1795.

What did the republic do in the year following the coup of 2 June 1793 to achieve such success? For one thing, it recruited enough soldiers by the pressure of the many agencies collaborating in the Terror. A levy of 300,000 proposed on 24 February

1793 was raised during the spring and summer, and then, on 23 August, Barère read out the eighteen articles of the famous "mass rising" *(levée en masse)*, which were immediately adopted and printed. The first article declared all Frenchmen to be at the service of the republic until the enemy had been driven from French territory—an expanding empire, in fact—and articles 8 to 12 ordered all bachelors and childless widowers under twenty-six to assemble at their nearest district towns in battalions under banners marked "The French people standing up to tyrants." As a result of this initiative, 300,000 or 400,000 joined up, and a year later another 750,000 were recruited. In spite of the many draft dodgers, deserters, and men exempted for various reasons, the enormous population of France furnished enough troops.

Carnot organized them in divisions of about 10,000, each one complete with cavalry and horse-drawn artillery and trained to combine in larger units. He improved the armies by such things as better medical care, by driving away women camp followers, and by stopping the election of officers. The problem of reconciling military subordination and discipline with social equality was slowly solved by promoting capable officers of modest family background, young patriotic generals like Hoche, Marceau, and Bonaparte, and by executing generals suspected of treachery, such as Custine (on 27 August 1793) and Houchard (on 15 November 1793).

Dictatorial methods obtained food, barracks, horses, fodder, materials for weapons, and other equipment. Under Robert Lindet a three-man Food and Supplies Commission, founded on 22 October 1793, soon had some 500 employees in the Hôtel de Toulouse and agents in the provinces. The commission had authority to requisition, buy, import, and transport food as necessary and to establish prices and priorities for its distribution. The task of enforcing maximum prices that had been set for grain on 4 May 1793 and for all other foods and fuels on 29 September proved impossible, but the commission did manage to keep the armies and cities supplied. Contractors and subcontractors were used, as of old, but kept in line like everyone else by threats of the guillotine. Meanwhile, the revolutionary armies of *sans-culottes* roamed about, hunting for food, valuables, weapons, and bell metal. Jeanbon Saint-André's improved navy collaborated by engaging a British fleet off Ushant so that a convoy of American grain was able to reach Brest on 9 June 1794. Seven ships of the line were lost on that occasion; one of them was *Le vengeur du peuple,* which fought until it sank on "the glorious first of June" in a famous duel with HMS *Brunswick.*

The armaments industry was organized mainly by Prieur de la Côte-d'Or. Steel, weapons, and powder being the primary necessities, he soon hired a number of distinguished scientists, notably the mathematician Gaspard Monge and the chemists Jean-Henri Hassenfratz and Louis-Bernard Guyton de Morveau, to improve materials and methods. They tested weapons on the proving ground at Meudon and even had a hydrogen balloon flying over the battlefield at Fleurus. An Arms and Powder Commission was appointed in February 1794 to direct and assist manufacturing. It was able to requisition as workshops monasteries and churches, such as the big Chartreux Convent in Paris, "formerly devoted to silence, to idleness, to boredom, and to regrets, but now a picture of worthwhile industry."[28] In Paris nearly 5,000 workers eventually turned out 600 muskets a day, and other factories in provincial towns also increased production. Groups of volunteers washed the saltpeter (potassium nitrate) out of urine-soaked cellars and decaying organic matter in gardens to produce the vital ingredient in gunpowder and also found the necessary charcoal potash. Some of the Paris sections organized the sewing of uniforms, and "national workshops" appeared here and there to make boots.

Much was done by dictatorial methods and patriotism, but huge sums of money were needed at every turn. These were paid in the paper *assignats* first issued in 1790 on the security of nationalized Church property. Made legal tender as early as 17 April 1790, these *assignats* ceased to bear interest and became simple bearer notes, like our own in the twentieth century, on 18 November following. They had been devised to pay off the huge debts inherited from the *ancien régime* but were easily adapted to war financing. On 8 April 1793 the hard-pressed Convention ordered all government purchases and all payments to soldiers to be in *assignats,* and three days later it prohibited the circulation, sale, and purchase of gold and silver. A limit of

2.4 billion livres, set by the Convention earlier on 24 October 1792, was soon passed as the printing presses turned out *assignats* for the republic. By the time these presses were ceremonially broken on 19 February 1796 almost 40 billion livres had been issued and the resulting inflation had rendered the *assignats* worthless. In the critical years 1793–94, however, they hovered between 20 percent and 50 percent of their face value and therefore served well enough.[29]

Once the French armies had begun to fight beyond the French frontiers, a new source of money, food, and equipment appeared. As early as 19 September 1793 two representatives on mission to the army in the north, Narcissse Trullard and Théophile Berlier, wrote to General André Gigaux: "We do not think we should make war today like fools, as we did last year. We must live at the expense of the enemy. We believe that the bulk provisions for the army, the grain, fodder etc. may be removed for the benefit of the Republic, which may be unfortunate for individuals, but which we may do as conquerors."[30] Carnot made a policy of this principle. On his advice the French armies plundered occupied countries systematically, spending *assignats* when necessary. This did not interfere with the looting of personal valuables by individual soldiers. The Netherlands were, it seems, more carefully treated in the belief that Dutch wealth was largely in the form of credit abroad, but parts of Germany and Italy and Belgium, with its numerous wealthy Church properties, were badly plundered.

A disregard for the rights of property, whether in France or abroad, was not part of Jacobin political thinking. Nor was a managed economy, in which economic freedom was sacrificed to requisitioning, fixed prices, and detailed regulations. Jacobins in the Convention shared with the Girondins, and the general public, a belief in laissez-faire principles, though not quite in the same fanatical form as the Physiocrats of the previous generation. The managed economy of 1793–94 grew out of practical and political necessity, not out of economic theory. The effort to meet the wartime emergency and the urgings of the populace in the Paris sections combined to make the Jacobins build up a controlled economy empirically step by step. Even so, the *sans-culottes* of the sections, and in particular the *enragés* socialist group—

Varlet, Roux, Leclerc, Léon, and Lacombe—tried to make the Committee of Public Safety go further than it was prepared to go in the direction of social equality.[31] The general leveling, symbolized by the universal *tutoiement* that would make all people feel equal, was an idea of the *sans-culottes* more than of the Jacobins.

The dechristianizing campaign, too, was forced upon the government by the *sans-culottes* and a minority of enthusiasts among the Jacobins. Only a few of the representatives on mission persecuted the clergy with the vigor of Dartigoeyte in the Haute-Garonne and of Javogues in the Loire Department, who on 21 December 1793 ordered all churches converted into clubs and temples of reason, civic centers where people could read and discuss official papers and laws.[32] It was dictatorial minorities that renamed the villages to get rid of the ancient saints' names. Only a few ex-clergy became fanatical dechristianizers, such as Fouché's friend Étienne-Jean-François Parent, who as a terrorist in the Clamecy district (Nièvre) had his own brother arrested in 1794 and turned a deaf ear to his mother's appeals.[33] It was the revolutionary armies of *sans-culottes* that went about the countryside forcing priests to marry, plundering churches, and urinating in chalices in front of the astonished peasantry. The Jacobins attacked the Church for its wealth and its counter-revolutionary bent, but with no evident desire to destroy it. In general, the Committee of Public Safety consisted of deists, not atheists like Georges-Auguste Couthon and some of the Committee of General Security. Robespierre described the Feast of Reason held at Notre-Dame Cathedral as a *mascarade* and was, indeed, so hostile to the dechristianizing campaign that he aroused the suspicion of the Commission of General Security. His views were empirical and practical rather than doctrinaire.

The genius of the Jacobin dictators was in using the force of popular emotions to mobilize the nation for war. Fear was the principal emotion: fear of invasion, of starvation, of conspiracy, of foreigners, and of counterrevolutionaries. Robespierre and his colleagues were haunted by a dread of plots and saw conspirators everywhere, and in this they were one with the populace. Nearly as strong as fear was the national patriotism that inspired courage and sacrifice, as well as a republican campaign against the selfish private interests that might so easily have destroyed the republic. At every turn the governing committees were able to win support for the general welfare of the nation with an appeal to collective emotions. "Young men shall go into battle," the law of the "mass rising" proclaimed on 23 August 1793. "Married men shall forge weapons and transport food supplies; women shall make tents and uniforms and serve in hospitals; children shall tear up rags for bandages; old men shall betake themselves to the public squares to excite the courage of the warriors and to preach the hatred of kings and the unity of the Republic." Only a minority of soldiers or civilians answered calls like this spontaneously in a spirit of self-sacrifice, but the complex emotions of revolutionary equality and fraternity enabled minorities to assault those elites of wealth or privilege that stood aloof. The genius of the Jacobin dictators lay, in the last analysis, in the ability to give the nation civil leadership in a war that might so easily have led to a military coup d'etat like that of 1799. They satisfied the popular sense of justice by matching death on the battlefield with death on the scaffold.

The Populace in Revolution and Counterrevolution

I. Sans-culottes *and Other Republicans*

The common people who are supposed to have supported the Jacobin dictatorship of 1793–94 are elusive. There can be no doubt of the alliance, tacit and uneasy though it was, by which the Paris sections and the Jacobin government established their rule in a coup d'etat of 31 May–2 June 1793. But whether the section militants were "the people" or even representative of "the people" is far from certain. *Le peuple* was a vague term, full of mystical emotion, to republican democrats of the French Revolution. When royal sovereignty gave way to popular sovereignty, "the people" appeared to them to be clothed in the glory that had hitherto surrounded the throne. *Mon souverain,* as Robespierre called them, were always right whatever they did, right in their interpretation of the legislative process, right even in their massacres and murders. Danton spoke of the "supreme tribunal of the people's vengeance."[1] This view of the people's place was quite different from the view prevailing among the public in general.

The majority in the National Assembly, in 1794 as in 1789, thought of itself as representing the nation and held the constitution sacred. The people were represented as part of the nation, and from 10 August 1792 they could take part in the governing process as full citizens and voters. Even after abolishing the distinction between active and passive citizens, even after proclaiming a democratic republic, the majority in the National Convention believed in a popular sovereignty expressed in the constitutional process of representation. Even the Jacobin minority, in command of the Convention after 2 June, saw the people's political role in constitutional terms. The sovereign people should elect their deputies, one for every 40,000, and let them govern. The primary task of government was "to guarantee the enjoyment of men's natural and imprescriptible rights, which are equality, liberty, safety and property."[2] On 24 June 1793 these principles were developed in the 124 clauses of a Jacobin constitution and in the 35 clauses of a Declaration of the Rights of Man and the Citizen. In these, the ruling Jacobin minority gave the people a much greater place in government than heretofore but laid down principles of representation, due process, and the rule of law. Nowhere did it declare that crowds of *sans-culottes,* or common folk under any other name, might take the law into their own hands, terrorize officials and political opponents, and impose their will on the legislature.

The violence of the *sans-culottes* posed an acute problem for the Jacobin government. How could the sovereign people be denied the right to exercise their sovereignty as they saw fit? Could the people's elected representatives legitimately lay down rules for the sovereign people? The Jacobins were never able to reconcile their constitutional principles with their mystical view of popular sovereignty. One of the problems was that the people did not behave as republican democrats believed they would and should behave. It was a problem similar to the one facing parents who feel they have no right and no need to discipline their children: Confronted with the abusive behavior of undisciplined children, they alternate between patient suffering and violent outbursts. The left wing was morally paralyzed in this way even before the dictatorship of 1793–94. A few hours after the purges and massacres of 10 August 1792, the surviving part of the Legislative Assembly took a patient view of the popular violence around them. It listened respectfully while Santerre, the provisional commander of the National Guard, cast the previous day's doings in the most favorable light possible. "I must admit," he declared, "that the people's anger was only too just. Drawn inside

[the Tuileries] in the consoling hope of a desirable reconciliation, they saw themselves shot down, their friends and brothers
pitilessly massacred. Unable to restrain their resentment, they
sacrificed the criminals to their vengeance. But the people had
been so long provoked that [surely] you will find they gave a
great example of moderation in dealing with the enemies of liberty."[3] Here already was that rosy Robespierrist view of the Paris
mob seen through the prism of Jacobin ideology.

By the summer of 1792 the doctrine of popular sovereignty
had evolved into a defense of violence, revolutionary "justice,"
and popular terrorism. The ruling Jacobins shared this view in
1793 and 1794 as they tried to interpret and lead the forces carrying them along. On 5 September 1793, for instance, Danton
expressed it in the Convention packed with crowds of the populace calling for an armed force of their own: "I know that when
the people presents its needs, when it offers to march against its
enemies, no other measures should be taken but those it presents itself: for they have been dictated by the national genius."
As the historian R. R. Palmer puts it, "The revolutionary leaders
. . . meant by 'the people' something higher and nobler than the
people they saw."[4] Some, like Camille Desmoulins, were gradually disillusioned by the blindness and immorality of the populace, but others blamed popular excesses on bad advice. In this
way the sovereign people remained, like the sovereign kings of
old, forever good but sometimes led astray, *surpris,* by their
advisers.

The historian who shakes off Jacobin ideology sees the *sans-
culottes* of Paris and other cities not as the sovereign people in
general but as militant minorities. The assemblies of the forty-
eight sections were attended by small, convinced minorities, and
the popular societies never had more than about 10 percent of
the section populations.[5] The political leaders in the sections
numbered only in hundreds even in 1793 and 1794. Some 343
sat on the Civil Committees created by municipal laws of May
and June 1790 and reorganized after 10 August 1792, about 454
in the Revolutionary Committees, and besides these, another 500
or 600 were politically active. The great majority in the sections,
which had total populations ranging from 4,000 to 25,000, seldom, if ever, took part in revolutionary demonstrations. On the

major political occasions, indeed, "popular" demonstrations were planned by small central committees. The insurrections of both 10 August 1792 and 31 May–2 June 1793 were, as we have seen, planned by such committees.[6]

The activists in the forty-eight sections were, furthermore, a social hierarchy, by no means the sort of egalitarian brotherhood their rhetoric suggested. The dominant groups, such as the revolutionary planning committees mentioned above, were middle-class intellectuals, and the majority of activists were socially above the laboring poor. The 144 citizens elected by the forty-eight sections in July 1793 to be ready to serve on the Paris Commune included 2 engineers, 2 clergymen, 5 teachers, 8 lawyers, 9 doctors, 9 government employees, 10 artists, and several big businessmen.[7] The ideologists among them believed in social equality, but more typical were *sans-culottes* such as Jacques-Maurice Duplay, a master cabinetmaker with whom Robespierre lodged, owner of three houses, father-in-law of the Convention deputy Lebas. Duplay would not have his workmen at his table because this was not done. At this level were the men of the Civil Committees, a quarter of whom lived on incomes from property and workshops. More than one-tenth of them were architects, sculptors, painters, lawyers, or other professional men, a few were entrepreneurs or manufacturers, and the rest were tradesmen or shopkeepers.

The Revolutionary Committees were lower in the social scale but still consisted mainly of self-employed shoemakers, carpenters, barbers, engravers, and the like. The militants not on these committees were even lower in the social scale, but scarcely more than one-fifth of them were wage earners even in this group. The mass of the hungry poor, perhaps 70,000 in Paris at the time, may have been among the followers but were nowhere to be seen among the leaders. They were the political clientele of the better-off tradesmen, shopkeepers, and professional men. Militancy was a luxury possible only for those with some funds.[8] So various were the *sans-culottes* in background and occupation that they did not form a social class any more than the Jacobins did. In fact, they cannot be socially defined at all, and this is why we have to fall back on their own name for themselves.

The politics of the so-called popular movement was partly a

matter of popularity or patronage by leaders practiced in the art of gathering followers. Several earlier section leaders, such as Desmoulins, Marat, and Danton, had been so successful in winning support that they had risen into the ranks of the Convention after 10 August 1792. In 1793 and 1794 the *enragés* formed a large circle of followers, as did the Cordeliers Club, now a rallying center for the section societies. Another circle formed around the famous journalist of *Le Père Duchesne*, Jacques-René Hébert. Two of his friends, François-Nicolas Vincent and Charles-Philippe Ronsin, formed a large group of their own, almost a party, including many clerks in the War Ministry.[9] The chiefs of staff in the Paris *armée révolutionnaire*, some forty *sans-culottes* and army officers, dispensed places to a numerous clientele in autumn 1793. For example, the second-in-command (second to Ronsin), Servais-Baudoin Boulanger, a Belgian journeyman jeweler, was supported by the Halle-au-Bled Section, where he was active, by the Committee of General Security, and by the Robespierre clan. He himself was a member of the Jacobin Club. Once in place, he promptly hired two neighbors as chief clerk and adjutant general.[10] The same story could be told over and over.

These and most of the other *sans-culottes* leaders who worked out the political strategy of the movement were literate, even educated, men who are not easily classified with the populace. Jacques Roux, for instance, was from a leading family of Pranzac in Angoumois. Among the nine on the Central Committee of 31 May–2 June 1793, for instance, were Jacques Marquet of the Bonne-nouvelle Section, the printer of Hébert's *Père Duchesne*, and Jean-François Varlet, the clever young postal clerk of the Droits de l'Homme Section, one of the *enragés* socialists. They were joined by Claude-Emmanuel Dobsen from the Cité Section, who was soon to be a judge and president of the Revolutionary Tribunal. Most of these and their kind had been constitutional monarchists or moderates earlier and became revolutionary republicans only after 10 August 1792. "As for the mass," Soboul tells us, "apart from the hatred of aristocracy and the summary way of dealing with it, such as massacre in particular, they do not seem to have been endowed with any great political feeling or sense."[11] This was true, too, of the rank and file of *sans-culottes* in the civil *armées révolutionnaires*. They were primarily interested in basic necessities and their prices.

More than all else, the mass of the *sans-culottes* wanted enough cheap food. Their anxiety on this score distinguished them from the men of the National Convention, the Jacobin clubs, the public in general, and even their own leadership. Since the middle of the eighteenth century the educated public had imbibed theories of economic freedom, of laissez-faire, along with liberal political ideas. Such ideas haunted even such egalitarian thinkers as Pierre-Sylvain Maréchal (1750–1803).[12] For merchants, landowners, and even peasant proprietors, the Revolution had been partly a struggle against the regulations and taxes of "tyrannical" government. The central and municipal governments had long ago learned to control the supplies and prices of grain in the interests of consumers, and it was as consumers that the *sans-culottes* agitated for assured provisions at fixed prices. Being self-employed tradesmen and shopkeepers, most of them wanted lower prices rather than higher wages. But the management of food prices and supplies entailed bureaucratic controls, inspections, and penalties that were anathema to the educated public in general. Many experienced administrators knew that efficient management was possible and necessary, and the Jacobin dictatorship was eager to manage the national economy temporarily as part of the war effort. On this misunderstanding was the political alliance of Jacobins and *sans-culottes* based. The Committee of Public Safety was willing to control food supplies and prices but not to achieve that measure of social equality that was the ideal of the *sans-culottes,* and of the *enragé* utopians in particular. Not even the Jacobins really understood *sans-culottes* thinking on this score.

Wherever the populace imposed its will, the trade in food and other basic necessities was managed by its direct intervention. This was in an old tradition. In May 1775, to cite only one prerevolutionary case, the common folk in the Paris region had invaded local markets to enforce fair prices rather than suffer by the free trade Turgot had ordered. Large crowds had tried to pillage grain cargoes in July and August 1789, and the crowds that had brought the royal family to Paris on 5–6 October 1789 had been mainly anxious about food. On 25 February 1793 there were mass invasions of grocers' and chandlers' shops in Paris to dictate lower prices, and similar violence in the days following to obtain sugar, soap, and coffee at lower prices. By summer 1793 prices had risen steeply since June 1790 owing to inflation, bad harvests, and wartime disruptions: wheat by 27 percent, rye 20 percent, potatoes 700 percent, beef 136 percent, and mutton 63 percent.[13] The maximum prices for grain and fodder decreed on 4 May were soon abandoned, and the chief purpose of the uprising on 4–5 September 1793 was to force the government to establish a new general price ceiling. When thousands of people shouted, *"Du pain! Du pain!"* and Hébert, Pache, and Chaumette came forward with plans for controlling the economy, the government once more decreed national maximum prices on 11 September and a general price ceiling on 29 September. Across the country, meanwhile, hoarders and profiteers were being denounced, arrested, and executed. Economic life could not be controlled, it seemed, except by force.

As a result of the same uprisings of 4–5 September, the government established a civil armed force of *sans-culottes* whose main purpose was to procure food in the countryside and see that it reached Paris. This was the *armée révolutionnaire,* some 6,000 strong, led by Ronsin under orders from the Paris Food Commission (Commission des subsistances). Contingents of this force went about the Paris region, making sure that wheat and rye from the harvest fields reached the city markets. To do this, they had to watch the stocks of the big farmers and of some threescore villages, including Gonesse (Seine-et-Oise) on the two great northern routes out of Paris. The Paris *armée révolutionnaire* was soon imitated in a haphazard way by about sixty other departments and by towns suffering from chronic food shortages. Incidental to this work, the *arméés révolutionnaires* arrested suspects, seized valuables from nobles, churches, and the wealthy, and tried to destroy Church life in a dechristianizing campaign.

Most of the rank and file of the Paris *armée* were *sans-culottes* from the forty-eight sections, family men in their thirties and forties, tradesmen, shopkeepers, or wage earners with a common view of the world. The rank and file of the *sans-culottes* typically lived and thought in groups or gangs. They were suspicious of privacy, individuality, and the secret ballot, would brook no dissent, and believed in sharing opinions and votes as well as food. They believed that all men should do useful work with their hands, and they had no respect for artists, scholars, scientists, and other such "idle" people. Austere in some ways, they denounced idleness, fancy dress, obscene writing, prostitution, and philandering. Convivial, they ate and drank as merrily as they could. Ganglike, often drunken, they thought women inferior, priests effeminate, and Christianity a plot against their manhood. Patriotic, they sang stirring songs, attended civic banquets, planted trees of liberty, and encouraged their children to recite the Declaration of the Rights of Man. Self-righteous, they knew an aristocrat, a counterrevolutionary, or a hoarder when they saw one and could kill him or see him killed without any apparent qualms of doubt or pity. Fraternal and idealistic, they tried to do away with poverty as well as wealth and dreamed of a world of small properties wherein all would have enough and none too much. But their concerns were mainly local; they had little interest in the national or international matters that interested the deputies to the Convention and other members of the educated public.[14]

In 1793 and 1794 the *sans-culottes* imposed the clothing and manners of the populace on French society in general. Woe to people who dressed or behaved as the public used to do! Workingmen's trousers *(pantalons)* were essential, instead of the breeches *(culottes)* hitherto worn by the middle classes and the nobility. The red Phrygian cap *(bonnet rouge)*, emblem of the freed slave, was widespread early in 1792 and served after 10 August as a symbol of *sans-culotte* political power, though Pétion and Robespierre had argued against it in the Jacobin Club on 15 March 1792 in favor of the *cocarde tricolore*.[15] The periwig had, of course, long gone, and wigmakers were numerous among the unemployed. The short jacket, or *carmagnole,* and the pike completed the dress of the typical *sans-culotte.*

People were to be addressed as *citoyen* or *citoyenne* instead of *monsieur* or *madame* and were to refer to each other in the familiar *tu* and *toi* instead of the polite *vous.* On 31 October 1793 a deputation from all the popular societies of Paris asked the Convention to outlaw the word *vous.* Neither the Convention nor even its ruling committees would go so far, but they conformed in dress and manners as long as the *sans-culottes* were a ruling force. Bowing, kissing women's hands, or clapping one's own was considered royalist; instead of clapping, a republican was to shout "Bravo!" Many *sans-culottes* gave up their Christian names in favor of heroes' names, ancient, modern, or mythical—Brutus, Gracchus, Anaxagorus, William Tell, Benjamin Franklin—or names from nature—Amaranthe, Balsamine, Pigeon, Tabac—or even splendid composites like Immortelle-Victoire, Miel-Erasme, or Dugommier-Pignon.

The *sans-culottes* were city folk. Many were from provincial towns with which they kept in touch, but not many had rural or peasant backgrounds. With a pathological suspicion of farmers, they visited the countryside mainly to find food in it, plunder it, and abuse it.[16] As city men they were part of that small minority of the French population that lived in towns and so can scarcely be described as representative of the masses. The masses in eighteenth-century France were peasants living in villages, hamlets, or lonely farms, rural folk quite different from the *sans-culottes*. But even in their cities the *sans-culottes* were no more than minorities. They were, in fact, those few from various walks of life who were sufficiently interested in public affairs to attend the meetings of section assemblies and committees and to attend to the events of their time in response to vigorous leadership. Among them were men from the urban populace who in the special circumstances of 1792–94 had the opportunity and the imagination to impose their will upon the public and so to become, in a sense, part of it.

II. *Chouans and Other Counterrevolutionaries*

In 1793 and 1794 there were as many counterrevolutionaries as revolutionaries in France, probably more. "By 1795–6," write the historians Le Goff and Sutherland, "a majority of French citizens were probably in some sort of revolt against the Republic."[17] The peasantry, some five-sixths of the population, was divided, and a large but indeterminate proportion of the peasants had turned their backs on the Revolution. That counterrevolutionary part is often left out of historical accounts because it was fragmentary, inarticulate, and not immediately successful. Looking ahead, however, we can see that it already formed a popular basis for the consulate, the empire, and the Bourbon restoration. We have to ask ourselves why, for example, the recruiting of Napoleon's huge armies over more than a decade aroused less resistance among the peasantry, all things considered, than the recruiting of smaller armies in 1793 and 1794. The counterrevolutionary elements in France were ultimately stronger than the revolutionary elements, and this was as true for the peasantry as for other social classes. The peasants cannot be dismissed, moreover, as merely ignorant masses blindly following their seigneurs and priests, for research shows this idea to be revolutionary propaganda and quite unfounded. The question that remains is why so many rural folk were monarchist, Roman Catholic and counterrevolutionary while others were republican, anticlerical, and revolutionary. Somehow the counterrevolutionary masses in the countryside must be accounted for in the history of 1793 and the years following.

Peasant resistance scarcely showed itself until 1792 and not on a large scale until 1793. The uprisings of the Great Fear in July 1789 are not thought of as counterrevolutionary (though the National Assembly at the time had its doubts) because they expressed resistance to the seigneurial regime and furnished pretexts for sweeping reforms in the countryside. But they also expressed the hostility of the rural community to outside authority, essentially the same hostility we find in 1793 and 1794. Local considerations were at the root of peasant behavior in the Revolution, as at other times. Once the republic began to make demands of the peasantry, a new resistance developed very quickly. The complaints of 1788–89 were forgotten in 1793 and 1794, but new complaints were not lacking.[18]

Some regions found the new taxes of the Revolution much heavier than those of the *ancien régime*. By trying in 1791 to make taxes rational, fair and equal, the Constituent Assembly condemned large numbers of peasants to pay more. The merits of the new *contribution foncière* on agricultural revenues and the *contribution mobilière* on chattels or movable wealth were lost on those who had earlier paid less. In Upper Brittany, for instance, the new system almost doubled the burden of taxes. The same was true of other provinces formerly taxed less as *pays d'état*. The seigneurial dues and the tithe were no longer collected, and that was a considerable benefit; but in 1793 a "forced loan" increased the tax burden—by half in the *département du Nord*. For one reason or another the new system of taxes did not bring universal contentment to the French countryside.[19]

The abolition of the tithe and the feudal dues was of greater benefit to peasant proprietors than to tenants, and so were the sales of property confiscated from the Church, the emigrant nobles, and other victims of the Revolution. Here was a persistent source of conflict in rural communities. Peasant proprietors benefited by the Revolution much more than peasant tenants. From early in 1791, when confiscated Church lands were first put up for auction, the better-off peasants acquired more and more land. So did the townspeople, always ready to buy land as a secure investment in an insecure world. These landowning groups tended to be republicans and supporters of the new regime. Property was the basis for the revolutionary liberalism expressed, for example, by Paul-Louis Courier, an army officer from a peasant family, who loved the constitution of 1791 and the charter of 1814, but neither the Robespierrist nor the Bonapartists regime, and who hated capitalists' buying up land as a speculation. Peasant tenants with less to lose were inclined to become hostile to landowners and to the Revolution. The western regions of Upper Brittany, Anjou, and Poitou, where counterrevolution was strong, had large numbers of sharecroppers and other tenants.[20]

Peasants without any incentive to respond to the calls of the republic were inclined to resist conscription for military duty. As early as 15 August 1792, 1,000 gathered at Saint-Ouen-des-Toits in Maine on the borders of Brittany, crying that they would fight only for the king and the pope and that the buyers of Church property should fight for the nation. Among those the gendarmerie arrested were the Cottereau brothers, former salt smugglers, nicknamed *chouans,* a name that soon applied to rural counterrevolutionary guerrillas in general.[21] Such movements were sporadic until 10 March 1793, when a veritable army of resistance to conscription appeared at Saint-Florent-le-Vieil in Anjou and roused western France in general.[22] Then no less than fourteen western departments rose against the efforts to conscript 300,000 men for the army.

The peasants who acquired Church lands were inclined to put up with the revolutionary religious policy more willingly than those who did not. But in general, as historians agree, the Civil Constitution of the Clergy was the strongest incentive to counterrevolution among the peasantry. Rural communities were strongly attached to their priests. From spring 1791 large numbers of clergy who would not take the oath were replaced with others who would, a vast majority in Flanders and the West. When a nonjuring priest remained in a village, he often became the leader of a counterrevolutionary faction opposed to the new constitutional priest and his supporters. The pope encouraged resistance when he took a stand against the Civil Constitution in April 1791, and the royal family encouraged it further by their flight to Varennes in June. Animosity to the revolutionary authorities on this score grew over the next two years and contributed more than anything else to the passionate outbursts of 1793. Late in 1793 and in 1794 the dechristianizing efforts of the representatives on mission, of the *armées révolutionnaires* and of Jacobin authorities here and there across the country were a further provocation. Peasants all over France resisted the new calendar with its ten-day "week," the revolutionary cults and festivals with their tree-planting ceremonies, and the marauding forces that seized church bells for the metal and forced curés to marry while trying to turn churches into meeting halls.

Efforts to provision the cities and the armies by controlling the distribution of grain caused much bitterness in the countryside. "Requisitioning," often only a euphemism for official theft, and all the regulations to keep grain flowing into Paris, Rouen, Marseilles, Toulouse, and other cities were enforced by the Jacobin representatives on mission and then by the *sans-culottes* in the civil *armées révolutionaires*. These were seen as outsiders sending the precious food supplies to unknown destinations. The price ceilings decreed in May and September 1793 pleased the *sans-culottes* but antagonized the peasants. To make things worse, the revolutionary authorities in Paris and the provincial capitals were inclined to see malevolence and hostility everywhere and so stirred up hostility by tactless violence.[23] The mere presence of an *armée révolutionnaire* in a district aroused antagonism by impugning the people's patriotism. Bad feeling was not universal, but most farmers opposed a policy conceived in the interests of the towns, and they found willing allies in the many administrators trying to keep grain for local use. Rural hostility did much to cause the terrible food shortages of 1795. In Richard Cobb's words, "Dearth was a great divider."[24]

Yet another source of rural discontent was the promotion of poor but ambitious men to positions of authority. With their strong sense of hierarchy, peasants in the *département du Nord* resented the "dregs of the people," the *gens sans aveu*, who rose in the revolutionary process of denunciation and democracy.[25] In the Massif Central the mountain peasants persisted in following local seigneurs and other notables. In Upper Brittany rural communities were "rigorously deferential."[26] The revolutionary message of equality scarcely reached the mass of peasants, and in general they remained indifferent to the great national cause preached by rapacious, irreligious strangers from the towns. Among peasant extremists even the terms *nation* and *citoyen* became dirty words. Innumerable incidents like the arrest of five Flemish farmers in June 1793 for parading a donkey on the road with a *cocarde tricolore* on its head are reported.[27]

Much resentment everywhere expressed the ancient antagonism of the country people to the towns whence came the revolutionary changes and forces. This was a political antagonism, not the conflict of different social classes. Until the 1790s government had rarely intruded in local affairs, and the priest had been virtually the only permanent outside official. Lawyers, intruders from the towns, were generally hated in the countryside. The ancient rural-urban conflict may not have been so great as to warrant the sweeping sociological theories of Paul Bois and Charles Tilly, but all studies show it to have been one of the major causes of discontent.[28] Resentment of the city was, after all, the peasant equivalent to provincial resentment of Paris at other social levels. Both need careful qualification, but both were everywhere apparent. Bred in these ancient resentments, rural communities were all the more ready to take offense at the imperious revolutionary messages from outside.

The map of counterrevolutionary feeling among the peasants is not yet clearly drawn, but some features are established. In southern France, communities in the Vivarais, the Velay, and other populous mountain regions of the Massif Central tended to be more counterrevolutionary than those in the plains. In the department of the Loire the Terror remained essentially a phenomenon of the plain, an urban phenomenon which imposed itself on those rural communities of the surrounding countryside that were easily accessible.[29] The mountain folk remained hostile to a revolution that came from the lowlands with its alarming attacks on the familiar religious, economic, and social order. Feuds and vendettas led clans to take sides on political matters and to wage bitter struggles, like the one between the Vadier and Darmaing clans in the Ariège Department or the one between the Labastide and Lanteiris clans at Chamborigaud near Génolhac (Gard).[30] In the Gard Department, around the ancient provincial capital of Nîmes, counterrevolution was strong in Roman Catholic circles because the Revolution had brought Protestants to the fore, freeing them from the cruel bondage imposed by Louis XIV. The same was true of the regions to the west around Montauban and Alès. In Corsica the counterrevolutionary movement by which Paoli led the island to renounce its union with France and to join Great Britain in 1794 was a return to the Corsican political tradition interrupted by French annexation in 1768. Counterrevolutionary activity, variously inspired, can be plotted all through a zone shaped like an inverted letter *T*, down the Rhône and throughout Provence to the southeast and across Languedoc to the southwest.[31] Most of all, hostility to the Revolution was strong in the western regions of Poitou, Anjou, Brittany, Maine, and even farther north in Normandy, Picardy, and Flanders.

What effect counterrevolutionary cities had on the peasantry remains unclear. The federalist revolts of summer 1793 in Lyons, Marseilles, and Toulon were not simple in their inspiration. Much of the federalist hostility to the Jacobin government in Paris grew up among the royalists, Girondins, and other "moderates" in the towns, where their ranks were swelled by the dispossessed officeholders of the *ancien régime*. But in Lyons the revolutionary government was also opposed by the sections and the popular clubs, composed mainly of silk weavers under lead-

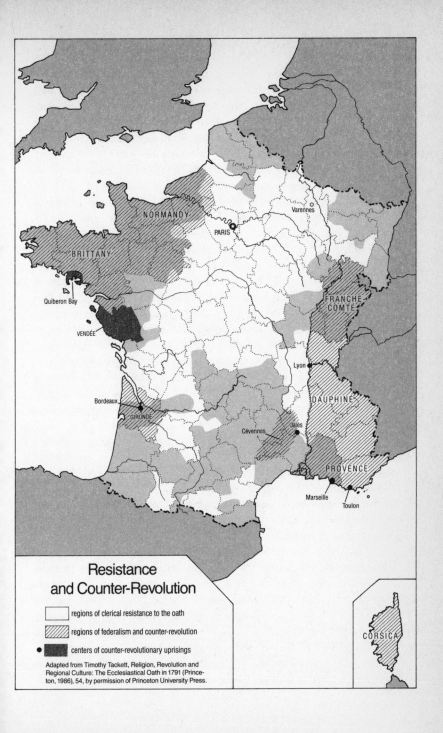

Resistance and Counter-Revolution

NORMANDY

BRITTANY

Quiberon Bay

VENDÉE

Varennes

PARIS

FRANCHE COMTÉ

Lyon

Bordeaux

GIRONDE

DAUPHINE

Cévennes

Alès

PROVENCE

Marseille

Toulon

regions of clerical resistance to the oath

regions of federalism and counter-revolution

• centers of counter-revolutionary uprisings

Adapted from Timothy Tackett, Religion, Revolution and Regional Culture: The Ecclesiastical Oath in 1791 (Princeton, 1986), 54, by permission of Princeton University Press.

CORSICA

ers like the experienced Patriot, Denis Monnet (1750–93).[32] All these had little to do with counterrevolution among the peasantry, whose leaders typically came from small market towns or villages: Joseph Puisaye from Mortagne in the Perche, west of Paris; Georges Cadoudal from Kerléano near Auray; his colleague Louis-Charles-René de Sol de Grisolles (1761–1836) from Guérande in Brittany; Jean-Nicolas Stofflet from Lunéville on the Meurthe River in Lorraine.

Peasants broke out into violent rebellion in two principal ways. One was in the "armies" of the Vendée, hordes of men, women, and children led by "generals" in attacks upon towns and villages. La Rouerie recruited thousands for his Association bretonne in 1791 and 1792, but most of the Vendean armies were afoot between March and December 1793. Badly armed, lacking the sustaining forces of the State, vainly hoping for allies at home and abroad, especially from England, these movements were soon exhausted, annihilated, and the survivors driven to the underground warfare of the Chouans. So cruel and devastating was the repression that some of its students are ready to describe it as genocide.[33] Pathetic victims of the Revolution, these peasants rank in history with the peasant armies in England in 1381, in Germany in 1525, in Russia in 1762 and 1819, and at many other places and times.

The guerrilla warfare of the Chouans in the west was more sustained and more widespread. Murder in the night on country roads was its principal manifestation.[34] Its victims were leaders, public figures, and supporters of the Revolution. The typical Chouan was a young farmhand in his twenties or a tenant farmer ready to aid the expected royalist forces whenever they might appear but committed in the meantime to destroying as many revolutionary agents and sympathizers as he could. Tens of thousands flourished in the bocage terrain of hamlets and isolated farms in enclosed fields and hedgerows east of Le Mans (Sarthe) and north of La Roche-sur-Yon (Vendée) as far as Rouen. Working in bands in districts they knew well, they were essentially local, and "the ferocious individualism of the local Chouan commanders" made subordination and cooperation difficult.[35] This difficulty was typical of the counterrevolutionary forces in general. Those few leaders with grander projects had the greatest difficulty in organizing collaborative forces, and Puisaye, for example, ultimately, on 17 September 1794, fled in a small boat to Jersey and thence to England. By that time the armies and tribunals of the republic had purged western France of hundreds of counterrevolutionaries and had imprisoned thousands more. But *chouannerie* was never stamped out and went on sporadically into the nineteenth century.

The Chouans must be distinguished in some respects from the murderous bands of criminals, such as the infamous *bande d'Orgères* in the Beauce district, and from the gangs of cutthroats (*égorgeurs*) who murdered thousands of the Jacobin and *sans-culotte* leaders and their followers in 1794, 1795, and later years. In their disrupting effects and their counterrevolutionary vengeance, however, there is little to choose between them. The men who killed some 2,000 popular militants in the region between the Swiss frontier and the Mediterranean were essentially no different from the Chouans who did the killing in the rural west. All over France the White Terror wreaked vengeance on the men of 1792–94 sporadically from the Thermidorian reaction of July 1794 until 1815, killing in all perhaps as many as the revolutionaries had killed in their regime of terror.[36] Once roused, the populace in town and country was hard to pacify. Civil order, public peace, and safety are delicate flowers and hard to establish, as the Thermidorian regime and the Directory found in the late 1790s.

TEN *The First Republic and Its Enemies, 1794–99*

THE First French Republic endured for more than five years after the Jacobin dictatorship had come to an end in July 1794. Until General Bonaparte's coup d'etat on 9 November 1799, the various political forces clashed and struggled within the terms of a liberal constitution. Certain groups resorted to violence, and the government did, too, on occasion; but in 1795 and 1796 the republic was ruled by moderate majorities which believed in the freedoms that had been established from 1789 to 1791. Those freedoms were major constitutional guarantees expressed in detail at the end of the first year in a new constitution of 22 August 1795, drafted by Pierre-Claude-François Daunou (1761–1840) and other Girondins, but it is easy to be blinded to them by the charges of corruption leveled at the republic. Every French republic, like all parliamentary regimes everywhere, has been accused of tolerating rich, selfish, predatory, decadent people.

In the 1790s the accusation was true but only a half-truth. Could any authority curb wealth and enforce principles of social equality without becoming oppressive and even tyrannical? Was freedom compatible with equality or with public virtue? It is not difficult to answer these questions in the negative by reviewing five occasions on which the regime resorted to violence in defense of the constitution: against a *sans-culotte* uprising on 20–21 May 1795, a royalist uprising on 5 October 1795, in an antiroyalist purge on 4 September 1797, in an anti-Jacobin purge on 11 May 1798, and in a purge of its own executive Directory on 18 June

1799. When the regime fell at last in a conspiratorial coup d'etat on 9 November 1799, it is tempting to declare that it was only getting its desserts. But these would be superficial judgments.

The men who governed France after 9 Thermidor (27 July 1794) are not so easy to judge. Four in particular are always taken to be representative, having all been regicides and active terrorists in the Convention, all in the Thermidorian conspiracy against Robespierre, and all prominent in the subsequent governments: Paul-François-Jean-Nicolas, Vicomte de Barras (1755–1829), a former officer in the royal army, corrupt and unscrupulous, known for organizing the repression of counterrevolution at Marseilles and Toulon and the defense of the Convention in July 1794 and October 1795; Louis-Marie-Stanislas Fréron (1754–1802), one of Barras's terrorist colleagues in the south, one of Danton's friends earlier, author of an influential journal, *L'orateur du people;* Philippe-Antoine Merlin de Douai (1754–1838), formerly a lawyer in the Parlement of Douai, one of those who drafted the Law of Suspects in September 1793, a minister of justice and a director after Thermidor; and Jean-Lambert Tallien (1767–1820), a lawyer's clerk and journalist, a member of the Commune of 10 August 1792, married to a famous banker's beautiful daughter, Thérèse Cabarrús. The careers of these and other Thermidorians make them seem like opportunists, unprincipled, cynical, and self-serving. In addition, their regime has always seemed dull and petty, sandwiched as it was between the colorful regimes of Robespierre's Terror (1792–94) and Napoleon's empire (1799–1815). And circumstances had changed so much since 1789 that the men look as if they had changed also.

Were the men of 1795 really much worse than the men of 1789 or the men of 1793? In judging the post-Thermidorian regime, we have to consider whether the high principles on which Robespierre and his colleagues terrorized the population by mass murder makes these men better than their successors. Was Barras more corrupt than Mirabeau? Did any Thermidorian abuse the power of public office more than the chairman of the Committee of General Security in 1793 and 1794, M.-G.-A. Vadier (1736–1828), whose principal endeavor was to build up a following and further the private interests of his own family?[1] Was

Talleyrand-Périgord any less scandalous or clever as a deputy to the Estates General in 1789 than as a minister for foreign affairs in 1796? Was Lazare Carnot any less efficient as a member of the Directory in 1795 than as a member of the Committee of Public Safety in 1793, or as a deputy to the Legislative Assembly in 1791—or, for that matter, as minister for war in 1800 or as minister for the interior in 1791? Were Lanjuinais, Reubell, La Révellière-Lépeaux, and others any worse in the legislatures of the Directory than in the earlier assemblies? Did the nation, in short, really elect more unprincipled adventurers to represent them in the late 1790s than in the early 1790s?

These questions cannot be fully answered here, but a brief answer lies in a statement by a French scholar, Frédéric Braesch. Writing of 1792, be it noted, not of 1795, he concluded with the sad reflection "For a few honest people, how many scoundrels, and for a few sincere men, how many unprincipled individuals, ready for any work, serving every régime."[2] In the reform of French institutions, on the other hand, the men of 1795–99 did not lag behind the men of 1789–94, and they managed to achieve a level of political civilization which, for France in that age, seems remarkable.

More than anything else, the post-Thermidorians lived with the heritage of the previous five years. Those years had given them, and all the survivors from the National Assembly, the Legislative Assembly, and the Convention, not only the burdens of reputation, enmity, and error that all politicians accumulate but also the benefits of political experience. They decided that what mattered above all else was the survival of the liberal political process first established in 1789. To prevent further tyranny of the sort they had just experienced and taken part in, they promptly established a rotating membership for the committees of Public Safety and General Security. The constitution the Convention published a year later expresses a clear determination to make the republic proof against all the forces that had threatened or overwhelmed it in recent years, Jacobin, sans-culotte, royalist, clerical, or foreign. The anarchy of crime, so widespread in the wake of the Terror, they also tried to deal with. The only danger not properly foreseen, because not yet experienced, was the military dictatorship that was to overwhelm the republic after Napoleon's coup d'etat of 1799.

The constitution provided for an elaborate system of election whereby property owners sent 750 middle-aged deputies to the Corps législatif in Paris, the heart of the republic.[3] Married or widowered deputies over forty years of age domiciled in France for at least fifteen years then drew lots for the 250 seats in an upper house, the Council of Ancients. The remaining 500 deputies sat in the Council of Five Hundred. Deputies were to sit for three years, and then one-third of them were to retire each year so that none sat for longer than six years. But the Convention also decreed that in the elections of 1795 the electors must choose two-thirds of the deputies from among the members of the Convention. As for the executive part of the government, the legislature was to elect a five-man Directory, closed to the elected deputies, and it was to choose the ministers and officers of state and to behave in general like a governing council. The ministers it chose were not to form a cabinet (section 151) but were to be answerable to the Directory one by one like the ministers of the monarchy. The men of the Directory were themselves hedged about by elaborate rules (sections 132–173): Their chairmanship was to rotate; they were to wear a special costume; each was to be accompanied by two guards, and the total directorial guard was to include 120 cavalry and 120 infantry; each was to have a salary equivalent to 50,000 myriagrams of wheat, or 10,222 quintals (section 173); none was to go abroad; their relatives were not to be eligible for appointment; and so on.

A new French constitution is like a New Year's resolution: a statement of good intentions that remain to be put into effect in the hurly-burly of the coming months. Everyone knows that written documents do not of themselves effect any change. When the Corps législatif met in 1795, all the old political antagonists found each other again in the new political arena. The circumstances were complicated, however, by the revolutionary legacy. On the one hand, many were embittered by the violent events of the previous years; on the other, many were chastened by the experience of how violence begets violence, billowing out in clouds of partisan revenge. It remained to see whether their newfound wisdom would prevail over their legacy of hatred. In the nine "Duties of a Man and Citizen" which stood—Oh, rare sight!—in the preface to the constitution of 1795 with the usual list of "Rights," we see a recognition that civil and political liberty depends upon personal morality.

"All the duties of a man and citizen stem from two principles engraved by nature on all hearts," reads the second duty. "Do not do unto others what you would not have them do unto you. Always do unto others the good you would like to receive." To this the fourth duty adds, "No one is a good citizen unless he is also a good son, a good father, a good brother, a good friend and a good husband." In these constitutional clauses this assembly of prodigal sons wise with the lessons of the years 1789–95 was sheepishly bringing in by the back door the Christian principles it had earlier driven out by the front. These principles were, of course, formulated as "natural laws" by the nation's philosophers of the moment, Cabanis (1757–1808), Chénier (1764–1811), Destutt de Tracy (1754–1836), Garat (1749–1833), Volney (1757–1820), and others in the Auteuil circle of "idéologues."[4] As early as August 1793, indeed, Constantin-François de Chasseboeuf, Comte de Volney, with Dominique-Joseph Garat's encouragement—Garat was then minister of the interior—had published a manual of morality for popular instruction, *La loi naturelle, catéchisme du citoyen français,* which served up the ancient Christian principles in a typical civic form.

Meanwhile, the Roman Catholic tradition had been kept alive among the public by various underground organizations, notably the secret societies known as the Aa, which had been founded at La Flèche (Sarthe) in 1630. A group of influential clergymen formed the Company of the Friends of Religion (Société des amis de la religion), which met weekly from November 1794 to 1806 to plan a revival of the Roman Catholic Church. Under the leadership of Henri-Baptiste Grégoire and an executive committee known as the United Bishops, and with some vocal public support, they persuaded the Convention to sanction a measure of religious toleration. It was set forth in a decree of 21 February 1795 drafted by Boissy d'Anglas. The price of toleration was a firm separation of Church and State, also laid down in that decree and confirmed in the constitution of 22 August 1795 (article 354).

But this only gave legal form to a separation that had existed in fact since the Terror. After all, clerical salaries had not been paid for a long time.

The leaders of Catholic revival carried on in spite of opposition in Rome and Paris. Following prerevolutionary Gallican and Jansenist ideas, they formed presbyteries to elect bishops and convened two national councils that might ratify what the United Bishops did. They translated the liturgy into French. They tried to reconcile the constitutional Church, with its devotion to the republic and its married clergy, and the traditional church. And in spite of much disagreement and difficulty, they succeeded in reviving formal Christianity in France. Inevitably associated with the republic, their constitutional Church did not survive Napoleon's Concordat of 1802 with its ultramontane reconciliation with Rome.[5] But their work shows the liberal inclinations of the First Republic after 1794. It proved to be anticlerical but tolerant, at least until it faced a political threat from rising right-wing forces, of which the Church was one.

The underlying political problem was to establish a liberal republic safe not only from its enemies but also from abuses of government power and from the violence of the populace. The Thermidorians, whatever their faults, were committed to liberal ideals. Freedom of the press was established, and soon there were many moderate journals of the kind that had flourished from 1789 to 1792. Tallien soon obtained the suppression of postal censorship and a formal guarantee that no government agency would open private letters. On 11 August 1794, the Comédie française theater reopened, after being closed for nearly a year, with a play called *Guillaume Tell,* played by actors recently let out of jail.[6] Within three months the Convention had obtained the release of about half the 8,500 people in the Paris jails. The Paris tribunal, stopped in its murderous course on 1 August 1794, was strictly regulated and lost half of its personnel on 28 December, shortly after it had sent the terrorists Jean-Baptiste Carrier, Jean Pinard, and Michel Moreau Grandmaison to their deaths on 16 December. It was abolished altogether on 31 May 1795, after it had sent its former prosecutor, Fouquier-Tinville, to his death earlier that month. The Convention received a deputation of the wives and daughters of guillotined deputies on 10 December 1794 with a view to restoring confiscated family property. Nine days later the Convention showed its liberalism by defeating a motion that all the men of the Terror be deported. The 67 surviving Girondin deputies were reinstated in the Convention, and so were 23 others who had gone on to join the federalist movement. This does not make Thermidorians of them, and it is important to avoid "the grave error of confusing Thermidorians with Girondins."[7] Many different groups collaborated in the midst of their political struggles to defend the First Republic in this liberal phase.

Few liberal steps were taken in this regime without a struggle. The Thermidorians and their allies were not in a secure position of command for months after the coup of 27 July 1794. They depended on political support and in their struggles played shamelessly on public emotions for their own political advantage. Many people had lost loved ones to the guillotine, to the prisons, or in massacres. Many had resisted military conscription in November 1792 and in 1793. Many others had resented the austerity of the Jacobin dictatorship, the war on the wealthy, and the egalitarian manners imposed by the *sans-culottes*. Many had never ceased to believe in a moderate, constitutional regime.

By no means all of the so-called *muscadins* (a term of contempt derived from a perfume of the time) were the fops who have so impressed historians of the Revolution. By no means all were the *"garçons-parfumeurs, garçons-marchands, commis-banquiers, clercs de notaire, agents de change"* or the children of the wealthy denounced from that day to this as the *jeunesse dorée*.[8] They were as socially mixed as were the *sans-culottes*, but fighting a moderate cause with *sans-culotte* methods. The Thermidorians had learned how to resist left-wing crowds with right-wing crowds. The *jeunesse dorée*, 2,000 or 3,000 in all, responded to the leadership of Barras, Tallien, and especially Fréron, rallied at the café de Chartres or des Cannoniers in the Palais-Royal, and surged about the city in the service of the Thermidorians singing a song of their own, "Le reveil du peuple," instead of "La Marseillaise." Groups of them assaulted Jacobins and fought pitched battles with groups of *sans-culottes*, while other "moderates" attended the section assemblies and began to take control of them. This was all the easier because the Paris Commune, a *sans-culotte* stronghold since 10 August 1792, had crumbled away on 28 July

1794. Similar movements occurred in provincial towns, such as La jeunesse bordelaise, formed on 6 August 1794.[9] In Paris this activity went on until 4–6 October 1795 (Vendémiaire), when the government used troops led by military generals, including Bonaparte with artillery, to crush a dangerously large demonstration of *jeunesse dorée.*

By the use of such forces and by parliamentary methods, too, Barras, Fréron, and Tallien, erstwhile terrorists themselves, denounced a former member of the Committee of General Security, Vadier, and three former members of the Committee of Public Safety, Barère, Billaud-Varenne, and Collot d'Herbois, so effectively that an investigation and then a trial, beginning on 22 March 1795, led to a sentence of deportation to the prison colony of Guiana. The sentence could not be carried out because of the British naval blockade, and first Vadier and then Barère managed to go into hiding. Meanwhile, the populace was ready, as ever, to lynch these latest victims.[10]

All this was only to be expected. The remarkable thing in these years is that a determined effort was made to establish the rule of law throughout the republic.[11] The first Directory, elected in autumn 1795, left partisan violence to the courts and tried to maintain the constitutional processes that might stabilize a liberal republic. They revived policies resembling the Girondin policy of September 1792 for creating a "departmental guard" and a law against *provocateurs* of murder and arson and resembling before that the efforts by Lafayette and the Constituent Assembly to establish political and civil liberties within a framework of law and order.[12] It is all very well to point out that they began to suspend civil and political liberties in 1797 and 1798. They saw the election results in 1797, when royalists were elected in large numbers, and in 1798, when many Jacobins were elected, as serious threats to the republic. The historian, safe from the practical consequences of mistakes in judgment, can fearlessly distinguish between the merely criminal activities of murder gangs and the political activities of royalist groups and Jacobin clubs, but the government of the republic could not afford to risk any such distinction. After all, royalists, Jacobins, and *sans-culottes* were proven enemies of liberal parliamentary process.

During the year between the events of 9 Thermidor and the

promulgation of the constitution of 1795 the *sans-culottes* pressed for the democratic constitution of 1793, which had never been implemented. On 21 March 1795 the Montreuil and Quinze-vingt sections petitioned the Convention to that effect and clashed with the *jeunesse dorée*. Behind the political pleas of the *sans-culottes*, however, were the physical hardships of that winter, an extraordinarily harsh one in which many people froze to death. Food shortages, furthermore, reached famine proportions that spring. These were, as usual, partly due to natural causes but were partly also due to disastrous blunders by the governing authorities. For a while early in the winter the Commission du commerce et des approvisionnements misjudged the situation and thought there was a surplus of grain. The Convention abolished the price ceiling *(maximum)* on 24 December 1794 in the name of free trade. Bread rationing was ordered but was not—perhaps could not be—enforced. At the root of the crisis was the resistance which the farmers opposed to requisitioning.[13]

After 9 Thermidor the commanding groups in the Convention did all in their power to restrict Paris and the *sans-culottes*. The Paris Commune fell on 11 Thermidor, and the new administration of the capital, set up by a decree of 31 August 1794, was thenceforth to be tightly controlled by the national government. The Revolutionary Committees in the forty-eight sections were undermined and then abolished; in the Droits de l'homme Section it last met on 5 November 1795.[14] On 24 August 1794 twelve large arrondissements were imposed on the sections, each with a comité de surveillance d'arrondissement, which resembled the moderate Civil Committees in composition and temperament. In 1795 and 1796 the Surveillance Committee of the Eighth Arrondissement, for instance, worked against the small groups of militants in the faubourg Saint-Antoine and by selective arrests left the discontented population almost leaderless.[15] Various clauses in the constitution of 22 August 1795 undermined the political life of the *sans-culottes*. "No individual, no partial meeting of citizens may assume sovereignty" (section 18). "No assembly of citizens may call itself a popular society" (section 361). "Citizens may exercise their political rights only in the primary or municipal assemblies" (section 363). "All citizens are free to address petitions to public authorities, but they must be submitted by individuals; no association may present a collective petition" (section 364). "Any armed gathering is an assault on the constitution and must be dispersed at once by force" (section 365).

The symbols of the *sans-culottes* and the ceremonies of the Terror began to disappear. On 6 January 1795 police inspectors reported hearing the terms *monsieur* and *madame* used everywhere in public.[16] As the *jeunesse dorée* began to parade about the town, people who were not tradesmen or artisans no longer felt any need to affect the dress of the *sans-culottes*. On 29 December 1794 a member of the Bonne-nouvelle Section caused an uproar by appearing in the section assembly in a *bonnet rouge,* and ten days later the police, weary of the public disturbances he was causing, ordered him not to wear it.[17] The cult of the revolutionary martyr Jean-Paul Marat, who personified popular violence, slowly died away under the pressure of hostile forces, especially the *jeunesse dorée,* always ready to pull down the busts of Marat everywhere erected in 1793 and 1794. A procession on 21 September 1794 to convey Marat's remains from the Cordeliers Section to the Panthéon by a ceremonial roundabout route proved to be small, damp, and anxious. And his tenure in the Panthéon turned out to be brief, as the Convention decreed his removal only four months later, on 8 February 1795.

Matters came to a head on 20–21 May 1795 (Prairial Year III), when crowds of *sans-culottes,* exasperated, confused, and desperate with hunger and misery, rose up in an insurrection as they had been doing since 1792. The Convention, no longer paralyzed by Jacobin democratic sympathies or by the fear of foreign aggression, organized a counterattack and put them down by force in a series of encounters that have been well described by George Rude and others.[18]

Meanwhile, the republic had also faced a growing Jacobin threat. The regime brought to power by the elections of 1795 announced its liberal intentions with a general political amnesty in November 1795. The Jacobin Club had been closed a year before on 14 November 1794, and its leaders hounded out of the popular society Défenseurs des droits de l'homme in the hospitable Quinze-vingts Section, "one of the last bastions of resistance to Thermidorian policy."[19] But now they began to recover in new clubs, such as the Panthéon Club in Paris and a few in the provinces such as the Club du Niveau in Bordeaux. Jacobin journals began to revive, too, in the new liberal atmosphere: René Vatar's *Journal de l'homme libre* (Paris) and *Le courrier de la Gironde* (Bordeaux). Certain individuals used the power of office to appoint Jacobins and to promote the Jacobin cause. A good example is Pierre Sotin, minister of police for five months, who protected and advanced Jacobins and took action against royalists until his sudden dismissal on 15 February 1798.[20]

In the elections of 1798 the Jacobins and *sectionnaires* won almost half of the seats in the Paris electoral assembly and were strong here and there in the provinces: in Ardèche, Bouche-du-Rhône, Corrèze, Haute-Pyrénées, Marne, Nièvre, Puy-de-Dôme, and Vienne.[21] Surviving Jacobin leaders of the Terror, such as Prieur de la Marne, Lindet, L.-J. Gohier (former minister of justice), and Pierre-François Tissot (1768–1854), were elected. Alarmed at this development, the Directory announced that a Jacobin party would not be tolerated and denounced it as a conspiracy against the republic. On 11 May a purge of Jacobins broke the movement further. Some historians lament these harsh measures as an interruption of the liberal political process, but can the Directory be blamed for taking steps to prevent a revival of the Jacobin Terror of 1792–94? Nothing in the history of Jacobinism warranted a trust in their newfound devotion to the constitutional political process. In July 1799 a new Jacobin Club was formed with about 3,000 members in the Salle de Manège in Paris but ordered closed only a month later. The movement was finally broken by the Bonapartist regime, which purged 62 Jacobin deputies for their opposition to the coup d'etat of 9 November 1799 and 100 more a year later in the affair of the "infernal machine" intended to blow up Napoleon.[22]

Throughout these years the republic was also threatened by royalists. These were numerous but weakened by an incapacity to sink their differences in a common cause. They might be reproached for lacking political common sense, except that the Thermidorians, who had plenty of common sense, are commonly reproached for being shifty and unscrupulous, for lacking, in fact, the impractical sincerity of the royalists. There is only a slight exaggeration in this comparison. Factious, proud, and jealous, the emigrant noblemen fell into three main groups according to convictions which they tended to hold with uncompromising religious fervor. The main body wanted the restoration of the king, who, after the supposed death of Louis XVII in 1795, was Louis XVI's brother, the Comte de Provence, the future Louis XVIII. He lived at Coblenz, at Verona, at Mitau, and finally in England. While he was still only regent for his young nephew, his Declaration to the French People (28 January 1793) made plain his intention to wipe out the Revolution and restore the absolute monarchy, and he confirmed this in a declaration at Verona on 24 June 1795. Large but indeterminate numbers of people in France and abroad shared the ancient religious commitment to this fat, intelligent Bourbon, who was to reign at last from 1814 to 1824.[23]

This movement of "pure" royalists committed to the Bourbon succession was rivaled by a powerful *parti des princes* rooted in the princely and provincial opposition to absolute monarchy that had flourished long before the Revolution. The princes who had opposed Louis XVI in the 1780s continued to do so in the 1790s. The large counterrevolutionary network built up by the Comte d'Antraigues from 1791 to 1793 was inspired as much by hatred of Louis XVI and the Bourbon monarchy as by opposition to the revolutionary republic.[24] D'Antraigues and his friends in and out of France wanted a decentralized feudal kingdom. In addition, these ancient *frondeurs* were joined by all who reproached Louis XVI and his followers for their liberal compromises with revolutionary governments.

The constitutional monarchists were a third royalist group at odds with the other two. In this movement must be counted the Feuillants and other monarchists who sat on the right in the revolutionary assemblies. Proscribed and hunted from 10 August 1792, surviving as best they could for the next two years, these royalists came back into the political arena after Thermidor with hopes of a political revival of monarchy. Their hopes and methods were quite different from those of Louis XVIII and the émigres, who were committed to intrigue, armed insurrection, and military invasion. Closer to practical politics, better aware of the profound changes brought about since 1789, the constitutional monarchists were readier for practical compromises. One of them, Antoine-Balthazard-Joseph d'André, wrote a conciliatory letter to Louis XVIII on 18 March 1796 and began to organize a royalist political campaign with a view to winning the elections of 1797.[25] This, one of the more practical royalist projects, drew together many disparate elements: Jacques Mallet du Pan, editor of the *Mercure;* the Institut philanthropique established in 1796 in Paris, Bordeaux, and other cities as a cover for moderate royalism; the men of the secret agency formed in Paris as early as 1791 by the Spanish ambassador, Comte Fermán de Núñez; the English organizer William Wickham and his French agents such as the young engineer, Louis Bayard, sent to Paris on 9 September 1795, when Wickham thought the republic might collapse.[26] They were encouraged by a royalist insurrection on 5 October 1795 (13 Vendémiaire year IV), by the Directory's official policy of repressing Jacobins, and by the spectacular public trial at Vendôme of Gracchus Babeuf's "conspiracy of equals" in summer 1796. In the elections of 1797 they were remarkably successful, but the government, alarmed at this success, organized a military repression and purged the royalists on 4 September 1797 (18 Fructidor Year V). The next day more than forty royalist newspapers were ordered suppressed.[27]

Not the least of the many threats to the First Republic was the widespread anarchy of revenge, the White Terror, directed against the men of 1792–94. It merges in the records with banditry, counterfeiting, and royalist insurgency, the motives of random crime being difficult to determine. All this was particularly savage in the southeast, where prisoners were massacred in the prisons of Lyons on 2 February and 4 May 1795, and about 100 Jacobin prisoners massacred in the Marseilles prisons on 5 June.[28] From 1795 to 1800, at least another 800 people were killed in streets, in fields, or in homes; murder became a daily occurrence in Lyons, Marseilles, and throughout the southeast. *Égorgeurs* and *sabreurs* attacked the Jacobin and *sans-culotte* terrorists of 1792–94 and the purchasers of confiscated property *(biens nationaux).*

A lot of this killing resulted from counterrevolutionary violence systematically organized by Roman Catholic groups like the Company of Jesus in Lyons and the Companies of the Sun in Provence. Much of it was the work of bandits who lurked in forests and hills in many regions, preying indiscriminately on travelers and the rural population: the *bande d'Orgères* in a region southwest of Paris centered on the Beauce granary district; François-Marie Salambier and his henchmen in the Flemish provinces; the *bande juive* in the Belgian departments and the Belgian border; various bands in Normandy, in the southwest from Toulouse to Bordeaux and elsewhere. For governing authorities it was difficult to distinguish between political violence and merely criminal violence, especially since any murder, whatever the real reason, could easily be disguised as political. The government usually surmounted this difficulty by imputing political motives to all criminals.

Against gangs of criminals that mingled inextricably with the White Terror the First Republic defended itself, as it did against Jacobins and *sans-culottes* on the left, royalists and Chouans on the right. None of these brought it down; it survived them all for more than five years. The republic was brought down at last in 1799 by General Napoleon Bonaparte with the support or acquiescence of all those in France ready to follow a successful military leader in a policy of national expansion. First among these were the millions of patriots, "Jacobins," or "neo-Jacobins" who believed in a patriotic revolutionary crusade for the expansion of France and the French nation, *la grande nation*.[29] Vadier, the Jacobin chairman of the Committee of General Security, had a typical vision of the day when "the tricolore would flutter over the Thames, when the Carmagnole would be heard in the streets of London, the 'modern Carthage,' and when *sans-culottes*, exhausted by the effort of invading Britain, would relax after their labours on the woolsack of the House of Lords."[30]

French aggression beginning in April 1792 provoked a defensive reaction on the part of European neighbors, and the coalitions they formed to oppose French armies aroused French patriotism even in circles that were scarcely revolutionary. Royalists and Jacobins, revolutionaries and counterrevolutionaries, *sans-culottes* and peasants all could agree in denouncing the Machiavellian schemes of foreign coalitions to humiliate and divide the French nation. "The patriotism of the men of the Revolution, Girondins and Montagnards," writes a historian of the Rev-

olution, "has a religious character and implies a veritable ethic.
With most of them, the sacred love of the fatherland took the
place of divine love."[31]

The creed of national patriotism brought with it a xenophobic anxiety about foreign conspiracy at every stage in the French
Revolution. One of the most persistent themes in both revolutionary and counterrevolutionary circles was the fear of foreign
machinations. This was manifested at different social levels and
in various political milieus. Most Jacobins believed in a foreign
counterrevolutionary plot of diabolical proportions led by the
kings of Europe, imagining far more unity, method, and cunning than ever existed in fact among the counterrevolutionary
forces.[32] As a consequence, to smear a public figure with the
suspicion of secret foreign alliances was as effective a way of
bringing him down as the suspicion of corruption. The demise
of the royal family and the monarchists in 1792, of the Girondins, Dantonists, and Hébertists in 1793 was based partly on the
suspicion of links abroad. Foreigners in general were held suspect during the Terror. In a burst of magnanimity on 26 August
1792 the Legislative Assembly had conferred French citizenship
on Thomas Paine and a few other foreign "friends of Liberty."
But on 1 August 1793 the Convention decided that all English-
men domiciled in France since 14 July 1789 must leave the country, and it went on to harass foreigners in general. On 24 June
1795 the people of Lyons were ordered to expel foreigners almost
as a matter of course in an effort to pacify the city.

The national cause drew Frenchmen together. "If there was
one common sentiment among Frenchmen of the middle and
lower classes," writes a student of Paris, "it was their devotion to
the *patrie*. Enragés and Girondists, labourers and shopkeepers,
men and women, became zealous partisans of the fatherland."[33]
From summer 1793 on the *sans-culottes* had a xenophobic hostility to foreigners and treated them all as suspects, even as enemies.[34] The sections watched foreigners closely and sometimes
refused them *cartes civiques*.

The *sans-culottes* . . . developed a revolutionary chauvinism not very far
removed from militarism and expansionism, while at the same time
turning inwards, with the result that there was a revulsion at both pop-

ular and government levels in the early months of 1794 against the "cosmopolitans" in Cloots's circus of professional, national-costumed refugees. By the summer of 1794, the surviving *sans-culottes* had become as wildly, madly xenophobic as Robespierre, Saint-Just and Barère.[35]

Chauvinism, nationalism, revolutionary imperialism form one of the deepest currents of the revolutionary era, binding together men of different social levels and different political views. Here is one of the fundamental elements in the interpretation of the First Republic and its ultimate demise. That interpretation is complicated by a widespread view of Napoleon's coup d'etat of 9 November 1799 as a right-wing conspiracy, part of a conservative reaction against the democratic left-wing forces of the republic. Faced with a dangerous coalition of foreign enemies and the threat of a Jacobin dictatorship to organize the national defense, the notables of the republic threw themselves into the arms of the generals, or so runs this common theory.[36]

There is, of course, much to be said in favor of this theory, but it leaves out of account the millions who rallied to Napoleon as first consul and then as emperor. By one means or another, especially by brilliant military victories, Napoleon gained the support of the great majority of Frenchmen. His armies were full of loyal peasants and lacked neither horses nor hardware; his legislative assemblies included no fewer than 330 men from the assemblies of the Directory and 57 from the earlier assemblies; his administrative services were full of men with long service back through the revolutionary years even to the reign of Louis XV. At least 629 of the 1,539 members of the Convention and the Constituent Assembly held office under Napoleon. Of the 281 men who served as prefects under Napoleon, 81 (30 percent) had once sat in a revolutionary assembly. From 1801 to 1805 the proportion approaches a half. Well over a quarter of Napoleon's prefects were noblemen. If the wastage by death and old age, and the rise of a new generation, are taken into account, these figures seem remarkably high.[37]

Popular or public opposition to Napoleon comparable with the opposition to previous regimes is scarcely to be found before 1814. As early as 7 February 1800 he held a plebiscite, and although it was rigged to secure a favorable vote, there is no evidence in it of much opposition to the new regime.[38] The working classes of the faubourg Saint-Antoine, lately so active in the revolutionary crowds, were ardent Bonapartists. Their young men joined Napoleon's armies with enthusiasm, and the military glory of victories and conquests made the populace in general put up with the hardships of daily life.[39] Again, several score deported Jacobins seem like the martyred minority of a larger movement, but it must be remembered that Bonaparte and his fellow generals were also Jacobins, the flower of that army built up by Carnot, Saint-Just, and Robespierre in 1793 and 1794. It would be hard to deny, too, that Napoleon won more support by his Concordat of 1801 with the papacy than the republic had won by its separation of Church and State on 21 February 1795. The effect of reviving noble rank and title in 1806 is harder to gauge, but there was no lack of candidates for the Bonapartist nobility. Many of them, like Abbé Sieyès, had been opponents of nobility in the revolutionary years.

As Georges Lefebvre remarked, "an authoritarian govern-ment was indispensable for saving the Republic as long as its adversaries collaborated with foreigners."[40] Against a patriotic national union under General Bonaparte the republic could not stand. The national aspirations of the French nation were stronger, in short, than its liberal aspirations. This, it must be stressed, was largely because the populace shared them. Only parts of the public, the "political nation," could understand par-liamentary government based on freedom and civil order, due process of law, an organized opposition, and an agreement to disagree. But the national and imperial struggles against the nation's enemies could be understood and shared by the great majority of Frenchmen. It was on the basis of their common support that Napoleon overthrew the Republic on 18 Brumaire Year VIII (9 November 1799) and founded his Consulate regime and, a few years later, his empire.

ELEVEN *A New Leviathan**

A national civil service grew up during the French Revolution. Greater in size, authority, and power than the
monarchy's administrative services, it survived every
political change, served every government in the revolutionary
years, and throve in their service. From April 1792 on continual
warfare stimulated and strengthened the civil service in the
national war effort. A new Leviathan was born during the French
Revolution. It was still there in 1799 for Napoleon to use. It is
still there today. Yet its story is seldom told because it seems at
first sight incongruous with a revolution for liberty and equality,
because Alexis de Tocqueville concluded in a famous study "that
administrative centralization is an institution of the ancien régime,
and not the work of the Revolution or of the Empire,"[1] and
because a casual review of the central administration can easily
mislead the reader to think that nothing significant was added
to it during the Revolution. A glance at the administration of the
provinces shows, for example, that the royal intendants were
abolished in principle by a law of 14 December 1789 (article 9)
on local government; they gradually gave way to the new departments in the course of 1790; and their successors, the prefects,
were not appointed until ten years later. In the revolutionary
decade elected authorities appear to have held power in the
provinces.

*In this chapter I have made much use of Michel Bruguière's brilliant *Gestion-
naires et profiteurs de la révolution*, Paris, 1986, 339 pp., and of Jacques Godechot,
Les Institutions de la France sous la révolution et l'empire, Paris, 1951; Edith Bernardin, *Jean-Marie Roland et le ministère de l'intérieur (1792–1793)*, Paris, 1964; C. H.
Church, *Revolution and Red Tape: The French Ministerial Bureaucracy 1770–1850*,
Oxford, 1981, 425 pp.; and J. F. Bosher, *French Finances 1770–1795: From Business to Bureaucracy*, Cambridge, England, 1970.

Four revolutionary changes outweigh all these considerations. First, the principle of national sovereignty gave the National Assembly the power it needed to destroy all intermediate authorities, all rivals to its own power. Armed with new authority, the Assembly and its successors did away with the provincial estates, the sovereign courts, the Church, the tax farms, the corps of financiers, the noble oligarchies in towns, in armed forces, and in the countryside. The central government and its civil service then had fewer and weaker rivals than ever before.

Secondly, the National Assembly defined itself and its successors as the legislature and created a separate executive power of government. As the Declaration of the Rights of Man and the Citizen puts it, "[p]reservation of the rights of man and the citizen require the existence of public forces. These forces are therefore established for the benefit of all . . ." (article 12). The forces of the state were henceforth supposed to be exercised in the name of the nation, in which resides (says the declaration, article II) the "principle of all sovereignty." The *nation*, not the *people*, as in the United States, was to be sovereign. The nation and the State played (and play) a characteristically greater part in the French constitution than in the American or British constitutions. Voluntary or local power was (and is) restricted.[2] Thus, for instance, the local hospital boards, the boards of education, and the independent university boards of regents or governors, with so much responsibility in Britain and the United States, never developed very far in France. Indeed, the arm of the French State grew longer and stronger in the French Revolution when it began to act in the name of the nation under the authority of the most sacred revolutionary principles. Even that measure of local and provincial government provided in the constitution of 3 September 1791 quickly fell victim to strong central governments. Mirabeau complained with his usual perspicacity about a rising thicket of regulations and limitations that seemed intended for "man bound by civil government rather than man free in nature."[3]

Thirdly, the revolutionary assemblies assumed responsibility for borrowing, taxing, and spending processes hitherto managed by the great corps of venal financiers; for some of the judicial and administrative services hitherto in the hands of the great corps of venal magistrates; for parts of government in the *pays d'état* hitherto directed by the provincial estates and sovereign courts; and for social welfare, education, and much else hitherto managed by the Church. These old authorities had employed *bureaux* of clerks, *premiers commis,* and other officials, who in the Revolution were either suppressed or else "nationalized" and brought into the civil service.

In a fourth sphere of change, the revolutionary assemblies created new ministries, tidied up the various administrative services, and reorganized them according to deliberate plans. The purpose was to render ministries and their *bureaux* economical, efficient, rational, and functional. In short, revolutionary assemblies needed a civil service, and they reformed it to make it stronger and more useful.

The work of the assemblies themselves rightly takes first place in any history of the French Revolution. But this need not blind us to the power of the executive services they fashioned out of the monarchy's old *bureaux.* After all, the legislators could do little or nothing without such services. "No right is fully guaranteed," Sieyès wrote, summing up a prevailing idea in July 1789, "if it is not fully protected by a relatively irresistible force."[4] The new civil service, relatively irresistible, was one of the most enduring creations of the French Revolution, but its novelty appears only through careful study. The financial administration is perhaps best treated separately from the rest, and both may be profitably introduced with a summary of some thoughts expressed by reformers in the *bureaux* and the revolutionary assemblies. They shared certain fundamental notions about the executive part of government.

I. The Bureaucratic Revolution

The public first began to use the term *bureaucratie* in the reign of Louis XVI, not many years before the French Revolution. A minor *philosophe,* Louis-Sébastien Mercier, then used the term several times in his journal, *Le tableau de Paris* (1783–89, 12 vols.), and defined it as "a word created in our time to designate in a concise and forceful manner the extensive power of mere clerks

who, in the various bureaux of the ministry, are able to implement a great many projects which they forge themselves or find
quite often in the dust of the bureaux, or adopt by taste or by
whim" (vol. IX, p. 57). A journalist and future deputy to the
National Convention, Jean-Louis Carra, complained in 1787 about
"the frightful *Bureaucratie* which exists and which is such that
what made seven or eight departments under abbé Terray now
makes twenty-seven or thirty."[5] This new word was an early sign
of revolutionary changes in the government and in its relations
with the governed. With these changes came certain ideas which
help explain what was happening. Whether these ideas caused
the changes is not clear, but they were certainly part of an ideology sweeping through the French public during the revolutionary years. Some of Louis XVI's ministers, notably Jacques
Necker, were imbued with these ideas, and so were a majority of
the deputies to the revolutionary assemblies.

One of these ideas was that a government was a kind of
machine or a set of machines. Almost unconsciously the public
began to think of the *bureaux,* the ministries, and the government in general as mechanical and to press this analogy as far as
possible. Some men, no doubt, had thought of human organizations as machines even in the seventeenth century, when
thinkers like René Descartes (1596–1650) and Isaac Newton
(1642–1727) were studying the universe as a machine.* But by
1789 the machine had become an obsessive image in France.
The influential Abbé Sieyès sprinkled his pamphlets with metaphors like the "social machine," the "political machine," and the
"springs of the public machine."[6] Deputies to the National
Assembly and the National Convention often referred in their
speeches to the "wheels," the "mainspring," or the "regularity"
of the administration. "In government as in mechanics . . . ," a
member of the Committee of Public Safety said in 1793.[7] Such
metaphors are to be found in most speeches and pamphlets of
that generation.

*Even Thomas Hobbes (1588–1679), who used the very different analogy of the
human body in his influential study of the State, was drawn to the mechanical
image: "For what is the heart but a spring; and the nerves, but so many strings;
and the joints but so many wheels, giving motion to the whole body, such as was
intended by the Artificer?" (*Leviathan, or the Matter, Form, and Power of a Common-
wealth, Ecclesiastical and Civil* [1651], ed. Michael Oakeshott, Oxford, 1960, p. 5).

Behind this mechanical vocabulary was the idea that all parts of the government should be organized as logically, simply, and efficiently as machines. Government agencies ought to be economical and functional. The revolutionary assemblies were continually trying to remove useless employees, duplication of effort, waste of every kind. Here was one motive for the laws of 2 October 1791, 14 January 1792, 20 March and 8 April 1793, ordering ministers to submit lists of their employees. The dozens of tables compiled in response to these instructions show an interest in costs and ministerial structure as well as in the political activities of the employees. In their concern for economy and efficiency the assemblies were taking up the work of reforming officials like Vivent Magnien (1744–1811), who had tried to reform the customs service; Mahy de Cormeré (1739–94), who had long tried to improve the whole system of indirect taxes; and Antoine-Jean-Baptiste Auget de Montyon (1733–1820), so imaginative in the field of public administration.

Enlightened officials such as these were also moved, like the revolutionary public as a whole, by the compelling idea of social utility. This was the idea that governments should serve the interests of the nation, not the interests of governing officials or political groups. Under the monarchy, official posts and all government employment had been awarded to the relatives and friends of men patronized at court. Employment in the king's service was a gift, a favor, a reward, like a title or a pension, and it raised the employee above the common herd. To serve the king or one of his officials was not to serve the public but to enjoy a measure of sovereign power. Abuses of government office did not end in the French Revolution, as anyone may discover even now by entering a French consulate, a prefecture, or a French post office, where petty officials are often rude, overbearing, and contemptuous of the public. But since the Revolution these have been supposed to serve the public. The principle of public service was clearly enunciated by the writers of the Enlightenment and adopted by the general public in the French Revolution. As the deputy Mounier said to the National Assembly in July 1789, "the government exists for the interests of the governed and not of those who govern; no public function may be considered as the property of those who perform it; the principle of all sovereignty resides in the nation."[8] This idea often took a more general form, as, for instance, in the words of a minor but typical writer in 1782: "The purpose of all government is to stop the efforts of private interests from harming the general interest."[9] Or Jean de Vaines (1733–1803), formerly Turgot's *premier commis des finances,* writing in 1790 just before he became one of the commissioners of the national treasury, "Private interests have now no refuge but in the general interest".[10] Hundreds of similar lines are to be found in speeches and pamphlets of that time.

The idea of social utility implied that the government should employ paid servants. This was a revolutionary idea. For centuries the monarchy had been served by noble officials whose dignity and honor prevented them from accepting salaries. A salary or wage was a mark of subordination, a curb on a man's independence, and a stain upon his honor. A noble official or one who hoped to become noble was reluctant to be dependent in this way on anyone except the king himself. A magistrate, an army officer, or a high-ranking financier was content to receive rewards, gifts, fees of office, returns on capital invested in a venal office, revenues from seigneurial estates, or even fraudulent profits, but he did not want to accept a salary. The emoluments of a venal office were acceptable because he remained his own master in the king's service. As Mirabeau remarked to his constituents in 1790, "Wasting or stealing public funds was not regarded as dishonorable under the ancien régime; but to be seen as a wage-earner *[salarié]* was felt to be dishonorable." He went on to argue that these old ideas would have to change. "Every public official in a free state should be salaried."[11] The clerks in the *bureaux* had, of course, always been paid, but by the higher officials or ministers who had hired them, not by the Crown. Clerks had never been civil servants at all; they had been only the employees of the officials they worked for.

A measure of civil equality was needed to remove all the venal, aristocratic impediments to bureaucratic subordination. Here is an unfamiliar side to the principle of equality adopted in 1789. In the name of equality, as it was then understood, privilege was denounced and destroyed so that a national civil service could be formed. This was laid down in the constitution of

22 August 1795 (article 351): "There exists among citizens no other superiority than that of *fonctionnaires public*, and that relatively only to the exercise of their functions." Before the Revolution the intendants of finance had been unwilling to work for the finance minister, Jacques Necker, because he was a social inferior, a mere commoner, a successful bank clerk. Thus, a bureaucratic hierarchy could scarcely be formed in the social hierarchy of the monarchy.

In establishing civil equality, the revolutionary assemblies were scotching an evil that had been held up to the light as long ago as 1679 by Abbé Claude Fleury. "Privileges do harm," he wrote in his book *Droit public en France* (1679), "by the multitude and the venality of offices. Through them, private individuals free themselves from laws and taxes. Common laws [*droits communs*] are scorned and become odious because they apply only to the miserable part of the population."[12] Sieyès developed the same thoughts in his *Essai sur les privilèges* (1788), and the *Moniteur* denounced the venality of offices early in July 1789.[13] A privilege seemed to those who had it like a right or a freedom, but there could be no rule of law so long as exceptions were granted to the privileged few. And the rule of law, the expression of the General Will, was the only guarantee of liberty.

As equal citizens, government officials could be paid and integrated in a bureaucratic hierarchy. They could also be addressed as equals and expected to regard members of the public as fellow citizens. The *ancien régime* had adopted an elaborate protocol to mark differences in social rank. Much thumbed manuals of protocol, still found today among the surviving records of the *bureaux,* laid down complicated rules of address and went into details about the length of paper and the wording of letters.

Write to the Grand Masters of Waters and Forests, the Farmers General [of Taxes], the *Régisseurs,* the Receivers General of Finances and other private persons in note form *[en billet]* avoiding the word "honour," and beginning, for example, "I have received, Monsieur, the letter you have taken the trouble to write to me . . . ," and signing off thus: "I am very sincerely, Monsieur, your obedient servant & etc." Or again, "To women, unless they are of inferior status [*état subalterne*], write in note form [*en billet*], ending with these words, "I am with respect, Madame, your & etc."[14]

All this was changed in the Revolution.

Officials of the civil service were expected to behave as employees of the nation. No longer could they speak as the servants of the king and his high and mighty gentlemen. Neither elaborate courtesy nor arrogance was to be endured from them. This trend reached its height in 1793 and 1794, when for some months even the formal pronouns *vous* and *vos* were abandoned in favor of the familiar *tu, toi,* and *tes*. But a permanent change in attitude was expected of officials.

> It has come to the ears of the Minister of the Interior [reads a ministerial circular of 11 April 1794] that a certain arrogance [*morgue*], a certain haughtiness in the necessary communications with our fellow citizens, still exists in the bureaux. These manners belonged to the era of pride [*orgueil*] and slavery. The peremptory and self-important attitude of the ancien régime should long ago have given way to a pleasant and obliging manner [*l'aménité et la complaisance*]. It is expressly recommended to chiefs of divisions to watch over their co-workers in this respect as in all others, and especially to set an example, as the Minister promises to do in the communications he has with them.[15]
>
> M. J. A. Herman
> Minister of the Interior

Underlying such changes was the idea that the officials were now servants of a nation of citizens equal in their citizenship, if not in other things. The National Assembly was trying to impose a new faith in the general ideas of nationality and of the virtues of the new national association that was to take precedence over other loyalties and over the individual will. Paradoxical though it may seem, liberty was expected to flow from the national or collective association which the Assembly represented. The civil service was to defend liberty by enforcing the laws made by the nation's representatives. "It is the authority of the law which assures general liberty . . ." said Mounier in a typical remark of the time.[16] "It was a profound error," Thouret added, "to treat the executive power [of government] as an enemy of national liberty. Is not the executive the power of the nation and derived, like the legislature, from the nation?"[17] In the eyes of the National Assembly, the liberty guaranteed by the constitution depended on the enforcement of the laws by the civil service and the courts.

II. A National Civil Service

The principle of national sovereignty gave the elected revolutionary assemblies great prestige and moral force. They and their committees were able to destroy rival authorities and to "nationalize" the agents and agencies that had served independent authorities in the kingdom. All, even the king, were to be made into citizens so that none might impose himself on the nation. None was to be above the law. The clergy, once obedient to Rome, were now ordered by the Civil Constitution of the Clergy (12 July 1790) to take an oath to the nation, and soldiers, too, were obliged to take an oath by decrees of 10 August 1789, 11 June 1791, and 3 September 1792.[18]

It was in this context that the Bourbon monarchy's historic collection of *bureaux* and private services were transformed into the relatively well-ordered civil service that is detailed in the *Almanach national* in the late 1790s. No particular government or group can be credited with this work. On the contrary, every government in the revolutionary decade used the administrative *bureaux*, added to them, and reorganized them. It would be difficult to exaggerate the effects of these changes, but some of them were so discreetly and so gradually made that they are easily overlooked. Most reforms were made piecemeal and came rarely to the forefront of public affairs. A review of the employees, especially the *premiers commis* and the *chefs de bureau*, might convey an impression of stability, as though nothing were happening, because the personnel of the *bureaux* changed remarkably little. But long bureaucratic careers do not show that nothing was changing in the *bureaux*.

The administrative services of the monarchy had consisted mainly of venal officials and the clerks they hired. The *bureaux* had been an official's personal employees, and he had paid them out of his funds. True, they could win retirement and other pensions on the royal treasury, but so could other citizens who were nobody's employees. For instance, two pensions of 600 livres were awarded in 1784 to two women who had never been employed, grand nieces of the dramatist Pierre Corneille. These pensions were no different from two others of 1,200 livres each granted in 1779 to Edmé-Pierre Frontier, aged thirty-three, for his services as a clerk at the French embassy in London, and "in consideration of a work of special correspondence concerning the navy with which he was entrusted during the same period."[19] Notwithstanding citations like this one, pensions did not come by right or as earned rewards; they came as grace and favor from the king's bounty.

Higher up the social scale, the royal officials who employed the clerks were not civil servants, either, in any modern sense of the term, because they had contractual links with the Crown. A venal official bought his office from a treasurer general of the *partie casuelle* (himself a venal official), from a previous owner, or his heirs, or else he inherited it from his father or brother, in the same way that he might acquire a house. The royal letters by which the Crown recognized his tenure of office came from a different source. A variety of fees and other emoluments were paid to him. Such was the situation of the royal intendants out in the provincial capitals, of the intendants of finance in charge of administrative *bureaux* in Paris and Versailles, of the receivers general and treasurers general who collected and spent royal revenues, of army officers who bought their commissions, and of a range of other royal officials.

Contractual links of a different type, six-year leases usually, bound the various farmers general and *régisseurs généraux* of taxes; and the companies of financiers to whom the Crown leased the naval and military victualing services, the postal and coach services *(messageries)*, and suchlike; and the orders of monks and nuns that contracted to run naval and military hospitals. The status of the Crown's officials was neither clear nor uniform. The hierarchy was a social system of patronage, not an administrative system of subordination. Every clerk had his patrons, his *protecteurs*, to use the French term of the day, and these pressed the claims of their clients, their *créatures* upon ministers, councillors, king, and royal relatives at every opportunity.

The monarchy had tried to supervise all these agents through the *bureaux* of the controller general of finances. The idea behind his department, the Contrôle général des finances, was that all money spent on work for the Crown might be recorded in sets of duplicate records, *contre-rôles,* permitting *contrôle* by the Crown. Hence the *bureaux* of the controller general followed and reported on all official services, everything from tax collections to supplying grain to Paris and building a naval base at Cherbourg. As the National Assembly "nationalized" these services, it grouped them in an appropriate ministry or other body together with the supervising *bureaux* from the Côntrôle général. Thus, for instance, the venal treasurers were organized as a national treasury together with the *bureaux* of the director general for the royal treasury hitherto in the Contrôle général. Thus, the royal mints were grouped with the Contrôle général's *bureau* for supervising mints, and the royal lottery was joined with the *bureau* for supervising lotteries, all in a new Ministry for Public Contributions, created on 27 April 1791. And thus the bridges and roads service (Ponts et chaussées) and its supervisory bureau from the Contrôle général were grouped in a Ministry of the Interior.[20]

The Ministry of the Interior, created by a decree of 27 April 1791, was a new power in the kingdom, a pillar of the administrative revolution, and an administrative symbol of national sovereignty. Curiously enough, it did not immediately come into its full power because the National Assembly began by putting many public services into the hands of elected authorities in cities and towns all over the kingdom. As organized in January 1792, the ministry was merely corresponding with all these provincial authorities about the "constitutional regime and the maintenance of public order." In this correspondence it was employing more than one-third of its clerks (47 of 137) and four of its six subdivisions.[21] But it had no permanent agents out in the provinces, only occasional visiting agents *en mission* and the secret network of sp:es and informers employed by the minister Roland in 1792 and probably by his successors.[22] The intendants of police, justice, and finance had disappeared from the provinces in 1790, and until Napoleon posted out prefects, the Ministry of the Interior maintained no strong presence there. As for the police that have now long served that ministry, they do not appear in the organization chart of 14 January 1792. The Gendarmerie nationale, made out of the old territorial police (maréchaussée) by a law of 22 December 1790, were attached to the War Ministry. The Paris National Guard was a semimilitary force answerable to the government of Paris (Commune). The police in other large towns were also put under the jurisdiction of the municipal government. The dictatorial committees of the Convention in 1793 and 1794 had police forces that were not under the Ministry of the Interior, either. At the end of 1795 the Directory created a Ministry of Police with a staff of about 200 who mostly observed and reported on political groups and the state of public opinion; and Napoleon, too, kept a Ministry of Police.[23] The Ministry of the Interior therefore lacked the forces that it was to acquire later, but from its very beginning it fell heir to many nationalized services.

First among these came services from the age-old provinces swept away in the Revolution. In their place the Constituent Assembly divided the kingdom into eighty-one roughly equal départements, each with a capital (chef-lieu). Paris and Corsica were added to the list, making a total of eighty-three departments. The capital was supposed to be no more than a day's walk from anywhere in the department, and with much patient negotiation and the expert advice of a mapmaker, Jacques-Dominique Cassini (1748–1845), Brittany was divided into five departments, Provence into three, and so on. These were in turn divided into districts, a total of 544 of them, but these were soon abolished by the constitution of 1795. As permanent as the departments, however, were the new municipalities, of which 40,411 were shortly named. These new arrangements were voted in principle as early as a law of 22 December 1789; the many decrees needed to bring them about were gathered into a general decree of 26 February 1790; the studies and surveys were made and the new administrative map of France was actually drawn before the end of 1790.[24] The Ministry of the Interior in Paris corresponded with the elected officials of departments, districts, and municipalities. These were soon discouraged by their arduous, thankless tasks, and few capable men offered their services. Most of the time the departmental administrations faithfully carried out orders from Paris.[25] It was only a matter of time before a permanent, central ministry would find ways of imposing itself on the entire country. This happened in 1800 under Napoleon Bonaparte, who swept away the electoral systems and appointed a prefect (*préfet*) to reside in the capital of each department and govern it under the authority of the central government.

The regulation of trade, industry, and the seaports fell to the ministry, as did the supervision of mines and mining, agriculture, the veterinary schools, the patenting of inventions, and the gathering of information and statistics on these matters. Reliable statistics about a people and their economic life are not easy to provide for, and the many questionnaires distributed in the revolutionary years brought small results even when the economist François de Neufchâteau became minister of the interior in 1797.[26] For much of this work whole *bureaux* were brought from the old controller general's department and carried on as before. But their field of operations grew wider as feudal domains, provinces with special status, and then foreign conquests all were integrated into France. When the provincial estates, the sovereign courts, the General Farm of Taxes, and some lesser bodies were suppressed, their functions and some of their personnel devolved upon the new civil service. When a new judicial system was put into effect in laws of 16–24 August 1790 and 16–25 September 1791, a new Ministry of Justice assumed many of the functions of the sovereign and seigneurial courts.[27]

As the Roman Catholic Church was "nationalized," many of its activities were distributed among secular authorities. Marriage was a knotty problem. Should it be in the charge of civil servants or of the constitutional clergy? After much debate it was made a civil act to be performed at a town hall, and a decree of 20 September 1792 ordered registers of births, marriages, and deaths to be kept in two copies, one by the municipality and the other by the department.* The constitutional monarchy, busy with many pressing problems, left social welfare to the clergy, and even the republican decree of 18 August 1792 abolishing

---

*The minimum age for marriage was set at fifteen instead of fourteen for men and thirteen instead of twelve for women. People under twenty-one, deemed minors, needed parental consent to marry. Even priests could now marry legally, and many did, though bishops struggled to prevent them from doing so. Divorce became legal by a vote of the Legislative Assembly on 20 September 1792.

the regular orders of monks and nuns made a special exemption for charitable orders. But there was a general understanding that the nation (i.e., the State) should take charge of poor, sick, hungry, and otherwise distressed citizens. In 1791 the Ministry of the Interior took over various *bureaux*—for beggars *(mendi-cité)*, charity, hospitals, etc.—from the controller general, though these were merely for what we might call "information, coor-dination, and planning."

The National Convention declared public assistance a right in a declaration of rights drawn up in 1793 (article 23). Various decrees followed: The legislature bound itself on 19 March 1793 to vote funds annually; the departments were ordered on 28 June 1793 to assist single mothers and foundlings; begging and charity were declared illegal on 15 October 1794; a prison for beggars was to be kept at the *chef-lieu* of each department. None of this worked very well; the social problems of that age being beyond the powers of government might perhaps have been bet-ter left to the clergy.

When the ministries were being reformed in spring 1791, some deputies, notably a former royal official, Pierre-Hubert Anson (1746–1810), urged the Assembly to set up a Ministry of Public Instruction. Here was a thorny subject. As the civil war of revolution and counterrevolution intensified, the government removed education more and more firmly from the Church. The Convention named a twenty-four-man Committee on Public Instruction to prepare a new system. A decree of 19 December 1793 established for the first time in France the principle of uni-versal primary schooling for children aged six to eight years, free in both senses of the word, and compulsory. Education, like social welfare, was thereby made a civil and national responsibil-ity, no longer to be left to the Church.

In practice, the establishment of schools and all that went with them was soon foisted off upon the authorities of the municipalities and the departments. Then, faced with the diffi-culty of putting their policy into effect, the Convention in November 1794 even removed the legal obligation to have chil-dren schooled, and in October 1795 it denied the funding that had been intended to make schooling free. Secondary and higher education also fell into neglect, and the *écoles centrales* planned in 1795 to replace both secondary schools and the twenty-two universities of the *ancien régime*, were never established.

Yet the principle and policy of centralized, national education had been established. Under the Directory, the Ministry of the Interior employed a director general of education. Inspection of schools by the national government was soon adopted in principle, and the ministry began to establish a system of school inspection.[28] In spite of the disagreements and hesitations of the legislators, education was already destined to come under the power of the national civil service. For when national governments "nationalized" the Roman Catholic Church, they assumed its centralizing, authoritarian power and inevitably became its heirs in the field of education. The process of teaching citizens the national message was, after all, much like teaching Christians the Catholic message. It is as a direct result of the French Revolution that schools and universities, teachers and professors are controlled today by a Ministry of National Education.

In all its activities the national government relied upon civil servants organized in *bureaux*. Experienced clerks writing letters and memoranda, keeping records with goose quills in paper ledgers were adopted by every organization in the 1790s much as electronic machines were adopted in the 1980s. Even the governing assemblies and committees needed them. In the system of *bureaux* the Constituent Assembly built up for its own use, it employed 7 clerks for its financial records alone. As early as summer 1793 the Committee of Public Safety was employing 26 clerks and secretaries to take and file minutes and to write dispatches. By the end of the year it had a staff of more than 100, and by July 1794 its staff numbered 523 under a director named Saint-Cyr Nuguès. Meanwhile, the Committee of General Security had come to employ 150 men under the direction of a certain Bugnaître. These and the Convention's other committees employed, all told, about 750 clerks in 1794 and more than 1,100 in 1795, these quite apart from the ministries and other agencies of the civil service, which were employing some 1,250 men in May 1793 and about 3,000 in 1795.[29]

Most of these men had been employed in the *bureaux* of the *ancien régime*. The organization and its purposes were new, but the men were not. Choosing at random in the personnel records, we find that C. A. Roussel (1751–1807), for instance, had worked for the *bailliage* of Rouen and then the General Farm of Taxes before joining the new Ministry of Public Contributions on 1 April 1792. At a higher level, André Regardin (1753–1834) was a director in the Régie général at Lyons until 1791,when he became one of the commissioners of the new Bureau of Accounting, and rose eventually to the Court of Accounts (1807– 34) and the Legion of Honor. As the new civil service grew and grew, there was no lack of employment in it for the personnel of agencies abolished in the Revolution. The Direction générale de la liquidation for winding up official bodies of the *ancien régime* employed many men from those very bodies. Among its *chefs de service* in May 1793 were such people as Dominique Desrenaudes, a former receiver in the General Farm of Taxes; Jean-François Carré, formerly employed in the domains administration; Jean-Baptiste Ythier, who once worked in the Parties casuelles, the agency that had sold royal offices; and Jerôme Bergerot, formerly a lawyer in the Parlement of Paris.[30] These are cited as examples.

Not all officials of the *ancien régime* were acceptable to the new civil service, and not all were willing to serve in it. The *cadres,* or politically significant officials, nearly all dropped out: the intendants, masters of requests, directors, venal officials in general, what might be called the managerial class of men named in the *Almanach royal.* Such *grands commis* were often from noble families that had served the monarchy for generations, or from rising families of magistrates, financiers, officers, and lesser courtiers eager to join the ruling classes of the monarchy. Owing their places directly to royal patronage, they were deemed to be loyal to the Crown and to be part of that vast, informal system of politics by which the Bourbons had ruled the kingdom. They disappeared with royal sovereignty like the magistrates in the sovereign courts, and some of them emigrated. Their fees and *gages d'office* were ordered stopped on 1 January 1791. There was no place for them in the national civil service created after 1789. G. I. Douet de la Boullaye (1734–97), for example, had a career as a councillor in the Parlement of Paris, a master of requests, intendant at Auch (1776), intendant of mines (1782), intendant of finances (1787), and he resigned on 30 September

1789. The few who stayed on, such as A. L. Chaumont de la Millière, who transferred to the Ministry of the Interior in 1791 with his *bureau* for bridges and roads, were arrested in 1793 or 1794 and fortunate if they escaped with their lives. The political process of appointment, by which men like Chaumont de la Millière and Douet de la Boullaye had been chosen to serve the *ancien régime*, passed in 1792 from king and court to the National Convention. This was what the republic meant in part to the civil service. The politics of appointment were now determined by the struggles of revolutionary factions. Posts were often filled by influential revolutionaries who arranged employment for their relatives and friends.

By 1793 the revolutionary government was being served mainly by *bureaux* of common clerks directed by *premiers commis* promoted from among their number. The safest and most successful were those from humble families with no visible connections at court, no firm roots in the governing classes, and no taint of monarchy. Their loyalty to the revolutionary assemblies representing the nation was assumed. Their services were indispensable even during the Terror of 1793–94, when they were intimidated like the moderate majority in the National Convention. The Convention kept a watch on civil servants lest their old loyalty to the monarchy prompt them to support movements of counterrevolution; suspects were arrested from time to time and ministries purged. But the great majority of clerks, and some higher officials too, passed quietly from one regime to another as apolitical civil servants.

III. *The Financial Administration*

The civil service gradually took charge of the collecting, holding, and spending of government funds. This was one of the great reforms of the French Revolution. Financial difficulties had provoked the monarchy to call the Assembly of Notables in 1787 and the Estates General in 1789 and were in that sense a major cause of the Revolution. Soon after the Estates General had reformed itself as a National Assembly, it began to see that the infamous debt was only a secondary or derivative problem. The basic problem, as Necker and other reformers had seen long before, was how to take command of the financial system in order to reform it. This was a political problem because privilege stood in the way. Historic privileges in matters of taxation were cherished by provinces and by noblemen. In the financial administration, however, the worst was the privilege of venal accountants to collect, hold, invest, and spend government funds—in short, to manage public financing for private profit. Families of accountants who owned their offices—farmers general of taxes, receivers general of finances, treasurers general, payers, purveyors of many kinds—had intermarried with the magistracy and the nobility to the point where they had become part of the ruling classes. They would have to be pulled down before the financial system could be reformed. Accordingly, the Assembly began to pull down the ruling classes and to reform the financial administration. The National Convention and its successors carried on the same task.

The political struggles have had their place in earlier chapters, and it is the administrative reforms, too often omitted in histories of the Revolution, to which we turn here. The first and greatest was the reform of the royal treasury. Before 1788 there was no central revenue fund, no organization in charge of the government's money, nothing that we could recognize as a treasury. What was called the "royal treasury" consisted of two venal keepers of the royal treasury, each with his own separate fund for receiving and paying, but they managed only a part of the king's revenues. More was received and spent by the great treasurers general of the spending departments, especially those for war, the navy, and the royal households. Scores of lesser treasurers received and paid out funds allotted to the sovereign courts, the bridges and roads service, the intendants and the provinces, the inspectors of manufactures, the book censors, the academies, the mines and mining *bureaux,* and all the other agencies paid by the Crown. Treasurers, payers, keepers, and all other accountants *(comptables)* kept accounts to send to the Chamber of Accounts, but these were not intended for the practical purposes of day-to-day government and were, in any case, submitted too late to be of any use. The controller general of Finances employed *bureaux* to keep records of government spending, but this type of control was too remote and too dependent on reports from accountants. In short, the government did not manage its own spending processes; venal accountants managed them in a system of profit-making enterprise.

Certain statesmen and officials saw the need for reforms in the financial administration, but there were many obstacles to be overcome. Jacques Necker took the first steps during his first ministry (1776–81), but these were largely undone, during the six years of reaction that followed, by ministers serving the interests of the frightened and angry financiers. Taking up Necker's projects in 1788, Loménie de Brienne was able to effect the first permanent reform of the treasury—its founding, really. He began with an edict and a regulation of March 1788 abolishing the venal offices of the two *gardes du trésor royal* and those of the treasurers general for war, the navy, the royal households, and other services. These financiers and their staffs were gathered into a single administrative body under a director, six administrators, and six *premiers commis*, all salaried officials.[31] So formed, the royal treasury comprised four specialized sections for war, the navy, the royal households, and debts and pensions. A fifth section coordinated and directed the whole, and each section was directed by a venal accountant turned salaried administrator. The treasury was henceforth to keep double-entry account books to help in controlling expenditures and in preparing annual accounts for the Royal Council each April. These accounts were to be published and matched by a budget which the Royal Council was to prepare annually. France had never had a budget before, and Loménie de Brienne published the very first one on 27 April 1788.

By August 1789, when these reforms were well established, the royal treasury was employing 264 men: 174 clerks, 4 *premiers commis*, 18 office boys, 4 cashiers, 1 controller, and 63 subtreasurers out in the provinces. Their salaries for 1789 totaled just over 1 million livres, including 50,000 livres for each of the five administrators, and they budgeted 134,000 livres that year for paper, candles, and other supplies.[32] This was already a large organization.

It soon became the nucleus of a very much larger one. In

May 1790 the treasury assumed responsibility for paying those parts of the public debt called the *rentes,* hitherto serviced by ten financial agencies, including the General Farm of Taxes, the receivers general, and the Paris city hall. The agent for settling claims on the treasury, Gérard-Maurice Turpin, and his *bureaux* were added to it on 15 August 1790. In autumn 1790, as the controller general's department was being dismantled, its treasury *bureaux* were transferred to the royal treasury. By a decree of 27 December 1790, several *bureaux* were transferred to it from the central *bureaux* of the suppressed receivers general of finances, and they were for correspondence with the district collectors of taxes. The treasury commissioners appointed and directed the new *payeurs généraux,* one or more for each territorial department, ordered by a law of 24 September 1791 to take over all the payments hitherto made by the venal treasurers for war, marine, etc. A law of 3–5 June 1793 brought to the treasury the Caisse de l'extraordinaire, set up earlier to manage the proceeds from the sale of Church and other confiscated property. *Bureaux* for managing the public debt were added on 24 August 1793 and 12 May 1794, and soon afterward the numerous *bureaux* for winding up the debts to venal officials and others *(liquidation).* As a result of these additions, the treasury had 488 employees in July 1793, 1,026 in January 1795, and 1,246 in April 1796.[33] Long before then it had become the commanding center of the financial system, with a consolidated revenue fund which enabled the government to keep track of its funds and to draw up a budget.

The elected assemblies kept firm control over the treasury through a responsible commission. So vital an organization could not be left to the king or his ministers or to any other executive group in the revolutionary years. On 26 May 1791 the National Assembly confined the king to a civil list of 25 million livres. For the same reasons, the assemblies would have no executive minister of finance, and it is a mistake to think of the minister of public contributions as such. No minister of finance was appointed until the constitution of 22 August 1795 allowed for one (section 150). Even then the ministers appointed were responsible to the Directory and were mainly technicians: Guillaume-Charles Faipoult de Maisoncelle (8 November 1795 to 1 January 1796),

Dominique-Vincent Ramel-Nogaret (14 February 1796 to 20 July 1799), and Robert Lindet (23 July to 10 November 1799). The revolutionary governments were haunted by a fear of ministers' evading legislative control and putting national revenues at the service of a government independently of the legislature. That was, indeed, how Napoleon's finance minister, Martin-Michel-Charles Gaudin, was to serve Napoleon throughout the fourteen years of his dictatorship. But the ministry Gaudin headed had been organized earlier during the Directory with a staff of about 1,650 divided into six sections (for direct taxes, indirect taxes, national property, émigré property, coinage and postal services, and a secretariat).

As for the collection of tax revenues, this, too, was nationalized early in the Revolution and put under the direction of the central government, particularly the Ministry of Public Contributions. The internal customs duties, the salt and tobacco monopolies (*gabelles* and *tabac*), and the excise duties on alcohol (*aides*) all were abolished during the second half of 1790. The hated duties on wine entering the gates of Paris and other cities (*octrois*) were abolished by a decree of 19 February 1791. A law of 16–19 August 1790 disposed of the old domains administration, of which the few surviving *bureaux* soon became parts of the Ministry of the Interior. The receivers and receivers general of finance were suppressed by a decree of 14 November 1790, in effect from 1 January 1791. Replacing them was a new body of district receivers, one for each of 543 districts (Paris, a district for some purposes, had special arrangements in this), and they were to be elected for six years by a majority vote in the administrative council of the district. These receivers were to answer to the district directory for some purposes and to the national treasury for others. Not unexpectedly, this system worked badly, and from 1793 on urgent needs of wartime governments were met by various supplementary agents sent out from Paris.

Thousands of employees in Paris and the provinces lost their jobs when the huge General Farm of Taxes and the Régie générale were suppressed by a decree of 27 March 1791. It is not clear how many were laid off and how many transferred to the growing civil service. A law of 20 March 1791, which the minister of public contributions tried to enforce, ordered that all new appointments to posts in the financial administration should be made from among former employees of the suppressed services. Many were employed by the new customs service *(régie)* concentrated on the national frontiers during the great reorganization of 1790–93. By the end of 1793 there were 592 employees at customs *bureaux* on the seacoasts, 788 in *bureaux* on the inland frontiers, and guards totaling more than 12,000 soldiers and sailors.[34] Here was a major force in the service of the central government.

The Constituent Assembly tried to shield the new financial services from the burden of the corrupt enterprises inherited from the *ancien régime*. This it did by treating the business of the *ancien régime* as a temporary, "extraordinary" settling of accounts, to be separated from the permanent, "ordinary" business of the new civil service. These two separate parts of the financial administration were to draw their funds from different sources. A Direction général de la liquidation, which had a staff of 220 by May 1793, was to wind up the *ancien régime,* buy back the venal offices, and settle all the old debts with paper notes *(assignats)* printed and distributed by a special Caisse de l'extraordinaire.[35] The decree of 17 April 1790 which provided for the *assignats* also abolished the paper *rescriptions, assignations,* and *billets* so widely used in the *ancien régime*. Issued in huge amounts against confiscated property of the Church and the emigrant nobles, these notes were intended to be received back from the public in payment for the confiscated property and burned.

This was an ingenious plan, and certainly there seemed no other way of raising the 320 million livres needed to reimburse the financiers for their lost venal offices and the 225 million owing to them in short-term loans *(anticipations)*. By August 1790 the total debt of the government, old and new, was reckoned at nearly 2 billion livres.[36] True, the theory of separating compensation *(liquidation)* from current financing tended to break down as fresh claims for compensation kept pouring in; for example, on 1 July 1790 the gunsmiths of Paris sent in a claim for 115,118 livres for the guns seized on 14 July 1789 by the crowds that had then captured the Bastille.[37] And after April 1792 the government began to draw on the *assignats* to meet wartime expenses. Huge inflationary sums in *assignats* were printed in the years 1792 to 1795, but this was an abuse of an ingenious method by which the National Constituent Assembly had turned confiscated Church property to immediate account. Whatever their faults and failings, these temporary financial arrangements permitted the legislative committees and collaborating officials to make a fresh start—that is, to develop the new civil service unencumbered with debts from the *ancien régime*.

As for government accounts, the old sovereign Chambers of Accounts, suppressed by a law of 2 September 1790, were replaced by a national Bureau of Accounting under commissioners responsible to the National Assembly. The daunting task of winding up the accounts of the *ancien régime* was not accomplished for many years. Only after long delays did the farmers general, the *régisseurs généraux,* the receivers general, and the other financiers wind up their business. They did not turn in their final accounts until years after their venal offices had been suppressed. But committees of the legislature never let these accounting tasks be forgotten. The governments of 1792–94 hastened accounting by their readiness to commit financiers to prison and the guillotine.

The revolutionary process of nationalizing government business began to come to an end in the Thermidorian regime of 1795. By then sales of confiscated property had been severely reduced, inflation had rendered the *assignats* nearly worthless, and foreign coalitions were threatening the republic. From autumn 1795 the government turned more and more to private businessmen for funding and military supplies. The Directory and Napoleon dealt with financiers, bankers, supply merchants, and foreign governments on a grand scale.[38] Public finance was exploited once more by private enterprise. Yet the revolutionary gains were not entirely forfeited in the twenty years 1795 to 1815, and the national civil service, especially the national treasury, remained to enforce a greater measure of state control than the Bourbons had achieved. The national bureaucracy remained. The financial reformers of the Restoration, such as Joseph-Dominique, Baron Louis (1755–1837) and Jean-Baptiste-Guillaume-Marie-Joseph-Seraphin, Comte de Villèle (1773–1854), and their successors did not have to repeat the work of Jacques Necker and the revolutionary National Assembly.[39] The July Monarchy (1830–48) continued the process of administrative change that had begun in the reign of Louis XVI and the early years of the Revolution.

The Revolution's Effects

THE French Revolution defies the brief summary, the rapid caricature, that would make it clear and simple. Its main stages convey no obvious underlying meaning. Of the American Revolution it is reasonable to say that it established American independence; of the Glorious Revolution of 1688 that it established parliamentary rule and drove James II and what he stood for out of England; of the Russian Revolution that it left Russia in the hands of a Bolshevik Communist dictatorship. No such formulation can reasonably be made for the French Revolution because it was not, in fact, a single unified event.

Any student of the French Revolution could, of course, reduce it to a single list of events. The monarchy of Louis XVI (it might run), challenged by its sovereign courts and other public groups, called a meeting of the Estates General, which declared itself to be a National Assembly and drew up a constitution. The limited monarchy thus created in 1789 was destroyed in 1792, and the king and queen were executed in 1793. The bloody First Republic, a brief circumstantial dictatorship, was soon brought down, leaving the country a prey to struggling factions. Meanwhile, an ideological war on kings, nobles, and priests had been waged since April 1792, but it very soon degenerated into a French imperial war for the conquest and plunder of Europe.

Where in all this, or in any other plain version, was *the* French Revolution? Some historians point to underlying political changes, others to social changes, and still others to new political and social ideas let loose in the world. With so many different phases and so much room for interpretation, it is hard to avoid the conclusion Alfred Cobban drew in 1954: that there was "no single French Revolution to be summed up in a single formula ... never *a*

French Revolution which you can be for or against."[1] What had occurred was a series of conflicts and upheavals which left their marks on France and on the entire Western world.

The revolutionary decade had one of its greatest effects as a new fund of ideas, principles, and examples. Frenchmen had been used to referring back to classical Greece and Rome or to the early Christian era of disciples, saints, and martyrs. A third field, looming close to home in history and in geography, was now added to the past. The Revolution echoed loudly through French life in the nineteenth and twentieth centuries. Revolutionary *journées** occurred in 1830, 1848, 1851, 1871, 1934, and 1968, to mention only a few. Political groups used the old revolutionary titles; perhaps 100,000 "Montagnards" were active in 1851. Many revolutionary figures were still alive, after all, as late as the Revolution of 1830: General Lafayette; General Jourdan; Abbé Sieyès; Abbé Henri Grégoire; Bertrand Barère; Jean Varlet, the *enragé;* Talleyrand; and such deputies as Boulay de la Meurthe, La Revellière-Lepeaux, Merlin de Douai, and Pierre-Louis Roederer. The families of certain revolutionaries carried on in public life for generations; notable is the Carnot family, of whom Sadi, Lazare Carnot's grandson, was elected president of the Third Republic in 1887. A certain Boissy d'Anglas who took part in the separation of Church and State in 1905 was a descendant of the Boissy d'Anglas who led the separation of Church and State by the law of 21 February 1795. The heritage of the French Revolution, variously interpreted, has encouraged French citizens, whatever their beliefs, to live in what they take to be the revolutionary (or counterrevolutionary) tradition. The history of the Revolution has come down even to the twentieth century as a national legend, a great drama in which people still take sides.

Robespierre's career, for instance, has never ceased to arouse contradictory responses. The socialist Pierre-Joseph Proudhon (1809–65) denounced Robespierre in the most violent terms (*"Ah!*

*Most of the events in the French Revolution were and are cited as *journées;* there was the *journée* of 14 July 1789, the *journée* of 10 August 1792, the *journées* of 31 May–2 June 1793, and so on. In French the word means "a dayful" or "a day's doings." The meaning may be understood in light of other French words with the suffix *ée,* such as *cuillerée,* which means "a spoonful," or *soirée,* meaning "an evening's doings."

je connais trop ce reptile . : ."); the poet Victor Hugo wrote of him sarcastically as the "revolutionary proof-reader"; the aged revolutionary Filippo Michele Buonarotti (1761–1837) wept at the mention of Robespierre's name; and the nineteenth-century revolutionary leader Armand Barbès (1809–70), sentenced to death and expecting to be executed, cried out, "Saint-Just, Robespierre, Couthon, Babeuf . . . pray for me!"[2] With the Revolution living on, as it were, in this way, the writing of schoolbooks or the naming of streets has called for tact and discretion.

Streets in Paris have been named for Danton, Carnot, and Lindet, but there is no rue Marat, rue Babeuf, or rue Robespierre. On 13 April 1946, soon after the liberation, a left-wing municipal council decided to rename the place and rue du Marché-Saint-Honoré after Robespierre. The prefect approved this decision on 8 June. The name of Robespierre began to appear on maps and official lists, but not on the street signs because the local residents opposed the change. On 3 July 1950 a new majority in the council reversed the decision and dropped the proposal, but it came up again in April 1958 near the bicentenary of Robespierre's birth (May 1758). This time the proposal was to rename the rue Saint-Hyacinthe, but it, too, was dropped when forty-five councillors voted against it and only forty-four in its favor. *"Vive Robespierre quand même,"* shouted one of the forty-four.[3]

I. *The Liberal Tradition*

Disagreement of this type arises from the varieties of the revolutionary tradition. One of the grandest is the liberal tradition of the years 1789–91 which, from that time to this, has aroused admiration, enthusiasm, and hope in France and in many other parts of the world. All over Europe and America in 1789 the public watched the French, one of the great nations, taking their destiny into their own hands and trying to rearrange their institutions for the benefit of all citizens. Frenchmen seemed to be realizing ideals expressed in the writings of Enlightenment thinkers and in the American Revolution. Henceforth all free men, all believers in justice and equality, could look upon France as a second home. Through all the tyranny and injustice of later years, the liberal tradition of government with an elected assembly acting under the terms of a written constitution has lived on.

During the first three-quarters of the nineteenth century that tradition was strong enough to oblige the ruling kings and emperors to have written constitutions, beginning with Napoleon's constitution of 13 December 1799 and continuing with Louis XVIII's charter of 1814. It was also strong enough to induce those rulers to tolerate elected legislative assemblies, but not to hold the executive part of the government responsible to the assemblies. The brief life of the Second Republic (1848–51) ended, like the First Republic, in the imperial dictatorship of a Bonaparte. From 1875 to 1940, however, France was ruled by a government responsible to a National Assembly, and this was not suspended even during the dark years of the Great War.

During the Second World War, from 10 July 1940 on, Marshal Henri-Philippe Pétain headed a military dictatorship subservient to the conquering German Third Reich, but even he respected the letter—though not the spirit—of the tradition by promising a new constitution "to be ratified by the Nation and applied by the assemblies that it [the Nation] will have created."[4] In fact, the regime's motto, *Famille, patrie, travail,* though it seemed acceptable at the time to a majority of French people, symbolized a reactionary, authoritarian regime that had broken with the revolutionary tradition. A commission appointed to draft a new constitution sprinkled its clauses with the word *liberté* and other language in the tradition of the French Revolution, but these drafts remained as dead as those of 1792 and 1793.

The constitution of 28 October 1946, a fine example of the genre, provided for an executive very much dependent upon the elected legislature, and General Charles de Gaulle overturned it in a coup d'etat on 13 May 1958, during the Algerian War crisis. The legislature had been hopelessly divided and deadlocked. The constitution of the Fifth Republic, dated 4 October 1958, began by reaffirming the Declaration of the Rights of Man (preamble) and the sovereignty of the people (*titre* I) but went on (*titre* II, and article 16) to endow the president of the republic with decisive authority in the government. In 1962 de Gaulle reinforced that provision of the constitution with a law providing for the popular election of the president. This allows the presidency to compete with the Assembly in representing the sovereign people. As a result, the president of the Fifth Republic stands in a political position not unlike that of the Bonaparte emperors, Napoleon I (1800–14) and Napoleon III (1852–70), who thought of themselves as representing the sovereign people.

The constitution of the Fifth Republic is the sixteenth, if you count one of 1814 that did not actually become law and if you count the series of constitutional acts in 1940; otherwise, it is the fourteenth. This entire constitutional history has been filled with variations on the themes of the first constitution drafted by the first National Assembly from 1789 to 1791. It is perhaps not too much to suggest, indeed, that the constitution has become a small special branch of French literature, not so well used as the novel, the short story, or the poem, of course, but with official origins and widespread influences, like those of the Church's liturgy in the eighteenth century.

The liturgical function of the French constitution appears clearest at moments of national crisis when a regime collapses with no strong paternal figure to take command. This occurred in 1830, 1848, 1870, and 1944. At such times the representatives of the sovereign people decide upon the form of government to come, as happened in 1789. In 1848 and 1944 provisional governments arranged for the election of a "constituent assembly"—that is, a national assembly for drafting a new constitution. When they had finished their work, these assemblies dissolved themselves so that elections could be held under the terms of the new constitution. These procedures closely resembled the procedures in the crisis of 1789.

On 7 August 1830, after the revolution against Charles X, the assembly of elected deputies declared "that the universal and pressing interest of the French people calls His Royal Highness Louis-Philippe d'Orléans . . . to the throne." On 17 February 1871, after the collapse of the Second Empire, the National Assembly, as "the repository of sovereign authority," named Adolphe Thiers the *chef du pouvoir exécutif* of the French Republic, exercising his functions "under the authority of the National Assembly."[5] Then it went on to pass a series of constitutional laws that laid the foundation of the Third Republic.

Thus, the National Constituent Assembly of 1789 established principles and a tradition, even though its own constitution was short-lived. Upon that heritage the nation may not maintain a regime for long, but it will "reconstitute" itself (*se constituer*) by due process now two centuries old. The liberal doctrines of the Revolution have been preserved and implemented in this way.

Modern liberal doctrines in their French form are based on eighteenth-century ideas of liberty and the General Will. "Liberty consists in the ability to do whatever does not harm another . . ." reads the Declaration of the Rights of Man and the Citizen (clause 4). "Its limits can only be determined by the law . . . [L]aw is the expression of the general will [clause 6]. Every citizen may speak, write and print freely [clause 11]. . . . All citizens have the right, by themselves or through their representatives, to have demonstrated to them the need for public taxes, to consent to them freely [clause 14]. . . . [P]roperty being an inviolable and sacred right, no one may be deprived of it except for an obvious requirement of public necessity . . ." (clause 17).[6]

These guarantees for the citizen have been substantial, in spite of the miscarriages of justice that might be found in the history of the last two centuries. Public guarantees have not protected every citizen against private vengeance, mob violence, police brutality, political spite, or terrorism, but they have maintained a good measure of safety for the individual in normal times. French streets in the nineteenth and twentieth centuries have been decidedly freer from robbers, footpads, and murderous gangs than have American streets.

As an example of liberal principles at work, the case of the French Jew Captain Alfred Dreyfus reflected widespread public concern for justice and the rights of the individual, and it lent further inspiration to the liberal cause. Arrested on 15 October 1894 for allegedly betraying military secrets, court-martialed on 19–22 December, and sent to the Devil's Island prison on 21 February 1895, Dreyfus was brought back for retrial, pardoned on 19 September 1899, reinstated on 15 July 1906, and then decorated with the Legion of Honor. In the political struggle over Dreyfus, a majority of the French public eventually responded to appeals for truth, liberty, and justice. These virtues come, of course, from the age-old Christian message as well as from the revolutionary message, but the outcome of the Dreyfus case did vindicate the Declaration of the Rights of Man and the Citizen.[7]

Since that time the French public has occasionally turned out in massive, spontaneous demonstrations of a liberal character. For instance, on 8 February 1962 about 15,000 demonstrated in Paris against the killing of four-year-old Delphine Renard by a terrorist plastic bomb. On that occasion a small unit of the police attacked the crowd and caused the death of 8 people who were smothered in a panic rush for the Charonne subway station. A few days later a funeral procession for the victims brought out more than 100,000 people, the largest demonstration since the Popular Front demonstrations of 1934–35, and this time the police had more sense than to intervene.[8]

One of the great struggles of French liberals in the nineteenth century was against the Roman Catholic Church and many of its members. For more than 100 years after the Revolution, France was divided over the place and power of Catholicism. The First Republic had remained anticlerical even after the reaction of Thermidor, and in 1798 General Louis-Alexandre Berthier had occupied Rome, declared it a republic, and taken Pope Pius VI as a prisoner to France, where he died on 29 August 1799. When General Bonaparte seized power a few months later, he soon began to negotiate with Pius VII to restore religious peace in France and to remove the influence of what he described as "fifty emigrant bishops, paid by England, who direct the French clergy today."[9] On 15 July 1801 he and the pope signed a concordat which was to endure until 1905. In it Napoleon made Pius VII swallow a bitter revolutionary pill: The clergy were to take an oath of obedience to the government, the Church was to acquiesce in the sale of its property, and the bishops were to be replaced by new men chosen by Napoleon. Pius VII would not recognize the organic articles which Napoleon added to give himself firm authority in religious matters, or the imperial catechism of 1806, teaching French children that Napoleon was emperor by divine right. Yet the concordat looked very much like another Napoleonic victory, especially when a later disagreement ended in Pius VII's being kidnapped on 6 July 1809 and held prisoner until Napoleon's fall in 1814. The Church's gains by the concordat were not immediately clear.

Gains there were, all the same. The old Gallican Church had been destroyed, and Napoleon did nothing to revive it, with the result that a decidedly ultramontane Church revived under the terms of the concordat. The Catholicism recognized by the French government as the "religion of the great majority of French people" was supported by the State but directed by the Vatican. By 1864 eighty of the ninety-one dioceses had adopted the Roman liturgy. The most numerous class of Frenchmen, the peasants, had never ceased to be Roman Catholic in the main. Among intellectuals, a few famous books, widely read, promoted Christianity in the wake of the Revolution: Chateaubriand, *Génie du christianisme* (1802); Lamennais, *Essai sur l'indifférence en matière de religion* (1817) and others of his writings; Joseph de Maistre, *Du pape* (1819); Montalembert's writings; and Renan, *La vie de Jésus* (1863). The returning emigrant nobles supported the Church in large numbers, and many of their sons and daughters went into religious orders.[10]

The clergy grew in numbers, wealth, and influence. This growth, though not steady or unopposed, was substantial. In 1814 some 700 priests were ordained, in 1821 some 1,400, and in 1829 more than 2,300. By 1869 there were 56,000 secular priests in France. The regular orders revived meanwhile, and by 1814 there were more than 12,000 nuns in France, and by 1861 more than 89,000 nuns and 17,700 monks. The *budget des cultes* swelled accordingly and reached more than 45 million francs by 1869. Among the laity the Society of Saint Vincent de Paul had more than 30,000 members in 1,300 branches by 1859. Priests had recovered much influence over women as of old and also over children.[11] On 15 March 1850, Frédéric, Comte de Falloux (1811–86) was able to put through the National Assembly his controversial law by which the Church was allowed to open its own schools freely, and bishops were allowed on the Conseil supérieur de l'instruction publique. Later another law of July 1875 allowed for Roman Catholic universities.

The Church and most of its clergy soon threw their weight behind conservative political forces and so clashed inevitably with republicans, socialists, and many liberals. Radical clergymen like Montalembert, Lamennais, and Lacordaire were exceptional. The returning emigrant noble families supported the Church, many bishops were drawn from them, and noblewomen entered convents in large numbers. As president of the Second Republic, Louis-Napoleon sent the French army to Rome in 1849 to destroy the Roman Republic of Mazzini and Garibaldi and to restore Pius IX to the papal throne. French troops went on guarding the Vatican until 1864. Many of the clergy had supported the Second Republic in its early stages, but most rallied quickly behind Louis-Napoleon after his coup d'etat of 2 December 1851. Later in the century the clergy were generally on the anti-Dreyfusard side in the crucial Dreyfus case and also favorably inclined toward the right-wing nationalists General Georges Boulanger (1837–91), Maurice Barrès (1862–1923), and Charles Maurras (1868–1952). In 1864 Pius IX circulated his *Syllabus of the Principal Errors of Our Time,* summing up all his earlier denunciations of liberalism, Protestantism, and rationalism and denouncing everything, indeed, except Roman Catholicism and his own judgment, which, six years later, he declared to be infallible. (*Pastor aeternus,* 13 July 1870).

The terrible social problems of the century seemed secondary to the French public in general, but Roman Catholics were particularly insensitive to the cry for social reform. The papacy did not even discuss social issues, publicly at least, until Leo XIII, provoked by Karl Marx's *Das Kapital* (1867), made a statement on the "condition of the working classes" in his *Rerum novarum* (15 May 1891). It was then a little late to be saying "some remedy must found, and found quickly, for the misery and wretchedness pressing so heavily and unjustly at this moment on the vast majority of the working classes." Socialists in France had been saying this since the French Revolution.

Anticlerical opinion in nineteenth- and early-twentieth-century France was not socialist, however, in its main inspiration. The clergy was opposed for a wide variety of reasons, most of them traceable to the French Revolution or to the *siècle des lumières* before it. The intellectual life of the academies and other learned societies revived and flourished in the nineteenth century. In 1886 there were no fewer than 655 *sociétés savantes* promoting

lectures, journals, and books in various learned fields.[12] State
schools and universities were staffed by teachers, many of them
former clergymen, who shared the humanism, the utilitarian-
ism, the faith in science, the notions of cultural relativity, and
the materialism of the famous eighteenth-century intellectuals.
The schoolmaster and the doctor opposed the priest in many a
French village. To them, the freedom of education claimed by
Catholics in the Falloux Law of 15 March 1850 seemed to mean
freedom for the clergy to win control of French youth and thereby
to work against the principles of 1789.

The Dreyfus case was a great turning point in the struggle
of clerical and anticlerical factions. During the late 1890s the
case became a competition between the part of the French public
inclined to defend the liberal cause of a citizen's rights and the
other part that put the dignity of State, army, and Church first.
The anticlericals won the national elections of April 1902 and
put into effect their policy of suppressing religious schools and
the regular orders that kept them. Monks and nuns laid down
their habits and left their flocks. Long before Dreyfus was declared
innocent (12 July 1906), anticlerical opinion encouraged President Émile Combes to break off relations with the Vatican in
summer 1904. Then, in a tense, thorny political conflict, Church
and State were separated by a law of 11 December 1905, which
passed by 314 votes to 233 in the Chamber of Deputies and 181
to 102 in the Senate. The *budget des cultes* was stopped; the
Church's property, confiscated. The number of ordinations fell
sharply. Here was another echo of the French Revolution. In
Pierre Miquel's words, "The Dreyfus Affair permitted the parliamentary régime to shatter the last obstacle to the control of all
the organs of the State by the representatives of the popular
[i.e., public] will."[13]

II. *The Popular Tradition*

The outcome of the Dreyfus case showed that in the course of
the nineteenth century a majority of the French nation had been
slowly won over to the liberal principles of the Revolution. In
the public defense of those principles consists the French civiliz-

ing mission in the world. The greatest task during the two centuries since the Revolution has been to bring the urban populace
and the peasantry into the national polity, a task presenting two
main difficulties. The first was the difficulty of recognizing, for-
mulating, and solving problems of poverty, hunger, misery, and
ignorance. Liberal doctrine had no solutions for these problems
and even encouraged the public to assume that property was
somehow merited or inevitable. When, in July 1830 and February 1848, the public was struggling for representative and
responsible government, for "freedom," the populace joined in
the struggle in the hope of some help in its own distress, some
solution to its material problems. There was a serious misunderstanding which led directly to the popular uprising of the June
Days (1848) and, in part, to the Paris Commune (1871).

On both occasions an elected government called upon the
army, which quelled these uprisings with a ruthless vengeance.
In June 1848 the army was assisted in its task of suppression by
a Garde mobile recruited from the populace.[14] Until the end of
the nineteenth century the French public were afraid of the
populace, *classes dangereuses,* and so maintained the National Guard
militia led during the Revolution by Lafayette. The National
Guard is now no more than a historic ceremonial force, but the
French police have carried on defending persons and property
against the populace. Like other police forces, they have been
practically incapable of distinguishing ordinary crime from popular distress in the hurly-burly of the streets. Meanwhile, liberal
governments have slowly moved toward practical solutions to
social problems. Already in 1838, the young Michel Chevalier,
later to be so active in the public works of the Second Empire,
published his *Des intérêts matériels en France,* proposing sweeping
improvements in the living conditions of the poor on the grounds
that a hungry man is not a free man. Slowly the huddled cities
and isolated villages were improved by public works projects.[15]
In these the governments of liberal regimes were moved by
political pressure from left-wing movements.

These, too, stemmed from the French Revolution and
inherited a tradition of violent insurrection from it. That tradition has, paradoxically enough, been the second of two main
impediments to the civilizing of the French populace. Parlia-

mentary elections and rules, parliamentary life in general, have always been public activities, not popular ones, but the doctrine of popular sovereignty proclaimed every Frenchman a citizen with the rights and duties of citizenship. The French revolutionary assemblies had thus "baptized" the populace and invited it to take part in public life. Incapable of parliamentary life, anxious, poor, often cold and hungry, crowds of the nineteenth-century populace exercised their share of sovereignty in violent street demonstrations like those of the French Revolution.

They did not, of course, need revolutionary doctrine to encourage them to riot; crowds had rioted like that from time immemorial. Nevertheless, the revolutionary tradition of popular insurrection has played no small part in the violence of the last two centuries. On 28 July 1830 Paris mobs defeated the troops of General Marmont, and this event "brought the people, particularly the people of Paris, back into politics in a way they had not been involved since the 1790s."[16] Some 659 people, 496 of them civilians, were killed in the fighting in Paris on 27–29 July 1830. On 31 July in Lyons an armed crowd raised barricades in the place des Terreaux and the mayor and prefect resigned so that the National Guard could elect a provisional government. On 21–22 November 1831 two days of murderous street fighting left the garrison at Lyons with more than 300 casualties, and April 1834 saw six more days of street fighting. An insurrection in Paris on 5–6 June 1832 killed 70 soldiers and wounded 290 more; a dozen more were killed by mobs on the right bank on 13 April 1834; and 18 were killed in the Society of the Seasons revolt on 12 May 1839.[17] Some 1,400 people died fighting in Paris during the June Days of 1848, and many more were imprisoned or deported. In December 1851, a peasant republican movement rose up sporadically in many parts of rural France, especially in the south and southeast, against Louis-Napoleon's imperial coup d'etat. The army and police put them down with difficulty and many casualties. In May 1871 the army subdued the Paris Commune by shooting perhaps 20,000 of the Paris populace. Smaller encounters of troops and people have occurred from time to time in the twentieth century. In 1944, in the wake of the Second World War, several thousands were murdered, most of them no doubt for collaborating with the German occupation forces.

It hardly needs to be said that people in France had obvious motives for rioting, had rioted long before the French Revolution, and would have rioted again without it. The point is that the Revolution bequeathed examples, a tradition, and a theory to popular insurrection which therefore attracted the leadership of certain intellectuals and politicians. An excellent example is the widespread *"Montagnard"* movement of secret societies that enrolled tens of thousands of peasants in the 1840s.[18] To such leaders, rioting crowds were not merely expressing their anxiety, anger, and misery but following in a grand revolutionary tradition, exercising their sovereign right, expressing the General Will, fulfilling prophecies, waging a titanic struggle against a historically defined enemy. "The French Revolution," Gracchus Babeuf had predicted in 1796, "is only the forerunner of a much bigger, much more solemn revolution, which will be the final one."[19] Babeuf had been executed for his heresies, but his colleague Filippo Michele Buonarotti, a Tuscan who had first gone to France in 1789, spent the rest of his long life founding secret societies in order to wage revolution for revolution's sake. The Revolution gave similar inspiration to Louis-Auguste Blanqui (1805–81) and other anarchists, such as Charles Gallo, who attacked the Paris stock exchange in 1886 with a revolver and a bottle of sulfuric acid; Auguste Vaillant, who was executed for exploding a bomb in the Chamber of Deputies at 4:00 P.M. on 9 December 1893; and Santo Geronimo Caserio, who in 1894 assassinated President Sadi Carnot (a descendant of Lazare Carnot, member of the Committee of Public Safety).

Meanwhile, socialists and communists likewise found inspiration in the French Revolution. Piotr Kropotkin, in *The Great French Revolution* (1909), regarded it as the source and origin of all communist, anarchist, and socialist ideas. Precursors with socialist thoughts are to be found in the eighteenth century, but the traditions and organization of French socialism go no further back than 1792–93. From the Hébertists and the *enragés* to Louis Blanc, Pierre Leroux, Pierre-Joseph Proudhon, Karl Marx and on to Jean Jaurès, Léon Blum, Maurice Thorez, and Dany *le rouge*, a great variety, a swelling host of intellectuals and political leaders have appealed to the populace to march behind them or to vote for them. Few, indeed, of these have been men of the people. The simple, tragic, prosaic motives of the populace they have sublimated in the rhetoric of their pamphlets, speeches, and treatises, torrents of them all embroidering or enlarging on left-wing ideas developed in the Revolution. Too many intellectual leaders, notably Karl Marx and his followers, carried away by what Guizot described in 1849 as the "idolatry of Democracy," have idealized the populace, somewhat as Robespierre did, and imagined it to be somehow better, purer, holier than the reading, writing, and ruling classes. Too few have seen, as Proudhon did, that "the heart of the proletarian is like that of the rich, a cesspool of babbling sensuality, a home of filth and hypocrisy. . . . The greatest obstacle which equality has to overcome is not the aristocratic pride of the rich, but rather the undisciplined egoism of the poor."[20] Too few have seen rioting folk for the insignificant minorities they were, scarcely representative of the French people, opposed on many occasions by the property-owning peasantry, which, even in 1939, constituted about two-thirds of the populace.

The popular tradition of the Revolution is a violent, illiberal, antiparliamentary tradition. This is because it is rooted in the revolutionary distinction of the populace from the public. Before, during, and after the Revolution the populace had a tendency to see problems in the shape of enemies to be found, faced, and destroyed. This tendency was an excellent moral basis for an army in wartime, and during the Revolution the populace made better soldiers than the mercenaries of earlier times whose motives had been profit and adventure. In domestic politics, on the other hand, a habit of blaming troubles on groups of fellow citizens and letting hatred lead on to mob, murder, and massacre raised more problems than it solved. The public in general knew this in the eighteenth and nineteenth centuries; the populace did not. Both had strong feelings of hostility toward "capitalists," "hoarders," the "two hundred families" of bankers, and others of that ilk and toward "traitors," "spies," "Jews," and foreigners in general. Large numbers of both also hated the clergy.

But the popular response to these feelings was to seek and destroy, whereas the public response was to debate, legislate, and reform. As a result of the eighteenth-century Enlightenment, the public saw that a well-ordered polity would protect the public interest against greedy private interests and that enforcing laws was better than wreaking vengeance. The populace meanwhile went on wreaking vengeance, as had the monarchy of old.

The pre-Enlightenment mind, which was to live on in the populace, thought it best to discourage profiteering, treachery, and crime by the harsh punishment of profiteers, traitors, and criminals. For example, the monarchy did not know how to protect its funds against fraud, but it knew how to make examples of fat financiers by the arrests, executions, and fines meted out by the occasional Chambre de justice. Again, the protection of the king's person was primitive on 5 January 1757, when Robert-François Damiens stabbed him with a knife, but no more primitive than Damiens's punishment in the place des Grèves, where he was publicly tortured to death.[21]

Voltaire, Rousseau, Beccaria, and other writers of the eighteenth-century Enlightenment turned the public in general against that sort of cruelty.[22] The public also learned that it was better to prevent crimes than to punish them. The National Assembly believed the national salvation to lie in enlightened laws and reforms. It did not usually look for scapegoats. But the populace learned little of all that. From 1792 to 1794 hoarders, traitors, and then priests, nobles, and "aristocrats" were sought and killed either by mobs or by public courts inclined, like the courts in Bourbon times, to please the populace. After the Revolution the liberal political process added to the variety of scapegoats, as various intellectual leaders competed for popular support.

The nobility, dispersed, persecuted, and despoiled from 1792 to 1794, seemed a smaller target than the rich *notables* who had survived, even profited by the Revolution. These, a mixed element soon referred to as *les bourgeois,* came into view. Anarchists and socialists of many varieties have shared a convenient myth of a bourgeoisie, an enemy that had escaped destruction in the French Revolution and remained to be destroyed by the nation as the nobility were supposed to have been destroyed. As the myth grew, two social classes, *peuple* and bourgeoisie, came to be identified in left-wing theory, which ran wildly ahead of any empirical investigation of social reality. The notion of a struggle between these two classes grew like an archetypal fairy tale, enabling political leaders and theorists to justify popular insurrection wherever it occurred. The Paris uprisings of 1830, 1848, and 1871 all could be fitted into a calendar of postrevolutionary expectations. Meanwhile, the populace occasionally gave vent to its anxiety, hunger, and fury against a general public still caught up in struggles for a liberal polity: a constitutional government consisting of an elected assembly, a responsible executive, a free press, and safety for persons and property.

One of the myths in the left-wing story is that the bourgeois were now the enemy because the nobility had been destroyed in the French Revolution. In fact, nobles began to return under the Directory in the 1790s and in a generation were able to recover a great deal of their property. Meanwhile, on 1 March 1808, Napoleon created about 1,500 knights, 1,090 barons, 388 counts, 31 dukes, and more than a dozen princes. Altogether, between 1808 and 1814 he bestowed some 3,263 titles upon men, about half of whom had not previously been titled.[23] Of Napoleon's 71 ambassadors, 31 were noble by birth. About one-third of the high dignitaries of the First Empire had belonged to the *noblesse* of the *ancien régime*. Altogether, between 1800 and 1830 more than 7,000 titles were granted by French rulers. The restored Bourbons named 164 prefects, of whom no fewer than 118 (70 percent) were from families that had been noble before the Revolution. Every regime from 1808 to 1879, except the brief Second Republic, rewarded supporters with noble titles. Nobles remained among the principal landowners in the nineteenth century and were also the richest (per capita) social group in France. It is true that they were no longer a ruling class and that their numbers were falling, as they had been since the seventeenth century, but their way of life was admired and imitated by middle-class people, many of whom adopted the particle *de* and endeavored to *vivre noblement* as of old. Even today in France, 1,000 families carry noble titles, 3,000 are considered legitimate nobles, and 15,000 claim to be noble.[24]

Another of the left-wing myths is that the new ruling class, the bourgeoisie, consisted of capitalists, bankers, and manufacturers. Marx's *Communist Manifesto* (1847) makes this point very forcefully. It is, however, a gross distortion of the facts. Of sixty men with portfolios under Louis-Philippe, only seven were businessmen and thirty-six were civil servants.[25] Land remained the basic form of French wealth because France was very slow to develop economically and to adapt to modern forms of great capitalism, which is characteristically international. The ruling elites were composed more of landowners than businessmen or financiers until the twentieth century. Most manufacturing in France was done in small workshops until well into the twentieth century. The rioting crowds of 1830, 1848, and 1871 were no more industrial wage earners than were the *sans-culottes* of 1793–94. There was certainly a great deal of misery and overcrowding and a shocking disparity of wealth and poverty, such as Émile Zola and other novelists portrayed, but the well-known picture of a capitalist bourgeois class of industrialists and financiers is a left-wing myth too often thoughtlessly repeated in general histories.[26]

III. *The National Tradition*

The liberal and democratic traditions derived from the French Revolution are inseparable from a national tradition that was born with them. "The representatives of the French people, constituted as a National Assembly . . . ," were, after all, the source of the Declaration of the Rights of Man and the Citizen, and they affirmed in it that "The principle of all sovereignty rests essentially in the Nation" (clause 3). In practice, furthermore, French nationalism has been much stronger than French liberalism, so much so that the liberal theory expressed in the Declaration of Rights has sometimes appeared to be only a stalking horse for the advancement of the French nation. In the cause of liberty, equality, and fraternity, French armies conquered and plundered all of continental Europe between 1793 and 1814. French government, French institutions, French taxes, French paper money *(assignats)*, even French weights and measures were forced upon the conquered nations, which were drained at the same time of money, horses, equipment, and even, after 1795, art treasures. Neighboring territories were annexed to France: Savoy, Nice County, Salm, the region between the Moselle and the Rhine, and (by a vote of the National Convention on 1 October 1795) all Belgium. These policies began under the revolutionary regimes years before Napoleon came to power.

The liberal message everywhere softened resistance to French conquest. The National Convention in declaring war in November 1792 offered "fraternity and help to all peoples who wish to recover their liberty," and minorities responded in all countries. *La grande nation* imposed itself on continental Europe in the guise of a deliverer from the tyranny of kings, nobles, and priests.

The national emotions and doctrines which then inspired the revolutionary crusade have never ceased to inspire French readers and writers of revolutionary history. Jacques Godechot, for instance, could not break away from the prevailing gallocentric assumptions even in his learned efforts to trace a wider Atlantic revolution. The idea of an Atlantic revolution brings into focus the long, deep tradition of Dutch, English, and Swiss resistance to absolute monarchy and the Protestant reformations in Germany, Switzerland, the Netherlands, and Scotland, reformations that were in fact revolutions by another name. But Godechot scarcely notices these. He passes over the parliamentary traditions, too, the freedoms of speech and of the press, and the measure of religious tolerance, established in northern European countries and the United States of America before the French Revolution, perhaps because they do not seem sufficiently revolutionary. He describes these countries, indeed, as "countries where revolutionary movements had failed earlier" (Jacques Godechot, *France and the Atlantic Revolution of the Eighteenth Century, 1770–1799*, London, 1971, p. 124).

He goes on to remark that "Protestant dissenters applauded the emancipation of religious minorities in France, the nationalization of the wealth of the clergy, and the reduction of papal power over the Church in France."[27] In this typical sentence Godechot forgets that the wealth of the clergy had been nationalized, and the pope's power not only reduced but removed altogether, in Great Britain centuries before the French Revolution. The British constitution was founded on these events. French religious refugees had been fleeing to Britain in their thousands

since the sixteenth century. True, the Protestant dissenters were
not yet emancipated in Britain, but they are scarcely likely to
have envied their French brethren for long. The brief liberal
interlude of 1789–91 soon ended in the holocaust of 1792–94
and subsequent outbursts of Terror, red and white. But in
Godechot's gallocentric view, all history leads on to the French
Revolution, for la grande nation is at the center of the world. It is
such typically unconscious nationalism that causes foreign
observers, even friends and francophiles, to describe the French
as "an insular people."[28] "France has always seen and understood the world", writes the Swiss Herbert Lüthy, "only as a pro-
jection of herself."[29]

In its most extreme form the cult of French nationalism
became a veritable religion. In Le peuple (1846) the historian
Michelet declared, "So many times France has given her life for
the world," as in the two "redemptions" of the world by Joan of
Arc and by the French Revolution. "My fatherland alone can
save the world," he went on to say in an effusion of patriotic
fervor shared by untold numbers of his countrymen.[30] In a different manifestation of the same cult, General Charles de Gaulle
was able to create the myth that in 1940 he took France to London and kept it there at No. 4 Carlton Gardens (just down the
street from where Louis-Napoleon had lived in 1871) until the
liberation of 1944. It is appropriate that the term chauvinisme,
adopted a century earlier to describe this extreme patriotism,
was a French term.[31]

The Revolution put all the force of national patriotism at
the service of the central government. Whatever the government ordained in the nation's name was henceforth justified by
the ideology of national sovereignty. Therein lay the source of
the vigorous national response to threatening foreign invasions
in 1792. The levée en masse, the nation in arms, now mobilized
French men, money, and munitions even more successfully than
king and Church had been able to do in the seventeenth century. Therein, too, lay the source of Napoleon's political authority after 1799. Emperor not of France but of "the French," he
led them on a national crusade of imperial conquest. They followed him so long as he led them to victory. Again and again in

the last 200 years, the stirring emotions of patriotism have moved French people to heroism and sacrifice. Defensive, as in the Franco-Prussian War and the First World War, French national force has awakened admiration and sympathy abroad; offensive, as in the Napoleonic Wars, it has led to defeat by touching chords of opposing national patriotisms among its victims. In either case an urgent national cause has tended to unite the French.

The national cause has proved capable, indeed, of bringing together otherwise irreconcilable groups. For instance, republicans and Bonapartists—strange bedfellows, indeed—worked for the same national cause in the 1830s and 1840s. This was because republicans and Bonapartists differed only in their politics, not in their devotion to France. The revolutionary and imperial armies had absorbed the aggressive nationalism of the populace, which had entered the army en masse, and Bonapartists shared what Georges Weill describes as *"la passion des républicains pour la grandeur nationale . . ."*[32] And as Theodore Zeldin remarks, "The peasants who voted for Louis Napoleon in December 1848 voted a few months later for the reddest republicans, as though for one and the same cause."[33] The *Union sacrée* during the Great War of 1914–18 was a manifestation of the same underlying cause, the same national "religion," and so was the political victory of Charles de Gaulle in the referenda and elections that followed his coup d'etat of 1958.

Nationalism has been firmly linked with militarism in the last two centuries. Many people, French and foreign, have remembered the Revolution as a military or imperial event. It was celebrated on its centenary, shortly after the Franco-Prussian War, as a series of military victories, *le salut de la patrie*, Valmy, Jemappes, and the glory of Lazare Carnot and of Generals Hoche, Marceau, and Desaix.[34] Still today the victors and victories of the Revolution are celebrated more than any other revolutionary themes in the naming of Paris streets. The revolutionary Generals Augereau, Bonaparte, Davout, Hoche, Jourdan, Kellerman, Kléber, Marceau, and Westermann all have streets named after them; the battles of Valmy and Jemappes (1792) each have a passage and a quai, and Valmy also has an impasse; the battles of Fleurus (1794) and Montenotte (1796) each have a rue. Meanwhile, members of the Committee of Public Safety will rarely be remembered in street names unless they are thought to have been military leaders. There is an avenue, a boulevard, and a rue Carnot, a rue Robert Lindet, and a rue Saint-Just, which is listed with all the other saints between the rues Saint-Julien-le-Pauvre and Saint-Lambert.

Another manifestation of French nationalism is the myth and cult of Napoleon which grew up soon after his death on Saint Helena in 1821 and flowered when Louis-Philippe and Lord Palmerston allowed Napoleon's remains to be brought back to France, carried slowly up the Seine in an ornate coffin mounted on a black boat with a cross at the bow, and deposited in Les Invalides hospital with great ceremony on 15 December 1840. The French public was deeply moved, and Victor Hugo wrote a poem, "Le retour de l'empereur" beginning, *"Sire, vous revenez dans votre capital. . . ."*[35] It was partly because of the Napoleonic cult that Louis-Napoleon, the nephew, was able to win the presidential elections of the Second Republic and then to seize power in 1851 as Napoleon III. Even strong liberal opponents like Adolphe Thiers were admirers of Napoleon I and saw the dangers of Napoleon III's regime too late. The cult of Napoleon is still strong in France. Schools continue to teach children to venerate Napoleon without regard for the European view of him as an upstart conqueror. I have heard a *chevalier de la Légion d'Honneur* argue heatedly that Napoleon created the first European union in a generous and farsighted policy which the British and their allies perversely thwarted.

IV. *The Bureaucratic Tradition*

The reforming governments of the French Revolution created a central administration, a set of executive government departments, very much larger and better organized than ever before. Under the monarchy, the administrative services had consisted of high officials *(magistrats)* and the clerks they chose to employ. Extremely personal, much affected by the venality of offices, organized according to the vagaries of patronage, not bureaucratic in any modern sense of the term, the old Bourbon administration had scarcely distinguished public funds and employees from private ones.[36] From the summer of 1789 the Constituent Assembly began to apply principles of utility or function and notions of mechanical organization or efficiency. It also "nationalized" the old administrative services, eliminating tax farms and venal offices.

At the same time it centralized French administration by eliminating the provinces and destroying all provincial authorities. "The language of the Constitution and the laws shall be taught to all," the Constitution Committee reported in September 1791, "and that multitude of corrupt dialects, which are the last remains of feudalism, will disappear; this is ordained by the nature of things."[37] The supporters of the provinces were subsequently defeated, and "federalism" was outlawed as a crime. Napoleon added much to this executive part of the government, though less than he is usually credited with, and it has remained large and powerful to this day. Every regime has used it in governing; none has tried to destroy it or to manage without it. Whatever is happening at the political level, whatever the National Assembly is doing, whether governments rise or fall, the administration carries on as it has done since the Revolution.

This administration is a fundamental part of French civilization. It embodies and fulfills an idea of the State that is planted in the mind of every French citizen. This idea originated long before the French Revolution, but the Revolution gave it clarity, permanence, and strength by removing all rival authorities and by investing the State with the authority of the nation. "Preservation of the rights of man and the citizen requires the existence of public forces," reads the Declaration of the Rights of Man and the Citizen (clause 12). "These forces are therefore created for the advantage of all. . . ." The French idea of the State, widespread and largely unconscious, prepares citizens for life in a country where central authority is usually present, usually in charge of things. It prepares them to suffer the officious, patronizing, sometimes nasty manners of petty officials accustomed to wielding public authority without regard for the dignity of the private citizen——unless he or she happens to be influential. France is a country in which schools, hospitals, or other public institutions are rarely directed by voluntary boards of citizens. It is a country in which the police act with enormous force and independence. There is no habeas corpus in French law. Legally the *préfet de police* may search a house, seize a letter from the post office, arrest a person and interrogate him, hold him prisoner almost indefinitely, and all without a warrant or any other judicial authority. All this the average Frenchman puts up with as normal and necessary.

France is also a country with pride in its administrative services and a high standard of recruiting. Top-ranking French officials—the *cadres*—are chosen from among the best graduates of the best schools. Statesmen and even writers not infrequently begin life as civil servants. Guy de Maupassant, Paul Claudel, and Paul Valéry, for instance, all served in ministries of the Third Republic.[38] The primary fact, however, is that the French civil service is organized differently from the British and American services. As well as the usual executive departments for foreign affairs, war, finance, transport, and so on, it has given a large place to several *grands corps de l'état* which have no equivalent in the English-speaking world. The first of these has been the Council of State (Conseil d'état), a body of 100 or 150 senior officials whose main task has been to see that no injustice is done to citizens by civil servants, to civil servants by citizens or to civil servants by one another. Another *grand corps de l'état* has been the Court of Accounts (Cour des comptes), which, as its name implies, examines and approves all government financial accounts; and a third has been the Corps of Inspectors of Finance *(inspecteurs des finances)*. There is a special corps of inspectors in every big government ministry, but the inspectors in the Ministry of Finance have become nationally and internationally famous for their quality and usefulness.[39]

To these should be added two other *grands corps:* the diplomatic corps and the prefectoral corps, also very prestigious. Louis XIV had built up a large, serviceable diplomatic corps, and the two or three dozen intendants of the *ancien régime* were in many ways the predecessors of the nineteenth century prefects. Because the intendants disappeared in the Revolution, and the prefects were not appointed until after Napoleon's law of 17 February 1800, there are some grounds for thinking that the prefectoral corps, at least, owed nothing to the French Revolution. Certainly the liberal principles of 1789–91 warranted a system of elected authorities, and such a system was in fact worked out for the departments, the districts, and the localities. Eighty-three *départements* and 44,000 *communes* (municipalities) were created. Characteristically, a uniform system was devised by the national government without reference to local variations, and the central government, never satisfied with it, seldom let it work for long. From 1792 to 1794 *commissaires* were sent out as the ruling emissaries of the central government. When the Directory endeavored to restore the electoral system, corruption, tyranny, neglect, local preoccupations, and civil disorder prevailed. The wartime needs of the central government were not met. The absence of a strong administrative presence out in the provinces seemed to be one of the causes of the situation in which Napoleon's coup d'etat was acceptable to so much of the public. From then on prefects governed provincial France for the central government, except from February to May 1848, when the Second Republic tried ineffectually to replace them with *commissaires de la république*. The prefects, roughly 100 in number, were too useful to the central government, for influencing elections as well as for ordinary executive purposes. Even in the Third Republic, which gave more initiative to the *communes* and their *conseils municipaux* in a law of 1884, the prefects retained much of their original authority. Their callous, authoritarian rule in Alsace and Lorraine after these provinces had been recovered in 1918 is a case in point.[40] The uses and prestige of the prefects admirably illustrate the bureaucratic tradition.

The Conseil d'état, the Cour des comptes, the *inspecteurs des finances*, the diplomatic and prefectoral services are elite groups of officials who are free to take on temporary tasks, usually in positions of command, almost anywhere in the civil service as directors of special *bureaux* or as inspectors or planners. They may be posted about here and there in France or in the French Empire, as the need arises. They are elites, too, in their education and selection. About one-third of them are recruited from the legal profession, the staffs of universities, and business and industry; but most of the rest come from the exclusive École polytechnique (founded in 1794), or from the University Faculty of Law and the École libre des sciences politiques (1872) by way of the École nationale d'administration (1945). Many more specialized schools for specialized corps are only slightly less prestigious: the École des ponts et chaussées (1775) for civil engineers, the École des mines (1783) for mining engineers, the École des chartes (1829) for archivists, and others. The competition to get into these and other such schools and from them into the appropriate *corps* is intense, and the prestige of the successful is correspondingly high. Efforts to free education in public affairs from state control and state service have failed. The École libre des sciences politiques was founded in 1871 and 1872 expressly for this purpose, but soon became another *grande école* for training the administrative elite.[41]

The French civil service is also powerful because the public sector is large. Few countries of Western Europe have had so much government management of economic life, not only of public utilities and transport systems but also of manufacturing, banks, and other businesses. Schoolteachers and university professors, too, are civil servants and constitute a large fraction of the civil servants (38 percent in 1964). In 1914 there were 489,000 French civil servants; in 1950 just over 1 million, which was twice the British figure; and in 1964 there were about 1.3 million, whose salaries absorbed one-fifth of the government's budget, their pensions another 3 percent. Superficially this huge administration looks as though it descends from the Bourbon administration of the seventeenth and eighteenth centuries, but it is in fact quite different in its structure and functioning. Closely studied, it can be traced back no farther than the French Revolution, in which modern French bureaucracy was born.

A Short Reading List

General

Cobban, Alfred, *The Social Interpretation of the French Revolution,* Cambridge, 1964. Original and provocative lectures.

Sutherland, D. M. G., *France 1789–1815: Revolution and Counterrevolution,* London, 1985. Detailed and balanced, especially on the social aspects.

Sydenham, Michael, *The French Revolution,* London, 1965. An excellent short introduction.

Thompson, J. M., *The French Revolution* (1943), various editions. With clear and factual explanations.

On the Eve

Baker, Keith, *Condorcet: From Natural Philosophy to Social Mathematics,* Chicago, 1975.

Darnton, Robert, *The Literary Underground of the Old Regime,* Cambridge, Mass., 1982. Essays on writing, printing, and publishing.

Doyle, William, *Origins of the French Revolution,* Oxford, 1980. An intelligent review of the question.

Egret, Jean, *The French Pre-Revolution, 1787–88* (1964), trans. W. Camp, Chicago, 1977. A detailed study of those two years.

Eisenstein, E. L., "Who Intervened in 1788? A Commentary on *The Coming of the French Revolution,*" *American Historical Review,* vol. LXXI (1965), pp. 77–103. An independent review of a vital point.

Girault de Coursac, Pierrette, *L'Education d'un roi: Louis XVI,* Paris, 1972. A new view of the king.

Hufton, Olwen, *The Poor in Eighteenth-Century France, 1750–89,* Oxford,

1974. A description of the populace.

————, "The French Church," in W. J. Callahan & David Higgs, *Church and Society in Catholic Europe of the 18th Century,* ed. Cambridge, England, 1979, pp. 13–33.

Hunt, Lynn, *Revolution and Urban Politics in Provincial France: Troyes and Reims, 1786–1790,* Stanford, 1978. The revolutionary crisis in the towns.

Kelly, G. A., "The Machine of the Duc d'Orléans and the New Politics," *Journal of Modern History,* vol. 51 (1979), pp. 667–84. A glimpse of princely opposition to the king.

Lefebvre, Georges, *The Great Fear of 1789* (1932), New York, trans. 1973. The peasant uprising of July 1789.

Taylor, George V. "Non-capitalist Wealth and the Origins of the French Revolution," *American Historical Review,* vol. LXXII (1967), pp. 469–96. An original study.

Wick, Daniel, "The Court Nobility and the French Revolution: The Example of the Society of Thirty," *Eighteenth-Century Studies,* vol. 13 (1980), pp. 263–84. Noble families in opposition to Louis XVI.

The Liberal Phase (1789–92)

Censer, Jack Richard, *Prelude to Power: The Parisian Radical Press, 1789–1791,* Baltimore, 1976.

Godechot, Jacques, *The Taking of the Bastille* (1965), trans., London, 1970. A detailed and interesting story.

Gottschalk, Louis, and M. Maddox, *Lafayette in the French Revolution From the October Days Through the Federation,* Chicago, 1973. A careful study of this central figure.

Kennedy, Michael, *The Jacobin Clubs in the French Revolution: The First Years,* Princeton, 1982. Across France, not only Paris.

Rose, R. B., *The Making of the Sans-culottes: Democratic Ideas and Institutions in Paris, 1789–92,* Manchester, England, 1983. The popular leaders and clubs at an early stage.

Scott, S. F., *The Response of the Royal Army to the French Revolution,* Oxford, 1978. How long did the army remain loyal?

The Terror

Brinton, Crane, *The Jacobins,* New York, 1930. A classic essay.

Greer, Donald, *The Incidence of the Terror During the French Revolution: A*

Statistical Interpretation, Cambridge, Mass., 1935. Who were the victims?

Hampson, Norman, *Danton*, London, 1978. Good reading.

Jordan, David, *The King's Trial*, Berkeley, 1979. Clear and simple.

Loomis, Stanley, *Paris in the Terror*, New York, 1964 and 1986. Marat's murder, Danton's trial, and Robespierre's fall.

Lucas, Colin, *The Structure of the Terror: The Example of Javogues and the Loire*, Oxford, 1973.

Palmer, R. R., *Twelve Who Ruled: The Year of the Terror in the French Revolution* (1941), various editions. The story of the Committee of Public Safety.

Rose, R. B., *The Enragés*, Sydney (Australia), 1968. A short, intimate account of a group of extremists.

Slavin, Morris, *The French Revolution in Miniature: Section Droits de l'Homme, 1789–1795*, Princeton, 1984. The story of one of the forty-eight Paris sections.

Soboul, Albert, *Les Sans-culottes parisiens en l'an II*, Paris, 1958, translated in part.

Thompson, J. M., *Robespierre*, Oxford, 1939, 2 vols. The fruit of long study.

Walter, Gérard, *Robespierre*, Paris, 1961, 2 vols., one volume on his life, the other on his work.

After 9 Thermidor

Lyons, Martyn, *France Under the Directory*, Cambridge, England, 1975.

Mathiez, Albert, *La réaction thermidorienne* (1929), trans. as *After Robespierre: The Thermidorian Reaction*, New York, 1965.

Rose, R. B., *Gracchus Babeuf*, Stanford, 1978.

Sydenham, M. J., *The First French Republic, 1792–1804*, London, 1974.

Woloch, Isser, *Jacobin Legacy: The Democratic Movement under the Directory*, Princeton, 1970.

Special Subjects

Blanning, T. C. W., *The Origins of the French Revolutionary Wars*, London and New York, 1986.

Bosher, J. F., *French Finances, 1770–1795: From Business to Bureaucracy*, Cambridge, England, 1970.

Bruguière, Michel, *Gestionnaires et profiteurs de la revolution*, Paris, 1986. Informed and original on the survival of financial officials during the Revolution.

Chaumié, Jacqueline, *Le réseau d'Antraigues et la contre-révolution, 1791–93*, Paris, 1965. Full of astonishing revelations.

Cobb, Richard, *The Police and the People*, Oxford, 1970, and *Reactions to the French Revolution*, Oxford, 1972. Learned but lively and full of real people.

Godechot, Jacques, *La Contre-révolution, 1789–1804*, Paris, 1961.

Harris, Jennifer, "The Red Cap of Liberty: A Study of Dress Worn by French Revolutionary Partisans 1789–94," *Eighteenth-Century Studies*, vol. 14 (1981), pp. 283–312.

Lucas, Colin, "The Problem of the Midi in the French Revolution," *Transactions of the Royal Historical Society*, vol. 28 (1978), pp. 1–25. A view of the Revolution in southern regions.

McManners, John, *The French Revolution and the Church*, London, 1969, New York, 1970. Short and clear.

Palmer, R. R., *The Improvement of Humanity: Education and the French Revolution*, Princeton, 1985. Sums up much recent scholarship.

Rude, George, *The Crowd in the French Revolution*, Oxford, 1959. A classic study of riots and rioters.

For Reference

Cabourdin, Guy, and Georges Viard, *Lexique historique de la France d'ancien régime*, Paris, 1978. A dictionary of institutions.

Cooke, James, *France 1789–1962*, Newton Abbot, England, 1975. A short historical dictionary of people, events, and institutions.

Godechot, Jacques, *Les Institutions de la France sous la révolution et l'empire*, Paris, 1951. Not easy to use, but irreplaceable.

Marion, Marcel, *Dictionnaire des institutions de la France aux XVIIe et XVIIIe siècles*, Paris, 1923. Old but still useful.

Scott, S. F., and B. Rothaus, *Historical Dictionary of the French Revolution, 1789–99*, London and Westport, Conn., 1985, 2 vols. Packed with information.

Notes

ONE
The French on the Eve of the Revolution

1. Jacques Dupâquier, *La population française aux XVIIe et XVIIIe siècles*, Paris, 1979, p. 82.

2. Alison Patrick, *The Men of the First French Republic: Political Alignments in the National Convention of 1792*, Baltimore, 1972, pp. 248–49, 292.

3. Georges Lefebvre, *Les paysans du nord pendant la révolution française*, Paris, 1924, p. 304; Régine Robin, *La société française en 1789: Semur-en-Auxois*, Paris, 1970, p. 190; T. J. A. Le Goff, *Vannes and Its Region*, Oxford, 1981, pp. 201–03; Olwen Hufton, *The Poor of Eighteenth-Century France, 1750–1789*, Oxford, 1974, p. 24; Maréchal de Vauban, *Le projet d'un dîme royale* (1689), pp. 2–4.

4. Jean Jacquart, "La production agricole dans la France du XVIIe siècle," *Le XIIe Siècle* (1966), p. 21; B. H. Slicher van Bath, *The Agrarian History of Western Europe, A.D. 500–1850*, London, 1963, p. 321; Robin, *Semur-en-Auxois*, p. 184; Pierre Goubert, "The French Peasantry: A Regional Example," *Crisis in Europe 1560–1660*, ed. T. Ashton, New York, 1967, p. 166; Le Goff, *Vannes* p. 154; F. Braudel and E. Labrousse, *Histoire économique et sociale de la France, 1660–1789*, Paris, 1970, vol. II, pp. 146–47; Anne Zink, *Azereix: La vie d'une communauté rurale à la fin du XVIIIe siècle*, Paris, 1969, passim.

5. Pierre Goubert, "Sociétés rurales françaises du 18e siècle: Vingt paysanneries contrastées," in *Conjonctures économiques, structures sociales, hommage à Ernest Labrousse*, The Hague, 1974, p. 376; Jean Meuvret, "Agronomie et jardinage aux XVIe et XVIIe siècles," in *Éventail de l'histoire vivante: Hommage à Lucien Febvre*, Paris, 1953, vol. II, pp. 353–62, and in *Études d'histoire économique*, Paris, 1971, pp. 153–62.

6. Arthur Young, *Travels in France During the Years 1787, 1788 &*

1789, ed. Constantia Maxwell, Cambridge, England, 1950, pp. 275 and 392.

7. R. C. Harris, *The Seigneurial System in Early Canada,* Madison, Wis., 1966, ch. 7, "The Roture"; Marcel Trudel, *Les débuts du régime seigneurial au Canada,* Montreal, 1974, ch. V, "Les censitaires."

8. Robert Forster, *The House of Saulx-Tavanes: Versailles and Burgundy, 1700–1830,* Baltimore, 1971; Michel Morineau, *Les faux-semblants d'un démarrage économique: Agriculture et démographie en France au XVIII siècle,* Paris, 1970, p. 17; Octave Festy, *L'agriculture pendant la révolution francaise,* Paris, 1950, p. 15.

9. Le Goff, *Vannes,* p. 158.

10. Édouard Bruley, "Nobles et paysans picards à la fin de l'ancien régime: Le marquis de Mailly et son receveur," *Revue d'histoire moderne et contemporaire,* vol. XVI (1969), p. 610.

11. Dupâquier, *La population française,* p. 69.

12. T. J. Markovitch, *Les industries lainières de Colbert à la révolution,* Geneva, 1976, p. 469; P. M. Jones, *Politics and Rural Society: The Southern Massif Central, 1750–1880,* Cambridge, England, 1985, p. 57.

13. Roger Dion, *Histoire de la vigne et du vin en France des origines au XIXe siècle,* Paris, 1959, pp. 32–33.

14. Paul Bois, *Les paysans de l'ouest,* Paris, 1971, p. 189.

15. Lefebvre, *Les paysans du nord,* p. 310.

16. Forster, *House of Saulx-Tavanes,* p. 165.

17. Ibid., p. 247.

18. Louis Merle, *La métairie et l'évolution agraire de la Gatiné poitevine de la fin du moyen age à la révolution,* Paris, 1958, pp. 189–91.

19. Pierre Goubert, *100,000 Provinciaux au XVIIe siècle,* Paris, 1968, p. 205.

20. Jean Meyer, *La noblesse bretonne au XVIIIe siècle,* Paris, 1966, vol. II, pp. 1188–91; Pierre de Saint Jacob, *Les paysans de la Bourgogne du Nord au dernier siècle de l'ancien régime,* Paris, 1960, p. 428.

21. Robert Forster, *Merchants, Landlords, Magistrates,* Baltimore, 1980, pp. 102–03.

22. Bois, *Les paysans de l'ouest,* p. 348; Colin Lucas, *The Structure of the Terror; The Example of Javogues and the Loire,* Oxford, 1973, p. 123.

23. Population figures are taken from Dupâquier, *La population française,* Maurice Garden, *Lyon at les lyonnais au XVIIIe siècle,* Paris, 1970, p. 248; François Lebrun, *Les hommes et la mort en Anjou,* Paris, 1971, p. 161; Jean-Claude Perrot, *Genèse d'une ville moderne: Caen au XVIIIe siècle,* The Hague, 1975, p. 265; Le Goff, *Vannes,* p. 44.

24. Louis Trenard, *Lyon de l'Encyclopédie au préromanticisme,* Paris, 1958, vol. I, p. 7.

25. W. H. Sewell, Jr., *Work and Revolution in France: The Language of Labor from the Old Regime to 1848*, Cambridge, England, 1980, ch. 2 to 5.

26. Abbé de Saint-Pierre, quoted in P. Dawson, *Provincial Magistrates and Revolutionary Politics in France, 1789–1795*, Cambridge, Mass., 1972, p. 35.

27. L. R. Berlanstein, *The Barristers of Toulouse in the 18th Century, 1740–93*, Baltimore, 1975, p. 3.

28. Georges Lefebvre, "Répartition de la propriété et de l'exploitation foncières à la fin de l'ancien régime," *Études sur la révolution française*, Paris, 1954, p. 206.

29. Olwen Hufton, *Bayeux in the Late Eighteenth Century: A Social Study*, Oxford, 1967, ch. 2 and pp. 248 and 281; Hufton, "The French Church," in *Church and Society in Catholic Europe of the Eighteenth Century*, ed. W. J. Callahan and David Higgs, Cambridge, England, 1979, pp. 13–33.

30. John McManners, *French Ecclesiastical Society Under the Ancien Régime*, Manchester, England, 1960, pp. 3–6.

31. Archives nationales, Paris, V^1 series.

32. Morineau, *Les faux-semblants d'un démarrage économique*.

33. Pierre Léon, "Structures du commerce extérieur et évolution industrielle de la France à la fin du XVIIIe siècle," *Conjoncture économique, structures sociales, hommage à Ernest Labrousse*, The Hague, 1974, pp. 407–32.

34. Markovitch, *Les industries lainières de Colbert à la révolution*, p. 457; François Crouzet, *De la supériorité de l'Angleterre*, Paris, 1985, chs. 2 and 3.

35. Louise Dechêne, *Habitants et marchands de Montréal au XVIIIe siècle*, Montreal, 1974, p. 363.

36. *Almanach royal*, Paris, 1753, pp. 436–37.

37. Paul Butel, *La croissance commerciale bordelaise dans la seconde moitié du XVIIIe siècle*, Paris Doctoral Thesis, Lille III, 1973, pp. 484 ff. and 501–05.

38. Yves Durand, *Les fermiers généraux au XVIIIe siècle*, Paris, 1970; J. F. Bosher, *French Finances, 1770–1795: From Business to Bureaucracy*, Cambridge, England, 1970, pt. I.

39. Jean-Pierre Poussou, *Bordeaux et le sud-ouest au XVIIIe siècle: Croissance économique et attraction urbaine*, Paris, 1983, pp. 64–65, 412; Poussou, "Les mouvements migratoires en France et à partir de la France . . . ," *Annales de démographie historique* (1970), p. 72 ff.; Garden, *Lyon*, pp. 31–39, 79; Jean-Pierre Gutton, *La société et les pauvres: L'exemple de la généralité de Lyon, 1534–1789*, Paris, 1970; Goubert, *100,000 Provin-*

ciaux, pp. 89–92, 109–16; Perrot, *Caen*, pp. 152, 156–66; Le Goff, *Vannes*, pp. 54–55.

40. William Doyle, *Origins of the French Revolution*, Oxford, 1980, p. 210.

TWO
The Social Hierarchy

1. Sarah C. Maza, *Servants and Masters in Eighteenth-Century France*, Princeton, 1983, pp. 46, 58, 190.

2. Forster, *House of Saulx-Tavanes;* François Bluche, *Les magistrats du Parlement de Paris au XVIIIe siècle*, Paris, 1960, p. 189.

3. Durand, *Les fermiers généraux*, pp. 131, 159.

4. Romuald Szramkiewicz, *Les régents et censeurs de la Banque de France nommés sous le consulat et l'empire*, Geneva, 1974, p. 148; Forster, *Merchants, Landlords, Magistrates;* on the bourgeoisie, see Joseph di Corcia, "Bourg, Bourgeoisie, Bourgeoisie de Paris from the Eleventh to the Eighteenth Century," *Journal of Modern History*, vol. 50 (1978), pp. 207–33.

5. J. F. Bosher, *The Canada Merchants 1713–1763*, Oxford, 1987; for Hugues, see Szramkiewicz, *Les régents*, p. 177; on the *pacte de famine* legend in the popular mind, see Steven L. Kaplan, The Famine Plot Persuasion in Eighteenth-Century France, *Transactions of the American Philosophical Society*, vol. 72 (1982).

6. Peter Gay, *The Enlightenment: An Interpretation*, vol. II, *The Science of Freedom*, New York, 1969, pp. 518–25; Jacques Proust, *Diderot et l'Encyclopédie*, Paris, 1967, p. 477; on Rousseau, Harry C. Payne, *The Philosophes and the People*, New Haven, 1976, p. 181.

7. George V. Taylor, "Revolutionary and Non-revolutionary Content in the Cahiers of 1789," *French Historical Studies*, vol. VII (1972), p. 501.

8. Albert Soboul, *Les sans-culottes parisiens de l'an II*, Paris, 1958, p. 412.

9. Keith Michael Baker, *Condorcet: From Natural Philosophy to Social Mathematics*, Chicago, 1975, p. 335.

10. Gouverneur Morris, *A Diary of the French Revolution*, London, 1939, vol. II, p. 483.

11. Hufton, *The Poor;* George Rude, *The Crowd in the French Revolution*, Oxford, 1959; Rude, *The Crowd in History, 1730–1848*, New York, 1964; Rude, *Paris and London in the Eighteenth Century*, London, 1969, pts. I and II; Jacques Godechot, *La prise de la Bastille*, Paris, 1965; Richard Cobb, *A Second Identity*, London, 1969, ch. 8; Louis Chevalier, *Classes laborieuses et classes dangereuses à Paris pendant la première moîtié du XIXe*

siècle, (1958), Paris, 1984, bk. II, pp. 283–430; Hervé Pommeret, *L'esprit publique dans le département des Côtes-du-Nord pendant la révolution, 1789–99,* Saint Brieuc, France, 1921, "Conclusion."

12. Cited in Hufton, *The Poor,* pp. 19–20.

13. A great deal has been written in this difficult field, much of it technical, abstract, and questionable. For the economics of French grain prices in general, see Meuvret, *Études d'histoire économique,* pp. 85–124; for the links between prices and the behavior of the populace, see George Rude, "Prices, Wages and Popular Movements in Paris During the French Revolution," *Economic History Review,* vol. VI (1954), pp. 246–67, reprinted in Rude, *Paris and London,* pp. 163–97; for Turgot's part see the biographies by Douglas Dakin (*Turgot and the Ancien Régime in France,* London, 1939) and Edgar Faure (*La disgrâce de Turgot,* Paris, 1961) and George Rude, "La taxation populaire de mai 1775 à Paris et dans la région parisienne," *Annales historiques de la révolution française,* 1956, pp. 1–43.

14. David Hunt, "The People and Pierre Dolivier: Popular Uprisings in the Seine-et-Oise Department (1791–1792)," *French Historical Studies,* vol. XI (1978), pp. 184–214.

15. Georges Lefebvre, *La grande peur de 1789,* Paris, 1932, p. 27; for the grain and flour trades, their management and regulation, see Kaplan, "The Famine Plot Persuasion in Eighteenth-Century France"; Steven L. Kaplan, *Bread, Politics and Political Economy in the Reign of Louis XV,* The Hague, 2 vols., 1976; and Kaplan, *Provisioning Paris: Merchants and Millers in the Grain and Flour Trade During the Eighteenth Century,* Ithaca, 1984.

16. Colin Lucas, "The Midi in the French Revolution," *Transactions of the Royal Historical Society* (1978), p. 7; on the populace's concern with food and prices in the Revolution, see Rude, *The Crowd in the French Revolution,* Richard Cobb, *The Police and the People: French Popular Protest, 1789–1820,* Oxford, 1970, pt. III, "Dearth, Famine and the Common People," and Soboul, *Les sans-culottes,* pp. 116–38, and Richard Cobb, *Terreur et subsistances, 1793–1795,* Paris, 1964, 396 pp.; on the clash of townsfolk and peasants, Richard Cobb, *Les armées révolutionnaires, instrument de la terreur dans les départements, avril 1793–floréal an II,* The Hague, 1963, vol. II, ch. 1.

17. Cited in Rude, *Paris and London,* pp. 50–51.

18. Hufton, *The Poor,* chs. III and IV. See also Daniel Roche, *Le peuple de Paris: Essai sur la culture populaire au XVIIIe siècle,* Paris, 1981; Soboul, *Les sans-culottes;* Rude, *The Crowd in the French Revolution;* and Cobb, *The Police and the People.*

19. E.g., by François Lebrun, *Les hommes et la mort en Anjou aux 17e*

et 18e siècles, The Hague, 1971, pp. 163–66; March Bloch, *Les caractères originaux de l'histoire rural française* (1931), Paris, 1952, 2 vols.

20. Alan Forrest, *The French Revolution and the Poor,* New York, 1981; Jeffry Kaplow, *The Names of Kings: The Parisian Laboring Poor in the Eighteenth Century,* New York, 1972; Jean-Pierre Gutton, *L'etat et la mendicité dans la première moîtié du XVIIIe siècle,* Lyons, 1973; Richard Cobb, *Reactions to the French Revolution,* London, 1972, ch. 5, "La bande d'Orgères, 1790–1799."

21. Lefebvre, *La grande peur,* p. 24; Lebrun, *Les hommes et la mort,* p. 291; Alain Molinier and Nicole Molinier-Meyer, "Environment et histoire: Les loups et l'homme en France," *La revue d'histoire moderne et contemporaine,* vol. XXVIII (1981), pp. 225–45.

22. Raymonde Monnier, *Le faubourg Saint-Antoine (1789–1815),* Paris, 1981, pp. 27–34; Cobb, *The Police and the People,* p. 227; Rude, *The Crowd in the French Revolution,* p. 58.

23. Rude, *The Crowd in History,* p. 6, and on the role of panic and rumor, p. 221 ff.; Roche, *Le peuple de Paris,* ch. 1.

24. E. N. Williams, ed., *The Eighteenth-Century Constitution 1688–1815: Documents and Commentary,* Cambridge, England, 1960, p. 414.

25. Arlette Farge, *Vivre dans la rue à Paris au XVIIIe siècle,* Paris, 1979, pp. 123–62; Roche, *Le peuple de Paris,* pp. 265–66; Hufton, *The Poor,* pp. 360–62; Lebrun, *Les hommes et la mort,* p. 419.

26. Pierre Rétat, ed., *L'attentat de Damiens: Discours sur l'évènement au XVIIIe siècle,* Lyons, 1979, pp. 256, 352–60.

27. David Bien, *The Calas Affair,* Princeton, 1960; Edna Nixon, *The Calas Case,* London, 1965.

28. Lebrun, *Les hommes et la mort,* p. 424; John McManners, *Death and the Enlightenment,* Oxford, 1985, ch. 11, "Death as an Instrument: The Public Execution"; and my own extensive reading of parish registers at Bordeaux, La Rochelle, and other towns in the southwest.

29. This aspect of the Enlightenment is one of the principal themes in many studies, for instance, Robert Mauzi, *L'idée du bonheur au XVIIIe siècle,* Paris, 1969; Proust, *Diderot et l'Encyclopédie;* Gustave Lanson, *Voltaire,* Paris, 1960; Peter Gay, *Voltaire's Politics: The Poet as Realist,* New York, 1959; and Alfred Cobban, *In Search of Humanity: The Role of the Enlightenment in Modern History,* London, 1960.

30. André Corvisier, *L'armée française de la fin du XVIIe siècle au ministère de Choiseul: Le soldat,* Paris, 1964, vol. I, p. 79; Roger Chartier, "Culture, lumières, doléances: Les cahiers de 1789," *La revue d'histoire moderne et contemporaine,* vol. XXVIII (1981), p. 93; and A. Farge and A. Zysberg, "Les théâtres de la violence à Paris au XVIIIe siècle," *Annales Économics, Sociétés, Civilisations,* 1970, pp. 984–1015; Farge, *Vivre dans la*

rue, pp. 123–62, "La violence de la rue."

31. Lucas, "The Midi in the French Revolution," pp. 22–25; Cobb, *The Police and the People,* pp. 85–92; see the excellent pages on popular violence in Nicole Castan, *Les criminels de Languedoc: Les exigences d'ordre et les voies du ressentiment dans une société pré-révolutionnaire (1750–1790),* Toulouse, 1980, "La violence," pp. 194–213.

32. Documents quoted in J. M. Roberts, ed., *French Revolutionary Documents,* Oxford, 1966, p. 149; Pierre Caron, *Les massacres de septembre,* Paris, 1935, p. 372.

33. Richard Cobb remarks on Rude's attitude in *The Police and the People,* pp. 85–92, "Popular Violence."

34. Soboul, *Les Sans-culottes,* pp. 576–80.

35. Caron, *Les massacres de septembre,* pp. 361, 469; this attitude of Caron and others is remarked on by Frédéric Bluche in *Septembre 1792, logiques d'un massacre,* Paris, 1986, pp. 18, 236.

36. Charles Tilly, *The Contentious French,* Cambridge, Mass., 1986, p. 404.

37. Hufton, *The Poor,* pp. 360–67.

38. "Le révolutionnaire est crédule," writes Richard Cobb *(Terreur et subsistances,* pp. 11–19).

39. Lebrun, *Les hommes et la mort,* p. 494; John McManners, *Death and the Enlightenment,* p. 125; on the primary schools, Harvey Chisick, "School Attendance, Literacy and Acculturation: Petites écoles and Popular Education in Eighteenth-Century France," *Europa* (Montreal), vol. 3 (1979–80), pp. 185–220.

40. Marc Bloch, *The Royal Touch: Sacred Monarchy and Scrofula in England and France* (1961), trans., London, 1973, p. 215; Lebrun, *Les hommes et la mort,* p. 396; and Timothy Tackett, *Priest and Parish in Eighteenth-Century France: A Social and Political Study of the Curés in a Diocèse of Dauphiné, 1750–91,* Princeton, 1977, p. 210.

41. Lebrun, *Les hommes et la mort,* p. 415.

42. Bois, *Les paysans de l'ouest,* p. 306.

43. Geneviève Bollême, "La littérature populaire," *Livre et société,* ed. François Furet, vol. I, p. 66.

44. Geneviève Bollême, *Les almanachs populaires aux XVIIe et XVIIIe siècles,* Paris, 1969; Robert Mandrou, *De la culture populaire aux 17e et 18e siècles: La bibliothèque bleue de Troyes,* Paris, 1964.

45. Georges Lefebvre, "Foules révolutionnaires," *Études sur la révolution française,* Paris, 1954, pp. 271–87; Lefebvre, *La Grande peur;* Rude, *Paris and London,* "The Pre-industrial Crowd," pp. 17–34.

46. Views of the populace in books by these influential writers are briefly discussed by Rude in *The Crowd in the French Revolution,* pp. 1–4.

47. Soboul, *Les sans-culottes,* p. 1031; Cobb, *Les armées révolution-naires,* p. 598; Lefebvre, *Les paysans du nord,* p. 883. On regional languages and dialects, R. R. Palmer, *The Improvement of Humanity: Education and the French Revolution,* Princeton, 1985, pp. 11, 183 ff.

48. Talleyrand, *Mémoires,* Paris, 1891, vol. I, p. 168. On the public in general see J. R. Censer and J. D. Popkin, *Press and Politics in Pre-Revolutionary France,* Berkeley, 1987.

49. Pierre Grosclaudes, *Malesherbes, témoin et interprète de son temps,* Paris, 1961, chs. III–VIII.

50. Among the largest pamphlet collections are those at the Newberry Library in Chicago, the Van Pelt Library at the University of Pennsylvania (the Maclure Collection), the British Library in London (the Croker Tracts), the John Rylands Library in Manchester, and, of course, the Bibliothèque nationale in Paris.

51. Doyle, *Origins of the French Revolution,* p. 213.

52. Harold T. Parker, *The Cult of Antiquity and the French Revolution: A Study in the Development of the Revolutionary Spirit* (1937), New York, 1965; R. R. Palmer, *The School of the French Revolution (Louis-le-Grand), 1762–1814,* Princeton, 1975, pp. 27–28; C. R. Bailey, "Municipal *Collèges:* Small-Town Secondary Schools in France Prior to the Revolution," *French Historical Studies,* vol. XII (1982), p. 372.

53. Daniel Roche, *Le siècle des lumières en province: Académies et académiciens provinciaux, 1680–1789,* The Hague, 2 vols.

54. Proust, *Diderot et l'Encyclopédie;* Robert Mauzi, *L'idée du bonheur;* Arthur M. Wilson, *Diderot,* New York, 1972; Jean-Claude Perrot, "Les dictionnaires de commerce du XVIIIe siècle," *Revue d'histoire moderne et contemporaine,* vol. XXVIII (1981), pp. 36–67.

55. Jean Petot, *Histoire de l'administration des ponts et chaussées, 1599–1815,* Paris, 1958, pp. 140, 186.

56. *Annales historiques de la révolution française,* vol. 41 (1969), p. 500; Alain Le Bihan, *Francs-Maçons et ateliers parisiens de la grande loge de France au XVIIIe siècle,* Paris, 1973.

57. Among the many studies of the Physiocrats, most of which exaggerate their importance, the best is still Georges Weulersse, *Le mouvement physiocratique en France de 1756 à 1770,* Paris, 1910, 2 vols.; their many writings are listed in Institut national d'études démographiques, *Économie et population: Les doctrines françaises avant 1800: Bibliographie générale commentée,* Paris, 1956, 689 pp.

58. André Bourde, *Agronomie et agronomes en France au XVIIIe siècle,* Paris, 1967, 3 vols., p. 1505; Roche, *Le siècle des lumières,* vol. I, pp. 61–62.

59. Robert Darnton, *Mesmerism and the End of the Enlightenment in*

France, Cambridge, Mass., 1968, p. 40.

60. Bluche, *Les magistrats du Parlement de Paris, XVIIIe*, p. 334.

61. Franklin Ford, *Strasbourg in Transition*, p. 210.

62. *Dictionary of Canadian Biography*, Toronto, vol. IV (1979), p. 565.

63. Archives départementales de la Charente maritime (La Rochelle), B 4055, François Couteau to Jean Brunet de Béranger, 17 December 1763.

64. Young, *Travels in France*, pp. 117, 174.

65. Lucas, "The Midi in the French Revolution," pp. 6–7.

66. Augustin Cochin, *Les sociétés de pensée et la révolution en Bretagne, 1788–89*, Paris, 1925, vol. I, p. 44.

67. Jacqueline Chaumié, *Le réseau d'Antraigues et la contre-révolution, 1791–93*, Paris, 1965, pp. 26–33.

68. Jean Egret, *La révolution des notables: Mounier et les monarchiens*, Paris, 1950.

69. Chartier, "Culture, lumières, doléances," p. 93, and George V. Taylor, in *Annales, Economies, Sociétés, Civilisations*, 1973, pp. 1495–1514; Palmer, *Improvement of Humanity*, p. 86.

70. Jean Egret, *Le Parlement de Dauphiné*, vol. II, p. 229.

71. Braudel and Labrousse, *Histoire économique et sociale*, vol. II, pp. 170–71; Petot, *Histoire de l'administration des ponts et chaussées*, pp. 322–27; Perrot, *Caen*, vol. I, p. 461; Guy Arbellot, "Arthur Young et la circulation en France," *Revue d'histoire moderne et contemporaire*, vol. XXVIII (1981), pp. 328–34; Jones, *Politics and Rural Society*, pp. 25–33.

72. Montesquieu, *De l'esprit des lois*, bk. XX, ch. 1.

73. The royal treasurer, Jacques Imbert, settled near Auxerre, the naval controller, Bréard, near Aulnay on the borders of Saintonge and Poitou, the royal storekeeper, Estèbe, at Pompignac near Bordeaux, and the royal purveyor general, Cadet, on various estates in the west. (See the *Dictionary of Canadian Biography*, Toronto, vols. III and IV.)

74. Crouzet, *De la supériorité de l'Angleterre sur la France*, ch. 5; Daniel Mornet, *Les origines intellectuelles de la révolution française*, Paris, 1937, ch. VIII; Mauzi, *L'idée de bonheur*, pp. 18, 235–36.

75. Voltaire, *Dialogues chrétiens ou préservatif contre l'Encyclopédie* (Pléiade edition, "Mélanges," p. 359); on anglomania in general, J. Grieder, *Anglomania in France, 1740–1789*, Geneva, 1985.

76. Grosclaude, *Malesherbes*, pp. 184–85, 287, 478–79, 674–76; Michael Kennedy, *The Jacobin Club of Marseilles 1790–1794*, Ithaca, 1973, p. 182; L. S. Mercier, *L'an 2440*, 1770, p. 445; Mauzi, *L'idée de bonheur*, p. 370, note; Gabriel Bonno, *La constitution britannique devant l'opinion française* (1931), New York, 1971, pp. 147, 152, 192; André Rémond,

John Holker, manufacturier et grand fonctionnaire en France au XVIIIe siècle, 1719–1786, Paris, 1946; Bourde, *Agronomie et agronomes,* pp. 277–310, 1522–23; Harold T. Parker, *The Bureau of Commerce in 1781 and Its Policies with Respect to French Industry,* Durham, N.C., 1979, pp. 109–13, 134–35.

77. Mona Ozouf, *La fête révolutionnaire, 1789–1799,* Paris, 1976, p. 263, note 1; *Encyclopédie méthodique, ou par ordre de matière; par une société de gens de lettres, de savans et d'artistes: Finance,* Paris, vol. I (1784), p. 145; Jones, *Politics and Rural Society,* p. 214; Kennedy, *Jacobin Club of Marseilles,* p. 182.

78. Dale van Kley, *The Jansenists and the Expulsion of the Jesuits from France, 1757–1765,* New Haven, 1975, 270 pp.; Jean Egret, "Le procès des Jesuites devant les parlements de France (1761–1770)," *Revue historique,* vol. CCIV (1950), pp. 1–27; D. G. Thompson, "The Confiscation of Jesuit Property in the District of the Parlement of Paris, *English Historical Review,* 1981; Palmer, *Improvement of Humanity,* p. 15.

79. Charles-Marguerite-Jean-Baptiste Mercier-Dupaty, *Lettres sur la procédure criminelle de la France dans lesquelles on montre sa conformité avec celle de l'inquisition . . . ,* n.p., 1788.

80. Martyn Lyons, "M. G. A. Vadier (1736–1828): The Formation of the Jacobin Mentality," *French Historical Studies,* vol. X (1977), p. 78; Harvey Chisick, "Institutional Innovations in Popular Education in 18th-Century France," *French Historical Studies,* vol. X (1977), pp. 41–73; and on every aspect, Palmer, *Improvement of Humanity, passim.*

81. Charles Rihs, *Les philosophes utopistes,* Geneva, 1970; Roche, *Le siècle des lumières,* pp. 199, 265; Proust, *Diderot et l'Encyclopédie,* p. 22; John McManners, *Ecclesiastical Society Under the Ancien Régime,* Manchester, England, 1960, pp. 38–40.

82. Jacqués Jallet, *Pièces rélatives à la démarche de messieurs les curés qui ont passé dans la salle nationale le 12 juin 1789 et les jours suivants,* p. 13 (British Museum, F 143 [3]).

83. Ibid., p. 32; Jallet, *Idées élémentaires sur la constitution,* 1789 (British Museum, F 143 [3]).

84. Perronnet, "Les assemblées du clergé de France sous le règne de Louis XVI," *Annales historiques de la Révolution française,* vol. 34 (1962), pp. 8–35.

85. R. Zapperi, "Sieyès et l'abolition de la féodalité," *Annales historiques de la révolution française,* vol. 44 (1972), pp. 321–51.

86. Mauzi, *L'idée de la bonheur,* p. 267.

87. Charles-Louis de Secondat Montesquieu, "Mes pensées 1720–1755," in *Oeuvres complètes,* ed. Daniel Oster, Paris (Macmillan), 1964, p. 875.

88. Perronnet, "Les assemblées du clergé," p. 13.
89. Baker, *Condorcet*, p. 62.

THREE
The Monarchy of Louis XVI

1. J. M. Gaudillot, ed., *Le voyage de Louis XVI en Normandie, 21–29 juin 1786*, Caen, 1967, passim.

2. No one has yet satisfactorily answered a question raised long ago by Augustin Cochin. He wanted to discover in detail how "a Christian and loyalist population had passed in ten months from a régime that was almost feudal to a state bordering on direct democracy." (Cochin, *Les sociétés de pensée*, p. 3.)

3. Jean Jaurès, *Histoire socialiste*, Paris, 1901–04, 4 vols.; Albert Mathiez, *La révolution française*, Paris, 1922–24, 3 vols., and many other books, notably *La vie chère et le mouvement social sous la Terreur*, Paris, 1927; Georges Lefebvre, *La révolution française*, Paris, 1951, and several other books, notably *Les Paysans du nord*; Soboul, *Les sans-culottes*, and several other books.

4. Lefebvre, *La révolution française*, p. 164.

5. Ralph E. Giesey, *The Juristic Basis of Dynastic Right to the French Throne*, Philadelphia, 1961.

6. E. Lavisse, "Étude sur le pouvoir royal au temps de Charles V," *Revue historique*, vol. XXVI (1884), p. 233, cited with respect in Michel Antoine, *Le conseil du roi sous le règne de Louis XV*, Geneva, 1970, p. 33.

7. Bloch, *The Royal Touch*, pp. 215, 224; Antoine, *Le conseil du roi*, p. 6; Lebrun, *Les hommes et la mort*, p. 398.

8. *Almanach royal, année M DCC LXXXIX, présenté à Sa Majesté pour la première fois en 1699*, ed. Laurent D'Houry, Paris, 1789.

9. Samuel F. Scott, *The Response of the Royal Army to the French Revolution: The Role and Development of the Line Army, 1789–93*, Oxford, 1978, pp. 5, 9, 67, 210.

10. *Almanach royal*, 1788, pp. 215–216; 1789, pp. 224–26 (but in my copy, pp. 223–24 appear between pp. 204 and 207); on the royal councils in general, the best study is Antoine, *Le conseil du roi*.

11. Maurice Bordes, *L'administration provinciale et municipale en France au XVIIIe siècle*, Paris, 1972, pp. 156, 159, contradicting a study by Ardascheff, an earlier authority on the subject; the intendants are listed in *Almanach royal*, 1789, pp. 259–67.

12. Pierrette Girault de Coursac, *L'education d'un roi: Louis XVI*, Paris,

1972, p. 169; Gaudillot, ed., *Le voyage de Louis XVI*, introduction by C. H. Pouthas.

13. Girault de Coursac, *L'education d'un roi*, pp. 145, 155.

14. J. Q. C. Mackrell, *The Attack on Feudalism in Eighteenth-Century France*, London, 1973, pp. 13–14.

15. Jean-Joseph Mounier, *Recherches sur les causes qui ont empeché les français de devenir libre*, Geneva, 1792, vol. I, p. 25.

16. A detailed study leading to this same conclusion is V. R. Gruder, "A Mutation in Elite Political Culture: The French Notables and the Defense of Property and Participation, 1787," *Journal of Modern History*, vol. 56 (1984), pp. 598–634.

17. Jean Egret, *The French Pre-Revolution*, trans., Chicago, 1978, p. xiv.

18. Mercer-Dupaty, *Lettres sur la procédure criminelle*, p. 91.

19. Egret, *French Pre-Revolution*, pp. 77–85.

20. Ibid., p. 73–74.

21. Marcel Marion, *Le Garde des Sceaux: Lamoignon, et la réforme judiciaire de 1788*, Paris, 1905, pp. 37–38.

22. Henri Carré, *La fin des parlements (1788–90)*, Paris, 1912, pp. 34–35.

23. J. F. Bosher, *The Single Duty Project: A Study of the Movement for a Customs Union in 18th-Century France*, London, 1964.

24. Jean-Paul Berthaud, *La révolution armée: Les soldats-citoyens et la révolution française*, n.d., p. 35; Georges Lefebvre, *Études orléanaises*, vol. II, p. 18.

25. Mornet, *Les origines intellectuelles de la révolution française*, p. 473.

26. Bosher, *French Finances*, pt. I.

27. Ibid., p. 256.

28. J. F. Bosher, *"Chambres de justice* in the French Monarchy," in *French Government and Society, 1500–1850*, ed. J. F. Bosher, London, 1973, ch. 2.

29. The basic work is C. E. Labrousse, *La crise de l'économie française à la fin de l'ancien régime et au début de la révolution*, 1944; more recent research is summarized in Braudel and Labrousse, *Histoire économique et sociale*, vol. II, 1660–1789, pt. III, and in *Conjoncture économique, structures sociales, hommage à Ernest Labrousse;* for the crisis of 1770, see J. F. Bosher, "The French Crisis of 1770," *History* (London), vol. LVII (1972), pp. 17–30; the work summarized therein has been questioned but by no means undermined, much less disqualified, by Morineau, *Les faux-semblants d'un démarrage économique*.

30. David L. Longfellow, "Silk Weavers and the Social Struggle in

Lyon During the French Revolution, 1789–94," *French Historical Studies,* vol. XII (1981), p. 11.

31. Braudel and Labrousse, *Histoire économique et sociale,* vol. II, p. 230.

32. Claude Fohlen, "The Commercial Failure of France in America," *Two Hundred Years of Franco-American Relations* (Papers of the Bicentennial Colloquium of the Society for French Historical Studies), Newport, R.I., 1978, pp. 93–120.

33. O. T. Murphy, *Charles Gravier, Comte de Vergennes: French Diplomacy in the Age of Revolution, 1719–1787,* Albany, N.Y., 1982, pp. 203, 474; Alfred Cobban, *Ambassadors and Secret Agents: The Diplomacy of the First Earl of Malmesbury at The Hague,* London, 1954.

34. D. L. Wick, "The Court Nobility and the French Revolution: The Example of the Society of Thirty," *Eighteenth-Century Studies,* vol. 13 (1980), p. 279.

35. Quoted in Albert Sorel, *Europe and the French Revolution: The Political Traditions of the Old Regime* (1885), trans., London, 1969, p. 36.

36. Ibid., p. 332; André Fugier, *La révolution française et l'empire napoléonien,* Paris, 1954, p. 8.

37. Jean Meyer, *La noblesse bretonne,* p. 1246.

38. Chaumié, *Le réseau d'Antraigues,* pp. 31–33.

39. Nora Temple, "Municipal Elections and Municipal Oligarchies in Eighteenth-Century France," *Government and Society in France, 1500–1850: Essays in Memory of Alfred Cobban,* ed. J. F. Bosher, London, 1973, pp. 87, 91.

40. L. A. Hunt, *Revolution and Urban Politics in Provincial France: Troyes and Reims, 1786–1790,* Stanford, 1978, p. 4; Philippe Sagnac, *La législation civile de la révolution française, 1789–1804: Essai d'histoire sociale,* Paris, 1898, pp. 7–10; William Doyle, *The Parlement of Bordeaux and the End of the Old Regime, 1771–1790,* Paris, 1974, pp. 5, 274, 287.

41. T. J. A. Le Goff and D. M. G. Sutherland, "The Revolution and the Rural Community in Eighteenth-Century Brittany," *Past and Present,* no. 62 (1974), p. 107.

42. P. S. Fritz, *The English Ministers and Jacobitism Between the Rebellions of 1715 and 1745,* Toronto, 1975, pp. 138–139.

43. Van Kley, *The Jansenists and the Expulsion of the Jesuits.*

44. Girault de Coursac, *L'education d'un roi,* p. 191.

45. Mollien, *Mémoires d'un ministre du trésor public, 1780–1815,* 3 vols. Paris, 1898, vol. I, pp. 8, 13.

46. Grosclaude, *Malesherbes,* chs. III, XV.

47. Wick, "Court Nobility and the French Revolution," pp. 263–

84; J. Egret, *The French Pre-Revolution*, p. 45; R. R. Palmer, *The Age of the Democratic Revolutions*, vol. I, pp. 185–372, 469–502; John McManners, "France," in *The European Nobility in the Eighteenth Century*, ed. A. Goodwin, London, 1953, p. 28.

48. Carré, *La fin des parlements*, pp. 68–69.

FOUR
Divine-Right Monarchy Undermined, *1774–88*

1. Lamoignon de Malesherbes (1721–94), a magistrate in the Cour des aides, was the son of Lamoignon de Blancmesnil (1683–1772), who was chancellor from 1750 to 1768 (Grosclaude, *Malesherbes*).

2. Jean Egret, *Louis XV et l'opposition parlementaire, 1715–1774*, Paris, 1970, pp. 219–26. Egret's many books and articles all have been drawn on for this chapter, though not all are cited in these notes.

3. *Lettres de Marie-Antoinette*, Paris, 1895, vol. II, p. 43, Marie-Antoinette to Joseph II, 22 September 1784.

4. Girault de Coursac, *L'education d'un roi*, p. 291 and ch. XI.

5. Louis XVI's ministers are difficult to judge because they have all too often been seen through the eyes of historians inclined to adopt the eighteenth-century views of one "party" or another. Thus, Turgot has usually been adored as an intellectual archliberal believer in free trade, Necker belittled as a shallow, pompous opportunist, Calonne admired as an intelligent and capable young statesman; but these are superficial impressions of men worthy of more careful assessments. The most informed studies of Turgot are Edgar Faure, *La disgrâce de Turgot*, and Douglas Dakin, *Turgot and the Ancien Régime in France*.

6. The fullest study of Necker's first ministry (1776–81) is Robert D. Harris, *Necker: Reform Statesman of the Ancien Régime*, Berkeley, 1979, but see also Bosher, *French Finances*, ch. 8; on Necker in general, see Jean Egret, *Necker, ministre de Louis XVI*, Paris 1975, p. 478, and the excellent study by Henri Grange, *Les idées de Necker*, Paris, 1974, 669 pp.

7. Murphy, *Vergennes*, p. 252; Marcel Trudel, *Louis XVI, le congrès américain et le Canada, 1774–1789*, Quebec, 1949, ch. 14; Gustave Lanctot, *Canada and the American Revolution, 1774–1783*, London, 1967, chs. 13 and 14.

8. There is no full study of Calonne, but for summaries of his policies see pp. 99–103; Egret, *French Pre-Revolution*, ch. 1; and Bosher, *French Finances*, ch. 9.

9. Quoted in Egret, *Necker*, p. 177.

10. Murphy, *Vergennes*, pp. 220, 232–33, 235, 240, 244, 257, 399, 456.

11. Jacques Necker, *De l'administration des finances de la France*, Paris, 1784, vol. II, ch. 11; Frédéric Braesch, *Finances et monnaie révolutionnaires (recherches, études et documents), deuxième fascicule*, Paris, 1936, "Le dernier budget de l'ancien régime," p. 202.

12. Durand, *Les fermiers généraux*, p. 84; Bosher, *French Finances*, ch. 9.

13. Herbert Lüthy, *La banque protestante en France de la révocation de l'édit de Nantes à la révolution française*, vol. II, Paris, 1961, pp. 658, 696–98.

14. Pierre Chevallier, ed., *Journal de l'assemblée des notables de 1787*, Paris, 1960, pp. XXIV, XXX, 61; Ernest Lavisse, ed., *Histoire de la France*, Paris, 1911, vol. IX, (1), pp. 324–25; Egret, *French Pre-Revolution*, pp. 4–5.

15. Vivian R. Gruder, "Paths to Political Consciousness: The Assembly of Notables of 1787 and the "Pre-Revolution" in France," *French Historical Studies*, vol. XIII (1984), pp. 323–56.

16. His wife, governess to the royal children, was forced to resign in October 1782 as a result of the scandal (Louis Petit de Bachaumont, *Mémoires secrets pour servir à l'histoire de la république des lettres en France*, vol. 21, London, 1783, pp. 155, 161, 166, 173, 184–86, 192; Lüthy, *La banque protestante*, vol. II, p. 689).

17. Chevallier, *Journal de l'assemblée des notables*, p. 75.

18. Braesch, *Finances et monnaie révolutionnaires*, fasc. II, pp. 61, 147; Egret, *French Pre-Revolution*, p. 54.

19. Chevallier, ed., *Journal de l'assemblée des notables*, pp. 41, 137, Lafayette to Louis XVI, 25 May 1787.

20. *Dénonciation de l'agiotage au roi et à l'assemblée des notables*, 1787.

21. Egret, *French Pre-Revolution*, p. 52; Chevallier, ed., *Journal de l'assemblée des notables*, passim.; Bosher, *French Finances*, ch. 10.

22. David D. Bien, "The Army in the French Enlightenment: Reform, Reaction and Revolution," *Past and Present*, no. 85 (November 1979), p. 93.

23. Egret, *French Pre-Revolution*, p. 33.

24. Egret, "La Dernière Assemblée du clergé de France (5 mai–5 aout, 1788)," *La revue historique* (1958), pp. 1–15.

25. For an explanation of treasury reform, see p. 260 (Chapter 11, part III).

26. *Almanach royal*, 1789, p. 563 ff.

27. J. L. Soulavie, *Mémoires historiques et politiques du règne de Louis XVI*, Paris, 1801, p. 245.

FIVE
The End of Divine-Right Monarchy

1. Bien, "The Army in the French Enlightenment," pp. 68–98.
2. Chaumié, *Le réseau d'Antraigues*, pp. 31–32.
3. Rude, *Paris and London*, p. 72.
4. Doyle, *The Parlement of Bordeaux*, pp. 277–81.
5. Egret, *French Pre-Revolution*, p. 179.
6. Dawson, *Provincial Magistrates and Revolutionary Politics*, pp. 71–75 and 174–75.
7. Quoted in Egret, *French Pre-Revolution*, p. 180.
8. Jean Egret, "La Fayette dans la première assemblée des notables (février–mai 1787)," *Annales historiques de la révolution française* (1952), p. 26.
9. Frédéric Braesch, *1789, L'année cruciale*, Paris, 1941, p. 42.
10. According to Jean Egret, for instance, "The revolutionary action of the Third Estate—as anyone will readily agree—was the work of a minority of new men who . . . intimidated, neutralized and swept away the hesitation and resistance of the traditional representatives of the Third Estate, too much involved in the system to fight it energetically." ("Les Origines de la Révolution en Bretagne (1788–9)," *La revue historique* [1955], p. 213.)
11. G. A. Kelly, "The Machine of the Duc d'Orléans and the New Politics," *Journal of Modern History*, vol. 51 (1979), p. 670.
12. Elizabeth Eisenstein, "Who Intervened in 1788?" (1965), in *The Social Origins of the French Revolution*, ed. Ralph Greenlaw, Lexington, Mass., 1975, p. 200.
13. Wick, "The Court Nobility and the French Revolution, pp. 264–65.
14. Forster, *Merchants, Landlords, Magistrates*, pp. 180–84.
15. Darnton, *Mesmerism*, pp. 72, 78; other public men active in the mesmerist group were Lafayette, d'Epremesnil, Nicolas Bergasse (a lawyer), Étienne Clavière (a Swiss banker), J. L. Carra (a journalist), Marquis Gouy d'Arsy, and Savalette de Langes (a financier in the royal treasury).
16. J. Egret, "La seconde assemblée des notables (6 novembre–12 décembre 1788)," *Annales historique de la révolution française* (1949), pp. 202–03.
17. William Doyle agrees with this conclusion in *Origins of the French Révolution*, p. 146.
18. Clear explanations of these and other practical matters may be

found in J. M. Thompson, *The French Revolution*, Oxford, 1943, reprinted several times.

19. Ruth F. Necheles, "The Curés in the Estates General of 1789," *Journal of Modern History*, vol. 46 (1974), p. 427.

20. James Murphy and Patrice Higonnet, "Les députés de la noblesse aux états généraux de 1789," *Revue d'histoire moderne et contemporaine*, vol. XX (1973), pp. 230–43.

21. E. H. Lemay, "La composition de l'assemblée constituante: Les hommes de la continuité?," *Revue d'histoire moderne et contemporaine*, vol. XXIV (1977), pp. 341–63; Alfred Cobban, *Aspects of the French Revolution*, London, 1968, pp. 109–11.

22. Bosher, "The French Crisis of 1770," pp. 17–30.

23. "Avis du Parlement de Dauphiné . . . au roi, 26 avril 1769," *Ephémérides du citoyen*, vol. I, 1769, p. 156, quoted in Kaplan, "The Famine Plot Persuasion in Eighteenth Century France."

24. Lefebvre, *Études orléanaises*, vol. I, p. 19 ff.

25. Longfellow, "Silk Weavers and the Social Struggle," p. 13.

26. Rude, *Paris and London*, pp. 75–76; Lefebvre, *La grande peur*, p. 51.

27. R. B. Rose, *The Making of the Sans-culottes: Democratic Ideas and Institutions in Paris, 1789–92*, Manchester, England, 1983, ch. 1 and 2; Melvin Edelstein," "Vers une sociologie électorale de la Révolution française," *Revue d'histoire moderne et contemporaine*, vol. XXII (1975), p. 529.

28. Egret, *Necker*, pp. 231–32.

29. Grange, *Les idées de Necker*, pp. 402–04.

30. Quoted in Gérard Walter, *Robespierre*, Paris, 1961, vol. I, p. 67.

31. Louis Gottschalk, *Jean-Paul Marat*, Paris, p. 37; Grosclaude, *Malesherbes*, pp. 659–63.

32. Grange, *Les Idées de Necker*, pp. 404–05.

33. Jean-Jacques Mounier, *Nouvelles observations sur les états-généraux de France*, Paris, 1789, p. 254.

34. Jallet, *Idées élémentaires sur la constitution;* M. G. Hutt, "The Role of the Clergy in the Estates General of 1789" and "The Curés and the Third Estate: The Ideas of Reform in the Pamphlets of the French Lower Clergy in the Period 1787–1789," *Journal of Ecclesiastical History*, vol. VI (1955), pp. 190–220, and vol. VIII (1957), pp. 74–92.

SIX
A Liberal Interlude, *1789–91*

1. The Constitution of 3 September 1791, in L. Duguit, H. Monnier, and R. Bonnard, *Les constitutions et les principales lois politiques de la France depuis 1789*, 7th ed., Paris, 1952, pp. 1–33.

2. *Procès-verbal de l'assemblée nationale imprimé par son ordre*, vol. XX, under date.

3. Edmund Burke, *Reflections on the French Revolution* (1790), London, 1910, pp. 49, 57.

4. The Declaration of the Rights of Man and of the Citizen, perhaps the principal statement of many made in those months, has often been reprinted. It appears in English translation in, e.g., R. W. Postgate, *Revolution from 1789 to 1906: Documents,* New York, 1962, p. 30, and in Georges Lefebvre, *The Coming of the French Revolution,* trans. R. R. Palmer, New York, p. 189. For the original French, see L. Duguit et al., *Les constitutions,* pp. 1–33; see also Gilbert Chinard, "La Déclaration des Droits de l'Homme et la Déclaration d'Indépendance d'aprés un document peu connu," *Cahiers d'histoire de la révolution française,* no. 1 (1946), pp. 66–90.

5. Pierre Duclos, *La notion de constitution dans l'oeuvre de l'assemblée constituante de 1789,* Paris, 1932, p. 94.

6. For an explanation of these administrative reforms, see Chapter 11.

7. Jacques Godechot, *Les institutions de la France sous la révolution et l'empire,* Paris, 1951, p. 48.

8. Voltaire, *Oeuvres: Mélanges,* ed. Jacques Van den Heuvel, Paris, 1961, p. 1415; Bien, *The Calas Affaire;* Nixon, *The Calas Case.*

9. Arthur Herzberg, *The French Enlightenment and the Jews,* New York, 1968, p. 353; François Delpech, "L'histoire des Juifs en France de 1780 à 1840," *Annales historiques de la révolution française,* 48e année (1976), pp. 3–46; Ruth Necheles, "L'emancipation des Juifs, 1787–1795," *Annales historiques de la révolution française,* 48e année (1976), pp. 71–86.

10. C. L. R. James, *The Black Jacobins: Toussaint l'Ouverture and the San Domingo Revolution,* 2d ed., New York, 1963; W. E. F. Ward, *The Royal Navy and the Slavers,* London, 1969.

11. Burke, *Reflections,* p. 109.

12. Bosher, *French Finances,* pp. 240–41.

13. On 24 September 1791 the Assembly passed a decree expressly depriving all African slaves of their rights as citizens.

14. Eric Thompson, *Popular Sovereignty and the French Constituent Assembly, 1789–1791,* Manchester, England, 1952, p. 56.

15. Marcel Reinhard, *La chute de la royauté, 10 août 1792*, Paris, 1969, p. 196; Rose, *Making of the Sans-culottes*, pp. 32–33, 61, 90.

16. Beatrice F. Hyslop, *L'apanage de Philippe-Égalité, duc d'Orléans (1785–91)*, Paris, 1965, p. 50 and pt. III.

17. Forster, *House of Saulx-Tavanes*, ch. IV.

18. Lefebvre, *Les paysans du nord*, pp. 842, 883; Jones, *Political and Rural Society*, p. 215; Hilton L. Root, *Peasants and King in Burgundy*, Berkeley, 1987, passim.

19. Jones, *Politics and Rural Society*, pp. 186–213.

20. *Archives parlementaires*, vol. XVIII, p. 354.

21. John McManners, *The French Revolution and the Church*, New York, 1969, p. 46; Timothy Tackett, *Religion, Revolution and Regional Culture in Eighteenth-Century France: The Ecclesiastical Oath of 1791*, Princeton, 1986.

22. Anne Fremantle, ed., *The Papal Encyclicals in Their Historical Context*, New York, 1956, p. 117.

23. Rude, *The Crowd in the French Revolution*, p. 55.

24. Berthaud, *La révolution armée*, pp. 39–46; Lt. Col. Louis Hartmann, "Les officiers de l'armée royale à la veille de la révolution," *La revue historique*, vol. 100 (1909), p. 243; *Almanach royal*, 1789, pp. 157–69, and 1790, pp. 156–68.

25. Rude, *The Crowd in the French Revolution*, pp. 154–59, 172–74; Felix Markham, *Napoleon and the Awakening of Europe*, London, 1954, pp. 44–49.

26. George Rude, Albert Soboul, Richard Cobb, Kare Tonnesson, and others.

27. Louis Gottschalk and Margaret Maddox, *Lafayette in the French Revolution from the October Days Through the Federation*, Chicago, 1973, pp. 203–08.

28. Duclos, *La notion de constitution*, p. 151.

29. Roger Doucet, *L'esprit public dans le département de la Vienne pendant la révolution* (Mémoires de la Société des Antiquaires de l'Ouest, 3e série, 1908, tome III), Poitiers, 1909, p. 22.

30. Lefebvre, *La grande peur;* for popular insurrection in Paris in this period, Godechot, *La prise de la Bastille*, and Rude, *The Crowd in the French Revolution*, ch. 4.

31. Rude, *The Crowd in the French Revolution*, pp. 65–76.

32. Egret, *La révolution des notables*.

33. Gottschalk and Maddox, *Lafayette*, pp. 78, 90, 249, 446.

34. M. L. Kennedy, "The Foundation of the Jacobin Club and the Development of the Jacobin Club Network, 1789–1791," *Journal of Modern History*, vol. 51 (1979), pp. 701–33.

35. Keith Baker, "Politics and Social Science in Eighteenth-Century France: The *Société de 1789*," in *French Government and Society*, ed. Bosher, pp. 208–30.

36. Kelly, "The Machine of the Duc d'Orléans and the New Politics," pp. 668–70.

37. Eric Thompson, *Popular Sovereignty*, p. 119.

38. S. F. Scott, "Problems of Law and Order During 1790: The "Peaceful" Year of the French Revolution," *American Historical Review*, vol. 80 (1975), pp. 859–88; Gwynne Lewis, *The Second Vendée*, Oxford, 1978, ch. 1.

39. Hunt, *Revolution and Urban Politics*, p. 136.

40. Lefebvre, *Les paysans du nord*, p. 375.

41. Marc Bouloiseau et al., eds., *Oeuvres de Maximilien Robespierre*, vol. VI, *Discours 1789–90*, Paris, 1950, pp. 86, 203, 227, 237, 268, 611.

42. *L'ami du peuple*, vol. III, no. 263 (23 October 1790) p. 5, cited in Bouloiseau, et al, eds., *Oeuvres de Maximilien Robespierre*, vol. VI, p. 552.

43. F. Braesch, ed., *Le Père Duchesne d'Hébert*, Paris, 1938, vol. I, p. 282; Walter, *Robespierre*, vol. II, p. 360.

44. Pétion de Villeneuve, *Oeuvres*, 1793, 3 vols., vol. II, p. 261.

45. Gottschalk, *Jean-Paul Marat*, p. 49.

46. Braesch, ed., *Le Père Duchesne*, p. 374, dated 28 November 1790.

47. Chaumié, *Le réseau d'Antraigues*, p. 46.

48. Rude, *The Crowd in the French Revolution*, p. 82.

49. Kennedy, *The Jacobin Clubs in the French Revolution*, ch. XV; on the Feuillants, Georges Michon, *Essai sur l'histoire du parti feuillant: Adrien Duport*, Paris, 1924.

50. Rude, *The Crowd in the French Revolution*, pp. 89–91.

SEVEN
1792: War and the Monarchy's Fall

1. Gottschalk and Maddox, *Lafayette in the French Revolution*, ch. VI, "The Favras Plot"; T. C. W. Blanning, *The Origins of the French Revolutionary Wars*, London and New York, 1986.

2. Duguit et al., *Les constitutions*, p. 31; Roberts, *French Revolution Documents*, vol. 1, p. 430; J. M. Thompson, *Documents of the French Revolution*, Oxford, p. 166.

3. Georges Michon, *Robespierre et la guerre révolutionnaire*, Paris, 1937, p. 21.

4. Quoted in Claude Bowers, *Pierre Vergniaud, Voice of the French Revolution*, New York, 1950, p. 166.

5. Baker, *Condorcet,* p. 308.

6. J. Christopher Herold, ed., *The Mind of Napoleon,* New York, 1961, p. 206.

7. R. F. Necheles, *The Abbé Grégoire, 1787–1831,* Westport, Conn., 1971, p. 115.

8. On the Girondins, M. J. Sydenham, *The Girondins,* London, 1961, 252 pp.; Patrick, *Men of the First French Republic;* and Darnton, *Mesmerism.*

9. Alan Forrest, *Society and Politics in Revolutionary Bordeaux,* Oxford, 1975, p. 40; Sydenham, *The Girondins,* pp. 101–03.

10. Baker, *Condorcet,* p. 304.

11. On the war, André Fugier, *La révolution française,* chs. I and II; Jacques Godechot, *La grande nation: L'expansion révolutionnaire de la France dans le monde de 1789 à 1799,* 2d ed., Paris, 1983, ch. II–VIII; T. C. W. Blanning, *The Origins of the French Revolutionary Wars,* London, 1986.

12. Alfred Cobban, "British Secret Service in France, 1784–92," *Aspects of the French Revolution,* London, 1968, ch. 10; D. B. Horn, *Great Britain and Europe in the Eighteenth Century,* Oxford, 1967, pp. 68–85.

13. Jean Vidalenc, *Les émigrés français, 1789–1825,* Caen, 1963, p. 453 and passim; Donald Greer, *The Incidence of the Emigration During the French Revolution,* Cambridge, Mass., ch. IV and pp. 127–32.

14. Ernst Wangermann, *From Joseph II to the Jacobin Trials,* Oxford, 1959, p. 66.

15. Chaumié, *Le réseau d'Antraigues,* p. 34 passim.

16. Ibid., p. 38.

17. Reinhard, *La chute de la royauté,* p. 255; Godechot, *La contre-revolution 1789–1804,* ch. XII.

18. Loc. cit.

19. Godechot, *La grande nation,* p. 123; S. F. Scott, *Response of the Royal Army to the French Revolution.*

20. Godechot, *La grande nation,* p. 124.

21. Reinhard, *La chute de la royauté,* p. 277 ff.

22. Walter, *Robespierre,* 1961, vol. II, p. 259 (1 May 1792).

23. Roberts, *French Revolution Documents,* pp. 487–90.

24. Gottschalk and Maddox, *Lafayette in the French Revolution,* vol. II, p. 57; Rude, *The Crowd in the French Revolution,* p. 78.

25. Rude, *The Crowd in the French Revolution,* p. 89.

26. Morris, *A Diary of the French Revolution,* pp. 457–60.

27. Scott, *The Response of the Royal Army,* p. 152 ff.

28. "Though remaining liberal (in 1848), Europe repudiated socialism and disorder," writes Charles Pouthas ("The Revolutions of 1848," *New Cambridge Modern History,* vol. X [1960], p. 399).

29. Rude, *The Crowd in the French Revolution*, p. 89, for casualties on the Champ-de-Mars.

30. Chaumié, *Le réseau d'Antraigues*, passim.; and Reinhard, *La chute de la royauté*, pp. 283, 379 ff.

31. Kennedy, *The Jacobin Clubs in the French Revolution*, p. 260.

32. Ibid., p. 262.

33. Reinhard, *La chute de la royauté*, p. 232.

34. Ibid., pp. 15–112.

35. Ibid., p. 365.

36. This paragraph is based on Rose, *Making of the Sans-culottes*.

37. Rude, *The Crowd in the French Revolution*, pp. 95–98.

38. Rose, *Making of the Sans-culottes*, p. 150.

39. Morris, *A Diary of the French Revolution*, vol. II, p. 452.

40. The story of events in July and August 1792 is taken from F. Braesch, *La commune du dix Août 1792: Etude sur l'histoire de Paris du 20 juin au 2 décembre 1792*, Geneva, 1911; Albert Mathiez, *Le club des Cordeliers pendant la crise de Varennes et le massacre du Champ de Mars*, Paris, 1910; Rude, *The Crowd in the French Revolution*, ch. 7; J. Chaumié, *Le réseau d'Antraigues*, ch. II–VIII; Reinhard, *La chute de la royauté;* Morris Slavin, *The French Revolution in Miniature: Section Droits-de-l'Homme, 1789–1795*, Princeton, 1984. ch. IV; Norman Hampson, *Danton*, London, 1978, ch. II–V.

41. The fate of two-thirds of the Legislative Assembly after 10 August is still obscure. *"Le côté droit était atterré,"* Cambon told the Convention on 10 November. *"Il ne restait que 200 à 206 députés, ceux qui avaient conservé la confiance publique en votant contre Lafayette, qui puissent parler encore . . . le Corps législatif, je suis honteux de le dire, était accablé"* (Pierre Caron, *Les massacres de septembre*, pp. 229–30). Danton was elected minister of justice by 222 of the 284 deputies "who still thought it safe to attend the Assembly" (Hampson, *Danton*, p. 74).

42. All sources agree that a massacre occurred but disagree on the numbers; Kenneth Margerison, *P.-L. Roederer: Political Thought and Practice During the French Revolution*, Philadelphia, 1983, p. 92.

43. Paul D'Hollander, *Religion et révolution en Haute-Vienne, 1791–1802*, thèse de troisième cycle (Paris), 1984, p. 82; Caron, *Les massacres de septembre*, pp. 363–410.

44. Many scattered studies tell of these and other such events; for instance, Hunt, "The People and Pierre Dolivier," p. 211; R. M. Andrews, "L'assassinat de J. L. Gérard, négociant lorientais," *Annales historiques de la révolution française*, vol. 40 (1967), pp. 309–38.

45. Caron, *Les massacres de Septembre*, pp. 103–20, 435, 469; Bluche,

Septembre 1792, p. 22, citing documents in Archives Nationales F7 4426 and 4622.

46. Braesch, *La commune du dix Août 1792*, p. 543.

47. Rose, *Making of the Sans-culottes*, pp. 101–04; Maurice Genty, "Le mouvement démocratique dans les sections parisiennes," *Annales historiques de la révolution française*, 54e année (1982), p. 141; Slavin, *The French Revolution in Miniature*, p. 119; Braesch, *La commune du dix août*, p. 273 (the comment on the Cordeliers).

48. Braesch, *La commune du dix août*, pp. 272–5.

49. British Museum Library (Croker Tracts), F 829 (10), 64 pp.

50. Reinhard, *La chute de la royauté*, p. 607.

51. A study both scholarly and readable is by David P. Jordan, *The King's Trial: Louis XVI vs. the French Revolution*, Berkeley, 1979.

52. Pierre Caron, *La première terreur (1792)*, vol. I, *Les missions du conseil executif provisoire et la commune de Paris*, Paris, 1950, ch. II; Godechot, *Les institutions de la France*, p. 240.

53. Braesch, *La commune du dix août*, pp. 250, 377–79, 414.

54. Ibid., pp. 464 ff. and 756 ff.

55. Godechot, *La grande nation*, ch. III; Reinhard, *La chute de la royauté*; Fugier, *La révolution française et l'empire napoléonien*, pp. 68–84.

56. Braesch, *La commune du dix août*, p. 1119.

EIGHT
The First People's Republic, *1793–94*

1. Fugier, *La révolution française et l'empire napoléonien*, p. 20.

2. Sydenham, *The Girondins*, pp. 194–96.

3. Morris Slavin, *The Making of an Insurrection: Parisian Sections and the Gironde*, Cambridge, Mass., 1986, chs. V and VI.

4. For examples, Albert Mathiez, *Girondins et Montagnards*, Paris, 1930; Sydenham, *The Girondins*; Patrick, *Men of the First Republic*; C. Perroud, *Recherches sur la proscription des Girondins, 1793–1795*, Paris, 1917.

5. This view was most forcefully and fully presented by Albert Mathiez in many books and articles.

6. Norman Hampson, *Will and Circumstance: Montesquieu, Rousseau and the French Revolution*, London and Norman, Okla., 1983, p. 271.

7. Sydenham, *The Girondins*, appendix A; Alison Patrick put this figure down to 178 (*Men of the First Republic*, p. 16); Jacqueline Chaumié and Albert Soboul listed 137 (A. Soboul, ed., *Girondins et Montagnards (actes du colloque à la Sorbonne 14 december 1975)*, Paris, 1980, pp. 53–60.

8. Sydenham, *The Girondins*, p. 207.

9. Michel Pertué, "La liste (of 9 May 1793) des Girondins de Jean-Paul Marat," *Annales historiques de la révolution française*, 53ᵉ année (1981), pp. 379–89.

10. Patrick, *Men of the First Republic*, pp. 17–26.

11. Sydenham, *The Girondins*, p. 229; T. A. DiPadova, "The Girondins and the Question of Revolutionary Government," *French Historical Studies*, vol. IX (1976), pp. 432–50.

12. Gary Kates, *The Cercle Social, the Girondins, and the French Revolution*, Princeton, 1985.

13. C. J. Mitchell, "Political Divisions Within the Legislative Assembly of 1791," *French Historical Studies*, vol. XIII (1984), pp. 381–83.

14. Edith Bernardin, *Jean-Marie Roland et le ministère de l'intérieur (1792–1793)*, Paris, 1964, p. 615.

15. Kennedy, *The Jacobin Club of Marseilles*, p. 115.

16. Emile Campardon, *Le tribunal révolutionnaire de Paris*, Paris, 1866, vol. I, p. 69.

17. Donald Greer, *The Incidence of the Terror*, Cambridge, Mass., 1935, p. 97 ff.

18. Soboul, ed., *Girondins et Montagnards*, p. 346.

19. Patrick, *The Men of the First Republic*, pp. 256–60.

20. There seems no other explanation of the contrast between the moderate Girondin remnant of the Legislative Assembly in August 1792 and the large Jacobin support from that same group later.

21. Robert J. Caldwell, "André Amar and the Fall of the Mountain," *The Proceedings of the 1973 Consortium on Revolutionary Europe*, ed. Harold T. Parker, Gainesville, Fla., 1975, pp. 94–106.

22. Campardon, *Le tribunal révolutionnaire de Paris*, vol. I, p. 7.

23. Ibid., vol. II, p. 191.

24. Ibid., vol. I, pp. 57–81 (17 July 1793); Forrest, *Society and Politics in Revolutionary Bordeaux*, p. 241.

25. Lucas, *Structure of the Terror*, p. 272.

26. Le Comte Fleury, *Carrier à Nantes, 1793–1794*, Paris, 1897, 518 pp.

27. Cobb, *Les armées révolutionnaires*, vol. II, pp. 554–58; Cobb, *Reactions to the French Revolution*, pp. 77–94.

28. Marc Bouloiseau, *The Jacobin Republic, 1792–1794* (1972), trans. Cambridge, England, 1983, p. 139.

29. Bosher, *French Finances*, 273–74.

30. Étienne Charavay, ed., *La correspondance général de Carnot*, Paris, 1897, vol. III, p. 172, vol. IV, pp. 531, 564, 684 ff.

31. R. B. Rose, *The Enragés: Socialists of the French Revolution?*, Melbourne, Australia, 1965.

32. Martyn Lyons, *Révolution et terreur à Toulouse,* Toulouse, 1980, p. 88; Lucas, *Structure of the Terror,* p. 288.

33. Simone Waquet, "Jacobins et presse provinciale sous le directoire: Bias Parent et *Le questionneur,*" *Annales historiques de la révolution française,* vol. 57 (1985), p. 74.

NINE
The Populace in Revolution and Counterrevolution

1. Walter, *Robespierre,* vol. II, p. 66, vol. I, pp. 106–07; Françoise Theuriot, "La conception robespierriste du bonheur," *Annales historiques de la révolution française,* vol. XL (1968), pp. 207–26; Cobban, *Aspects,* pp. 138–39; Campardon, *Le tribunal révolutionnaire,* vol. I, p. 7.

2. Duguit et al., *Les constitutions,* p. 62.

3. *Archives parlementaires,* vol. 48, p. 14 (11 August 1792).

4. Soboul, *Les sans-culottes,* p. 171; Palmer, *Twelve Who Ruled,* p. 137.

5. This paragraph is based on Soboul, *Les sans-culottes,* pp. 442, 599, 633 ff.; Rose, *Making of the Sans-culottes,* passim; and Kare Tonnesson, *La défaite des sans-culottes,* Oslo, 1959, p. 341. Things were no different in the provinces; only about 10 percent of the adult population of the Haute-Vienne Department, for instance, attended *sociétés populaires,* and scarcely 5 percent of that membership was drawn from the populace (D'Hollander, *Religion et Révolution en Haute-Vienne,* 1984, p. 155 ff.)

6. Slavin, *The French Revolution in Miniature,* pp. 147–54; and *Making of an Insurrection,* ch. V.

7. Palmer, *Improvement of Humanity,* p. 148; and on Duplay, Soboul, *Les sans-culottes,* p. 1030; Soboul, "Robespierre and the Popular Movement of 1793–94," *Past and Present,* no. 5 (May 1954), pp. 54–70; Tonnesson, *La défaite,* p. 358.

8. Lucas, *Structure of the Terror,* p. 301; Tonnesson, *La défaite,* p. XV.

9. Soboul, *Les sans-culottes,* pp. 700 ff., 810–11, 843; Cobb, *Les armées révolutionnaires,* pp. 117, 146.

10. Cobb, *Les armées révolutionnaires,* p. 103.

11. Soboul, *Les sans-culottes,* p. 1031; Cobb, op. cit., p. 598; Tonnesson, *La défaite,* p. 349, ascribes a greater political consciousness to the *sans-culottes.*

12. Maurice Dommanget, *Sylvain Maréchal: L'égalitaire*, Paris, 1950.

13. Soboul, *Les sans-culottes*, pt. I, ch. 1.

14. R. C. Cobb, "The Revolutionary Mentality in France, 1793–1794," *History*, vol. 42 (1957), pp. 181–96; Cobb "Quelques aspects de la mentalité révolutionnaire," in Cobb, *Terreur et subsistances, 1793–1795*, pp. 3–53; Soboul, *Les sans-culottes*, passim; Lucas, "The Problem of the Midi in the French Revolution," pp. 18–19.

15. Jennifer Harris, "The Red Cap of Liberty: A Study of Dress Worn by the French Revolutionary Partisans in 1789–94," *Eighteenth-Century Studies*, vol. 14 (1981), p. 292; Roche, *Le peuple de Paris*, ch. 6, "Le vêtement populaire."

16. Cobb, *Les armées révolutionnaires*, p. 183.

17. Donald Sutherland, *The Chouans: The Social Origins of Popular Counter-Revolution in Upper Brittany, 1770–1796*, Oxford, 1982, p. 305; T. J. A. Le Goff and D. M. G. Sutherland, "The Social Origins of Counter-Revolution in Western France," *Past and Present*, no. 99 (1983), p. 65; Colin Lucas, "The First Directory and the Rule of Law," *French Historical Studies*, vol. X (1977), p. 215.

18. Bois, *Paysans de l'ouest*, p. 96.

19. Sutherland, *The Chouans*, p. 137; Lefebvre, *Les paysans du nord*, pp. 565 and 577.

20. Lefebvre, *Les paysans du nord*, p. 407; Sutherland, *The Chouans*, p. 308.

21. François Dornic, *Histoire du Maine*, Paris, 1973, pp. 103–04.

22. T. J. A. Le Goff and D. M. G. Sutherland, "Religion and Rural Revolt in the French Revolution: An Overview," *Religion and Rural Revolt*, ed. Janos M. Bak and Gerhard Benecke, Manchester, England, 1984, pp. 124–45.

23. Cobb, *Terreur et subsistances*, ch. VII, "Le ravitaillement des villes sous la terreur"; Cobb, *Les armées révolutionnaires*, p. 401.

24. Cobb, *Les armées révolutionnaires*, p. 405; Cobb, *Paris and Its Provinces, 1792–1802*, London, 1975, ch. 4; Cobb, *The Police and the People*, pp. 217–18; Tonnesson, *La défaite*, p. 8.

25. Lefebvre, *Les paysans du nord*, p. 842.

26. Lucas, "The Problem of the Midi in the French Revolution," p. 14; Sutherland, *The Chouans*, p. 220.

27. Lefebvre, *Les paysans du Nord*, p. 811.

28. Bois, *Paysans de l'ouest*; Charles Tilly, *The Vendée*, New York, 1964.

29. Lucas, *Structure of the Terror*, p. 32; Cobb, *Reactions to the French Revolution*, p. 26.

30. Lyons, "M. G. A. Vadier (1736–1828), p. 82; Lewis, *The Second Vendée*, pp. 141–45.

31. J. P. M. McErlean, "Le royaume Anglo-Corse (1794–1796): Contre-révolution ou continuité?," *Annales historiques de la révolution française*, 57e année (1985), pp. 215–35; Le Goff and Sutherland, "Religion and Rural Revolt," p. 127.

32. C. Riffaterre, *Le mouvement anti-Jacobin et anti-parisien à Lyon et dans le Rhône-et-Loire en 1793*, Lyons, 1912, 2 vols.; Bill Edmonds, "A Study in Popular Anti-Jacobinism: The Career of Denis Monnet," *French Historical Studies*, vol. XIII (1983), pp. 215–51.

33. Reynald Secher, *Le génocide franco-français: La Vendée vengée*, Paris, 1986, and Secher, *La Chapelle-Basse-Mer, village vendéen*, Paris, 1986.

34. D. M. G. Sutherland, *The Chouans*, Oxford, 1982.

35. Maurice Hutt, *Chouannerie and Counter-Revolution: Puisaye, the Princes and the British Government in the 1790s*, Cambridge, England, 1983, vol. I, pp. 65–67 and 96.

36. Cobb, *The Police and the People*, p. 134; Cobb, *Reactions to the French Revolution*, ch. 5.

TEN
The First Republic and Its Enemies, 1794–99

1. Lyons, "M. G. A. Vadier (1736–1828), pp. 90 and 99; two excellent general studies of these years are Martyn Lyons, *France Under the Directory*, Cambridge, England, 1975, and M. J. Sydenham, *First French Republic*.

2. Braesch, *La commune du dix août*, p. 281.

3. Duguit, *Les constitutions*, pp. 73–109, and Peter Campbell, *French Electoral Systems and Elections Since 1789*, London, 1958, p. 52.

4. M. S. Staum, *Cabanis: Enlightenment and Medical Philosophy in the French Revolution*, Princeton, 1980, p. 169.

5. R. F. Necheles, "The Constitutional Church, 1794–1802: An Essay in Voluntarism," *Proceedings of the Consortium on Revolutionary Europe*, Gainesville (Florida), 1974, pp. 80–90; Jacques Godechot, *Regards sur l'époque révolutionnaire*, Toulouse, 1980, ch. 5, "Quel a été le rôle des Aa pendant la révolution?"

6. François Gendron, *La jeunesse dorée: Épisodes de la révolution francaise*, Quebec, 1979, p. 110.

7. Jacqueline Chaumié, "Les Girondins," *Girondins et Montagnards*, ed. Albert Soboul, p. 24.

8. Gendron, *La jeunesse dorée*, pp. 356–406, conveys an impression

of crowds as mixed as the *sans-culottes.*

9. Forrest, *Society and Politics in Revolutionary Bordeaux,* p. 247.

10. Leo Gershoy, *Bertrand Barère, a Reluctant Terrorist,* Princeton, 1962, chs. 14 and 15.

11. Lucas, "The First Directory and the Rule of Law," pp. 231–60.

12. T. A. DiPadova, "The Girondins and the Question of Revolutionary Government," pp. 437–38.

13. Tonnesson, *La défaite,* p. 8 and passim in chs. 1 and 6.

14. Slavin, *French Revolution in Miniature,* ch. IX.

15. Monnier, *Le faubourg Saint-Antoine,* pp. 138–46.

16. Tonnesson, *La défaite,* pp. 114–15.

17. Gendron, *La jeunesse dorée,* pp. 121–23.

18. Rude, *The Crowd in the French Revolution,* ch. 10; Tonnesson, *La défaite,* chs. X–XIV.

19. Monnier, *Le faubourg Saint-Antoine,* p. 136.

20. Isser Woloch, *Jacobin Legacy: The Democratic Movement Under the Directory,* Princeton, 1970, p. 102 ff.

21. This paragraph is based on ibid.

22. M. J. Sydenham, "The Crime of 3 Nivôse (24 December 1800)," in *French Government and Society,* ed. Bosher, ch. 13.

23. W. R. Fryer, *Republic or Restoration in France?, 1794–97: The Politics of French Royalism,* Manchester, England, ch. 1; David Higgs, *Ultraroyalism in Toulouse from Its Origins to the Revolution of 1830,* Baltimore, 1973, chs. 1 and 2.

24. Chaumié, *Le réseau d'Antraigues.*

25. Fryer, *Republic or Restoration in France?,* p. 126 ff.

26. Harvey Mitchell, *The Underground War Against Revolutionary France: The Missions of William Wickham, 1794–1800,* Oxford, 1965, p. 69 ff.

27. Woloch, *Jacobin Legacy,* p. 377.

28. These two paragraphs are based on Cobb, *Paris and Its Provinces,* ch. 5; Cobb, *Reactions to the French Revolution,* chs. 4 and 5; Cobb, *The Police and the People,* pp. 131–50; Lewis, *Second Vendée,* and Denis Woronoff, *The Thermidorian Régime and the Directory, 1794–1799,* trans. Cambridge, England, 1984, pp. 20–28.

29. Godechot, *La grande nation,* chs. VIII and XX.

30. Lyons, "M. G. A. Vadier (1736–1828)," p. 89, quoting *Le moniteur,* vol. XIX, p. 326.

31. Chaumié, "Les Girondins," p. 41.

32. E.g., Kennedy, *The Jacobin Club of Marseilles,* p. 181.

33. Slavin, *French Revolution in Miniature,* p. 344 and all of ch. 12.

34. Soboul, *Les sans-culottes,* pp. 208–09 and 609.

35. Cobb, *The Police and the People,* p. 130.
36. See, for example, Georges Lefebvre's classic, *Napoleon* (1936), 4th ed., Paris, 1953, bk.1.
37. These figures come from ibid., p. 76; Cobban, *Aspects of the French Revolution,* p. 111, and E. A. Whitcomb, "Napoleon's Prefects," *American Historical Review,* vol. 79 (1974), pp. 1091–95.
38. Claude Langlois, "Le plebiscite de l'an VIII," *Annales historiques de la révolution française,* 44e année (1972), pp. 43, 231, 390.
39. Monnier, *Le faubourg Saint-Antoine,* p. 287.
40. Lefebvre, *Napoleon,* p. 573.

ELEVEN
A New Leviathan

1. Alexis de Tocqueville, *L'ancien régime et la révolution* (1856), bk. II, ch. 2, title.
2. For discussion of this theme see, for instance, Brian Chapman, *Introduction to French Local Government,* London, 1953, and Herbert Lüthy, *France Against Herself: The Past, Politics and Crises of Modern France* (1953), trans., New York, 1955, ch. 5, "The State Apparatus."
3. Pierre Duclos, *La notion de constitution,* p. 94.
4. Abbé Sieyès, *Préliminaire de la constitution,* July 1789, p. 20 (British Library), 934 g 3 [4].
5. Jean-Louis Carra, *Un petit mot de réponse,* 1787, p. 48.
6. Sieyès, *Vues sur les moyens d'exécution dont les représentants de la France pourront disposer en 1789,* 1789, pp. 2, 5, 109; *Essai sur les privilèges,* 1788, pp. 25, 30.
7. Clive Church, *Revolution and Red Tape: The French Ministerial Bureaucracy 1770–1850,* Oxford, 1981, p. 86.
8. Jean Belin, *La logique d'une idée-force: L'idée d'utilité sociale et la révolution française, 1789–92,* Paris, 1939, p. 37.
9. Pierre-Louis-Claude Gin, *Les vrais principes du gouvernement français démontrés par la raison et par les faits par un français,* Geneva, 1782, p. 35.
10. Jean de Vaines, *Des moyens d'assurer le succès et la durée de la constitution,* 1790, p. 13.
11. Bernardin, *Jean-Marie Roland,* p. 196.
12. Guy Thuillier, "Comment les français voyaient l'administration au XVIIe siècle: Le droit public de France de l'abbé Fleury," *La revue administrative,* no. 103 (1965), p. 21; a second edition was published in its centenary year, Claude Fleury, *Droit public de France,* 2 vols., new ed., 1769 (British Library 230 F 18, 19).

13. *La gazette nationale ou moniteur universel,* vol. I, introduction, p. 39, *"De la vénalité des charges"* (Bibliothèqùe nationale, Gr. fol. LC^2 113).

14. Archives Nationales, F^{30} 110^1, mss.

15. Archives Nationales, F^{1B} 1–2.

16. Belin, *La Logique d'une idée-force,* p. 75.

17. L. Duguit, "La séparation des pouvoirs et l'assemblée nationale de 1789," *Revue d'économie politique,* année 7 (1893), p. 353 (Thouret on 8 August 1791); *Correspondance inédite du constituant Thibaudeau 1789–1791, publiée par Henri Carré et Pierre Boissonnade,* Paris, 1898, p. 12.

18. Marcel Reinhard, "Observations sur le rôle révolutionnaire de l'armée dans la révolution française," *Annales historiques de la révolution française,* vol. 34 (1962), p. 171.

19. Archives Nationales, DX2, Calonne's pensions, décision du Roi, 21 November 1784; *État des pensions sur le trésor royal,* 1789, vol. I, p. 224.

20. Petot, *Histoire de l'administration des ponts et chaussées,* troisième partie.

21. Archives Nationales F^{1B} 1–2, *Etat des bureaux du ministère de l'intérieur.*

22. Bernardin, *Jean-Marie Roland,* p. 402 ff.

23. Church, *Revolution and Red Tape,* p. 159.

24. British Library, 28 d 4 (5 May 1790); Albert Mirot, *Manuel de géographie historique de la France,* 2d ed. 1950, vol. II, p. 396 ff.; Nicholas Richardson, *The French Prefectoral Corps, 1814–1830,* Cambridge, England, 1966; Pierre Henry, *Histoire des préfets,* Paris, 1950, 360 pp.; Brian Chapman, *The Prefects and Provincial France,* London, 1955, 246 pp.

25. Lyons, *France Under the Directory,* p. 166; Godechot, *Les institutions de la France,* p. 101.

26. Bertrand Gille, *Les sources statistiques de l'histoire de France des enquêtes du XVIIe siècle à 1870,* Paris, 1964, pp. 118–21.

27. Edmond Seligman, *La justice en France pendant la révolution française,* Paris, 1901, vol. I, pp. 160–63.

28. Felix Ponteil, *Histoire de l'enseignement, 1789–1965,* Paris, 1966, bk. I, pp. 9–156; Paul Gerbod, "Les inspecteurs généraux et l'inspection générale de l'instruction publique, 1802–1882," *La revue historique,* vol. 236 (1966), pp. 79–106; Godechot, *Les institutions de la France,* pp. 383, 461.

29. Church, *Revolution and Red Tape,* pp. 81, 128, 139, and 142; British Library, FR 552 (30 September 1791).

30. Michel Bruguière, *Gestionnaires et profiteurs de la révolution,* Paris, 1986, see "Notices biographiques."

31. Bosher, *French Finances*, ch. 11.

32. Archives Nationales, D VI 8 and D X 3.

33. Bosher, *French Finances*, pp. 231–53.

34. *États présentés à la commission des douanes par les régisseurs, imprimés par ordre de la convention nationale le 2 frimaire an II,* Paris (Bibliothèque nationale, Lf¹³⁰ 5 and 6); Bosher, *The Single Duty Project.*

35. *État des citoyens employés dans les bureaux de la direction générale de la liquidation,* 15 May 1793 (Bibliothèque nationale, Lf¹⁵⁷ 10).

36. *Archives parlementaires de 1787 à 1860, recueil complet des débats législatifs et politiques des chambres françaises,* vol. 10, p. 90 (from a report of the Finance Committee on 18 November 1789); and vol. XVIII, pp. 343, 354 (a report dated 27 August 1790).

37. Archives Nationales, D VI 6: a printed letter from the *arquebusiers* of Paris to the Finance Committee, dated 1 July 1790.

38. Louis Bergeron, *Banquiers, négociants et manufacturiers parisiens du Directoire à l'Empire,* Paris, 1978.

39. Michael Bruguière, *La première restauration et son budget,* Paris-Geneva, 1969.

TWELVE
The Revolution's Effects

1. Cobban, *Aspects of the French Revolution,* p. 108.

2. Georges Weill, *Histoire du parti républicain en France 1814–1870,* Paris, 1928, p. 134; James Joll, *The Anarchists,* New York, 1964, p. 48.

3. Walter, *Robespierre,* vol. II, pp. 380–85.

4. Duguit, *Les constitutions,* p. 358.

5. Ibid., p. 286.

6. Ibid., pp. 1–3; there are many English translations of the Declaration, such as in R. R. Palmer's translation of Lefebvre, *The Coming of the French Revolution,* and later editions.

7. Douglas Johnson, France and the Dreyfus Affair, London, 1966; Guy Chapman, *The Dreyfus Case: A Reassessment,* London, 1955; Pierre Miquel, *L'affaire Dreyfus,* Paris, 1961.

8. *Le monde hébdomadaire,* no. 695, dated that same week.

9. Lefebvre, *Napoleon,* p. 126.

10. David Higgs, *The Nobles in Nineteenth-Century France: The Practice of Inegalitarianism,* Baltimore, 1987. ch. 6.

11. Theodore Zeldin, *France 1848–1945: Ambition and Love,* Oxford, 1979, p. 292; and on this subject in general, John McManners, *Church and State in France, 1870–1914,* London, 1972; and Philip Spencer, *Politics of Belief in Nineteenth-Century France,* London, 1954.

12. Robert Fox, "Learning, Politics and Polite Culture in Provincial France: The Sociétés Savantes in the 19th Century," *Historical Reflections*, vol. VII (1980), "The Making of Frenchmen," p. 544.

13. Miquel, *L'affaire Dreyfus*, p. 123.

14. Mark Traugott, *Armies of the Poor: Determinants of Working-Class Participation in the Parisian Insurrection of June 1848*, Princeton, 1985.

15. Louis Girard, *La politique des travaux publics du second empire*, Paris, 1952.

16. David Pinkney, *The French Revolution of 1830*, Princeton, 1972, p. 367; Tilly, *Contentious French*, p. 384.

17. J. M. Merriman, ed., *1830 in France*, New York, 1975, pieces by David Pinkney, R. J. Bezucha, and J. M. Merriman.

18. Ted W. Margadant, *French Peasants in Revolt: The Insurrection of 1851*, Princeton, 1979.

19. Joll, *The Anarchists*, p. 40.

20. Ibid., p. 67; F.-P.-G. Guizot, *Democracy in France*, London, January 1849, preface.

21. Rétat, ed., *L'attentat de Damiens*, pp. 352–60.

22. See above, pp. 39 and 49 (Chapter 2).

23. Higgs, *The Nobles*, pp. 8–14.

24. Edward Whitcomb, *Napoleon's Diplomatic Service*, Durham, N.C., p. 3; Richardson, *French Prefectoral Corps*, p. 179; Thomas J. Beck, "The French Revolution and the Nobility: A Reconsideration," *Journal of Social History*, vol. 15 (1981), p. 228; and especially Higgs, *The Nobles*, passim.

25. Pinkney, *The French Revolution of 1830*, p. 283 note; Pinkney, *Decisive Years in France, 1840–1847*, Princeton, 1986, p. 5.

26. Pinkney, *Decisive Years*, chs. 1 and 2; Adeline Daumard, *La bourgeoisie parisienne de 1815 à 1848*, Paris, 1963; André Jean Tudesq, *Les grands notables en France (1840–49): Étude historique d'une psychologie sociale*, Paris, 1964, 2 vols.

27. Jacques Godechot, *France and the Atlantic Revolution of the Eighteenth Century, 1770–1799*, New York, 1965, pp. 124–25; Godechot, *La grande nation*, preface and ch. 1.

28. Denis Brogan, *The Development of Modern France (1870–1939)*, London, 1940, p. 687.

29. Lüthy, *France Against Herself*, p. 12.

30. D. G. Charleton, *Secular Religions in France, 1815–1870*, London, 1963, p. 36.

31. *Chauvinisme* derived from Nicolas Chauvin, a brave but excessively patriotic soldier of the republic and empire, originally from Rochefort, and the word entered the language through Cogniard's play *La Cocarde tricolore* (1831).

32. Weill, *Histoire du parti républicain*, p. 154.

33. Theodore Zeldin, *The Political System of Napoleon III*, London, 1958, p. 6.

34. Walter, *Robespierre*, vol. II, p. 188.

35. Adrien Dansette, *Louis-Napoléon à la conquête du pouvoir*, Paris, 1961, ch. 4; J. Lucas-Dubreton, *Le culte de Napoléon*, Paris, 1960, 468 pp.; J. P. T. Bury and R. P. Tombs, *Thiers 1797–1877; A Political Life*, London, 1986, ch. 8.

36. Bosher, *French Finances, 1770–1795.*

37. De Talleyrand-Périgord, *Rapport sur l'instruction publique fait au nom du comité de constitution à l'assemblée nationale, les 10, 11 et 19 septembre 1791*, Paris, 1791, p. 95.

38. Guy Thuillier, *Bureaucratie et bureaucrates en France au XIXe siècle*, Geneva, 1980, pp. 3–83.

39. F. Ridley and J. Blondel, *Public Administration in France,*, New York, 1965; Pierre Legendre, *Histoire de l'administration de 1750 à nos jours*, Paris, 1968.

40. Chapman, *The Prefects and Provincial France*, pp. 48–49.

41. Thomas R. Osborne, *A Grande École for the Grands Corps: The Recruitment and Training of the French Administrative Elite in the Nineteenth Century*, New York, 1983, p. 59.

Index

Public Instruction Ministry, 256
publiciste, Le, 201
publiciste de la république française, Le,
    181
Puisaye, Joseph, liv, 224–25
Puységur (councillor), 131

Quebec, 12*n*, 25, 54
Quesnay, François, 50

Rabaut Saint-Étienne, Paul, 119
Ramel-Nogaret, Dominique-Vincent,
    263
reading rooms, 51–52
receivers general of Finances, 97,
    103, 263
receivers of Finance, 263
Regardin, André, 258
régie, 97
Régie général, 258, 263
Reims, Terror in, 179
Rémy, Abbé, 81
Renan, Joseph-Ernest, 274
Renard, Delphine, 273
Rennes, 18–19
    Parlement at, 52
    resistance to Lamoignon's reforms
        at, 112–13
rental leaseholds, 10
Réponse de Monsieur Calonne à l'écrit de
    Monsieur Necker (Calonne), 70
republicanism:
    background of, 172–73
    Bonapartists and, 286
    Church and, 231
    civil service and, 259
    decline and fall of monarchy and,
        60–62
    democratic movement and, 173
    Estates General and, 128–29, 131–
        32
    First Republic and, 185, 207–8
    populace and, 210, 219
    sans-culottes and, 210
    Thermidorian regime and, 231
    war effort and, 181–82, 207–8
Rerum novarum (Leo XIII), 275
Research or Information Committee,
    193
Restoration, 265–66
"retour de l'empereur, Le" (Hugo),
    287
Reubell, Jean-François, 142, 228
Reunion Club, 188
"reveil du peuple, Le," 232

revolutionary armies, *see sans-culottes*
Revolutionary Committees, 193, 211–
    12, 234
revolutionary *journées,* 268
Revolutionary Tribunals, 181, 191,
    213
    of Paris, 193–95, 231
    victims of, 194–95
Revolutionary Women's Club, 201
Revolution of 1830, 268, 271
Richelieu, Armand-Jean du Plessis
    Cardinal et Duc de, 79–82
Richer, Edmond, 56
Richerists, 80, 122
Riot Act (1715), 38
Riot Act (1792), 169
riots, rioting:
    hunger as cause of, 33–35, 112,
        125–26, 277
    in Paris, 35, 92, 112, 125, 147,
        149–50, 153, 155, 169–71, 174,
        278, 282
    by peasants, 35, 125–26, 150, 153–
        54
    by populace, 33–35, 153–55, 277–
        80, 282–83
    provincial patriotism and, 53–54,
        114
    in response to rumors or sugges-
        tions, 37–38
    see also Terror
Robecq, Anne-Louis-Alexandre de
    Montmorency, Prince de, 97, 101
Robert, François, liv, 172, 174, 179
Robespierre, Maximilien Marie-Isi-
    dore, lv, 48, 116, 173, 180, 187,
    241
    Barbaroux's denunciation of, 190
    Brissot and, 186, 188–89
    Committee of Public Safety headed
        by, 195–98, 200–201
    conspiracy against, 227
    on dechristianizing campaign, 207
    execution of, 202
    fall of, 193, 202
    Hébertist executions and, 202
    historical depictions of, 191
    imperial expansion and, 182
    invasion of Tuileries and, 175, 177
    National Assembly and, 141, 151,
        154, 181
    Necker admired by, 128
    Paris Commune and, 188–89
    populace and, 154, 209, 211–13,
        216, 219, 280

Terror (*continued*)
  in rural communities, 222
  victims of, 178–80, 192
terrorism, 273
textilemaking, 24, 26
Thermidorian regime, 203, 225,
    226–42, 273
  constitution of, 226, 228–31, 234–
    35
  financial administration of, 265
  leaders of, 227–28
  legacy of, 228–29
  liberal phase of, 231–36
  resorts to violence by, 226–27,
    232–33, 235, 238
Théroigne de Méricourt (Anne-
    Joseph Terwagne), lix, 173
Thiers, Adolphe, 271, 287
Third Estate, 40, 53, 84, 118, 150
  conflict of upper orders with, 119–
    20
  in election of deputies to Estates
    General, 120–21, 123–28, 172
  internal quarrels of, 156
  liberal clergy and, 57–58
  Louis XVI's alliance with, 114,
    130–32
  National Assembly and, 130–32,
    133, 137, 140
  republican idea adopted by, 128–
    32
  revolution of, 129–30, 136, 153,
    158–59, 181
Third Republic, 268, 272, 289–90
Thirty Years' Peace, 24
Thirty Years' War, 96
Thorez, Maurice, 279–80
Thouret, Jacques-Guillaume, 140,
    250–51
Tilly, Charles, 42, 221
Tissot, Pierre-François, 236
Tocqueville, Alexis de, 243
Tollendal, Thomas-Arthur, Comte de
    Lally et Baron de, 72, 82, 150
Tondu, P.-H.-H.-M. (Lebrun), 177
torture, xiv, xvi, 38–39, 71–72, 109,
    281
Toulon, revolt against Jacobins in,
    199–200, 203, 222, 227
Toulouse, 18–19, 21, 28
  Parlement of, 82n
  sharecropping in, 10
Tourville, Anne de Cotentin, Comte
    de, 78n
Toussaint l'Ouverture, lix, 142

townspeople, 6, 17–29
  Church and, 18–19, 21–22
  country people vs., 220–21
  diets of, 8
  government and, 18–19
  impact of financial crisis on, 124–
    25
  instability of, 28
  lawcourts and, 18, 21
  manufacturing and, 18, 19
  peasant migrations and, 28, 37,
    124–25
  realms of activity of, 18–28
  rioting of, 35, 37–38
  trade and, 18, 23–28
  violence and cruelty of, 38, 41
trade, 18, 23–28
  financial crises and, 76–77
Treaty of Paris (1763), 78
Treaty of Versailles (1783), 78
tribunal criminel extraordinaire, 180
Tribunal of Seven, 199
Trudaine, Daniel-Charles, 49
Trullard, Narcisse, 206
Tuileries Palace, 198
  government defense of, 176–78
  invasion of, 168, 170, 174–78,
    210–11
Turgot, Anne-Robert-Jacques, lix, 34,
    115–16, 127, 214, 248
  anti-British policies opposed by, 95
  dismissal of, 93, 102
  on economy, 68, 76, 92–93, 96
  ruling classes and, 82–83
Turpin, Gérard-Maurice, 262

unemployment, 156
United Belgian Estates, 161
United Bishops, 230–31
University Faculty of Law, 290–91
upper class:
  Assembly of Notables and, 101,
    105–7
  child marriages among, 12
  Church revival and, 274–75
  counterrevolutionary activities of,
    158–59
  court politics and, 85–86, 117–18
  Crown reforms and, 92, 94, 96,
    112–14
  decline and downfall of monarchy
    and, 61–62, 80–84
  émigrés from, 162–63, 167, 171
  financial administration reform
    and, 260